# The Collapse of Heaven

HARVARD-YENCHING INSTITUTE MONOGRAPH SERIES 141

# The Collapse of Heaven

*The Taiping Civil War and Chinese
Literature and Culture, 1850–1880*

## Huan Jin

Published by the Harvard University Asia Center
Distributed by Harvard University Press
Cambridge (Massachusetts) and London 2024

Published by the Harvard University Asia Center, Cambridge, MA 02138

The Harvard University Asia Center publishes a monograph series and, in coordination with
the Fairbank Center for Chinese Studies, the Korea Institute, the Reischauer Institute of Japanese Studies, and other faculties and institutes, administers research projects designed to
further scholarly understanding of China, Japan, Vietnam, Korea, and other Asian countries.
The Center also sponsors projects addressing multidisciplinary and regional issues in Asia.

The Harvard-Yenching Institute, founded in 1928, is an independent foundation dedicated to
the advancement of higher education in the humanities and social sciences in Asia. Head-
quartered on the campus of Harvard University, the Institute provides fellowships for advanced
research, training, and graduate studies at Harvard by competitively selected faculty and
graduate students from Asia. The Institute also supports a range of academic activities at its
fifty partner universities and research institutes across Asia. At Harvard, the Institute promotes East Asian studies through annual contributions to the Harvard-Yenching Library and
publication of the *Harvard Journal of Asiatic Studies* and the Harvard-Yenching Institute
Monograph Series.

Library of Congress Cataloging-in-Publication Data

Names: Jin, Huan, 1986– author.
Title: The collapse of heaven : the Taiping Civil War and Chinese
    literature and culture, 1850–1880 / Huan Jin.
Other titles: Taiping Civil War and Chinese literature and culture, 1850–1880 |
    Harvard-Yenching Institute monograph series ; 141.
Description: Cambridge : Harvard University Asia Center, 2024. |
    Series: Harvard-Yenching Institute monograph series; 141 | Includes
    bibliographical references and index.
Identifiers: LCCN 2023027185 | ISBN 9780674295872 (hardcover)
Subjects: LCSH: Chinese literature—19th century—History and criticism. |
    War and literature—China—History—19th century. | War in literature. |
    China—History—Taiping Rebellion, 1850-1864—Literature and the
    rebellion.
Classification: LCC DS759.4.L58 J56 2024 | DDC 951/.034—dc23/eng/20230927
LC record available at https://lccn.loc.gov/2023027185

Index by Arc Indexing, Inc.

♾   Printed on acid-free paper
Printed in the United States of America

*To my parents*

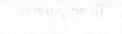

To my parents

# Contents

List of Illustrations     ix

Acknowledgments     xi

List of Abbreviations     xiii

Introduction     1

### PART I: COMPETING VISIONS OF HEAVEN AND HELL

1.   Heavenly Visions: The Taiping Alternative     25

2.   Revelations from Hell: A Qing Answer     67

3.   Order in Disorder: Personal Accounts of War     109

### PART II: MAKING SENSE OF THE PAST AND THE FUTURE

4.   Traces of History: A Literati Novel and Its Precedents     151

5.   Violence in Drama: The Reinvention of Community     204

6.   Fantasies: Transcendence and Defiance     245

    Conclusion     286

    Bibliography     295

    Glossary-Index     321

# Illustrations

## Figures

1.1     Cover page of *The Imperial Proclamation of the Heavenly Father.*     31

1.2     Cover page of an 1825 missionary tract.     31

1.3     Page from *The Taiping Heavenly Chronicle.*     32

1.4     An 1853 Taiping placard.     40

2.1     Illustration from Li Laizhang, "Instructions on Positions of Kowtow and Prostration."     87

3.1     Page spread from Shen Zi's diary manuscript.     119

3.2     Page spread from Shen Zi's diary manuscript.     130

3.3     Excerpt from Shen Zi's "Biography of Shen Fen."     134

4.1     Page spread from *Traces of Flowers and the Moon.*     154

4.2     Illustration of Wei Chizhu's ascension to Heaven.     195

5.1     Illustration from *Tears from a Man of Iron in Jiangnan.*     214

6.1     Xuan Ding, "Seeking Reclusion in an Ink Stone."     252

6.2     Portrait of Wang Tao.     253

## Maps

0.1     Territory controlled by the Taiping forces.     8

3.1     The town of Puyuan and its waterways.     122

# Illustrations

Figures

Maps

# Acknowledgments

I am forever indebted to those who refused to be victimized or silenced by historical violence and by the violence of history.

This book would not have been possible without the generous support of many people. Wai-yee Li exemplified to me with grittiness and grace what it means to meet the challenging paradox of language as both a vehicle for and an obstacle to truth. David Der-wei Wang showed me how to find freedom and strength in literature and arts, and what it means to hold the intellectual community together with generosity and kindness. Robert E. Hegel, who led me onto this career path, helped me with abundant experience. Ann Blair welcomed me into the community of book historians and has been a constant source of support ever since. Jie Li motivated me with her spirited curiosity, resolute inquisitiveness, and insightful comments. Shigehisa Kuriyama broadened my horizons by leading me to discover unexpected connections through the linkage of time.

I feel fortunate to have begun this scholarly journey with Lu Kou, Ming Tak Ted Hui, Chen Liu, Huijun Mai, Graham Chamness, Billy French, Heng Du, Feiran Du, Guangchen Chen, and Miya Qiong Xie. The spiritedness of Shih-Pei Chen, Hongsu Wang, and William Wai Him Pang helped me as much as their expertise on digital humanities. Ariel Fox, William Hedberg, Xiaoqiao Ling, Qiaomei Tang, Sakura Christmas, and S. E. Kile each inspired me in their own way. I thank Anh Tran for challenging me to stay centered and courageous through it all. My research has also benefited from conversations I had with a dynamic group of historians, including Rui Hua, Wen Yu, Joel Wing-Lun, Jonas Rüegg, Eric Schluessel, and Devin Fitzgerald. Yi Lu supplied me with not only homemade baked goods but also cheerful candor and many conversations across continents and oceans.

I would like to offer my thanks to Tobie Meyer-Fong, Steven R. Platt, Rania Huntington, William Charles Wooldridge, Ge Zhaoguang, Pamela Kyle Crossley, Yim Chi Hung, and Maram Epstein for their interest in this project. I am grateful for the encouragement I received from Ellen Widmer, Catherine Yeh, Ling Hon Lam, and Paize Keulemans while completing this book. I appreciate the helpful questions I received from audiences at the Association for Asian Studies, Academia Sinica, Chinese University of Hong Kong, and Dartmouth College where I presented portions of this research. Thanks also to my colleagues in Hong Kong: Yingzhi Zhao, Tze-ki Hon, May Bo Ching, Hsiao-t'i Li, Steven B. Miles, Jianmei Liu, Shengqing Wu, and Xiaolu Ma, who offered me support and advice at times of need. Lik Hang Tsui, Yu Luo, Chia-hui Lu, Binbin Yang, and Kam Siu Cheung provided me with invaluable comradeship in the past few years, for which I am deeply thankful. The hospitality I received from Siao-chen Hu, Chiung-yun Liu, Yuan-ju Liu, and Chao-heng Liao makes Academia Sinica a home for all my scholarly adventures.

I was able to access primary materials important to my research due to the kind help of librarians, especially Xiao-he Ma at Harvard-Yenching library and Qiuyan Shen at Jiaxing library. While writing this book, I received generous support from the Hong Kong Research Grants Council, Academia Sinica, Henry Luce Foundation/ACLS Program in China Studies, and the Asia Center and the Fairbank Center at Harvard University.

I am thankful for the two anonymous readers whose input helped improve this manuscript. I would also like to thank Vincent Goossaert for kindly sparing time to read and offer useful comments on one of the chapters. My editors made the material form of this book possible: Bob Graham, Kristen Wanner, and Qin Higley offered me suggestions with thoughtful expertise; Maura High went beyond what is expected from an editor to inspire me with friendship and love of literature. Any errors that remain are my own.

My deepest gratitude goes to my ancestors and my parents, Jin Chengri and Piao Yingyu, for planting in me the seeds of curiosity about language and knowledge, and for cultivating them with strong love.

The immense scale of the war registers in different ways in the many contemporary and near-contemporary documents that have survived, ranging from personal accounts like Shen Zi's, through manifestos and religious tracts, to essays, drama, and fiction. In the manifestos, for example, we have dramatic statements of the colliding visions of the Taiping rebels and the Qing government. In 1853, after the rebels had established their capital in Nanjing, and the Taiping War was at its height, the Taipings published a placard entitled "Receiving the Mandate of Heaven to Attack the Barbarian" ("Fengtian taohu" 奉天討胡), which reads in part:

> Since China has been saturated with the nefarious influence of the Manchus, a perilous fire burns the heavenly dome; excessive poison pollutes the polestar; the stench of blood spreads across the four seas; the air of wickedness is harsher than that of the five barbarian groups. . . . Now having known God, the real Father, all of you should forsake demonic traits and become human beings. On Earth, you shall enjoy unparalleled glories; in Heaven, you shall relish boundless blessings.
>
> 自滿洲流毒中國，虐燄燔蒼穹，淫毒穢宸極，腥風播於四海，妖氣慘於五胡 . . . 爾等本身既認識上帝親爺，脫鬼成人。在世榮耀無比，在天享福無疆。[3]

In response, Zeng Guofan 曾國藩 (1811–1872), the most powerful Qing leader in the suppression of the Taipings, issued "Denouncing the Yue Rebels" in early 1854:

> The offending rebels . . . slaughtered millions of people and trampled through counties and towns beyond a five-thousand-mile radius. . . . This is not only a disaster for our Qing empire, but an inexplicable catastrophe for Confucian moral teachings since the beginning of Heaven and Earth. . . . This has indeed infuriated all the gods and spirits, who in the great yonder would implacably seek reparations for the shame and slander.

---

3. *TPTGYS*, 1:108, 112. All translations in this book are my own unless noted otherwise.

# Introduction

On the afternoon of September 9, 1860, Taiping rebel troops arrived west of Puyuan in Zhejiang Province.[1] Shen Zi 沈梓 (1833–1888), a native of Puyuan, had been closely observing the development of hostilities in Zhejiang Province over the previous few months, and he received the news of the Taipings' arrival with great anxiety. Wanting to devise an escape route for his family, he went for divination at a local temple. While piously waiting for his lot from the bodhisattva, Shen Zi could not have foreseen the violence and destruction he would eventually bear witness to and endure. The war would kill his daughter, wife, and four siblings, and these deaths were just a tiny fraction of the estimated death toll of twenty million during the Taiping War (1851–1864), one of the most destructive civil wars in human history.[2]

---

1. Shen Zi, *BKRJ*, 8:22.

2. Scholars have come up with different estimates of the number of people who died during the Taiping War. Tobie Meyer-Fong follows William Hail's estimate of twenty million, as do I; see Meyer-Fong, *What Remains*, 1, n. 1. In comparison, the estimated death toll of soldiers and civilians in the American Civil War is about 0.67 million. See Faust, *This Republic of Suffering*, xii. Meyer-Fong also contrasts the numbers of deaths in these two wars in *What Remains*, 1, n. 4.

# Abbreviations

| | |
|---|---|
| ATPTGGS | *Aodaliya cang Taiping tianguo yuanke guanshu congkan* 澳大利亞藏太平天國原刻官書叢刊 |
| BKRJ | Shen Zi 沈梓, *Bikou riji* 避寇日記, modern reprint in *Taiping tianguo* 太平天國 |
| DKLY | Wang Tao 王韜, *Dunku lanyan* 遁窟讕言 |
| HYH | Wei Xiuren 魏秀仁, *Hua yue hen* 花月痕 |
| LSYSG | Li Shangyin 李商隱, *Li Shangyin shige jijie* 李商隱詩歌集解 |
| MZY | Handan mengxing ren 邯鄲夢醒人, *Meng zhong yuan* 夢中緣 |
| SBSH | Wang Tao 王韜, *Songbin suohua* 淞濱瑣話 |
| SYLZ | *Shengyu lingzheng* 聖諭靈徵 |
| SYML | Wang Tao 王韜, *Songyin manlu* 淞隱漫錄 |
| TFTXSZ | *Tianfu tianxiong shengzhi* 天父天兄聖旨 |
| TPTGYS | *Taiping tianguo yinshu* 太平天國印書 |
| WXRZZ | *Wei Xiuren zazhu chaoben* 魏秀仁襍著抄本 |
| YYQDL | Xuan Ding 宣鼎, *Yeyu qiudeng lu* 夜雨秋燈錄 |

逆賊 . . . 荼毒生靈百萬，蹂躪州縣五千餘里 . . . 此豈獨我大清之
變，乃開闢以來名教之奇變 . . . 斯又鬼神所並憤怒，欲雪此憾於冥
冥之中者也。[4]

The Taiping rebels portray the China ruled by the Manchus as an uninhabitable and foul landscape that has been burned and polluted, and then hold out the promise of heavenly blessings with the aim of inciting people to rebellion. Zeng Guofan's proclamation justifies Qing retaliatory actions by blaming the Taiping rebels for the massive destruction and their unprecedented attack on Confucianism's moral ground; it even claims that the supernatural realm will take up arms along with the Qing armies to punish this outrage.

These two proclamations from the opposing sides of the conflict belong to the genre of "a calling to arms" (xi wen 檄文). This genre typically solicits and justifies violence through a rhetoric constructed upon binary categories of virtue and vice, authority and illegitimacy.[5] Characterized by its ostentatious expository style and its emphasis on hostility, xi wen is a verbal performance of violence, but it also constitutes and catalyzes acts of violence.[6] Both parties use xi wen to present an antithesis between orthodox and heterodox through a rhetoric of malice, savagery, Heaven, Earth, gods, and spirits. Both associate the enemy with the metaphor of "poison" (du 毒), a dangerous substance that spreads insidiously and pervasively to destroy people's minds and bodies. Both emphasize the vast scope of the catastrophe in spatial and temporal terms, and conclude with a call for divine forces to do justice to the catastrophe on Earth. Even though they were in opposite camps, under the duress of the conflict their rhetoric is the same, using similar

4. "Tao Yue fei xi" 討粵匪檄 in Zeng Guofan, Zuben Zeng Wenzheng gong, 3:1579. The Taiping rebels were from today's Guangdong and Guangxi Provinces. "Yue" is an ancient name for the two provinces, so in Qing sources the Taipings are often referred to as "Yue rebels."

5. On the characteristics of xi wen, see Lian Qiyuan, Mingdai de gaoshi bangwen, 238. See also Zhong Wai sanwen cidian (Zhang Yongjian, ed.), 1330.

6. I agree with the poststructuralist view that "naming itself is an act of coercion, and that hate speech performs what it declares." See Butler, Excitable Speech, 19. On the relationship between language and violence in modern society, see Dawes, The Language of War.

images and tactics for similar ends. In writings revolving around the Taiping Civil War, intense phrases, images, and rhetoric on violence, as shown in these *xi wen*, are portable across boundaries of genres and media, from political incitements and religious coercion to individual testimonies and literary reminiscences. Such a confluence of discourses, symptomatic of a war waged between two opposing belief systems, deeply transformed Chinese literary and cultural landscapes.

## Heaven's Collapse

To engage people urgently with a chaotic present, both political regimes present an apocalyptic vision—the cosmic-scale failure alluded to in the title of this book. This "sense of an ending," however, does not appear only in *xi wen* writings; it pervades Chinese literary and cultural realms from the 1850s to the 1880s. In describing the Taiping War, writers frequently evoked apocalyptic imagery: "Heaven collapses and Earth crumbles" (*tian beng di che* 天崩地坼). The term "Heaven" requires some comment: as it can refer simply to the sky, but also, in the Chinese tradition, to the ultimate and omnipotent Power, it is thus imbued with religious, political, and moral meanings.[7] In this study, I

7. In Confucianism, Heaven is the highest moral judge, as in Confucius's statement, "If one is found guilty by Heaven, no prayer could redeem him" 獲罪於天，無所禱也. *Lunyu zhu shu*, vol. 3, 7b. My translation. Much has been written on the meaning of *tian* in Confucianism. There is a helpful summary of the word's meaning in Ames and Rosemont, *The Analects of Confucius*, 47–48. See also Eno, *The Confucian Creation of Heaven*. In the Daoist classic *Daode jing*, Heaven is represented as an impersonal process that ruthlessly exercises its power over the human realm. For instance, the *Daode jing* reads, "Heaven and Earth are not benign. They treat everything in the world as straw dogs" 天地不仁，以萬物為芻狗. *Zhuangzi nanhua zhenjing*, 5:10b. In political discourse, the legitimate ruler of China is called "the Son of Heaven" (*Tianzi* 天子) who receives "the Mandate of Heaven," a phrase often used in political discourse to justify the downfall of an old dynasty and the rise of a new one. In Chinese mythology and religions, Heaven is the realm where immortals and gods reside in eternal bliss and exercise their power on Earth. See Zhu Tianshun, *Zhongguo gudai*, 7–61, where Zhu explains the origins and roles of the deities and gods in Heaven, and 253–72 on ancient worship of *Tiandi* 天帝 and the Mandate of Heaven. In the literary tradition, Heaven is often an illusory realm, where a man has encounters with goddesses, enjoying a series of physical, emotional, and sometimes spiritual engagements

focus on the meanings associated with moral and political justice, as well as with figures of celestial transcendence in literary and cultural realms. With regard to the latter, specifically, attempts to seek solace in literary tropes and imagination. I read these as evidence of the crumbling and collapse of the traditional political, literary, and cultural structures figured in the phrase "collapse of Heaven." Hence, throughout my book, I use this phrase to refer to the profound reshaping of the Chinese literary and cultural milieu from the 1850s to the 1880s, when Chinese society was witnessing not only a collapse in the political and moral order but also the erosion and disruption of long-held beliefs. I found Anders Engberg-Pedersen's salient observation about the Napoleonic Wars (1803–1815) applicable also to the Taiping Civil War: "While clearly marked as a historical event, war was nevertheless not a historical fact but an elusive phenomenon, a blurry object that required a new aesthetics, a new set of forms, new morphologies," and thus literature should be "read as a way of dealing with the complex epistemic regime of war."[8] In the case of the Taiping Civil War, I argue that under the extreme violence, late imperial literary and cultural paradigms began to unravel, giving rise to new modes of sentiment and expression that mark the beginning of Chinese literary modernity. In addition to rethinking the beginning of Chinese literary and cultural modernity, my book offers a comparative perspective on studies about war, rhetoric, and media to engage with discussions of the nineteenth-century global moment.

The collapse did not happen all at once, but in four major stages. The initial stage began around 1840, when social, economic, and cultural order in the southern frontiers fell apart under increasing foreign influences. Even before the First Opium War (1839–1842), Western missionaries had been disseminating religious pamphlets in Canton; they distributed the texts discreetly, but preached openly to people in the streets.[9] With the new treaty ports established by the Nanking Treaty

---

with them before he returns to the human realm. A good example of this tradition is chapter 5 of *Hong loumeng*, in which the protagonist visits the Illusory Realm. I discuss this chapter and its nineteenth-century re-creation in chapter 4.

8. Engberg-Pedersen, *Empire of Chance*, 5–6.

9. From the eighteenth century to the early nineteenth century, the Qing policy on Christianity, except for a few moments, was increasingly restrictive. For instance,

(1842), thousands in the Canton area lost their jobs, the Hakka people among them; to survive, many became bandits in the mountainous areas in the southeastern provinces. As Philip Kuhn points out, the poverty-stricken Hakka communities, who were especially susceptible to Taiping ideology, would constitute the heart of the Taiping movement.[10]

The second stage began in 1843, when a Hakka man, Hong Xiuquan 洪秀全 (1814–1864), declared that the true Heaven had been revealed to him and that he was the son of God, thereby opening the way for a millenarian movement.[11] In 1836, he was given a book by a Western missionary while taking the civil service examination in Guangzhou. Entitled *Good Words to Admonish the World* (*Quan shi liang yan* 勸世良言), this book was written by Liang Fa 梁發 (1789–1855), a woodblock carver who had become the first Chinese Protestant minister. Upon returning to his home from this, his third, failed attempt at the examination, Hong Xiuquan fell gravely ill. For weeks, he was confined to bed, experiencing manic episodes and hallucinations. However, he recovered from the illness and resumed preparing for the examinations, working in the meantime as a teacher. In 1843, Hong Xiuquan failed a fourth time. By chance, he reread the book the missionary had given him and found in it what he believed was the key to the strange dreams and hallucinations he had experienced while ill: the place he had visited was Heaven, and the old man who claimed to be his father was God. The mission he believed God had entrusted to him was to carry out a holy war to salvage the corrupted world and to deliver the Chinese people to Heaven. This chance encounter between Hong Xiuquan and the first Christian pamphlet written by a Chinese author led

---

the Qianlong Emperor (r. 1735–1796) arrested many Christians; the Jiaqing Emperor (r. 1796–1820), imposing even sterner restrictions, ruled that the believers in Christianity were "bandits." See Ma Tingzhong, "Qing wangchao," 225.

10. Kuhn, "Origins of the Taiping Vision"; see also his *Rebellion and Its Enemies.*

11. Boardman, *Christian Influence*; see also his "Millenary Aspects." However, Vincent Shih points out that the Taiping ideology is a more complex system, encompassing not only Christianity but also Chinese orthodoxies such as Confucianism, Daoism, and Buddhism. Shih, *The Taiping Ideology.* For a comprehensive and captivating account of Hong Xiuquan and his vision, see Spence, *God's Chinese Son.*

ultimately to a surge of religious fervor in the mountainous areas of Guangxi fueled by Hong's apocalyptic vision. In January 1851, what began as a regional religious movement transformed into an epic uprising against the Qing government with the proclamation of the Taiping Heavenly Kingdom.[12]

The third stage in the collapse was the Taiping Civil War. Moving down the Yangtze River, the Taiping rebels took over Changsha and Wuhan, the capitals of Hunan and Hubei Provinces, respectively. By the time the Taipings seized Nanjing and established their capital in 1853, their army had grown to three million.[13] The Taipings soon controlled most of the lower Yangtze River and launched expeditions toward the north and west.[14] The initial Qing government response to the Taiping uprising was delayed and incompetent. However, by the summer of 1853, an army that started in Hunan as a local resistance militia evolved into a solid force supporting the Qing army. From 1854, the Taipings and the Qing troops took turns controlling major cities along the Yangtze River, including Changsha, Wuhan, Jiujiang, Suzhou, Ningbo, and Hangzhou. The constant warfare in the Jiangnan region, as Tobie Meyer-Fong has shown, caused tremendous suffering and destruction for local

12. The early development of the Taiping movement puzzles and fascinates scholars. See Wagner, "Operating in the Chinese Public Sphere" and *Reenacting the Heavenly Vision,* and Weller, *Resistance, Chaos, and Control in China.* The translation of the name of God, as Reilly points out, was also important for the Taiping religion as it attracted many followers. (See Reilly, *The Taiping Heavenly Kingdom.*) The literal translation of "Taiping" is "Great Peace." Historically, the term was used to describe a peaceful and harmonious society that exemplifies a traditional political ideal. Several religiously motivated rebellions in China were inspired by the pursuit of the vision of "Taiping," including the Yellow Turban Rebellion (184–200s) that propelled the disintegration of the Han dynasty (202 BCE–9 CE, 25–220 CE) and the Taiping Rebellion itself. Therefore, by naming the regime "Taiping *tianguo*," the rebel leaders conveyed a millenarian vision and evoked the history of ancient rebellion.

13. Zhang Dejian gives an estimate of three million. See Zhang, *Zei qing huizuan,* 2:852–53. Cui Zhiqing's estimate of the size of the Taiping troops in 1853 is more conservative, at no more than one million. See Cui Zhiqing, *Taiping tianguo zhanzheng quanshi,* 1:651.

14. On military development during the Taiping War, see Li Chun, *Taiping tianguo junshi shi.*

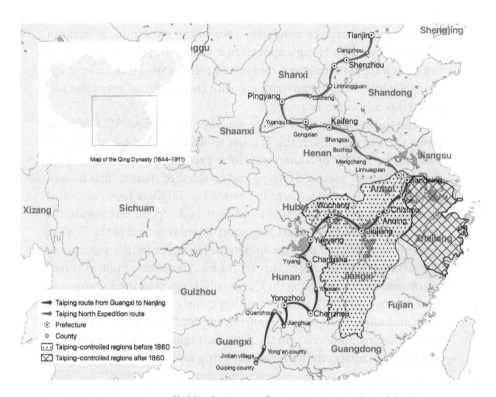

MAP 0.1. Territory controlled by the Taiping forces, 1851–1864. Adapted, by the author with William Wai Him Pang's help, from China Historical Geographic Information System, version 5.

communities.[15] Toward the war's later stage, foreign involvement exerted a strong influence on the war's outcome.[16] From 1862 to 1863, sometimes with the help of foreign militaries, the Qing army recovered many cities in Jiangsu and Zhejiang Provinces. Nanjing remained the Heavenly Kingdom's capital, but not for long. A Qing force led by Zeng Guoquan 曾國荃 (1824–1890), younger brother of Zeng Guofan, rebuilt military camps outside of Nanjing and besieged the city. In July 1864,

15. The destruction caused by the war and the subsequent restoration of order are described in Meyer-Fong, *What Remains*. Responses to personal losses within the family of the prominent Jiangnan scholar, Yu Yue 俞樾 (1821–1907), are discussed by Rania Huntington in her book, *Ink and Tears*.

16. Platt, *Autumn in the Heavenly Kingdom*.

Zeng Guoquan breached the city walls and slaughtered the city's people. Thus, Hong Xiuquan's alternative "Heaven," together with the Taiping Heavenly Kingdom, met its downfall.

Compared with the previous stages, the fourth and final stage may seem less well delineated, but its influence is just as significant and far-reaching. After the war ended, the corruption of the Qing government, the scale of violence and suffering, the repeated foreign invasions, as well as the chaos that reigned for a decade and half, were recorded in bleak reflections of the war and its aftermath. Nevertheless, political, social, and economic order was gradually reestablished on the local level and coincided with the rise of Han military leaders of the Qing, especially Zeng Guofan and his followers. The redistribution of local resources went hand in hand with the "Self-Strengthening Movement" that flourished from the 1860s to the 1880s, a series of reforms that affirmed Confucianism but adopted Western military technology in response to various Qing defeats. For many male Han elites who had endured the Taiping War, the changes in the sociopolitical milieu offered them the hope of entering officialdom based on their military merits or on contributions made to the local community during the war. Those who survived and benefited from the postwar power redistribution went on to shape late Qing politics.

## Resonances across Time

The period of the Taiping War was not the first time China was gripped by a sense of imminent apocalypse. Many nineteenth-century writers find in the events of the Taiping Civil War echoes of the traumatic Ming-Qing dynastic transition in the seventeenth century. For example, authors of fiction and drama sought to come to terms with the Taiping War by referencing literary and historical models such as *The Peach Blossom Fan* (*Taohua shan* 桃花扇), the early Qing canonical southern play (*chuanqi* 傳奇) that tells the story of a tragic romance against the background of the fall of the Ming dynasty (1368–1644 CE).[17] Various

---

17. On the entanglement of romance and history in *The Peach Blossom Fan*, see C. H. Wang, "The Double Plot of *T'ao-hua shan*," 9–18; Wai-yee Li, "The Representation

early Qing texts about the Ming-Qing transition, including the famous witness account *An Account of Ten Days in Yangzhou* (*Yangzhou shiri ji* 揚州十日記), were unearthed in the late Qing era.[18] These models from the fall of the Ming are evoked and adapted by nineteenth-century writers to make sense of contemporary war and violence; at the same time, these models summon traumatic memories of dynastic change that were vehemently suppressed after the Qing consolidation of power.

In describing events such as the Ming-Qing dynastic transition and the Taiping Civil War, late imperial Chinese writers use the expression *jie* 劫. In Buddhist cosmology, *jie* (*kalpa*) designates an extremely long unit of time that marks a complete cycle of the creation and dissolution of the universe. Deriving from that original Buddhist concept, *jie* in the Chinese context describes events of apocalyptic proportions. With the concept of *jie*, people recognize and identify the pattern of historical time as marked by political catastrophes that have occurred and returned, and will occur and return again perpetually. During the late Ming and late Qing dynasties, *jie* also often appeared in Daoist spirit-writings to admonish people to follow moral teachings and avoid cataclysm; with the Taiping War, the eschatological discourse of the Daoist spirit-writing tradition culminated.[19] In writings from the 1850s to the 1880s, the phrase "calamity of the red ram" (*hong yang jie* 紅羊劫) often showed up in reference to the Taiping Rebellion. This is partly because traditionally, the year of the "red ram" (*hong yang* 紅羊) in the Chinese sexagenary cycle was associated with major political disasters deemed unavoidable since they were Heaven's will.[20] Even though the

---

of History in *The Peach Blossom Fan*," 421–33; Struve, "History and *The Peach Blossom Fan*," 55–72.

18. This text only appeared in the public in the second quarter of the nineteenth century. On the dating and discovery of this account, see Struve, *The Ming-Qing Conflict*, 251.

19. Goossaert, *Making the Gods Speak*, 201, 273, 274, 291.

20. The years of *bingwu* 丙午 and *dingwei* 丁未 in the traditional Chinese calendar are associated with national calamities. In the sexagenarian cycle, *bing* 丙, *wu* 午, and *ding* 丁 are associated with the fire, and *wei* is associated with the goat (or ram). The phrase "red ram" is used to refer to the years of *bingwu* and *dingwei* when political disasters happen.

year of "red ram" did not actually occur in the period of the Taiping War, people used this term to describe the catastrophic scale of the event, especially because *hong yang* is homophonous with the combined surnames of Hong Xiuquan and Yang Xiuqing 楊秀清 (1821?–1856), two major leaders of the Taiping Rebellion.

In seventeenth-century discourse, *jie* was primarily associated with political upheaval; in writings generated during the Taiping period, however, we find another common usage of *jie*: as both the cause of, and the means of making sense of, an individual's sufferings. The wish to bring meaning to an individual's *jie* is often expressed through the trope of "banished immortals," in which divine beings banished for wrongs committed in their heavenly lives are subjected to finite sufferings on Earth that eventually help redeem them and let them regain their celestial positions. In addition, *jie* also serves to explain personal ordeals caused by karmic retribution or conditions beyond one's control in this lifetime.[21] Inspired by these usages of *jie*, writers presented themselves as banished immortals in narrating their own existence during their calamitous times. An excellent example of how *jie* is used as a critical concept for making sense of the calamity on both the collective and individual levels is the *chuanqi* play written by Zhu Shaoyi 朱紹頤 (1833–1880), titled *The Calamity of the Red Ram* (*Hong yang jie* 紅羊劫).[22] The play was written in 1854, after Zhu fled from Nanjing, which by that time had become the Taiping Heavenly Capital. The first scene, "The Calamity Begins," presents the outbreak of the war and family separation; the last scene, "The Calamity Ends," fantasizes about the conclusion of the war and family reunion. Through the mediation and theater of *jie*, the public tragedy becomes personal as much as the personal tragedy becomes public.

---

21. On the narrative frame of *jie* in Daoist novels about individuals' cultivation and attainment of immortality, see Lee Fong-mao, *Xu Xun yu Sa Shoujian*, 335–42. As Meyer-Fong observes in *What Remains*, in local gazetteers and morality books produced after the Taiping War there was a strong tendency to explain historical changes through schemes of religious and moral retribution. My study shows that innovations in nineteenth-century political rhetoric and literary experiments reveal both yearning for and disillusionment in those long-held beliefs.

22. Zhu Shaoyi, *Hong yang jie*, 1.

The Taiping legacy lives on into the present time in various forms, for better or worse, especially when the spirit of rebellion is evoked in the name of nationalism and revolution during moments of national crisis. In the present, the historical events subsumed under the rubric "Taiping" are characterized in distinctive ways depending on the purpose and assumptions of those using the term. In mainland China, the story of the Taiping movement is ideologically driven; a prime example is the exhibition titled "The Path of Rejuvenation" at the National Museum of China (2011–present), where the Taiping Rebellion is presented as the forerunner of the twentieth-century Communist Revolution.

Many Chinese scholars writing about this period have followed the line taken by the National Museum exhibition. Western historians, by contrast, do not emphasize the moral and political implications of rebellion (*qiyi* 起義), but read in the term "rebellion" the violent nature of the Taiping resistance to the Qing government. In recent years, historians such as Meyer-Fong and Stephen Platt have taken to using the term "the Taiping Civil War" to emphasize the equivalence of the Qing government and the Taiping regime as two political entities with distinct ideologies. The events of the time do indeed constitute a "civil war," not only because the Taiping Heavenly Kingdom was established in opposition to the Qing empire, but also because the political repercussions of the Taiping movement, manifested in the form of numerous local uprisings, had spread throughout China.

## Rewriting the Times

The Taipings' reckoning with the fundamental structure of Chinese society is exemplified by the calendar they designed. This calendar, which integrates the traditional Chinese lunar calendar and the Gregorian calendar, aimed to implement the Taiping millenarian vision by influencing people's everyday experiences on Earth. With such a new awareness, the Taipings demonstrated that they were ready to radically break from the temporal mode that sustained not only the Qing society at the time, but also the connections between that society and the past in which it was rooted. This Taiping temporal regime, against not only the Qing rule but also the entire Chinese imperial tradition, is an extreme example of how temporalities exploded during the nineteenth century.[23]

Although one of the heterogeneous temporal orientations during the Taiping period appears in the form of the Taiping calendar, most of those orientations are registered in narratives. This is because on both the personal and collective levels, the structure of existence reaches language in narrativity, which in turn has "temporality as its ultimate referent."[24] At the same time, as one of the essential cognitive tools, narrative plays a significant role in helping people make sense of their experiences, especially during disastrous times.[25] The sense-making processes about a catastrophic period of the Taiping War generated myriad forms of narrative, including Hong Xiuquan's delineation of the Taiping millenarian vision, personal accounts and memoirs, as well as fiction and drama relating to cultural reverberations of traumatic historical moments with the evocation of *jie*, which rejects a linear progression of time but offers a cyclical temporal complex.[26] Taken together, the writings that came out of Chinese culture from the 1850s to 1880s are examples of allegories not only of history but also of the extensive change in late imperial literary and cultural paradigms, with regard to configurations of individual fate and collective destiny situated within an uncertain time that is simultaneously a unity of past, present, and future.[27]

This book is a broad-ranging, multigenre, and multimedia study of writings produced during and in relation to the Taiping Civil War. I argue that Chinese literature from the mid- to late nineteenth century creatively manipulates a long tradition of writings on military and

23. My use of "temporality" stems from the Heideggerian analysis (simplified and with modification) that we exist "within time," and its descriptions of how our experience of time depends on our "care" for the world. See his famous *Being and Time*. Heideggerian time-analysis, however, has been challenged for its lack of moral concern toward others and toward historical and natural time. One of the major thinkers engaging in this debate is Paul Ricœur, who fully explores this question in *Time and Narrative*.

24. Ricœur, "Narrative Time," 165.

25. Mink, "Narrative Form as a Cognitive Instrument."

26. Ricœur, "Narrative Time," 165.

27. White describes this kind of writings as "artistic treatment of a real event . . . [that] transcends the truth." See his "Introduction," 149.

political violence dating back to the late Tang dynasty (618–907 CE) and especially the Ming-Qing dynastic transition. In doing so, I reconceptualize the Taiping War as a pivotal event in Chinese literary and cultural history, an event that is deeply rooted in a traumatic past. At the same time, I show the possibilities and processes of the first Chinese civil war inspired by utopian visions imported from the West, to shed light on understandings about wars in twentieth-century China that were also influenced by Western beliefs.

Drawing from studies of religion, history, and literature, I have chosen to focus on texts of political, archaeological, or literary significance. On a synchronic level, I show that these writings, as expressions produced at particular historical instances, exemplify shifting expectations of major narrative genres' social and aesthetic functions. On a diachronic level, I track networks of allusions to show that utopian and dystopian visions, nostalgic lamentations, and fantastic imaginings know no temporal and political boundaries in literary engagements with calamitous events. The conflicting yet mutually generative rhetoric and aesthetic modes in the writings I study unsettle simplistic dichotomies: if one of the modes is despair, it must be understood in the context of elation, just as orthodoxy must be seen in relation to heterodoxy, and despondency in relation to masochistic pleasure. Ultimately, we see the emergence of a culture characterized by apocalyptic sensibilities and yearnings for transcendence on both ideological and personal levels. Reading the many modes of narratives generated by an impactful historical event like the Taiping Civil War with temporal awareness, I show a glimpse of the deep structure underlying society or culture that might otherwise be obscured.

I begin in chapters 1 and 2 by tracing the ideological contest between the Taiping rebels and their Qing opponents, to rethink the meaning and practices of nineteenth-century Chinese religion. Meyer-Fong's influential book, *What Remains*, shows there was a strong tendency to explain the Taiping War through schemes of some sort of moral retribution in its aftermath. However, I show how internal changes in Taiping and Qing ideological discourses both present an antithesis of the heterodox and the orthodox in competition for ultimate political and religious authority. Their emphases on supernatural powers foreshadowed the Boxer Rebellion (1899–1901), a violent uprising against

Christianity and foreigners that was charged with beliefs in the super-natural.[28] As chapter 1 shows, the active usage of woodblock printing technology and the Taiping regime's institutionalization of prosely-tizing activities anticipate what Philip Clark observes about the usage of religious media in China from the late nineteenth century through the Republican period.[29] In fact, as Chuck Wooldridge shows, the rebels and their conqueror, the Qing government, projected their ideologies onto urban space through both material and nonmaterial means.[30] In addition, the ideological convulsions of the Taiping War can be in-cluded in what Vincent Goossaert describes as the "series of events" that led "a sizable segment" of Chinese elites to support campaigns against superstition in the late nineteenth century.[31]

With regard to the effects of the war on the arts, my investigation of a wide collection of genres shows how nineteenth-century writers' adaptations of a long literary tradition, in response to the war and its aftermath, reinvented the terrain of Chinese literature. Discussions of nineteenth-century Chinese literature tend to focus on Western impact, as shown in Patrick Hanan's work on the significance of the introduction of modern media and Keith McMahon's attention to the semicolonial historical context.[32] However, as my research shows, significant changes had been happening within the Chinese literary tradition since before the influx of Western technology and literature. These changes were accelerated and redirected by the war.

My exploration of the effects of the war on culture participates in the larger field that discusses the reverberations of national crises in Chinese literary tradition. Ellen Widmer exhibits the Zhan family's literary responses to the war; Rania Huntington has done an excellent exploration of immediate literary remembrances of this war in literary genres such as personal writings, short stories, and drama.[33] However,

28. Esherick, *The Origins of the Boxer Uprising*.
29. Clark, "New Technologies and the Production of Religious Texts."
30. Wooldridge, *City of Virtues*.
31. Goossaert, "1898: The Beginning of the End," 327.
32. Hanan, *Chinese Fiction of the Nineteenth and Early Twentieth Centuries*; McMahon, *Polygamy and Sublime Passion*.
33. Widmer, *Fiction's Family*; Huntington, *Ink and Tears*, "Chaos, Memory, and Genre," "The Captive's Revenge," and "Singing Punishment and Redemption."

I argue that it is equally important to situate these writings about the Taiping Civil War against a broader literary and cultural backdrop. The Ming-Qing dynastic transition, for example, "forced the domains of history and literature into a complex and riveting symbiosis."[34] Representations of history in twentieth-century Chinese fiction, as David Der-wei Wang has shown, highlight the "monstrosity" of perpetual violence passing across generations.[35] Therefore, focusing as it does on the literary and cultural artifacts of the Taiping Civil War—from the utopian ideals inspired by the West to the rejuvenation of Qing ideology, and from lyrical articulations of the self to phantasmagorical vistas arising from a bleak reality—this book adds to these discussions, showing how the writings of this period exhibit new visions of apocalypse as well as religious and political redemption, thus anticipating modern conceptions of selfhood and community.

## The Producers and Production of Texts

The writings I discuss were produced by two generations of writers from the 1850s to the 1880s. The span of forty years allows political and religious questions raised by the Taiping Rebellion to be at least temporarily resolved or put to rest with the restoration of Qing imperial order. All the writers, including Hong Xiuquan, received a Confucian education, but none succeeded in the civil service examinations. The oldest generation of these writers included Hong Xiuquan and the writers who undertook the project of reinterpreting Qing ideology to fight against the beliefs Hong Xiuquan introduced and disseminated. In comparison, the life stories of those who came of age after Hong Xiuquan's generation were quite different, as many were afforded new opportunities brought about by the rise of Zeng Guofan and the Han military officials in the Qing government. Still, others among this

34. Wai-yee Li, "Introduction," 1. At various places in *Women and National Trauma in Late Imperial Chinese Literature*, Wai-yee Li touches upon the issue of how the Ming-Qing dynastic transition was received in the nineteenth century. Peter Zarrow gives a more comprehensive exploration of this topic in "Historical Trauma."

35. David Der-wei Wang, *The Monster That Is History*.

younger generation, who were completely disillusioned with the civil examination system and with late Qing politics, sought cultural inspiration from the West and invested in modern print media. Each author found a unique way to confront and work with the feeling that "Heaven was collapsing." Hong Xiuquan sought to bring an absolute utopian Heaven to Earth.[36] The Qing literati who resisted the Taipings made the Mandate of Heaven central to their interpretation of the Qing Sacred Edict. The diarists cried out to Heaven as the ultimate yet merciless Being during moments of despair. The image of an omnipotent and implacable Heaven is further developed in fiction and drama, where writers sought to frame the *jie* of the Taiping War as an atrocity doomed to occur. The unfulfilled yearning for and ironic disenchantment with the ideal of Heaven is epitomized in their imaginations of themselves as divinely inspired or abandoned immortals.

The writers were able to express and disseminate their views of the "collapse of Heaven" through the various media forms I discuss. Ideas were translated into words, and words into texts. In its capacity to produce numerous copies of texts, print technology served as a vehicle for transmitting emotional and intellectual experiences to a mass audience. The pamphlets (printed by lithography outside of China) that missionaries brought to southeastern coastal regions triggered a wave of Taiping proselytization using traditional woodblock printing technology. The history of some Taiping texts can be traced to the 1840s, but all the texts I discuss were written or printed after 1850. As Taiping texts proliferated, Confucian classics were purged as much as possible from Taiping-occupied regions; contemporary personal accounts and literary creations were also destroyed in the violence and warfare. At the same time, Qing loyalists printed and distributed religious tracts that aimed to admonish the masses with traditional Confucian morality on a large scale. In the aftermath of the war, texts from both sides survived, and publishing played a significant role in restoring Confucian moral beliefs and creating war memories.[37] About two decades after the conclusion of the war, personal writings treating the recent trauma began to surface

36. Nineteenth-century missionaries placed tremendous importance on the translation of "Heaven"; see Reilly, *The Taiping Heavenly Kingdom*, 83, 85, 90, 104.

37. Meyer-Fong, *What Remains*, chap. 2, 20–63.

again in both manuscript and print forms including full-length novels, short stories about the strange, and *chuanqi* plays. Although *chuanqi* plays, printed in the 1880s with woodblock technology, circulated mostly among the inner circle of playwrights, the literati novel that concerned itself with the war was, in response to consumer appetite, immediately reprinted with modern typesetting technology for commercial purposes. The introduction of modern printing technologies and the establishment of the *Shenbao* publisher (Shenbaoguan 申報館) cultivated not only the burgeoning literary market but also the first generation of writers who wrote for and were published in modern media. Books, pamphlets, magazines, and newspapers—all products of the print technology—helped create and stoke the general despair and disillusionment. As a result, they inspired and reinforced a desire for the restoration of order as much as a desire for radical change.

## A Brief Conspectus

This book's chapters chart the changes to cultural discourses and literary forms under the pressure of the Taiping Civil War. Part I, "Competing Visions of Heaven and Hell," examines cultural and historical texts written or produced amid the war, contrasting the preaching of Taiping and Qing ideologies with meditations on personal plight and precariousness. Both the Qing and Taiping ideological discourses seek to persuade people to act in alignment with the moral and political future each prescribes, but the rumination of one individual (Shen Zi) on traumatic loss transforms the present by editing traces of the past. Part II, "Making Sense of the Past and the Future," looks at literary texts written for the most part in the aftermath of the war. In these texts, the Taiping catastrophe is presented in fictional and theatrical forms that deconstruct received topoi and anticipate future rounds of upheavals.

Each part consists of three chapters, each chapter focusing on a few major narrative texts that are representative of writings of the genre. Given the chronological order of the chapters, this book itself may be read as a narrative of the literary and cultural milieu of the second half of the nineteenth century. Nevertheless, like the texts I discuss, this "narrative" should be regarded as a tapestry woven of many temporal threads, as I show in my analysis of the interstices of authorial edits and textual variants, as well as textual and historical referentiality. The literary texts emanating from the Taiping War are the subject of my study, but threaded through the whole is how writers evoked and reinvented major literary classics from the Ming and Qing dynasties, including *The Peach Blossom Fan, Dream of the Red Chamber* (*Honglou meng* 紅樓夢), *Stories about the Strange from Liaozhai Studio* (*Liaozhai zhiyi* 聊齋誌異), and *Water Margin* (*Shuihu zhuan* 水滸傳).

Chapters 1 and 2 explore the reinvention of political and religious discourses as both Taiping rebels and Qing elites evoked divine forces to compete for ultimate authority to claim different forms of orthodoxies. Chapter 1, "Heavenly Visions: The Taiping Alternative," explores important edicts at the core of the Taiping textual universe. Traditionally issued by emperors, edicts are symbolic of imperial authority, so the act of publishing in this genre itself serves as a political statement. The hybridity of Taiping texts, in terms of ideas as well as printing features, reveals how they appropriated and exploited both Chinese and Western cultural traditions. Viewed as a continuum, these "sacred" texts show the expansion and evolution of the Taiping textual universe as it expurgates remnants of Confucianism, identifies the Manchu as the foe, and systematically rewrites China's entire history.

Chapter 2, "Revelations from Hell: A Qing Answer," examines significant transformations in Qing ideological discourse, which occurred partly in response to the heterogeneous religious beliefs on the rise in southern frontiers during the mid-nineteenth century. The major text that this chapter discusses is *Miraculous Proofs of the Sacred Edict* (*Shengyu lingzheng* 聖諭靈徵), a multivolume interpretation of the Sacred Edict, the foundational text for preaching Qing ideology. I argue that by melding Qing state ideology and popular religious beliefs, *Miraculous Proofs of the Sacred Edict* marks a significant moment of change in late imperial ideological discourse. The incorporation of popular religious elements, especially notions of Hell and retributive punishment, initiated a new genre using stories of retribution to vindicate the Sacred Edict. Ironically, these interpretive efforts resonate with the proselytizing approaches used by the Taiping rebels and inadvertently pose a potential challenge to the Qing emperor's legitimacy as transmitter of the Mandate of Heaven.

Taking an archaeological approach, chapter 3 ("Order in Disorder: Personal Accounts of War") examines private accounts written in wartime. Compared to the proselytizing texts discussed in chapters 1 and 2, which advocate certainty and stability, these accounts bear witness to calamitous events and the collapse of order. I focus in particular on a manuscript diary by Shen Zi as a historical, cultural, and literary phenomenon. Shen Zi made countless revisions to his notes and accounts as he revisited, recollected, and reconstructed traumatic memories of his own experiences and those of others. This meticulous editorial work can be read as a manifestation of a Confucian student's identity struggles during atrocious times. The causal connections that emerge from the repeatedly revised narrative reveal how Shen Zi attempts to reestablish his identity and agency by asserting a certain sense of control over what had transpired.

Part II covers the ways that conflict, violence, and the self are presented, often through the devices and genres of fiction. Chapter 4, "Traces of History: A Literati Novel and Its Precedents," investigates the full-length novel *Traces of Flowers and the Moon* (*Hua yue hen* 花月痕), which enjoyed immense popularity during the late Qing and early Republican era. In this work, the author, Wei Xiuren 魏秀仁 (1818–1873), presents a version of himself as the male protagonist, creating in the process a repository of personal memories that invoke tropes from literary classics such as *Dream of the Red Chamber* and *The Peach Blossom Fan*. However, his futile attempt to create such a self-image points to the irretrievable loss of those literary ideals as literati identities crumbled. The last eight chapters of the novel, characterized as they are by cynicism and fanciful optimism, invoke cultural memories of the seventeenth-century Ming-Qing dynastic transition only to reveal the author's deep disillusionment with traditional paradigms that promise to bring meaning to political calamities.

Chapter 5, "Violence in Drama: The Reinvention of Community," studies theatrical works revolving around individual trauma to serve as public remembrances and commemorations. In these plays, images of literati-turned-warriors who vanquish the Taiping rebels contrast with the protagonists discussed in chapters 3 and 4. Nevertheless, by looking back to *The Peach Blossom Fan*, a play about the Ming-Qing dynastic transition, and *Water Margin*, a novel about outlaws and insurrections, some of these dramatic renditions of political catastrophe and their celebrations of individual and local prowess coincidentally foreshadow the disintegration of the empire. The paratextual discourse emerging from prefaces and commentaries to the plays, written by the literati communities that survived the war, may have offered cathartic consolation to the violence and disintegration of families in the theatrical realm and in reality.

The last chapter, "Fantasies: Transcendence and Defiance," discusses the nineteenth-century reinvention of the tradition of the seventeenth-century classic *Stories about the Strange from Liaozhai Studio*. Two writers of the period, Xuan Ding 宣鼎 (1832–1880) and Wang Tao 王韜 (1828–1897), who supported opposing sides in the war, "fabulate" memories of unrestrained violence and inexplicable horrors in the forms of the deviant, the outlawed, and the grotesque. The effacement of the boundary between the realms of the fantastic and the real in their work, and the inadequacy of received moral and historical codes, create "fables" that break historical continuity, ironically echoing the Taiping claim that Earth has become an uninhabitable realm. The collapsing paradigm revealed by the fantastic, mystic visions, therefore, gestures toward infinite possibilities for the future.

Fabulation was not just an escapist dream, but a way forward from an impasse for all parties, including the Taipings. The turbulence from the 1850s to the 1880s was instigated, recorded, and negotiated through words as mediated in multiple forms. Writings from this period collectively communicate this impression: when Heaven was collapsing, people sought to resurrect fragments of anything remotely resembling stability and certainty by vying to invent a new Heaven, or struggling to piece back together the shattered fragments of Heaven. Ironically, the anomalous pictures they presented only called forth further disillusionment. However, as I will show, as traditional literary and cultural paradigms unraveled, new possibilities emerged for redefining both the making and the imagining of history. An extreme consequence of economic inequality, social exclusion, and racial antagonism, the Taiping Civil War opened up many new directions for the Chinese to engage with the past and the future.

PART I

*Competing Visions
of Heaven and Hell*

# CHAPTER ONE

# Heavenly Visions

## The Taiping Alternative

At the core of the Taiping ideology is this vision: God, the ultimate authority, is enraged and will let disasters befall China. Only if the Chinese people recognize and believe in the one true God can they be saved from the evil Manchus. This vision is also the self-stated cause, mission, and purpose of the Taiping movement.[1] Historians trace the connections between this vision and the Taiping movement from various perspectives. For example, both Rudolf Wagner and Jonathan Spence emphasize the importance of Hong Xiuquan's vision in the course of Taiping history.[2] Eugene Boardman interprets the purpose

---

Discussions of the Taiping placards and *The Taiping Heavenly Chronicle* in this chapter have appeared respectively in my journal articles, "Violence and the Evolving Face of *Yao* in Taiping Propaganda," *Journal of Religion and Violence* 6 (1), May 2018, 127–44 and "Authenticating the Renewed Heavenly Vision: *The Taiping Heavenly Chronicle (Taiping tianri),*" in *Frontiers of History in China* 13, no. 2 (2018), 173–92. I use relevant discussion with both journals' permissions.

1. Boardman traces the Christian texts that were probably available to the Taipings in *Christian Influence*. For more about the miscellaneous sources that framers of Taiping ideology might have drawn inspiration from, see Shih, *The Taiping Ideology*. From an anthropological perspective, Robert Weller argues that the numerous interpretive possibilities among their divine messages destabilized the Taiping ideology. See Weller, *Resistance, Chaos, and Control in China*.

2. Wagner, *Reenacting the Heavenly Vision*, 99; Spence, *God's Chinese Son*, 76.

of the Taiping movement as "provid[ing] otherworldly solace and . . .
inspir[ing] the realization of a Taiping Heaven on earth."[3] However,
Taiping ideology can be seen as operating not only on historical and
religious levels but also on linguistic, literary, and rhetorical levels,
which is evident if we look closely at a range of publications categorized
by the Taipings as "sacred." In this chapter, I investigate the Taipings'
innovative approaches to literature of persuasion for a mass audience
with inspirations from the West, as well as the historical significance
of this kind of literature. On one level, I show the interdependence of
Taiping internal and external power struggles; on another level, I un-
pack the textual constituents of Taiping ideology revolving around
binary concepts of orthodoxy and heterodoxy, and their reinventions
of various political, religious, and cultural discourses.

A key example of such reinventions is the Taipings' use of the term
*Tian* (天; literally, Heaven) to refer to "God." This term has particular
associations and connotations in Chinese traditional beliefs, quite different from those associated with Christianity and the Judeo-Christian
tradition. The Taipings were not the first to adopt this term to refer to
"God." *Tian* was one of the few terms to name the divinity selected by
Matteo Ricci (1552–1610), the seventeenth-century Jesuit who endeav-
ored to translate Christian ideas into Chinese. At the same time, the
Chinese notion of "Heaven" was foundational to imperial rule, so
adopting it for the Christian God could be interpreted politically as a
challenge to the system. Thus, both Jesuits and other Christian missionaries in the late imperial period avoided using *Tian* in the translation for God. The Taiping rebels, however, embraced *Tian* in their
discourse both to signify God's divine authority and to challenge Qing
rulership, to such an extent that, as Thomas Reilly observed, "the concepts of Heaven and Heaven's rule most radically shaped the developing Taiping movement."[4]

We see similar redeployments of elements in traditional discourse
of decrees and edicts issued in Taiping publications, which effectively
declared a rebellion against the Qing government. In imperial Chinese
history, both decrees and edicts were issued in the name of the emperor

3. Boardman, "Millenary Aspects of the Taiping Rebellion," 77.
4. Reilly, *The Taiping Heavenly Kingdom*, 104.

for an audience of either officials or masses.[5] Written in classical Chinese, these are very formal literary genres, often in prose but also occasionally in the form of verse. The earliest comprehensive work about Chinese literary thought, *The Literary Mind and the Carving of Dragons* (*Wen xin diao long* 文心雕龍), by Liu Xie 劉勰 (fl. 465–522), describes imperial edicts in this way: "As an emperor rules over his empire, his words have a mysterious effect . . . his voice is heard to the limits of the four borders. To accomplish this, he depends on the *zhao* 詔, or edict."[6] Used to proclaim imperial messages, edicts are meant to "reach far," as Liu Xie goes on to explain: "In making appointments and selecting the virtuous for such appointments, an edict should contain ideas as bright as the sun and the moon . . . in connection with the conduct of military expeditions, it should thunder forth in rolling majesty."[7] Unlike traditional imperial proclamations, however, the Taiping "sacred" texts exhibit influences from many genres, ranging from ballads to historical narratives. Furthermore, the physicality of these Taiping texts—their nature as objects—differentiates them from traditional imperial proclamations: the Taiping texts are hybrids of printing features from both traditional China and the West. As the Taiping Rebellion developed, the format and content of Taiping proselytizing texts changed along with it; these changes suggest struggles within Taiping leadership and their efforts to find a voice to communicate divinity to the masses. Taken together, the Taipings' search for political and religious authorities in these "sacred" texts appropriates, exploits, and disrupts important cultural traditions that symbolize the highest imperial authority. The

5. The authors of Taiping "imperial" proclamations were not just speaking in the name of Heaven: they styled themselves as heavenly beings, members of the "divine family," as they defined it: God, Jesus Christ, Hong Xiuquan, and Hong Xiuquan's son. When divine messages are mediated through these figures, the effect is that specific historical moments take on a supernatural character in which divine revelation and political authority validate one another, just as they do in existing Qing imperial political discourses. Harold Love writes about the role of "owner of words" in the public sphere, under the rubric of "declarative authorship." See Love, *Attributing Authorship*, 45. Wang Qingcheng notices but does not fully explore the significance of *zhao* in Taiping publications. See his *Taiping tianguo de wenxian*, 124.

6. Liu Xie, *The Literary Mind*, 145.

7. Liu Xie, *The Literary Mind*, 149.

Taiping rebels—as they declare—subverted not only the Qing government but also the entire imperial system.

## The Taiping Publications

The Taiping publications were central to their religious and political
endeavors and served as what we might now recognize as forms of
propaganda. In Jacques Ellul's definition, "propaganda" is "a set of
methods employed by an organized group that wants to bring about
the active or passive participation in its actions of a mass of individuals,
psychologically unified through psychological manipulations and incorporated in an organization."[8] With modifications, this concept provides a useful analytical tool to understand the social and cultural
functions of Taiping texts. Ellul uses the concept to discuss propaganda
in a modern society dominated by television and radio, but the concept
opens a fresh perspective on the modi operandi the Taipings used to
spread their beliefs to the masses: the Taipings consciously exploited
the various media forms available in their time to influence people's
beliefs and to impel them into political and military activities. In this
sense, the Taiping publications, which certainly carry great religious
significance, are also an early example of propaganda.

The Taipings were keenly aware of the power that ideologies have
over people. Claiming the Taiping ideology to be true orthodoxy, the
Taipings set themselves up in opposition to traditional beliefs such
as Confucianism, Buddhism, and Daoism, calling them "deviant
teachings." One of the earliest Taiping tracts analyzes the "pernicious"
influence of those beliefs:

> Once deviant teachings are promoted, people under Heaven all believe
> and follow them. After having believed and followed them for so long,
> people are used to seeing and hearing them; being used to seeing and
> hearing those teachings, people have them deeply ingrained in their
> minds; with these teachings deeply ingrained in their minds, people find

8. Ellul, *Propaganda*, 61.

it difficult to see their pitfalls; finding it difficult to see the pitfalls, people cannot transcend their boundaries.

邪說一倡，而天下多靡然信之從之。信從久，則見聞熟；見聞熟，則膠固深；膠固深，則難尋其罅漏；難尋其罅漏，則難出其範圍。[9]

This tract, circulated in the early days of the movement, is insightful in pointing out that people do not question existing beliefs because these beliefs have been deeply ingrained for a long time. The neat parallelism and sequential logic enact a strong rhetorical style of persuasion. From this simple observation, it was an easy step for the Taipings to argue that what they had to do was to make known the "truth" about God and to eradicate the "deviant teachings" at the foundation of the traditional beliefs. What's left unsaid in the quoted extract, though, is that the Taipings aimed to replace traditional beliefs with another ideology, a new system that would be as cohesive and widespread as the old system.

## Context and Function

The Taipings carried out cultural strategies with political force to promulgate their ideology.[10] They disciplined and punished people in the areas they controlled through military enforcement and organized rituals. To mobilize large congregations, the Taipings also used a practice called "preaching the principles" (*jiang daoli* 講道理).[11] Of all the Taipings' cultural strategies, however, it was their control of printed matter

9. *TPTGYS*, 1:18; Michael, *The Taiping Rebellion*, 2:40.

10. For example, the Taipings made every effort to recruit, enlist, and capture those who had a certain degree of literacy, and forced them to preach the Taiping ideology to the illiterate. See the transcription of an oral account by Liu Guizeng, *Yusheng ji lüe*, 4:373.

11. *Jiang daoli* is a term traditionally used to refer to religious teachings. This phrase is primarily seen in Buddhist religious texts. In contemporary Cantonese, this phrase is still used to refer to the preaching of Christianity. In some cases, more than ten thousand people from a city in a Taiping-controlled area could gather to listen to a session of "preaching the principles." For instance, once the Taipings occupied Wuchang, they transformed the Yard of Reviewing Horses (*yue ma chang* 閱馬場) to the Yard of Preaching Principles (*jiang dao chang* 講道場). Chen Li, "Taiping jun gongzhan Wuchang chengqu tu," 56.

that played the vital role, employing strategies influenced by both imperial censorship and proselytizing activities of Christian missionaries
in nineteenth-century China. One strategy was proscription: as early
as their 1851 declaration of the uprising, the Taipings forbade "evil
books" (*yao shu* 妖書), which encompassed almost all non-Taiping
books except for calendars and almanacs. After the 1853 establishment
of the Heavenly capital in Nanjing, the Taiping rebels began to destroy
"evil books" widely and systematically.[12] The Taipings balanced proscription with edification strategies. Around the same time as the bans
and burnings, the Taipings opened an office of print and initiated the
first major wave of Taiping publication.[13] In fact, following in the foot-
steps of Protestant missionaries such as Karl Gützlaff (1803–1851), the
Taipings treated proselytizing texts not as sacred objects but as means
of spreading ideas; as a result, their publications were prevalent in
many of the areas they passed through or controlled.[14]

## The Texts as Artifacts

The Taiping tracts have paratextual features embodying both Chinese
and Western influences. In figure 1.1, the cover of a Taiping tract features symmetrical patterns made up of auspicious mythical animals
such as dragons and phoenixes, as well as symbols of nature such as
ocean waves and mountain ridges. These patterns, under the name
"Edge of Sea and River" (*haishui jiangya* 海水江涯), symbolized

---

12. These strategies had disastrous consequences for private libraries and personal
collections in the Jiangnan area. See Lai Xinxia, *Zhongguo tushu shiye shi*, 275.

13. The earliest publication date indicated on extant Taiping materials is 1851.
Most extant Taiping texts were printed between 1852 and 1854. Wang Qingcheng,
*Taiping tianguo de wenxian*, 106–14. Sometimes the same title of a Taiping publica-
tion has various editions. In this book, I primarily use the editions preserved in
*ATPTGGS*, in addition to modern reprints and those digitized and made accessible
online by libraries.

14. Karl Gützlaff disseminated a large number of Christian pamphlets along
China's coastal frontiers. Lutz, *Opening China*, 267. The Taiping texts were so many
and so ubiquitous that both Zhang Dejian, a Qing official, and Augustus Lindley
(1840–1873), the British Royal Navy officer who joined the Taiping side during the
war, recorded this observation in their accounts. Zhang Dejian, *Zei qing huizuan*,
2:716; Lindley, *Ti-ping Tien-kwoh*, 147.

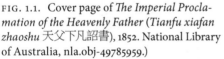

FIG. 1.1.  Cover page of *The Imperial Procla-mation of the Heavenly Father* (*Tianfu xiafan zhaoshu* 天父下凡詔書), 1852. National Library of Australia, nla.obj-49785959.)

FIG. 1.2.  Cover page of an 1825 missionary tract. TA 1977.75 C1825. Harvard-Yenching Library, Harvard University.

infinite prosperity and stability during the Qing dynasty. They were widely used on imperial robes worn by officials and emperors to designate authority. However, having the publication date on the cover is a Western feature, as seen on the Christian pamphlets distributed along the southeastern coast in China (an example is shown in fig. 1.2). Noticeably, the publication date appears on the cover of each Taiping print material. These dates are based on the Taiping calendar, which integrates the traditional Chinese lunar calendar and the Gregorian calendar.

The text of the Taiping tracts is presented in an unusual format: terms referring to those associated with Heaven, such as God, Jesus

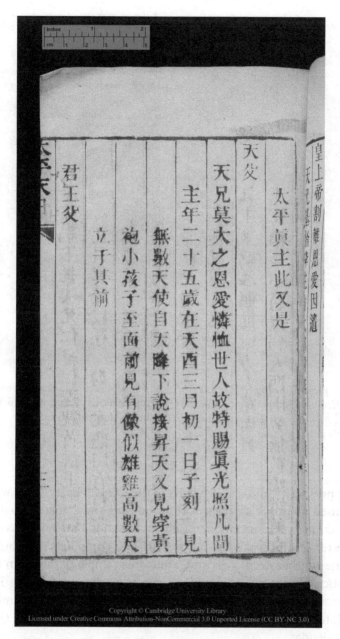

FIG. 1.3. Page from *The Taiping Heavenly Chronicle* (*Taiping tianri* 太平天日), 1862. Picture courtesy of the Digital Library of Cambridge University.

Christ, and Hong Xiuquan, are printed in superscript (elevated characters) of varying heights that follow a divine hierarchy. For instance, the layout of an 1862 tract consistently symbolizes reverence for God by making each reference to the deity stand alone in a column, with no indent downward (as illustrated by the second column from the right in fig. 1.3). In contrast, the content of a column that makes no mention of divine names is indented downward by four characters (as in the fifth to seventh columns from the right in fig. 1.3). The text's visual flow on the page is disrupted in the following pattern: Jesus Christ's name is one character lower than that of God, and the name of the Heavenly King is one character lower than that of Jesus Christ (as in the third and the fourth columns from the right, respectively, in fig. 1.3). Thus, the name of God hovers above the rest of the text. This design appropriates a standard practice across genres of Qing political and religious publications: whenever Qing emperors or important divinities are referred to, their honorific titles are made to stand out by their placement.[15] Elizabeth Perry, in her discussion of the Chinese Communist Revolution, identifies a practice she calls "cultural positioning": "strategic deployment of a range of symbolic resources (religion, ritual, rhetoric, dress, drama, art, and so on) for purposes of political persuasion."[16] As Perry observes, through cultural positioning, radically new messages, such as communism, obtained a less foreign appearance and were introduced to the target audience with greater ease. We can see cultural positioning at work in the Taiping movement, as the Taipings drew on both late imperial propagandistic practices and missionary proselytizing activities to make their ideology and methods seem less radical.

15. In early Taiping publications, the hierarchical order of divine names is not strictly observed, and the rectangular frame containing the main text is sometimes modified to fit the elevation of divine names; in later tracts, however, the print layout becomes more consistent. For instance, in one of the edicts that records God's descent from Heaven, the frame of the main body of the text in one edition is an irregular rectangle, whereas in another edition, all content is contained within a rectangular frame. See the two editions of *Tianfu xiafan zhaoshu* in the New York Public Library Digital Collections.

16. Perry, *Anyuan*, 4.

In addition to employing special design elements in their publications, the Taipings also carefully managed the books they produced. Between the title page and the text proper in the tracts produced after 1853, there is a list of approved Taiping texts' titles. As time went on, the number of works that were listed increased from fourteen to twenty-nine, suggesting an expansion of Taiping ideological discourse.[17] The titles of these publications appeared in the front matter in a hierarchical order based on their degrees of sacredness and can be divided into three categories: first are the most sacred works, including the Old and New Testaments of the Bible and the Taiping decrees and edicts; second are the earliest Taiping tracts and the manuals prescribing Taiping rituals and military principles; the third category comprises pragmatic texts such as educational primers and the Taiping calendar.

Categorized as the most sacred of the texts produced by the Taipings themselves, edicts and decrees functioned as scriptural texts.[18] Whereas some texts from the early stage of the Taiping movement use classical Chinese, most of these "sacred" texts are written in vernacular Chinese mixed with low-register classical Chinese, as do other Taiping publications. Some of these "sacred" texts were used to admonish people about the Taiping vision and moral codes, and some are essentially historical records of a (claimed) divine revelation.[19] The admonitions regularly appear on the lists of Taiping tracts printed after 1853, but the historical records appear only occasionally or not at all. This inconsistency may be due to power struggles within Taiping leadership or to deliberately restricted accessibility to sensitive information that might yield clues to those struggles. I look more deeply into these questions in the next section.

17. The list in the 1852 edition of *Tian tiao shu* has fourteen entries. Some 1853 tracts, for instance, *San zi jing*, have twenty-four entries. In the texts from 1858 and later, there are twenty-eight to twenty-nine titles. See Wang Qingcheng, *Taiping tianguo de wenxian*, 106–14.

18. Wang Qingcheng points out that the edicts issued by the "divine" family were used to admonish people about the Taiping vision and moral codes. See Wang Qingcheng, *Taiping tianguo de wenxian*, 142–43.

19. Wang Qingcheng, *Taiping tianguo de wenxian*, 142–43.

# Texts Listed as Approved

Of all the Taiping edicts and decrees, three texts regularly appear as approved reading: *The Taiping Edicts* (*Taiping zhaoshu* 太平詔書), *Promulgated Edicts* (*Banxing zhaoshu* 頒行詔書), and *The Edicts of the Divine Will Made during the Heavenly Father's Descent to Earth* (*Tianfu xiafan zhaoshu* 天父下凡詔書, two volumes). Published separately and meant to be disseminated broadly, each text assumes a distinct form.

## *The Taiping Edicts*

*The Taiping Edicts* is a collection of three foundational tracts circulated from the start of the Taiping movement: *The Song of Saving the World by Seeking the Fundamental Way* (*Yuan Dao jiu shi ge* 原道救世歌), *Admonitions to Awaken the World by Seeking the Fundamental Way* (*Yuan Dao xing shi xun* 原道醒世訓), and *Admonitions to Enlighten the World by Seeking the Fundamental Way* (*Yuan Dao jue shi xun* 原道覺世訓). According to various historical sources, these texts were written by Hong Xiuquan between 1844 and 1846.[20] The earliest extant edition of *The Taiping Edicts* dates to 1852. The titles of the tracts point not only to the texts' contents but also to what drives them: the phrases "saving the world" and "awaken the world" indicate a sense of urgency, and the key term in two of these titles, "seeking the fundamental way" (*yuan Dao* 原道), illustrates a rejection of established norms and a determination to be radical. Taken together, they stand as a triad of texts that communicate beliefs and claim religious authority for the Taipings at the beginning of the movement.

    *The Song of Saving the World* is a long ballad consisting of mostly rhymed heptasyllabic lines.[21] Its language is a mixture of vernacular and low-level classical Chinese. According to the text, everything is created by God/Heaven, and no other deity is involved in the process of creation. To be favored by Heaven, a virtuous man should eschew

---

20. Michael, *The Taiping Rebellion*, 2:24. The sources he mentions include *The Taiping Heavenly Chronicle*, Hong Rengan's introduction to Hong Xiuquan's background, and Hamberg's "*The Visions of Hung-Siu-tshuen.*"

    21. *ATPTGGS*, 1: 35–48, 77–86.

licentiousness, disrespect for parents, killing, robbery, sorcery, and gambling. The homilies against each vice, of varied lengths, occasionally evoke famous historical figures and metaphors, but the overall rhetorical style is plain and expository. Thus, as one of the earliest Taiping tracts, *The Song of Saving the World* introduces many elements that would appear in later Taiping discourse: moral admonition, usage of a mixture of both vernacular and classical Chinese, association between God and Heaven, and opposition to conventional imperial and religious authorities.

The second text in this collection, *Admonitions to Awaken the World*, is a prose treatise written in classical Chinese that ends with eight heptasyllabic couplets summarizing its central idea. Its format brings to mind other narrative forms such as historical chronicles and vernacular stories, where concluding couplets recapitulate the moral message of the prose. This treatise advocates for religious tolerance by envisioning all men and women on Earth to be followers of God. Despite the radical ideas in *The Song of Saving the World* and *Admonitions to Awaken the World*, these texts still observe certain generic conventions and do not rebuke other beliefs outright. However, in the third sacred text, the tone becomes graver, the rhetoric more hyperbolic, and the form more unconstrained.

The treatise *Admonitions to Enlighten the World*, the third text in the collection, begins by presenting an antithesis between God and the devil in classical Chinese, but ends with an appeal for people's participation in the Taiping cause in vernacular Chinese. According to this treatise, people should not subscribe to the heterodox belief in Yama Demon, because this spirit does not appear in any ancient text. The text concludes with a call for awakening to God and a reprimand for those who don't. In *Admonitions to Enlighten the World*, the tone is more urgent and absolute than in the earlier texts, showing the heightened opposition between the "orthodox" belief and the "heterodox" ones in Taiping ideological discourse.

The textual differences between the 1852 edition and the 1853 reprint of *The Taiping Edicts* provide important clues for understanding the development of Taiping ideology.[22] The most obvious change in the

22. Facsimiles of both editions are reprinted in the first volume of *ATPTGGS*.

1853 edition is the inclusion of a list of approved texts. In addition, though the 1852 edition preserves a reconciliatory attitude toward traditional moral and political authorities, the 1853 reprint aims to break all bonds with those traditions.[23] For instance, in the 1852 edition, the essential Confucian concept of humaneness/benevolence (*ren* 仁) is considered a means of saving a world in decline, but it is completely removed in the 1853 edition. At the same time, the 1853 edition, with its erasure of concrete historical examples and its mystification of the past, is a prime example of the emerging ambition to rewrite Chinese history.[24]

To bring in God and the Taiping "divine family" to occupy the place of absolute power, the 1853 edition of *The Taiping Edicts* removes the figures traditionally considered authorities in Chinese culture, such as emperors and the sages. To replace those figures, in the 1853 edition, God, the devil, and the heavenly law become the focal points of reference. Another significant change in the 1853 reprint is that it presents Heaven and Earth as a continuum where the spirits of Taiping devotees can travel without constraint.[25] Given the amount of violence and loss of life that occurred during the process of establishing the Taiping Heavenly Kingdom, the celebration of death as a path to Heaven indicates an intentional adaptation of Taiping ideology for political purposes. In sum, the 1853 edition institutes three distinct changes: it portrays the uprising against the Qing government as an ongoing heavenly battle, highlights the opposing ways of God and devil, and blurs the boundary between Earth and Heaven, life and death.

23. For another example, there are two 1852 editions of *Tian tiao shu*. One has Confucian content; the other does not. For bibliographical information about these two texts, see Wang Qingcheng, *Taiping tianguo de wenxian*, 98, 100. To compare the content of these two editions, the full version with the Confucian elements is in *TPTGYS*, 1:26–27, and the "cleansed" version is in *ATPTGGS*, 1:300.

24. See *Taiping zhaoshu*, 1:46 and *Taiping zhaoshu* (*chong ke ben*), 1:86. At the end of the 1852 edition, there is a ballad titled "Song of One Hundred Virtues" ("Bai zheng ge" 百正歌). Consisting of three to five characters in each verse, this ballad contrasts virtuous and immoral rulers in Chinese history. The 1853 edition makes significant changes to this perspective, intentionally leaving out all Chinese dynasties, and instead using the word "antiquity" (*gu* 古) to generalize—and thereby mystify—history.

25. *Tian tiao shu* (*chong ke ben*), 1:308–9.

## Promulgated Edicts

In 1847, when Hong Xiuquan and Feng Yunshan 馮雲山 (1815–1852), the two earliest Taiping leaders, had to leave the Taiping base at the Thistle Mountain in Guangxi Province because of Qing persecution, some of the followers who remained behind experienced a series of "spirit possessions" in which they believed they had directly experienced God and Jesus Christ. Until then, the movement emphasized worship, rather than direct revelation, and in fact was known as the "God-worshipping Society" (*Bai Shangdi hui* 拜上帝會). Because of the scarcity of historical records, little is known about how spirit possession exactly happened in the Taiping base. However, when Hong Xiuquan returned in 1849, these incidents of spirit possession among followers were "threaten[ing] to tear the movement apart."[26] Nevertheless, through his visions Hong Xiuquan asserted control by declaring a hierarchy within the leadership, with himself at the top: he affirmed Xiao Chaogui 蕭朝貴 (fl. 1820–1852) as the "medium" of Jesus Christ, Yang Xiuqing as the "medium" of God; Hong Xiuquan himself experienced a "heavenly vision" in which he was identified as "the Messiah."[27] These revelations established a clearer leadership structure and instilled some cohesion into the movement. Over the course of the years 1847 to 1856, the Taipings believed that the Heavenly Brother (Jesus Christ) and the Heavenly Father descended among them for many reasons, great and small: from giving political and military instructions to regulating Hong Xiuquan's domestic affairs.[28]

In 1851, Hong Xiuquan declared the establishment of the Taiping Kingdom and gave five of the senior Taiping leaders the title "king," with particular implied jurisdictions: the East King was Yang Xiuqing; the West King, Xiao Chaogui; the North King, Wei Changhui 韋昌輝

26. Weller, *Resistance, Chaos, and Control in China*, 94.

27. As Zhou Weichi points out, the images of God and the devil were also outlined in one of the conversations between Xiao Chaogui and Hong Xiuquan. Zhou Weichi, *Taiping tianguo yu* Qishi lu, 137.

28. In the following pages, I use the terms "Heavenly Brother" and "Heavenly Father" in describing incidents in which Xiao Chaogui and Yang Xiuqing serve as the mediums of these divinities: Xiao Chaogui as "Heavenly Brother" and Yang Xiuqing as "Heavenly Father."

(1823?–1856); the South King, Feng Yunshan; and the Wing King, Shi Dakai 石達開 (1831–1863). In 1853, the year the Taiping Heavenly Kingdom was established, the full-fledged vision featuring the heavenly battle between God and the Manchus was systematically laid out in three important placards issued by Yang Xiuqing and Xiao Chaogui. In that same year, the Taipings combined the contents of the placards into a tract titled *Promulgated Edicts*.[29]

During the late imperial period, the placard was, perhaps, one of the most important and direct media for spreading official information and ideas among the masses. Some placards survive, so we know what they looked like and how they might have functioned as media of communication. Serving a function similar to today's posters, a placard is much larger, and usually bears stamps and visual patterns symbolic of political authority. The first of the three Taiping placards, shown in figure 1.4, measures fifteen square feet. The textual content is set horizontally inside a frame 25.5" high by 68.4" wide; surrounding this frame is a wide border filled with patterns similar to, though more decorative than, those on the covers of Taiping tracts. The content printed on these three Taiping placards is of the genre *xi wen* introduced at the beginning of this book. Because the genre is so formal, the mere action of publishing *xi wen* demonstrates the Taiping regime's legitimacy and moral authority.

The placard reproduced in figure 1.4 and reprinted in *Promulgated Edicts* is titled "Receiving the Mandate of Heaven to Extinguish Demons; Saving the World and Pacifying People" ("Fengtian zhuyao, jiushi anmin" 奉天誅妖，救世安民).[30] It tells of a vision where the respective divine roles of Yang Xiuqing, Xiao Chaogui, and Hong Xiuquan are evoked either explicitly or implicitly through a historical narrative giving them key responsibilities. The text begins its portrayal of the cosmos with God's creation of the world. It goes on to say that God is omnipresent and omnipotent, naming three occasions when he

29. All extant Taiping placards have similar visual designs. The text is placed in a rectangular frame, surrounded by symbols that represent nature and imperial authority in traditional Chinese cosmology. Reprints of some Taiping placards are preserved in *ATPTGGS*.

30. I discuss the meaning of *yao* in these placards in my article, "Violence and the Evolving Face of *Yao*."

FIG. 1.4. An 1853 Taiping placard, "Receiving the Mandate of Heaven to Extinguish Demons; Saving the World and Pacifying People." National Library of Australia, nla.obj-6327160.

wielded that power forcefully. The first time, he was enraged and unleashed the Great Flood. The second time, he let Moses lead the Jews out of Egypt. The third time, he decided to extinguish humankind. This last time, Jesus Christ, the "Heavenly Brother," sacrificed himself to redeem people from their sins. We are then given a description of what is happening in the present era: as people continued to do evil, in *dingyou* year [1847], God sent down the Heavenly King (Hong Xiuquan) to enlighten the world. In the third month of *wushen* year [1848], God, feeling pity for the people entrapped by demons, descends to Earth through Yang Xiuqing. In the ninth month of the same year, Jesus Christ also descended through Xiao Chaogui. God and his heavenly sons will save the Chinese people from the Manchu demons, who had been the Chinese people's foes for centuries. After completing its outline of the Taiping heavenly vision, the text calls for "famous scholars" and "valiant heroes" to "rise up in righteousness and unfurl the standards, avenging yourselves upon your enemies with whom you cannot live under the same heaven, and together earning merits for yourselves in service to the Sovereign" 願各各起義，大振旌旗，報不共戴天之仇，共立勤王之勳.[31]

A significant development of *Promulgated Edicts* in comparison with *The Taiping Edicts*, as shown in the placard I will introduce, is the identification of Manchus as devils that must be wiped out. Though another famous *xi wen* piece in Chinese history, "Admonishing the Central Plain" ("Yu Zhongyuan xi" 諭中原檄), proclaimed by the Hongwu Emperor (r. 1368–1398) in 1367, also makes ethnic attacks against Mongolian rulers of the Yuan dynasty (1271–1368 CE), it does not demonize the non-Han rulers.[32] However, the Manchu rulers' sins are enumerated in the second of the three Taiping placards, titled "Receiving the Mandate of Heaven to Attack the Barbarian" ("Fengtian taohu" 奉天討胡). This placard expounds on the origins of the Manchu rulers and their sins, portraying them as a demonic alien that should be eliminated. First, the text sets up an antithesis between barbarian territory and China (*Zhongguo* 中國): the original "complete domain

31. *TPTGYS*, 1:108; Michael, *The Taiping Rebellion*, 2:144.
32. "Yu Zhongyuan xi" was allegedly written by Song Lian 宋濂 (1310–1381). See "Yu Zhongyuan xi," 1a–2b.

under Heaven" was Chinese (Han) and not barbarian. However, this changed as the descendants of a white fox and a red dog—the devious Manchus, who worshipped "the serpent demon, the Yama demon, and evil ghosts" (*shemo yanluoyao xiegui* 蛇魔閻羅妖邪鬼)—invaded, forcing the Chinese people to adopt their evil ways. A hundred thousand Manchus, claims the text, rule fifty million Chinese. Therefore, the Taiping cause is to take revenge on the Manchus. Those who follow the cause will ascend to Heaven, and those who do not will be trapped in Hell for eternity.

The third placard, titled "Saving All Chinese People Born of Heaven and Nourished by Heaven" ("Jiu yiqie Tiansheng Tianyang Zhongguo renmin" 救一切天生天養中國人民), seeks to convert all Chinese people to the Taiping cause. The text identifies all Chinese people as children of God, but points out that people have cast aside their belief in God to worship demons, including idols of Buddha, the serpent demon, and the red-eyed Yama demon. The text also states that "For China to rule the Manchu devils is like the master ruling the slave, which is proper, but for the Manchu devils to rule China is like the slave oppressing the master, which is improper" 以中國制妖胡，主御奴也，順也；以妖胡制中國，奴欺主也，逆也.[33] This statement evokes the master-slave relationship, which it seeks to invert rather than destroy. Therefore, even though the Taipings argue for an alternative religious and political vision, their way of thinking is dualistic, patterned after the polarized power structure of the Manchu rulers.

To combat the evil force of the Manchus, these *xi wen* texts evoke the ideal of the chivalric hero to characterize Taiping followers, attributing to them popular literature's stereotypical features of bandits, who rebel against a corrupt government.[34] As Vincent Shih points out, "The Taipings owed a great deal to the novels for the building of their ideology; both in the form of ideas and in the form of physical symbols."[35] For example, in the areas the Taiping rebels passed through, they distributed turbans to those who converted to Christianity. On the turban, the

---

33. *TPTGYS*, 1:112; Michael, *The Taiping Rebellion*, 2:150.

34. We see this characterization in different phrases, for example, *yingxiong* and *haojie* 英雄、豪傑. See *TPTGYS*, 1:33, 109, respectively.

35. Shih, *The Taiping Ideology*, 296.

three characters *zhong yi tang* 忠義堂 (the hall of righteousness and loyalty) were printed. This is the name of the hall where the heroes convened and planned military strategies in *Water Margin*, a sixteenth-century novel about 108 outlaws and their military forays against the imperial government. The Taipings also associated the Christian idea that all men were brothers with the literary representation of sworn brotherhood in *Water Margin* and *Romance of the Three Kingdoms* (*Sanguo yanyi* 三國演義), another well-known work of vernacular fiction.[36] One example is the following line from a Taiping ballad circulating at the time: "As loyal as the sun and the moon and as righteous as Heaven / At the Peach Garden the brothers make the vow" 忠同日月義同天，兄弟結拜是桃園.[37] The assertion of righteousness and loyalty in the first line of the ballad harks back to the theme of *Water Margin*. The second line refers to a canonical scene in *Romance of the Three Kingdoms*. In this novel, the protagonist, Liu Bei, a descendant of the Han imperial family, forms a brotherhood with Guan Yu and Zhang Fei, two virtuous men he serendipitously encounters in a peach garden. There they commit themselves to the cause of supporting the Eastern Han dynasty (25–220 CE), which has been ripped apart by rebellions and warlords. During the Taiping movement, when their unfolding history is narrated in the manner of traditional storytelling, it is likely that the storyteller as well as the audience—who were all participants in the Taiping movement—would want to see themselves through the lens of chivalric heroism.[38]

36. Vincent Shih discusses the cultural resonances between the Taiping ideology and vernacular novels including *Water Margin* in detail. See Shih, *The Taiping Ideology*, 290–95.

37. Cao Daguan, *Kou ting ji lüe*, 6:809.

38. The Taipings enlisted traditional forms and motifs in other ways, too, to promulgate their message. Until the publication of the first official Taiping history in 1862, stories about the origins of the Taiping movement were not only circulated in manuscript form but also by word of mouth. In these orally transmitted stories, narrative devices featured in Chinese storytelling as well as in vernacular stories and fictions—phrases and devices such as "speaking of" (*huashuo* 話說), "to put this aside for the moment" (*anxia buti* 按下不提), and "to explain it in the next chapter" (*xiahui fenjie* 下回分解) often appear. See Zhang Runan, *Jinling xingnan ji lüe*, 4:719 and Xie Jiehe, *Jinling guijia jishi lüe*, 4:656.

The image of rebellious heroes in the popular imagination contributed not only to the Taiping soldiers' imaginations about themselves but also to how Qing cultural elites imagined them. This may be best illustrated by the tussle between the Taipings and Qing cultural elites over the novel *Quell the Bandits* (*Dang kou zhi* 蕩寇志), a nineteenth-century sequel to *Water Margin*. Local elites printed and disseminated *Quell the Bandits,* with its clear agenda of eradicating outlaws, to counter the influence of *Water Margin*. The Taipings considered this elite response a serious threat. Immediately after capturing Suzhou in 1860, they destroyed all the printing blocks and copies of *Quell the Bandits* that they could find in the region.[39] Ironically, as chapters 5 and 6 will show, the Qing elites themselves turned to *Water Margin* to justify their fantasies of defeating the rebels with unauthorized military forces.

The 1853 placards established a comprehensive Taiping vision in the literary tradition of *xi wen*. In doing so, they present a discourse of violence in the name of God and Jesus Christ, in a call for arms against the Manchus that carried over into other forms. The core message of these placards was also preserved and disseminated in Taiping tracts. The Taiping soldiers, armed with popular imaginations of the rebellious heroes their ideology advocated, were expected to continue pushing for the total extermination of "the demons" who were not yet vanquished.

## The Edicts of the Divine Will Made during the Heavenly Father's Descent to Earth

As their movement developed, the Taipings also increased the number of seminal texts underpinning their ideology, as illustrated by the publication of two volumes of *The Edicts of the Divine Will Made during the Heavenly Father's Descent to Earth*, the first volume in 1852 and the second in 1853. Each volume presents a coherent narrative of an incident in which the "Heavenly Father" (in the person of Yang Xiuqing) descended to conduct an interrogation in the first case, and a

39. Yu Xun, "*Dang kou zhi* xu xu," 515–16; Qian Xiang, "Xu ke *Dang kou zhi* xu," 517–18.

punishment in the second. The texts, where dialogue rather than expository prose takes up most of the space, are written in vernacular Chinese in a plain language style. Even though the "Heavenly Brother" (in the person of Xiao Chaogui) and the "Heavenly Father" both issued sacred decrees, only the two incidents recounted in these volumes are presented in carefully constructed narratives under the title of "edicts." In addition, only these texts regularly appear in lists of Taiping-approved books, an unambiguous declaration of their status in the Taiping textual regime.

The mediation of divinity is rooted in the Chinese religious tradition that, as Laurence Thompson says, "used mediums for communicating with the spiritual realm. . . . The medium . . . is . . . the Chinese version of the Shaman, who by certain techniques puts himself into a trance, during which he is possessed by the spirit."[40] For example, on the occasions when Xiao Chaogui "passed" into Heaven as the Heavenly Brother, he fell into a state resembling a coma, or gave a shamanistic performance that involved expelling demons, or required the presence of various attendants and often an interpreter (usually Xiao Chaogui himself). The precise mechanism of a descent by the Heavenly Brother was unclear, but during the Heavenly Father's descents, a few components appeared consistently. For instance, a sedan chair was used to carry Yang Xiuqing. Yang also often summoned the prime minister and the officials, who pronounced edicts (chengxuan guan 承宣官) before a descent. Both the prime minister and the officials in these instances were women, a fact that points to the intriguing gender dynamics in Yang Xiuqing's palace, which I will illustrate in the examples of Zhu Jiumei 朱九妹 (fl. 1853) and Fu Shanxiang 傅善祥 (fl. 1853) in chapters 4 and 6. When a ritual of divine descent ended, the Heavenly Father most often announced, "I am returning to Heaven" 朕回天矣; after that, he would revert to his own human identity as Yang Xiuqing and confirm the divine revelation.[41]

The first volume of *The Edicts of the Divine Will Made during the Heavenly Father's Descent to Earth* records the Heavenly Father's

40. Thompson, *Chinese Religion*, 23.

41. At the end of the ritual of descent, the Heavenly Brother also announced his return to Heaven.

prosecution of a defector named Zhou Xineng 周錫能 (d. 1851), whose betrayal was detected through an efficient intelligence service Yang Xiuqing used to gather information. The description of this event is preceded by Hong Xiuquan's testimony of his knowledge about the divine "descent," which authenticates the following description of events.

This framing narrative begins with a specific date and is told from Hong Xiuquan's perspective. After hearing Feng Yunshan's brief report that the Heavenly Father (in the person of Yang Xiuqing) has descended and detained Zhou Xineng, Hong Xiuquan praises the omnipotent God and expresses his gratitude for heavenly grace. Hong refers to himself as *quan* 全, a usage implying the addresser's humble position and intimate relationship with the addressee. Here, he creates the impression that he is speaking to God. The narrative then relates the making of the text: Hong Xiuquan orders Wei Changhui to record the Heavenly Father's edicts. Wei then orders two Taiping officials to keep the record, which Hong Xiuquan then reviewed and edited a few days later. Within the frame of Hong Xiuquan's narration, Taiping officials reference "the Heavenly Father, the Supreme High Sovereign."[42] The mediation of the divine is complex, involving not only Hong Xiuquan but also various witnesses; in this process the text reveals a hierarchical structure on the receiving end of this divine manifestation. Intricate mediation of divinity through the hands of several agents, as chapter 2 will show, is an important narrative design also in Qing proselytization texts seeking to establish a connection with Heaven.

Hong Xiuquan's frame narrative suggests that he had authority and control over the event recorded, but the Taiping officials' supposedly "objective" narrative offers a different perspective. In their account, the focus of the record is the trial conducted by Yang Xiuqing (as the Heavenly Father) in which he interrogates the accused Zhou Xineng, a former Taiping follower bribed by the Qing government to assassinate Taiping leaders. Prior to the trial, Yang Xiuqing had collected information from spies he had planted among the Taiping followers. On the day of the trial, the Heavenly Father "descended" to Earth and

---

42. For an 1852 edition, see *TPTGYS*, 1:96; for an 1853 edition, see *ATPTGGS*, 1:212. In the 1853 edition, Hong Xiuquan refers to himself as *zhen* 朕, a self-reference used by emperors in Imperial China.

interrogated Zhou Xineng about his plot. Throughout the trial, the exchanges between the Heavenly Father and Zhou are characterized by short sentences with enigmatic, highly repetitive phrases characterized by Taiping ideology, similar to a catechism. This excerpt is a characteristic example of the conversation:

> The Heavenly Father said, "Zhou Xineng, who is it that is now speaking to you in the person of the East King?"
> Zhou Xineng said, "The Heavenly Father, the supreme Lord and Great God."
> The Heavenly Father said, "And who is the sun?"
> Xineng replied, "The sun is my Sovereign, the Heavenly King, the true sovereign of all the kingdoms of the world."
> The Heavenly Father said, "Over what breadth of space does the sun shine?"
> Xineng replied, "He illuminates the entire world."[43]

Zhou was able to respond correctly to the questions or prompts of the Heavenly Father, who kept emphasizing his omnipresent and omnipotent power. However, Zhou continued to deny all the charges. Nevertheless, when the Heavenly Father revealed Zhou's interactions with the Manchu general Sai Shang'e 賽尚阿 (1794–1875) one by one, Zhou gave up and made his remorseful confession. At the end of the trial, Zhou was sentenced to a brutal death. The narrative pattern of the culprit who persists in denying charges but eventually confesses when presented with specific evidence is also vital in some Qing proselytization texts and court case fiction, as chapter 2 will show.

The narrative concludes with an idealized response that brings in numerous voices to condemn the traitor and affirm the Heavenly Father's righteousness and authority. Zhou, the defector, "suddenly discovered his conscience" 一時良心發見 before his execution and repented.[44] His wife pointed her finger at him and bitterly condemned him for betraying Heaven's will. In addition, the Taiping official who

---

43. *TPTGYS*, 1:97; Michael, *The Taiping Rebellion*, 2:89. This dialogue is the same in the 1852 and 1853 editions I consulted.

44. *TPTGYS*, 1:102. This line is the same in both editions I consulted.

didn't immediately report the traitor's plot to the Heavenly King was chained at the city gate for public display. The official called the Taiping brothers to wake up and be vigilant for treasonous schemes, pleading that the traitor be killed with one thousand cuts. The entire edict concludes with the remarks from the palace ladies: "Who would have known that the Heavenly Father, the Great God, was directing all affairs and that he would so suddenly come down to the world to point out the true situation. Their plot did not succeed; on the contrary they shall sink into Hell and bear eternal misery. Alas!" 誰知天父皇上帝有主張，忽然下凡，指出真情，謀事不成，反陷地獄受永苦矣。哀哉。[45] In this well-orchestrated representation of the audience's response at the end of the edict, the moral reverberations of defection are heard in the wife's charges, which signify broken familial bonds; in the official's calls for military vigilance; and in the palace ladies' exchanges, which symbolize criticism from the masses. A traitor is thus isolated ethically, politically, and socially through the constructed responses of an ideal group of audiences to validate Taiping ideology.

The second volume of *The Edicts of the Divine Will Made during the Heavenly Father's Descent to Earth* bears a publication date of 1853. In this volume, an omnipresent perspective is used to narrate the accounts, with Hong Xiuquan's viewpoint entirely erased. Neither is there any reference to the ministers who recorded the events. These changes suggest that in 1853, the authority of Yang Xiuqing was established in the Taiping regime. In the second volume, power struggles between Yang Xiuqing and Hong Xiuquan are dramatically enacted. The major incidents described in the second volume include the following: on December 24, 1853, the Heavenly Father (in the person of Yang Xiuqing) descends to regulate Hong Xiuquan's domestic affairs, instructing him to contain his temper when interacting with his son and palace ladies. The Heavenly Father almost flogs Hong Xiuquan in public, but eventually decides to pardon him. Yang Xiuqing, at least temporarily, has the upper hand. However, the power struggle between Hong Xiuquan and Yang Xiuqing concludes with the latter's premature death in 1856, in the massacre that became known as the Tianjing

45. *TPTGYS*, 1:103; Michael, *The Taiping Rebellion*, 2:97. This line is the same in both editions I consulted.

Incident, in which Hong Xiuquan supported Wei Changhui in killing Yang Xiuqing and his 20,000 followers.

## Texts Not Listed as Approved

From 1853, many tracts consistently show up in extant lists of titles of approved Taiping texts; however, some Taiping decrees and edicts appear only occasionally, and some do not appear in any known list.[46] There are several questions we may ask about the texts themselves, notably: How do the format and content of the listed and unlisted texts differ? What do we learn from these texts about the evolution of Taiping ideology and the Taiping movement? Time—or more specifically, temporality, as I show in this section—is an important theme running through the three texts under focus, which are both scriptures and historical narratives about divine revelations at the same time. Among the "sacred" texts that almost do not appear in any known list of approved publications are *The Sacred Decrees of the Heavenly Brother* (*Tianxiong shengzhi* 天兄聖旨, two volumes), *The Sacred Decrees of the Heavenly Father* (*Tianfu shengzhi* 天父聖旨), and *The Taiping Heavenly Chronicle* (*Taiping tianri* 太平天日). Little is known about the publication history of *The Sacred Decrees*, but the printing features of *The Taiping Heavenly Chronicle* yield much information about Taiping publications in the later stage of the Taiping movement.

### The Sacred Decrees of the Heavenly Brother and The Sacred Decrees of the Heavenly Father

No precise publication date is associated with extant editions of *The Sacred Decrees of the Heavenly Brother* (two volumes) and *The Sacred Decrees of the Heavenly Father*. The former records the descent of Jesus

---

46. The omission/inconsistent inclusion of these titles may be due to either (or both) of two reasons: first, uncertainties and changes in Taiping internal politics caused inconsistent printing policies; second, the Taipings restricted access to some records of internal power struggles in order to control information and maintain centralized power.

Christ (the Heavenly Brother) to Earth from 1848 to 1852. The simple
print format suggests that the two volumes of *The Sacred Decrees of the
Heavenly Brother* were likely first printed before the Taipings' attempts
to systemize their publications in 1853.[47] However, we may infer that
this text was reprinted after 1860.[48] *The Sacred Decrees of the Heavenly
Father* records the descent of God (the Heavenly Father) to Earth from
1854 to 1856, so it was probably first printed during or after 1856. In
terms of content, *The Sacred Decrees of the Heavenly Brother* highlights
themes of faith and perseverance in the early stage of the Taiping
movement, unlike the accounts of the Heavenly Father's descent, which
reinforce authoritarianism and absolutism.

The rather brief entries comprising these *Decrees* appear under
specific, chronicled dates. All the incidents in *The Sacred Decrees of
the Heavenly Brother* are associated with specific locations and dates.
For instance, one entry begins: "At Pingshan, the Heavenly Brother
compassionately descended" 天兄勞心下凡，時在平山.[49] In comparison, *The Sacred Decrees of the Heavenly Father* does not record the
location of divine revelations, possibly because the Heavenly Father is
presented as issuing his edicts primarily in the Taiping palaces in
Nanjing. This change is indicative of the kind of political stability—
albeit transient—the Taiping regime had achieved in its struggle with
the Qing government.

Most records in the two kinds of *Decrees* are statements of the
Heavenly Brother and the Heavenly Father and their dialogues with
Taiping followers. The narrative style is terse, and the language style

47. Wang Qingcheng suggests that in order to assert information control, the
Taiping rebels wrote many "sacred edicts" in manuscript form and forbade them to
be widely circulated. See Wang Qingcheng, *Taiping tianguo de wenxian*, 141. This may
help us understand why *The Sacred Decrees of the Heavenly Brother* and *The Sacred
Decrees of the Heavenly Father* are rarely found on known lists of approved Taiping
materials. A similar example is *Taiping tianri*, the only complete history written by
the Taipings, which will be discussed shortly.

48. The same applies to *The Sacred Decrees of the Heavenly Father*, which, unlike
other texts discussed in this section, appears on the lists of approved texts in two
extant Taiping publications. I follow Wang Qingcheng's argument that extant editions
of *The Sacred Decrees of the Heavenly Brother* and *The Sacred Decrees of the Heavenly
Father* are both reprints made after 1860. Wang Qingcheng, *TFTXSZ*, 183–87.

49. Wang Qingcheng, *TFTXSZ*, 6.

an odd mixture of classical and vernacular phrasing. The entries in *The Sacred Decrees of the Heavenly Father* begin with a synopsis of, or the lesson to be drawn from, the incidents described, suggesting an effort to assert control over the interpretation of the text, probably by Yang Xiuqing. These summaries bring to mind the "storyteller's manner" of vernacular stories, where the lesson or moral to be drawn comes in the storyteller's voice.[50] Moreover, the summaries also recall the moralizing admonitions placed at the beginning of popular religious texts.

The entries in these *Decrees* may be seen as examples of what Hayden White calls "annals." According to White, annalists compile all the records of historical events that they find without weighting or shaping them into a coherent narrative; history in this mode of representation can appear endless and incomprehensible.[51] In the Taiping *Decrees*, we see no narrative development and cohesion, but instead only discrete records of moments in which divinity is manifested in ordinary time. The juxtaposition of two temporal modes—the human time of annals, and that of God and Heaven—creates repercussions worth mentioning briefly here. It may not be a fatal flaw in such texts as the *Decrees*: the yearning for and imagination of the temporal experience of eternity is often communicated through descriptions of momentary revelations of eternity. Eternity lies *within* each instant of divine revelation, and each instant *embodies* eternity. However, in Taiping discourse, the sessions of spirit possession are fragmentary, spontaneous, and episodic. If these possessions were put into coherent narratives, it would be difficult to control their meanings. These kinds of annals betray "the absence of any consciousness of a social center."[52] The Taipings did eventually develop a social center, but it did not emerge until the publication of *The Sacred Decrees of the Heavenly Father* in 1856, when "correct" readings of the Heavenly Father's enigmatic utterances were established.

The two Taiping *Decrees* record not only the divine descent and ascent of the Heavenly Father and the Heavenly Brother but also the

50. Idema, *Chinese Vernacular Fiction*, 40.
51. White, "The Value of Narrativity," 8. For his discussion of "chronicle," see 16–22.
52. White, "The Value of Narrativity," 11.

audience's active participation in those rituals. The trance possessions of the Heavenly Father and the Heavenly Brother are inherently dramatic because they reflect "society and show actions and processes in front of an audience; in other words, they have 'public reflexivity.'"[53] For the audience of the ritual of divine descent, the processes are "a source of collective identity," because by participating in the ritual performance, the audience becomes an integral part of the Taiping movement.[54] In the textual account of the processes of the divine descent, the audience's active engagement in the event plays as pivotal a role as the divine itself. In doing so, these records establish the reciprocal relationship between "divinity" and ordinary people on Earth; in addition, the incidents they describe serve as concrete evidence for the overarching Taiping cosmological and historical visions. This kind of audience's participation, however, does not expand to include the readers as an imaginary audience, so the text is an enclosed system both inscribing and inscribed with permanence and sacredness.

Titles and terms of address and other language terms with symbolic meaning seem paramount to establishing a structure of authority in *The Sacred Decrees of the Heavenly Brother*. For example, important Taiping leaders would themselves "ascend to Heaven," see the Heavenly Brother there, and then descend to Earth. We see this happening in the case of Wei Changhui, who joined the Taiping movement relatively late and donated a considerable portion of his family fortune to the uprising. In the eighth month of 1849, this text reports, the Heavenly Brother descended (through Xiao Chaogui) and asked Wei Changhui, "Wei Zheng (Wei Changhui), what do you call Xiao Chaogui?" 天兄諭韋正曰：韋正，爾呼朝貴為何乎. Wei Changhui was slow to respond. Watching this, Hong Xiuquan asked, "Heavenly Brother, is Wei Zheng one of our humble brothers, in Heaven?" 天兄，韋正在高天與小弟們是同胞否. The Heavenly Brother seemed to be forgiving and answered, "His heart is the same as ours" 他同朕們總是共條腸也.[55] There are three participants in this scene: Wei Changhui, Hong Xiuquan, and

---

53. Turner, "Are There Universals of Performance," 10–11.

54. Stephenson, *Ritual*, 48.

55. Wang Qingcheng, *TFTXSZ*, 16–17. Note the mixture of classical Chinese (爾), vernacular Chinese (小弟們), and dialect (共條腸).

Xiao Chaogui. Although there are some potential obstacles to Wei Changhui's initial acceptance into Taiping leadership, those worries are set aside by the Heavenly Brother as represented by Xiao Chaogui. About half a month later, the Heavenly Brother summoned Wei Changhui's father, telling him that the entire Wei family would receive glory by following the Taiping cause.[56] A few days after this meeting between the Heavenly Brother and his father, Wei Changhui was quick to recognize the "Heavenly Sister-in-law" when the Heavenly Brother descended again, indicating his full assimilation into the Taiping discourse, and by extension, the Taiping cause.[57] Wei Changhui was later awarded the title of North King by Hong Xiuquan.

In a similar fashion, also in *The Sacred Decrees of the Heavenly Brother*, we find that even the ordinary Taiping soldiers had to know the ritual terms and their implications. They too bore the responsibility of deciphering and responding to divine messages correctly. Their performance of this ritual signifies acceptance of Taiping ideology and affirms their assimilation into the Taiping leadership. The text cites an example: before an important 1851 battle in Sanli, the Heavenly Brother summoned the Taiping soldiers by military unit to "bring them to Heaven" and to instruct them on heavenly teaching. The soldiers all responded properly, except for one man. As his punishment, he was discharged by the Heavenly Brother and sentenced to one hundred blows.[58] In another incident, the Heavenly Brother summoned 400 new recruits and "judged them one by one. He requested them to be careful about what they had to say, and made the soul of each of them ascend to Heaven" 逐一斷過，要謹口，逐一超升各魂上天堂.[59] For the Taiping soldiers, as well as the Taiping leaders, recognizing Xiao Chaogui as the Heavenly Brother enabled them to transform themselves: ordinary people on Earth were empowered by the divine that they collectively desired, created, and recognized. Furthermore, as the divine was to be mediated through Yang Xiuqing, Xiao Chaogui, and Hong Xiuquan, religious reverence assumed the form of personal idolization.

56. Wang Qingcheng, *TFTXSZ*, 18.
57. Wang Qingcheng, *TFTXSZ*, 55.
58. Wang Qingcheng, *TFTXSZ*, 88.
59. Wang Qingcheng, *TFTXSZ*, 37.

The Heavenly Brother, as channeled by Xiao Chaogui, adapted his messages in *The Sacred Decrees of the Heavenly Brother* to focus on the varied psychological needs of different audiences in order to boost their military morale. When the imprisonment of some Taiping followers caused fear in the community, he referenced the crucifixion of Jesus Christ—which he framed as his own experience—to convince people of future salvation: "There will be more suffering in the future. Who came to bear witness when I was nailed to death on the cross in a foreign country? The more suffering, the better. You should not panic" 後還有苦也。朕當日在番郭被人釘死十字架，有誰人知乎？越苦越好，爾們不必慌也。[60] This statement evinces the transtemporal and transspatial nature of Taiping vision: In nineteenth-century China, Xiao Chaogui evokes the first-century crucifixion of Jesus Christ in Jerusalem to validate the Taiping millenarian vision, so his "divinely inspired" voice speaks of past, present, and future in a single phrase. "You should not panic" directly addresses and activates the audience, who are lower-ranking Taiping officials. At times, the Heavenly Brother found that even Hong Xiuquan needed to be encouraged: "Xiuquan, you have to build up your aspiration, hold up the country to show people, and win glory for the Heavenly Father and the Heavenly Brother's principles" 秀全，爾要增起志氣來，頂起江山畀人看，爭起爾天父天兄綱常也。[61]

Even though *The Sacred Decrees of the Heavenly Father* is also about divine descents and ascents, both its format and focus differ from *The Sacred Decrees of the Heavenly Brother*. On each occasion of the Heavenly Father's descents, the varied types of audiences, who were primarily Taiping leaders (the "kings"), are recorded more explicitly. For example, the Heavenly Father's punishments for transgressors were meted out in the presence of Taiping kings, but it was not necessary for Hong Xiuquan to be there, implying that the Heavenly Father's authority (as channeled through Yang Xiuqing) was higher than Hong Xiuquan's.[62] Another kind of audience convened for the Heavenly Father's interrogations of traitors and the elevation of the East King's status,

60. Wang Qingcheng, *TFTXSZ*, 19.
61. Wang Qingcheng, *TFTXSZ*, 46.
62. Wang Qingcheng, *TFTXSZ*, 104.

which occurred before all the Taiping kings, including Hong Xiuquan—whose witness to those occasions probably further substantiated Yang Xiuqing's power.[63] The Heavenly Father's instructions on books and symbols, however, did not involve the kings: they were given to the officials (female in this instance) serving the East King, or the officials involved in preparing the Taiping documents.[64] When the Heavenly Father pardoned criminals and supported the disadvantaged, Yang Xiuqing usually received these messages in a dream.[65] Divinity, therefore, was revealed only to those who were chosen to reinforce the Heavenly Father's power and will.

## The Taiping Heavenly Chronicle

The sacred edicts of the Heavenly Father (in the person of Yang Xiuqing) and the Heavenly Brother (in the person of Xiao Chaogui) put the Heavenly King (Hong Xiuquan) in a position subordinate to Yang Xiuqing and Xiao Chaogui. *The Taiping Heavenly Chronicle*, the only coherent historical account written by the Taiping rebels, however, portrays Hong Xiuquan as the sole representative of divinity on Earth. The publication of *The Taiping Heavenly Chronicle* in 1862 was significant because signs of the Taiping Kingdom's decline were already evident. Underpinned by a logic that shows a thorough integration of the millenarian vision with history, the narrative offers a mythic vision of the Taiping uprising, reverently presenting Hong Xiuquan as the single religious and political leader of the movement.

The immediate context for the writing and publication of *The Taiping Heavenly Chronicle* begins in 1856, when the Taiping millenarian vision starts to break up. The Tianjing Incident, in which Yang Xiuqing and his followers were wiped out by Wei Changhui with support from Hong Xiuquan, occurred the same year.[66] Not long afterward, Hong sentenced Wei to death, under the pretext that he had killed too many

---

63. Wang Qingcheng, *TFTXSZ*, 119, 124.

64. Wang Qingcheng, *TFTXSZ*, 102, 111.

65. Wang Qingcheng, *TFTXSZ*, 111–14, 121, 126.

66. An earlier version of the rest of this section appeared in Huan Jin, "Authenticating the Renewed Heavenly Vision."

innocent people. Wing King Shi Dakai, disillusioned, left Nanjing to
lead the Taiping military push called the "North Expedition," in which
he later died. Hong Xiuquan thus lost his last comrade in the leadership
group with whom he had started the movement. He was on his own
until 1859, when his cousin Hong Rengan 洪仁玕 (1822–1864), who had
been studying with Western missionaries in Hong Kong since 1852,
arrived in Nanjing. Hong Xiuquan soon appointed Hong Rengan to be
the Shield King, a new title; in that role, Hong Rengan undertook a
series of political, social, economic, and cultural reforms that rejuve-
nated the kingdom. But the changes came too late. Starting in May
1862, cities the Taiping rebels had conquered one after another were
lost to the Xiang army led by Zeng Guofan.[67] The Taiping rebels' military and political setbacks undermined the deep convictions powering
the millenarian movement and put it in grave danger.[68] Thus, it was
crucial for the Taiping rebels to adjust their ideological discourse to
accommodate the changes in leadership that had occurred.

The adjustment came in 1862, when the Taipings issued *The Taiping
Heavenly Chronicle*. Proclaimed as "Edict I" on its inside cover, *The
Taiping Heavenly Chronicle* holds a particularly significant status
among the Taiping edicts, as shown by its title page and the copperplate
print technology used to produce the book. In a font smaller than the
one used for the title, a paragraph gives information about the production and publication of the book: "This book was announced in
the winter of *wushen* year [1848]. Now in *renxu* twelfth year [1862] of the
Heavenly Father, the Heavenly Brother, the Heavenly King, and the Taiping Heavenly Kingdom, it is printed from copper plate and published
with the central authority's commission" 此書詔明於戊申年冬，今
於天父天兄天王太平天國壬戌十二年欽遵旨准刷印銅板頒行.[69] *The
Taiping Heavenly Chronicle* is the only Taiping text printed from copper plates, an expensive and prestigious printing technique normally
only used by imperial authorities. The high production quality of the

67. Luo Ergang, *Taiping tianguo shigang*, 108. By February 1863, according to Zeng
Guofan's judgment—which proved to be true in historical hindsight—the Taiping
rebels had already lost their chance to prevail. Also see Platt, "Introduction: War and
Reconstruction in 1860s Jiangnan," 7.

68. Festinger, *When Prophecy Fails*, 28.

69. *TPTGYS*, 1:50.

book conveys an aura of authority echoed by the emphasis on the date of 1848 as the year in which the book was first announced. The evocation of a long prehistory to the book adds to the sacredness of the text by extending the temporal span of its influence, and yet, ironically, this statement also implies a sense of insecurity, in its attempt to establish the authority of history to bolster the book's prestige. The pre-1860 Taiping texts give only their publication years on the title pages, whereas *The Taiping Heavenly Chronicle* lists the Heavenly Father, the Heavenly Brother, and the Heavenly King there too, emphasizing the pedigree of the "divine family." In 1862, since the "voices" of God and Jesus Christ were no longer heard, the Heavenly King became the only legitimate authority to transmit truth on behalf of God and Jesus Christ.

Compared with other Taiping texts, the hierarchical order of divine beings' names in *The Taiping Heavenly Chronicle*, as shown in the page layout, demonstrates a consistency we do not see elsewhere (see fig. 1.3). For instance, although in other Taiping texts, the terms "Supreme High Sovereign" (*huangshangdi* 皇上帝) and "Heavenly Father" (*Tianfu* 天父) are used alternately to designate God, *The Taiping Heavenly Chronicle* uses the single term "the Heavenly Father, the Supreme High Sovereign" (*Tianfu shangzhu huangshangdi* 天父上主皇上帝) throughout. In addition, Hong Xiuquan's family members are incorporated into his visionary dream, and the way they are represented in the page layout indicates the restructured political milieu of the Taiping Kingdom. The book introduces, for the first time, Hong Xiuquan's parents and assigns them a specific divine status: "the father of the Sovereign" (*junwang fu* 君王父) and "the mother of the Sovereign" (*junwang mu* 君王母). The print layout of *The Taiping Heavenly Chronicle* shows the parents as second only to God and equivalent to Jesus Christ in status. The fact that Hong Xiuquan's parents have acquired divine status reflects the changes that had happened in the Taiping Heavenly Kingdom since 1856: Hong Xiuquan deliberately assigned leadership roles to more family members, and thus essentially rebuilt the center of power, making it into one dominated by the Hong family.

*The Taiping Heavenly Chronicle* is the only full-fledged account of the Taiping Rebellion written by the Taiping rebels themselves. It comprises three major segments: a summary of the book of Genesis and the story of Jesus Christ, the visionary journey made by Hong Xiuquan in Heaven, and Hong Xiuquan's proselytizing activities on Earth. The entire narrative ends in the eleventh month of *yisi* (乙巳, 1847), when the Qing government began to persecute Taiping followers. Written in a mixture of classical and vernacular Chinese, *The Taiping Heavenly Chronicle* does not have a narrative frame or moral admonition.

This version of Taiping history begins with God's creation of the world and how he subsequently brought disasters down on the world as punishment for various infractions by human beings; Jesus Christ is praised for sacrificing his life to redeem humans. With this groundwork laid, the account moves to the story of Hong Xiuquan and the movement itself. It gives a comprehensive description of Hong Xiuquan's heavenly journey. We are told that on the first day of the third month in the year of *tianyou* (1837), a great number of angels descended to Earth to welcome and receive Hong Xiuquan as he ascended to Heaven. In Heaven, he witnessed many marvels and met with God, who explained his distress at the state of the world and identified the devil and Confucianism as the causes of human misery. Confucius was eventually forgiven—but he was forbidden ever to come down to Earth. The narrative continues with an account of a heavenly battle between God and the devil in which Hong Xiuquan played a major role, for which God gave him the name "Completeness" (*quan* 全). Hong Xiuquan enjoyed such happiness that he was reluctant to return to Earth. However, with God's reassurance that divine power would always come to his assistance, and that he would find on Earth a book of enlightenment, Hong Xiuquan returned to the human realm.

The history then turns to events on Earth. In the year of *guirong* (1843), Hong Xiuquan read a book titled *Good Words to Admonish the World* and was enlightened as to the meaning of his heavenly journey. Thereupon, Hong Xiuquan started to proselytize. He first convinced his immediate family of his vision, and then the Hong clan and other villagers. Among the first group of followers he attracted were Hong Rengan and Feng Yunshan. In the year of *jiachen* (1844), Hong Xiuquan, Feng Yunshan, and the other Feng brothers who had converted, started to travel, reaching Guangdong Province. In the year of *dingwei* (1847), he obtained the Old and New Testaments from the British missionary Issachar J. Roberts (1802–1871). The same year, Hong Xiuquan was robbed of all his personal belongings, but when a group of strangers helped him, he interpreted the act of generosity as evidence of God's revelation. Hong Xiuquan traveled on, destroying shrines and temples, railing against local spirits, and attracting followers. The history ends at the eleventh month of the year, with Hong Xiuquan traveling to Gui County.

The intention to produce a finished account of Hong Xiuquan's visionary journey is apparent in *The Taiping Heavenly Chronicle,* as the text provides elaborate images of God and the devil—two critical symbols in apocalyptic discourse—as well as details of Hong Xiuquan's interactions with them. In Hong Rengan's description of Hong Xiuquan, which Theodore Hamberg (1819–1854) incorporated into his 1854 account, the God that Hong Xiuquan saw was an old man with golden hair dressed in a black robe.[70] On an occasion in 1848, God was for the first time described by the Heavenly King, the Heavenly Brother, and the Western King as they conversed "in Heaven." God, according to their descriptions, is a man with a voluminous golden beard extending to his stomach, who wears a tall hat and black dragon robe.[71] *The Taiping Heavenly Chronicle* adds more details to this image of God: "His physiognomy is absolutely impressive, his frame is absolutely tall and large, his posture is absolutely solemn, and his clothes are absolutely pristine" 像貌最魁梧，身體最高大，坐裝最嚴肅，衣袍最端正.[72] Another noteworthy change between the earlier accounts and the later one is in God's demeanor. In Hamberg's account, God is a sorrowful, weeping man; in *The Taiping Heavenly Chronicle,* he is a furious and authoritative supreme being. As for the image of the devil, an 1853 placard describes it as a snake demon (*shemo* 蛇魔) with red eyes. *The Taiping Heavenly Chronicle,* however, fleshes out this figure: it has a square head, red eyes, and a putrid body. The devil could change shape: it did not want to leave Heaven, so it metamorphosed into various forms, such as

70. Hamberg, *The Visions of Hung-Siu-tshuen,* 10.

71. *TFTXSZ,* 3–13. Their conversation as recorded in *The Sacred Edicts of the Heavenly Brother* is deemed by scholars to be the formal establishment of God's concrete image in Taiping ideology. Zhou Weichi gives a detailed comparison of the image of God in various Taiping accounts in his *Taiping tianguo yu* Qishi lu, 129–37.

72. *TPTGYS,* 1:36.

a snake and a louse. The devil's shape-shifting is archetypal within Taiping discourse: images of the religious and political enemies of the Taipings changed at various stages of the movement.

Unlike God and the devil, Confucius has little if any part in Western Christian discourse, but he is an important figure in Taiping ideology. Confucius already appears briefly in Hong Rengan's early account, as recorded by Hamberg, and in the sacred edicts issued by the Heavenly Brother. *The Taiping Heavenly Chronicle*, however, represents Confucius more concretely. During Hong Xiuquan's heavenly journey, as recounted in *The Taiping Heavenly Chronicle*, God shows him three books: the Old Testament, the New Testament, and the Confucian classics. God tells Hong Xiuquan that there are many wrong teachings in Confucian books, and that he is disappointed that Confucius is better known than he (God) is among Chinese people. Confucius "at first came up with forced arguments, but eventually became speechless and silently contemplative" 始則強辯，終則默想無辭.[73] He tries to escape from Heaven, but is captured and brought back by Hong Xiuquan under God's orders. The juxtaposition here of Confucian canons with the Bible demonstrates how the Taiping rebels envisioned knowledge from the West and from traditional China. The conflict between God and Confucius in Heaven that the Taipings recount can be seen as mirroring how the rebels struggled to find a place for Confucianism in their discourse as they changed their attitude toward the Confucian classics after 1853.[74] Therefore, by making Confucius part of Hong Xiuquan's heavenly journey, albeit with certain reservations, *The Taiping Heavenly Chronicle* integrates acceptance of Confucianism into Taiping discourse of their vision.

The prime invention of *The Taiping Heavenly Chronicle*, however, is to establish Hong Xiuquan as the central authority in Taiping ideology. The title in Chinese, *Taiping tianri* ("Greatness, Peace, Heaven,

73. *TPTGYS*, 1:38.
74. Because of Yang Xiuqing's praise of the value of Confucian classics and the worth of Confucianism when he "mediated" God, in spring of 1854, the Taiping rebels changed their policy; Confucian works could be circulated after being officially edited and censored (the Taipings established a special office for censoring books). This is one among many initiatives in which Yang was instructed by God. See Wang Qingcheng, *Taiping tianguo de wenxian*, 222.

and Sun," or "A Time of Great Heavenly Peace"), indicates the text's uniqueness as a source of authority. This phrase appears only once among all surviving Taiping materials in a Taiping placard dated 1853: "What a great fortune for people in the world to be born at this time to witness *Taiping tianri*" 世人何其大幸。生遇其時，得見太平天日.[75] Taiping discourse referred to Hong Xiuquan, the protagonist in the narrative, as the "sun" from the beginning of the movement. The flexible translation of *ri* invites a metaphorical association between the sun, which symbolically drives away darkness with light, and Hong Xiuquan and the Taiping movement under his leadership.

Manipulations of narrative perspective also establish Hong Xiuquan's central status in *The Taiping Heavenly Chronicle*. In the first segment of the narrative, the omniscient perspective implies an omnipresent divine authority. The narrative opens with God's creation of the world.[76] This retelling of the beginning of the world has an apocalyptic implication: I am telling you the truth, and my telling of the beginning enables me to reveal the ending. The second and third sections of the book, following the Genesis section, are narrated from a limited third-person perspective and center on Hong Xiuquan's actions and psychological states. The descriptions of his internal states are critical in building the connection between the realms of Heaven and Earth. At the beginning of the heavenly journey, Hong Xiuquan is described as reluctant to leave his family on Earth behind. Little is revealed about his psychological state during the heavenly journey, but toward the end of his stay in Heaven, Hong Xiuquan's unwillingness to leave Heaven is frequently mentioned. In doing so, the narrative emphasizes Hong Xiuquan's sacrifice for the Chinese people and reaffirms divine sanction as the source of Hong Xiuquan's worldly authority. In addition, Hong Xiuquan's feelings prepare the readers for the transition to the next segment describing his activities on Earth.

In the third section of *The Taiping Heavenly Chronicle*, the moment of Hong Xiuquan's revelation is described in detail. After reading the Christian pamphlet, *Good Words to Admonish the World*, he "contemplated the content of the book over and again and remembered what

75. *TPTGYS*, 1:107.
76. *TPTGYS*, 1:36.

he had seen in Heaven and on Earth in the *dingyou* year. Comparing these experiences with [descriptions in the Christian pamphlet], he noticed that what they said agreed with each other. The king [Hong Xiuquan] then was enlightened" 將此書所說反覆細勘，因想起天酉年升天及下天所見所為之情，一一與此書所說互相印證，若合符節。主乃悟。[77] Hong Xiuquan's reflections continue after he starts to proselytize in mountainous areas. On the occasion when Hong Xiuquan was robbed of all his belongings by bandits, he interpreted the strangers' assistance as a manifestation of divine intervention. Told from the first-person point of view, this episode engages the audience with activities in Hong Xiuquan's mind, lending credibility to the account. This particular episode takes up four folio pages in the book, and because there is no punctuation (as in other traditional Chinese books), the boundary between Hong Xiuquan's physical actions and his internal activities is ambiguous. At the same time, the high placement of the name of God on the page layout foregrounds his omnipresent power and authority.

If the manipulation of narrative perspectives explains how Hong Xiuquan's absolute power on Earth derives from the divine, the construction of time reveals another aspect of the underlying structure of *The Taiping Heavenly Chronicle*. As a text that defines an alternative origin of Chinese history, *The Taiping Heavenly Chronicle* evokes the cyclical temporality with which dynastic rises and falls are traditionally interpreted in Chinese thoughts.[78] As events could be measured on Earth, a linear temporality substitutes for the cyclical one once mythical time is translated into historical time. The earthly calendar used here, however, is based on the unique Taiping calendar system that symbolizes their assertion of power over cosmology. At the beginning of the second section of the book, earthly calendrical time is explicitly emphasized: "The King was then twenty-five. At midnight, on the first day of the third month in the year of *tianyou* [1837], he saw numerous angels descend from Heaven" 主年二十五歲，在天酉三月初一日子

77. *TPTGYS*, 1:43.
78. Pankenier, "Temporality and the Fabric of Space-Time," 141.

刻，見無數天使自天降下。[79] The specification of time—here, the precise hour of Hong Xiuquan's ascension—is likely ritualistic rather than realistic. Temporal precision is particularly important in apocalyptic discourse, for "the tendency to set specific dates . . . appears . . . as the natural functioning of the psychology of the audience."[80] When an experience in one realm could be measured in the other realm in temporal terms, it establishes a connection between the transcendental and the mundane. In the context of *The Taiping Heavenly Chronicle*, this precise calendrical time marks the moment when a mystical, remote antiquity meets the "present" moment as a new cycle in history begins.

However, time as Hong Xiuquan experienced it in his visionary journey is not to be calculated by the worldly Taiping calendar. The sense of historicity and linearity is deconstructed by adverbs concretizing Hong Xiuquan's actions. For instance, terms such as "immediately," "instantly," and "at this time," are used repeatedly to describe Hong Xiuquan's visionary experience in a dramatic way; they convey a sense of urgency. This drama taps into one of the critical aspects of apocalyptic psychology: the end is near, and fear and the urge to escape have to be addressed immediately. Such a way of measuring time, which does not pass the same way that earthly, historical time does, makes sense only in specific contexts; thus, in the Heavenly realm, Hong Xiuquan's interactions with God and the divine battle with the devil are contained in a self-sufficient narrative.

The temporal connection between Heaven and Earth appears again with the transition from Heaven to Earth in this sentence: "Between the Sovereign's ascension to Heaven on the first day of the third lunar month and his descent to Earth, it had been about forty days" 主自三月初一日升天，至送下凡時約四十餘日。[81] The symbolic meaning is

---

79. *TPTGYS*, 1:36. The Taiping calendar inherits the traditional *ganzhi* system to mark cycles of years, but the Taiping rebels changed some characters in the *ganzhi* system for auspicious meanings. For instance, the year of *tianyou* evoked here is the year of *dingyou* in the *ganzhi* system. They have replaced *ding* 丁 with *tian* 天 to designate divine authority. Luo Ergang made a detailed comparison between the Taiping calendar and the *ganzhi* system. Luo Ergang, *Tianli kao*.

80. O'Leary, *Arguing the Apocalypse*, 80.

81. *TPTGYS*, 1:41.

unmistakable, given the importance of the number forty in Judeo-Christian discourse.[82] The ritual time of Hong Xiuquan's ascension is announced once more, whereas the length of the period of his "descent" from Heaven back to Earth—his return to lucidity—is not specified: "Though the Heavenly Father, the Supreme High Sovereign had admonished him [Hong Xiuquan] in detail, when he was in the human realm, he was still unable to come to full awareness of that in his heart" 天父上主皇上帝雖吩咐甚悉，既在凡間時，則未能盡醒然於心也.[83]

Hong's eventual descent is given a specific time marker: the morning of a day in the sixth month of *guirong* year (1843), which was probably when Hong Xiuquan came to a revelation while rereading *Good Words to Admonish the World*.[84] The *Taiping Heavenly Chronicle* was the first text to explicitly address the significance of the missionary pamphlet *Good Words to Admonish the World* in Taiping discourse, and it establishes an important fact: that the Taiping rebels traced the genealogy of their ideology beyond mere Western influence. It also foregrounds Hong's personal encounter with the enlightening text. At the same time, the encounter is only described in part, since the narrative leaves out the date of 1836, when Hong Xiuquan received the pamphlet outside of the examination hall in Guangzhou.[85] With this omission, *The Taiping Heavenly Chronicle* elides Hong Xiuquan's previous identity as a Confucian student. Therefore, even though the precise evocation of time may seem constructive, it is also deconstructive, because concealed and suppressed information always poses a potential threat to an existing discourse.

As if to validate the authenticity of the heavenly vision, the narrative on the following pages of *The Taiping Heavenly Chronicle* emphasizes the precise treatment of time in its description of Hong Xiuquan's proselytization. In great detail, Hong Xiuquan's every move is recorded, and the enumeration of names and places echoes the lists of names and places in the Bible. Given that Hong Xiuquan had been

82. One of the tests for Jesus was his sojourn in the desert for forty days as described in the New Testament.

83. *TPTGYS*, 1:41.

84. Hamberg, *The Visions of Hung-Siu-tshuen*, 14.

85. Hamberg, *The Visions of Hung-Siu-tshuen*, 14.

reading and editing the Bible diligently in his later years, this episode in *The Taiping Heavenly Chronicle* may very well emulate that text. In any event, the meticulous emphasis on concrete dates contrasts starkly with the strange temporality of the heavenly journey. Ultimately, these time markers serve a primarily rhetorical purpose rather than generating substantial meaning.

The narrative cuts off after the eleventh month of *yisi* (乙巳, 1847), when Hong Xiuquan received news that Feng Yunshan, an important leader of the nascent movement, had been captured. Therefore, the history presented in *The Taiping Heavenly Chronicle* is incomplete, its implication being that the actualization of the moral/divine promise is an ongoing process, to be advanced as time progresses. On the first page of *The Taiping Heavenly Chronicle*, a similar message is communicated by the subtitle "Imperial Edict I" ("Zhaoshu yi" 詔書一), which indicates that more edicts of *The Taiping Heavenly Chronicle* would follow. Were there an "Edict II," however, it would have demanded a narrative construction even more skillful than the first one—because the narrative thus far represented events in 1846 and 1847. When God "sent" messages through Yang Xiuqing and Jesus Christ "sent" messages through Wei Changhui, both figures would downplay Hong Xiuquan's importance among the Taiping leaders, and the stories involving them would challenge the power dynamic presented by *The Taiping Heavenly Chronicle*. Before the Taipings could continue writing their history, the Taiping regime met its downfall.

Among all the Taiping publications, those meant to be treated with the most religious and political reverence illuminate our understanding of the politics and struggles involved in the Taipings' quest for Heaven. This chapter looked at the core of the Taiping textual universe, beginning with ballads and treatises that appealed for religious tolerance, and ending in the chronicle of Hong Xiuquan's messianic mission. Words, narratives, ritual performances, and printed matter all constituted indispensable components of the modus operandi that mediated the divine. Through appropriations and exploitations of literary genres symbolizing the highest imperial authority, the Taiping "sacred" texts constitute textual manifestations of their political and religious agenda to overthrow not only the Manchu government but also the entire imperial system. With their use of vernacular language, engagement with the audience, and employment of narrative devices, the Taipings reinvented the literature of persuasion to spread an epistemological discourse inspired by the West as a state ideology in China. As the next chapter shows, some Qing elites responded to Taiping proselytizing endeavors through a precarious re-creation of Qing ideological discourse.

CHAPTER TWO

# Revelations from Hell

## A Qing Answer

Among nineteenth-century China's popular beliefs were those centered on Hell and the punishments stemming from the idea of moral retribution, "a belief ... at the heart of the earliest indigenous Chinese religious and political vision."[1] These beliefs are summoned and used in both Taiping and Qing discourses of the period—on the one hand, to convert people to the Taiping vision of Heaven, and on the other, in the service of Qing state ideology. Chapter 1 looks at the Taiping use of such beliefs; this chapter turns to the Qing. In rather unexpected ways, the works local elites produced to voice Qing religious and moral orthodoxies turned out to be just as "revolutionary" in terms of their religious and political implications. Notably, there is the publication of *Miraculous Proofs of the Sacred Edict* (*Shengyu lingzheng* 聖諭靈徵), a text by an unnamed author, which invokes the supernatural power of Hell to vindicate Qing state ideology.

A mixture of various political, legal, religious and cultural traditions, *Miraculous Proofs* reveals how nineteenth-century elites strove to promote state ideology. This book draws from various influences: the Qing emperors' Sacred Edict—a compilation of sixteen maxims; religious tracts about moral retribution and manuals about self-cultivation; and

1. Brokaw, *The Ledgers of Merit and Demerit*, 30.

popular literature such as storytelling and precious scroll (*baojuan* 寶卷) performance that is characterized by alternating prose and verse. The production and promulgation of *Miraculous Proofs* in various regions from the 1850s to the 1880s reflect the pressing need felt by the Qing elites, who used indigenous religion to communicate Qing orthodox values and combat heretical beliefs.[2] This book may have first been printed in mid-nineteenth-century southwestern China at an early stage of the Taiping Rebellion.[3] Bringing together Qing state ideology and the popular beliefs represented in morality books (*shanshu* 善書), *Miraculous Proofs* presents a vision of Hell where moral transgressions would be severely punished.[4] In this vision, the divine and human realms have a close relationship, with their analogous features forming a "judicial continuum" in which "the judicial mechanisms of this world can interact and even overlap with those of the underworld."[5] In 1885, *Miraculous Proofs* was brought to Hunan Province and reprinted by a Qing official, who evidently felt that it could still be useful to the state in the postwar context.[6] *Miraculous Proofs* is an important work

2. When early missionaries first came to China, they were also inspired by the Sacred Edict and imitated this text to proselytize Christianity. See Yao Dadui, *Xiandai de xiansheng*.

3. One of the prefaces of the edition of *Miraculous Proofs* I examine is dated 1885. Other prefaces are dated earlier, which I will discuss in more detail in the following pages. Lin Shanwen suggests that *Miraculous Proofs* may have been first printed around 1856; I agree with this hypothesis. See Lin Shanwen, *Qingmo Shengyu xuanjiang*, 14, 22.

4. In late imperial China, morality books constitute a popular literary genre that preaches orthodox ethical values and admonishes people to do good deeds. This genre is fully explored in Tadao Sakai, *Zōho Chūgoku zensho no kenkyū*. A brief introduction to this genre in English can be found in Brokaw, *Ledgers of Merit and Demerit*, 3.

5. Katz, *Divine Justice*, 2, 59.

6. After the Taiping War, the Xiang Army from Hunan Province was sent to settle in frontier areas such as Xinjiang. They carried with them both morality pamphlets and relevant printing projects. For example, the anti-Christian activist Zhou Han, who was a Xiang army veteran, used to run a printing house in Xinjiang. See Schluessel, *Land of Strangers*, 56. A pamphlet by Zhou Han titled *In Accord with the Imperial Edict: Complete Illustrations of the Heretical Religion* (*Jinzun Shengyu bixie quantu* 謹遵聖諭辟邪全圖) is reproduced in missionary Griffith John's 1891 book, *The Cause of the Riots in the Yangtse Valley: A "Complete Picture Gallery"* with his commentary. First printed in Hankow in 1891, *The Cause of the Riots* is fully digitized in MIT's Visualizing Cultures project and accessible online: https://visu alizingcultures.mit.edu/cause_of_the_riots/cr_book_01.html.

representing a popular trend that interprets the Sacred Edict with beliefs of supernatural retributions at an early stage.

*Miraculous Proofs* and the Taiping tracts choose different gods to worship and different religious visions to follow, but they share similar kinds of rhetoric and sentiments, and all emphasize the presence of an audience for divine revelations. Whereas the Taipings sought validation through Christianity-influenced notions of Heaven and God, the author of *Miraculous Proofs* turned to the ancient principle of the Mandate of Heaven, the god of literature and culture (Wenchang di 文昌帝), and Lord Guan Yu (Guandi 關帝).[7] There were also significant differences in narrative strategy and in the authorities underpinning their respective ideologies. For example, unlike the Taiping texts, *Miraculous Proofs* makes no attempt to historicize the instances of divine manifestation; instead, it presents an ahistorical discourse of moral retribution. Nevertheless, both *Miraculous Proofs* and Taiping discourse mainly use local dialect and vernacular Chinese to appeal to the masses. They also share a similar kind of apocalyptic sentiment. To convince people of this need and the immediacy of divinity, both the producer of *Miraculous Proofs* and the Taipings emphasize the "acting out" of divinity as channeled by characters (in text and reality, respectively) with an audience's presence as the essential means of verifying divine revelations. In the case of *Miraculous Proofs*, the god of literature and culture and Lord Guan Yu are part of the Qing official pantheon; therefore, by evoking these deities, the author of this book attempts to make it an extension of Qing imperial authority. However, ironically, *Miraculous Proofs* opens up a hermeneutic space that is potentially subversive to Qing state ideology; its publication is part of the long

7. *Miraculous Proofs* refers to Guandi 關帝 as Guan sheng dijun 關聖帝君. Guandi, or Lord Guan Yu, was the apotheosized hero Guan Yu (162–220) from the time of the Three Kingdoms. The myths of Guandi became increasingly popular first in local cults and later in drama and fiction in late imperial society. See Haar, *Guan Yu*, 78. During Qing times, the state orchestrated the local cult of Guandi with institutional changes. See Duara, "Superscribing Symbols," 783–84. Goossaert observes that during the Taiping War, Lord Guan Yu emerged as a prominent deity of the elite tradition, and there were "an overwhelming number of eschatological texts featuring Guandi (Lord Guan Yu) that were produced in the immediate war context." See Goossaert, *Making the Gods Speak*, 277.

process of decentralization extending to Qing frontiers in the nineteenth century.[8]

## The Traditions of *Jiaohua* and Moral Retribution

### Teaching the Sacred Edict

*Miraculous Proofs* is one of the endeavors for carrying out the Confucian ideal of teaching and transforming (*jiaohua* 教化), which underlay the practice of education and governance in traditional China. The goal of *jiaohua* should be achieved in a subtle and gentle manner, so that the minds of the target audience could be effectively transformed, which in principle should incite proper action.[9] Considered an efficient means of promulgating state ideology, *jiaohua* drove several public initiatives in traditional China. During the Song dynasty (960–1279 CE), Neo-Confucian thinkers created and implemented a village compact (*xiangyue* 鄉約) system to promote Confucian moral principles in local academies.[10] At the time, this social practice was restricted to students of Confucianism. However, at the beginning of the Ming dynasty, the Hongwu Emperor (r. 1368–1398) issued the *Great Imperial Mandate* (*Da gao* 大誥) and the *Imperial Placard of Instructions to the People* (*Jiao min bangwen* 教民榜文), which required each village and each *li* (group of 110 households, 里) to regularly preach Confucian moral exhortations.[11] By the late Ming, the imperial policy on regular

8. Eric Schluessel discusses how the Xiang Army leaders and soldiers governed Xinjiang with an enclosed administrative system that led to its de facto independent state in the financial crisis of the late Qing. See Schluessel, *Land of Strangers*, chap. 2, especially p. 79.

9. George Orwell observed that successful propaganda often presents its messages obliquely and is therefore usually not recognized as propaganda. See Orwell, *Seeing Things as They Are*, 144–47.

10. Übelhor, "The Community Compact (Hsiang-yüeh) of the Sung."

11. See Tadao Sakai, *Zōho Chūgoku zensho no kenkyū*, 1:61–77. Prescribed by the government during the founding reign of Ming, this system in theory designated every 110 households a community. The Qing perpetuated the *lijia* system for tax-collection purposes, but by the 1700s, it was losing its effectiveness. See Hucker, *A Dictionary of Official Titles*, 303.

proclamation was neither carefully observed nor abided by. Nevertheless, because of the expansion of literacy and a burgeoning publishing industry, Neo-Confucian thinkers like Wang Yangming 王陽明 (1472–1529) were eager to spread Confucianism to the smallest units of the state power system.[12]

State ideology was institutionalized more systematically during the Qing dynasty, with control and sanctions in line with the principles of *jiaohua*. The gradual process began with the proclamation in 1670 of the Sacred Edict of the Kangxi Emperor (r. 1661–1722). This text comprises sixteen maxims that merged Confucian ethics with state discipline and punishment. On its surface, the Sacred Edict shares the goal of *xiangyue* in bettering local communities through Confucian principles of self-cultivation. Looking more closely, however, we see that the text puts an equal emphasis on the authority of laws and regulations.[13] The emperor's preface to the full edict explains: "The era of the most perfect government does not rely only on laws and regulations, but regards teaching and transformation as paramount. . . . That is because *faling* 法令 [laws and regulations] could impose proscriptions for a short period of time, whereas teaching and transforming lasts long. If one relies only on laws and regulations without prioritizing

---

12. Wang Yangming proposed the idea of the community compact, according to which commoners would convene at the local level to practice Confucian rituals, discuss local matters, and report on the people's good and bad deeds. Wang Yangming's vision in regulating the local community through self-governance can be traced back to the first reign period of the Ming dynasty, when imperial power exerted strong control over local communities by placarding walls with laws and regulations. In 1370, for instance, the wealthy in Jiangnan area were summoned to the capital to listen to the emperor's admonition, which was printed and placarded soon afterward. See Tan Qian, *Guo que*, 361:264. It was compulsory to post imperial placards in *yamen* 衙門 (local offices) and *shen ming ting* 申明亭 (pavilions—sites for declaring and elucidating Confucian principles) in local counties; these placards were issued with great frequency during the Hongwu era. Local officials who neglected this responsibility might be subject to the penalty of execution made harsher by torture. This practice was stopped after the Yongle era (1403–1424). See Guo Jian, *Zhonghua wenhua tongzhi*, 37.

13. Scholars such as Ogaeri Yoshio, Victor Mair, and Zhou Zhenhe trace the cultural history of the derivatives of the Sacred Edict, but all treat the sixteen maxims as a mere text without considering the fact that they should be contextualized within the entire edict issued.

teaching and transforming, it is like discarding the root to focus on the tip of the branch" 至治之世，不專以法令為事而以教化為先 . . . 蓋法令禁於一時而教化維於可久，若徒事法令而教化不先，是捨本而務末也.[14] This preamble justifies the importance of the Confucian Sacred Edict based on the limitations of laws and regulations. Paradoxically, it also evokes the imposition of laws and regulations as the primary means of achieving social control. Such a tension between benevolence and punishment constitutes the internal logic upon which the maxims are constructed.

Each maxim of the Sacred Edict is seven characters long and is written in the format "Do X in order to achieve Y." Each "X" is a Confucian moral principle of individual self-cultivation, and each "Y" pertains to the betterment of community achieved through individuals' exercise of the principles. For instance, the first maxim reads, "Devote yourselves to filial piety and fraternal devotion, in order to give due importance to relationships of normative human relations" 敦孝弟以重人倫.[15] The following fifteen maxims continue this focus on relationships within the boundaries of family and lineage since they highlight concepts such as filial piety, brotherly submission, and communal harmony. Noteworthy is the seventh maxim, "Extirpate strange heterodox principles, in order to exalt the correct doctrine" 黜異端以崇正學, which shows an antiheterodox agenda predating the Taiping Civil War in Qing ideology.[16] However, a thematic shift becomes apparent by the eighth maxim, which unmistakably brings law into the discourse: "Lecture on the laws, in order to warn the ignorant and obstinate" 講法律以儆愚頑. This maxim brings people's attention to the law, and hence the imperial power that imposes the law. As a continuation of this shift, the last six maxims represent society as being full of perils and threats, and individual members of society having the potential to become "the ignorant and obstinate" who contribute to these perils and threats. At the end of the Sacred Edict, in the maxim "Remove enmity and anger,

14. A 1661 edict by the Kangxi Emperor, compiled in Zhou Zhenhe, *Shengyu guangxun jijie*, 507.

15. Translation from Mair, "Language and Ideology in the Sacred Edict," 325–26, with my own modification.

16. The same applies to the interpretive discourse revolving around the Sacred Edict, as shown in Mair, "Language and Ideology in the Sacred Edict."

in order to properly value the body and life" 解仇忿以重身命, benevolence in "teaching and transforming" is completely replaced by the ruthless coercion of state legislation that physically polices and punishes the people.

Interpretations of the maxims of the Sacred Edict were shaped by concrete historical and geographical factors.[17] Local officials and literati voluntarily prepared the interpretations without state intervention, but in a few cases, their efforts were acknowledged by the Qing emperor. The derivative nature of the exegetical texts resembles the various versions of narratives sharing the same plot skeleton, in which each version discloses the storyteller's distinctive agenda. The language of the interpretations ranges from classical Chinese to local dialect, and sometimes stories and pictorial aids are used to illustrate the maxims.[18] Some interpretations attach Qing legal codes to each maxim, therefore showing an even keener awareness of the implementation of the law in comparison to other texts.[19] However, despite the cultivation of exegetical discourse surrounding the Sacred Edict, the idea of omnipresent deities and punishment in Hell hardly exists in this discourse before the mid-nineteenth century. *Miraculous Proofs* marked the pinnacle of the

17. Both Zhou Zhenhe and Victor Mair discuss this issue in their works. Many morality books were produced in Hubei Province from the eighteenth century onward, and some of them include content about the Sacred Edict. See Lin Yu-ping, "'Hanchuan shanshu' de lishi bianqian"; Jia Ping, "Lun Hanchuan shanshu"; Liu Shouhua, "Cong baojuan dao shanshu."

18. Zhang Yichen describes the generic traits of the texts surrounding the Sacred Edict. See Zhang Yichen, "Qingdai Shengyu xuanjiang lei shanshu." You Zi'an's "Cong xuanjiang Shengyu dao shuo shanshu" introduces the most popular kinds of exegetical texts (ten in number) of the Sacred Edict. The most important interpretation written in classical Chinese is the Yongzheng Emperor's (r. 1722–1735) *Shengyu guangxun*, proclaimed in 1722. Liang Yannian's *Shengyu xiangjie*, written in 1676, uses stories and pictures to illustrate each maxim. See *Shengyu guangxun jijie yu yanjiu*, 598.

19. Chen Bingzhi's *Shengyu helü zhijie* combines vernacular interpretation and laws that are relevant to each maxim under discussion. The preface to the extant edition of this text shows that before 1679, the Sacred Edict was already "known to each household." See *Shengyu guangxun jijie yu yanjiu*, 596. As Zhang Ting observes, some books preaching the Sacred Edict popularized the Qing code and "included a large amount of accurate legal information." Zhang Ting, *Circulating the Code*, 155. She also traces the history of community compact (*xiangyue*) and the cultural history of the Sacred Edict, 148–51.

decentralization process in the developing of the exegetical discourse of the Sacred Edict. This text might have signaled an early stage of the genre of "story that preaches the Sacred Edict" (*Shengyu xuanjiang xiaoshuo* 聖諭宣講小說), which integrates religious elements with the principle of the Sacred Edict through storytelling.[20] From the 1870s to the end of the Qing dynasty, this subgenre in the interpretive discourse surrounding the Sacred Edict became especially popular.

## Moral Retribution through Divinity

In the world presented in *Miraculous Proofs*, the underlying principle is the moral retribution presiding over people's everyday activities, as shown in one of the most popular morality books of the late imperial period, *Tract on Divine Action and Response* (*Taishang ganying pian* 太上感應篇). When the Qing dynasty was first established, the Shun-zhi Emperor (r. 1643–1661) seems to have tried to incorporate both imperial edicts and popular religion into the Qing ideological system. Not only did he continue advocating the Hongwu Emperor's "Six Edicts" ("Liu yu" 六諭), he also decreed that the popular text *Tract on Divine Action and Response* (*Taishang ganying pian* 太上感應篇) should be translated into the Manchu language and be read among high officials.[21] However, *Tract on Divine Action and Response* never formally entered Qing discourse centered on the Sacred Edict.

The short *Tract on Divine Action and Response*, with only twelve hundred characters, presents a judicial administration derived from the connection between human beings and the divine. The text begins with a line from the *Chronicle of Zuo* (*Zuo zhuan* 左傳) that emphasizes human agency in the making of one's life: "Calamity and good fortune do not come through gates [of themselves], but are summoned only by men themselves" 禍福無門，唯人自召.[22] It says that the spirits in Heaven and in one's body oversee people's deeds, reporting on their

20. On "story that preaches the Sacred Edict," see Geng Shuyan, "Shengyu xuanjiang xiaoshuo."

21. You Zi'an, *Shan yu ren tong*, 24.

22. *Taishang ganying pian ji shi*, 10. Translation from Legge, *The Chinese Classics*, 5:502.

conduct to the Heavenly Tribunal (*Tiancao* 天曹), which then adjudicates people's life spans and the quality of the remainder of their lives. Touching on every aspect of daily life, the text lists 26 good deeds and about 170 evil deeds. The evil deeds include greed for wealth and power, transgression of gender boundaries, and involvement in quarrels with relatives and community members, as well as violation of religious and customary rules. All transgressions shorten one's life. If people have done so much wrong that they cannot pay off their karmic debt in this life, the responsibility of paying off their moral debt will be transferred to their descendants. However, if one repents in a timely fashion, one can still be redeemed and possibly hope for immortality. The quantification of karmic retribution at the end of *Tract on Divine Action and Response* brings to mind calculations of morality in sixteenth-century books of "ledgers of merit and demerit." In such ledgers, the accumulation and deduction of merit are meticulously calculated based on people's each action and intention. Many ledgers of merit and demerit borrow supernatural elements from Buddhism, Daoism, and popular religions, so sixteenth-century Confucian elites had to justify their use of those books.[23] The ledgers provided a forum for debates on issues such as "the connection between virtue and social status, the proper approach to self-cultivation, and the relationship between people and their fate" in the sixteenth century.[24]

The view of the netherworld in *Miraculous Proofs* is heavily influenced by the Buddhist image of Hell, which spread through the mediation of the popular tract *Jade Records* (*Yuli zhibao chao* 玉歷至寶鈔) during the nineteenth century.[25] As Jonathan Spence shows, *Jade Records*

23. For example, Yuan Huang's case in Cynthia Brokaw's discussion, chap. 2, 61–109. The recourse they eventually found was to focus on their current life and emphasize the diligent observation of moral rules in these books, according with the central idea of self-cultivation in Neo-Confucianism. Goossaert shows there is a strong Daoist influence on morality texts during the Taiping period in Goossaert, "Competing Eschatological Scenarios."

24. Brokaw, *Ledgers of Merit and Demerit*, 25.

25. It should also be pointed out that these visions are far from mainstream Buddhism. See Duan Yuming, "*Yuli zhibao chao.*" The edition that Duan Yuming considers to be closer to the original edition was published in 1890, and the dates appended to the preface of the text range from 1809 to 1855. *Yuli* has multiple editions, and it also bears several titles, though the differences of the titles do not necessarily

was widely circulated in southern China when the Taiping Rebellion was on the rise.[26] The world set up in *Jade Records* shares its structure and imagery with that of *Miraculous Proofs*.[27] At the beginning of *Jade Records*, the ten kings in the netherworld who are in charge of the ten levels of Hell gather to celebrate the birthday of Ksitigarbha Bodhisattva, who is feared and respected by all the kings.[28] The bodhisattva, out of compassion for those who committed wrongs while oblivious to the consequences, commanded the kings of Hell to document the punishments endured in Hell and then summon a virtuous man to transmit the text to the human realm. Reportedly, a Daoist priest named Without Obsession (Danchi 淡癡) was chosen to be the virtuous transmitter, and it was his disciple Refraining from Infatuation (Wumi 勿迷) who published this text.

The netherworld in *Jade Records* is structured as ten major Hells, each of them having sixteen subordinating small hells. After death, a deceased person embarks on the path to the netherworld (*Huangquan lu* 黃泉路). Before arriving at Hell, which is located beyond the ocean, people's merits and demerits are calculated: the virtuous ones ascend directly to Heaven as immortals; the ones whose positive and negative karma balance out achieve immediate rebirth as human beings; and those who have done more wrong than good remain in the netherworld. On the first level, those who have done wrong come to the Terrace of Mirror of Karmic Debt (*Niejing tai* 孽鏡台) to see their

---

mean difference in content. Among all the titles, including *Yuli chao zhuan jing shi* 玉歷鈔傳警世, *Yuli zhibao chao* 玉歷至寶鈔, *Yuli zhibao bian* 玉歷至寶編, and *Ci'en yuli* 慈恩玉歷, what remains constant is the component of *Yuli* 玉歷. According to Wang Jianchuan and Lin Wanchuan, *Yuli* may mean the forms of human being and immortals that contrast with ghosts in the netherworld. See Wang Jianchuan and Lin Wanchuan, "Ming Qing minjian zongjiao jingjuan wenxian daoyan," 9–10; You Zi'an, *Shan yu ren tong*, 208. Some scholars have argued for Daoist influence on *Yuli baochao*; see Li Ji, "*Taishang ganying pian* wenben laiyuan." Also see Goossaert, "Une théologie chinoise de l'au-delà."

26. Spence, *God's Chinese Son*, 38–46.

27. Because printing and disseminating morality books were considered ways of accumulating merit, many people hired printers to print these books. Though morality books were printed in large numbers, they are not well-preserved. The edition of *Precious Jade Records* I consulted was printed in 1920 by an unknown publisher.

28. On the ten kings, see Teiser, *The Scripture on the Ten Kings*.

negative karma reflected in a huge mirror. All wrongdoers, after receiving punishment in each level of Hell, get their karmic balance re-
evaluated: those who have received their fair amount of punishment
go directly to the tenth level, whereas others continue their punishment
by torture. Most wrongdoers have to go through each of the ten levels;
in the tenth level, people exit the netherworld to be reborn.[29]

The central point of *Jade Records* is that people are punished com-
mensurately with how reprehensible they are. Even relatively light punishments are horrifying. Deeds that usually evade the punishment of
earthly law, such as making a profit from prescribing unknown med-
icines to people, not having sympathy for the elder or the younger
generation, and not repaying benefactors with loyalty and gratitude,
are all penalized in the netherworld. Sinners have their tendons cut,
bones scratched, eyes gouged, and skin peeled—just to name a few
mechanisms of punishment. Those who hurt the natural world by causing forest fires, poisoning fish in rivers, and killing birds have their
hearts minced and bodies soaked in human waste. Being disrespectful
toward one's parents or parents-in-law is among the worst offenses: one
will be born as a beast in all future lives. The most extreme torture
applies to those who set fire to a person's houses or disseminate por-
nography: they will be bound to heated bronze pillars and condemned
to the Avīci Hell, where they endure eternal suffering. Though this
extreme moral vision of punishments does not have an actual parallel
in Qing imperial legal codes, in reality, the imperial government imposed severe punishments on convicted criminals, exploiting the fra-
gilities and sensitivities of the human body and thereby creating a
symbolic representation of imperial despotism.[30] The bodily degrada-
tion of transgressors in *Jade Records*, which is further developed in
*Miraculous Proofs*, may be seen as an intensified version of this aspect
of Qing legal life manifested in popular beliefs.

29. However, those who committed or even considered suicide during their
lifetime, as well as the Buddhist and Daoist priests who omitted words or parts of the
sutra while performing the ceremony to deliver the deceased, have to endure
additional suffering before entering the second level.

30. Examples and discussions on this topic can be found in Brook, *Death by a
Thousand Cuts*.

Morality books such as *Tract on Divine Action and Response* and *Jade Records* were broadly disseminated, but there were few attempts to interpret the Sacred Edict using beliefs in supernatural retribution. This changed with the publication of *Miraculous Proofs*, which combined the discourse surrounding the Sacred Edict and the worldview of the netherworld in morality books, to scrutinize people's conduct in everyday life, imposing discipline on people's bodies and minds at every single moment. In doing so, this text integrates imperial ideological and legal systems—which influence people through external regulations—and by-then popular religious beliefs, which implanted an afterlife purgatorial system in the minds of the people. Imaginations of judgment, consequently, became especially important during this process of integration, as they connected the human realm and the divine world with the "judicial continuum."

## Miraculous Proofs in the Tradition of Morality Books

In addition to its connections with the interpretive discourse centering on the Sacred Edict and with important popular religious texts about moral retribution, *Miraculous Proofs* should also be situated within the tradition of morality books produced in southwestern China. The many printing houses in Sichuan Province might have also contributed to the popularity of morality books in this area.[31] As Yasuki Abe shows in various studies, preaching the Sacred Edict through stories of moral retribution became popular in southwestern China around the mid-nineteenth century; the 1852 publication of *Essential Summaries of the Proclamation* (*Xuanjiang jiyao* 宣講集要) marks the beginning of this trend.[32] *Essential Summaries* is probably the first book to use stories of moral retribution to interpret the Sacred Edict, and it features prefaces attributed to the god of literature and culture (Wenchang di 文昌帝), the god of blessings (Fuyou di 孚佑帝),

31. Wang Yangang, "Lun Qingdai Shengyu xuanjiang."
32. Yasuki Abe, *Hōkō densetsu no keisei*. A general description of the form and content of *Xuanjiang jiyao* can be found in Lin Yu-Ping, "'Han Chuan shanshu' de lishi," 629–32.

and Lord Guan Yu.[33] These popular deities were also invoked in the practice of spirit writing or planchette writing (*fuji* 扶乩) in late imperial China.[34] *Miraculous Proofs* was probably influenced by *Essential Summaries,* given its evocation of the same deities. However, unlike *Essential Summaries, Miraculous Proofs* constructs a systematic vision of the netherworld and uses imageries of Hell to vindicate the principle of moral retribution; this innovation suggests possible influences from *Tract on Divine Action and Response* and *Jade Records.*

## The Physical Characteristics of Miraculous Proofs

The two extant copies of *Miraculous Proofs* are different editions. The edition examined by Zhou Zhenhe (Zhou edition) has eight volumes. The edition I consulted at Kyoto University (Kyoto edition) consists of six volumes.[35] This chapter focuses on the Kyoto edition, which is the reprint of the Zhou edition with modifications: on the interior of its cover page, there is an alternative title of *Essential Summary of Miraculous Proofs of the Sacred Edict* (*Shengyu lingzheng zhaiyao* 聖諭靈徵摘要).[36] Among the Zhou edition's three prefaces cited in his study, two are preserved in the Kyoto edition.

---

33. Wenchang was in charge of culture and the civil examinations. His official title of lord was conferred in the Yuan dynasty, and he became increasingly popular in late imperial times. See You Zi'an, *Shan yu ren tong,* 238–40. Fuyou di is one of the names of Lü zu 呂祖, or Lü Dongbin 呂洞賓, a popular Daoist deity in late imperial China. In 1805, the Jiaqing Emperor (r. 1796–1820) conferred on him the title of "god of blessings." During the Qing dynasty, Lü zu's status was elevated in the hierarchy of Daoist deities. See Lai Chi Tim, "Ming Qing Daojiao Lü zu."

34. You Zi'an, *Quanhua jinzhen,* 54–58.

35. The Kyoto edition is the only copy I found in library catalogs. Though contemporary scholar Zhou Zhenhe mentions *Miraculous Proofs* in his *Shengyu guangxun jijie,* he does not indicate where he saw this book. In the edition I saw, *juan* corresponds to *ce* (volume): one *juan* equals one *ce.*

36. Some excerpts of the earlier edition could be found in Wang Yangang, "Lun Qingdai Shengyu xuanjiang," 106–7. My comparison between several excerpts of the earlier edition and their corresponding passages in the reprint suggests these excerpts are identical.

The various dates and locations appended to the prefaces of the Kyoto edition suggest that *Miraculous Proofs* was probably reprinted multiple times between 1855 and 1885 in different regions with modified titles. The pagination of the first volume of *Essential Summary of Miraculous Proofs* also suggests there were various rounds of republication: the prefaces dating to 1855 are placed at the beginning of the book, and are paginated separately from the possibly forged prefaces dating up to 1849, which are paginated together with the rest of the book. In between these groups of prefaces is an 1885 preface with no page number, suggesting that it may be a later addition. By 1885, the book had been adopted by Qing officials to facilitate the spread of state ideology. The prefatory writings allow us to reconstruct its publication history: in southwestern China, *Miraculous Proofs* was first printed around 1855, and was eventually brought to Hunan Province to be reprinted in 1885 under the additional title of *Essential Summary of Miraculous Proofs.*

The producer of *Miraculous Proofs* first needed to legitimize his work by attributing its authorship to deities and incorporating an epilogue by a Qing political authority, Chang Ming 常明 (d. 1817). The epilogue, which also appears in the Zhou edition, is dated 1800, the earliest date associated with the book. Chang Ming served at that time as the provincial governor in Yunnan. His epilogue is most likely authentic. However, its content does not concern the *Miraculous Proofs,* but another vernacular interpretation of the Sacred Edict, one that had been widely circulated in China since it was written in 1726.[37] The writer of *Miraculous Proofs* seems to have "recycled" Chang Ming's text and printed it in his book to increase its credibility.

The attributions of authorship to divine beings are found in other, later prefaces. After the earliest date, 1800, the next earliest seen in both the Zhou and Kyoto editions is 1805, which is penned in a preface entitled "The Original Preface of *Miraculous Proofs*" ("*Shengyu lingzheng yuan xu*" 聖諭靈徵原序), attributed to Lord Guan Yu. A closer examination of the content of the preface, however, shows this date (1805) was likely forged later. Another preface, attributed to the god of literature and culture, dates to 1849. Neither preface is associated with a location. Another two prefaces dated 1855 are attributed to two Daoist

37. Zhou Zhenhe, *Shengyu guangxun jijie*, 623.

immortals respectively: the god of blessings and the god of Heaven and sun (Qingxuan jiuyang shangdi 青玄九陽上帝), who allegedly descended to the Huangni Village in Yunnan Province.

The latest date associated with *Miraculous Proofs* in the Kyoto edition is 1885, a date penned after a preface attributed to Liao Changming 廖長明 (fl. 1885), who was then serving as the regional military commander in Hunan Province. In the preface, Liao describes how he was intrigued by the book when he first arrived at his post. He proposed that *Miraculous Proofs* was a hybrid genre formed by merging morality books and the Sacred Edict, so it "moves people most. Upon reading the book, people are warned and cautioned in their hearts" 最易感動，使人觸目警心.[38] Liao's reprinting and dissemination of *Miraculous Proofs* suggests this book, at least in the Hunan area, was fully integrated into Qing ideological discourse together with the supernatural elements it introduced. The amalgamation of various religious traditions in *Miraculous Proofs,* and the gradual subsumption of it within Qing official ideological discourse in the 1880s, illustrates how after the Qing victory against the Taiping Rebellion, local cults gained official support.[39]

The physical features of the *Miraculous Proofs* I examined suggest this book was intended to be associated with imperial authority and meant for mass dissemination. The body of the text is printed on bamboo paper, a low-cost paper that is often stigmatized for its low quality. However, the type of bamboo paper used to print this edition is stronger, thicker, and paler, and features higher printing quality compared to nineteenth-century prints of cheap vernacular fiction, Protestant pamphlets, and Taiping propagandistic materials.[40] In the Kyoto edition, a purple slip of paper with a rectangular frame in its center is glued to the left side of each volume's cover. In the middle of that frame, the title, *Miraculous Proofs of the Sacred Edict* (*Shengyu lingzheng* 聖諭靈徵),

38. *SYLZ*, 1: not paginated.

39. Qing government's support for local cults is discussed in Goossaert, "1898: The Beginning of the End," 326. After the Boxer Rebellion, this support for local cults waned, 328. Goossaert views "local cults" as synonymous of "(local) religious structures," 318.

40. On bamboo paper and the range of its quality, see Chia, *Printing for Profit*, 26. She also explains this issue in more detail in 327n.

appears. In the bottom half, a couplet printed in a smaller font reads, "In total, there are six volumes, retributions are fully manifested therein; / The essential summary is made known, and wicked hearts should repent instantly" 全部六本，果報畢現；摘要以聞，惡心速變. Surrounding this frame is the pattern known as "edge of sea and river," which is similar to those on extant Taiping placards. The slips attached to all six volumes are the same, though none gives a specific volume number. This suggests the slips were produced in large numbers to accommodate the book's mass production. The reverse of the front cover page is decorated with more elaborate patterns of dragons in clouds that symbolize imperial authority. At the center of the page, a frame contains the alternative book title, *Essential Summary of the Miraculous Proofs of the Sacred Edict*.

The page contents and layout of *Miraculous Proofs* reveal attempts to put various authorities that have been evoked into certain hierarchical order. Following the title page are two tables of contents: the first lists the Shunzhi Emperor's six maxims, and the second lists the Kangxi Emperor's sixteen maxims. This table of contents is printed with sophisticated, multilayer color-printing technology (*taoyin* 套印): the characters are printed in black ink, and the patterns and the frames are printed in pink.[41] Surrounding the frame of the table of contents, there are "S"-shaped dragons at its top, bottom, and the inner long edge. All printing features emphasize imperial authority. The other table of contents lists all the prefatory writings. The tables of contents and prefaces take up so many pages that they make up nearly the entire first volume. Superscript is also used to symbolize reverence to authorities in *Miraculous Proofs*.[42] However, the issue here is how to visually represent imperial, divine, and cultural authorities on the page layout: Should there be a hierarchical order for these authorities? Practically, which name should be more elevated, and by how much? These questions about the visual alignment symbolizing religious/political/cultural

41. It is possible that the original color has faded.

42. Daoist texts of the period adopt such visual markers to honor the emperor or the Daoist deities. Most texts are concerned exclusively with Daoist deities. An exception is a copy of *Taishang baofa tushuo* 太上寶筏圖說 printed in 1889. In this text, in the few cases where both emperor and Daoist deities are mentioned, the print layout suggests greater reverence for Daoist deities.

authorities are echoed in the physical layouts of the Taiping publications. In the layout of *Miraculous Proofs*, these authorities are generally treated equally. Some inconsistency, however, does occur: in the general table of contents, Lord Guan Yu is placed one character higher than the Kangxi Emperor. In volume 1's table of contents, however, the hierarchy of these two is reversed. Such occasional disorder does not apply to the whole book, but it shows that a religious authority may possibly challenge the absolute status of the Qing emperor. The treatment of Confucius is especially intriguing: in the sample page, his name is still elevated from the text proper, but appears lower in comparison with both the Qing emperor and the various deities. This visual alignment suggests that in the world presented in *Miraculous Proofs*, Confucius may be deemed less powerful than the imperial and divine authorities. In contrast, of all authorities, Heaven and the supreme God (Shangdi 上帝), as I will explain later, are always represented with the greatest reverence.

## *The Contents of* Miraculous Proofs

In *Miraculous Proofs*, the interpretation of each of the Kangxi Emperor's sixteen maxims has four components: (1) the Yongzheng Emperor's amplification, (2) the 1726 vernacular interpretation that was widely circulated in the eighteenth century, (3) the cases of revelation from Hell, and (4) Lord Guan Yu's brief admonishment. Each maxim is illustrated by several stories. Among all maxims, the first one—about Confucian familial ethics—is the most extensively expounded upon, to such an extent that the stories illustrating that maxim take up two-and-a-half of the six volumes. This maxim, "Devote yourselves to filial piety and fraternal devotion, in order to give due importance to normative human relations," is broken down to concrete familial relationships, such as those between a principal wife and a concubine, an adopted son and his foster parents, and even between pairs of sisters-in-law.

The explanatory stories seek to include every possible role one may assume in familial and local communities. The order in which the stories are arranged shows that priority is given to the relationships between parents and children. Those touching on the subject of the first maxim include: "A Daughter Who Failed to Be Filial" 女子不孝, "Being Unfilial toward a Divorced Mother" 不孝出母, "A Son Being Unfilial toward His Stepmother" 前子不孝後母, "The Foster Parents Forbid Their Son to Be Filial to His Biological Parents" 撫親阻子行孝, and "A Stepmother Fails to Cherish Her Stepson" 後母不慈前子. Besides the stories falling under this rubric, there are illustrations of the relationships between uncle and nephew, husband and wife, and between brothers as well as between sisters-in-law; for example, "The Nephew Being Unfilial toward His Maternal Uncle" 外侄不孝舅父, "[A Wife] Being Disrespectful toward Her Husband" 不敬其夫, "[A Man] in Discord with His Brothers Because of His Children" 為兒女不和弟兄, "[A Woman] in Discord with Her Sisters-in-Law Because of Words [arguments, rumors, etc.]" 為言語不和妯娌. Such exhaustiveness in the categories and descriptions should be viewed in the context of Qing society, where laws and policies sought to bind everyone within certain familial relationships.[43]

Like Taiping edicts about the divine descents of the Heavenly Father and the Heavenly Brother, *Miraculous Proofs* seeks to illustrate divinity through individual incidents. The central scene in almost all stories is an interrogation in Hell, which is represented as a conversation between the wrongdoer and the king of Hell. For instance, in "Man Who Trusted People's Treacherous Words on Bad Terms with His Brother" 信人言不和弟兄, Rao Chunshan, a man who died of dysentery when he was forty years old, is interrogated in the netherworld. He tries to argue with the king of Hell but to no avail.

The king of Hell addresses him with these words:

Despicable slave, in your life, because of your credulity of other people's words, you have sued and quarreled with your brother for seventeen times in total. Every time it was like that. None of the quarrels was based on true evidence. Despicable slave, why were you so credulous?
狗奴一生聽旁人之言與兄弟角業興訟，都是這種故態。並無一次是真。狗奴，你為何要輕信呢?

43. See Sommer, *Sex, Law, and Society.*

Trying to defend himself, Rao Chunshan argues,

> I only figured that their words were true, so I trusted them. Now my
> honorable King, you have revealed the truth to me. It is all because those
> people of rotten mouths added elements to the stories that I was deceived.
> I beg you, my king, to punish them.
>
> 小人只想人言是真，我才聽信。今蒙大王指示。這才是他們那些爛牙
> 吧的，添言添語哄了小人。還望大王處置他們。

The king of Hell proceeds to deliver his moral admonition:

> Making up and spreading rumors to cause disharmony between brothers
> is a big crime. Doubtless, they will be sent to Hell where their tongues
> will be pulled out. However, even if people's words are true, you should
> not have believed them . . . Even if it is something you see with your own
> eyes and hear with your own ears, you should be tolerant and yielding,
> instead of harboring anger and resentment. How can you be hostile
> against your brother because of other people's words?
>
> 捏言造謗，使人弟兄不和，這是大罪, 拔舌地獄，固是不容他的。但人
> 言就是真的，狗奴也不可信 . . . 就是你親耳聽得，親眼看見，也當寬
> 容忍讓。不可藏怒宿怨。何可因人之言就成仇恨呢?[44]

The dialogue between the king and the man being judged and cas-
tigated concerns mundane matters in daily life. The king uses very simple classical Chinese, but the wrongdoers mainly use southwestern
Mandarin.[45] These features have the effect of blurring the boundary
between the imaginary netherworld and the human realm. In addition, the transgressor and the king of Hell engage in an interrogation
based on the accusation and evidence presented by the king, as pros-
ecutor and judge; the chain of logic is meticulously constructed, to
such an extent that it seems tedious. The strict adherence to moral
propriety (maintaining a good relationship with one's brother) and

---

44. *SYLZ*, 3:7a.

45. For instance, in the cited example, *lan yaba* 爛牙吧 (rotten mouths) comes
from southwestern dialect.

the enumeration of all the factors that compromise the man's position, however, imply the potential difficulty of maintaining the absoluteness of this moralistic picture in reality.

The punishments meted out in Hell seem to be modeled on the court-like setting in which the Kangxi Emperor's Sacred Edict was preached. It was a common practice for the heads of local communities to observe people's daily conduct and to solicit reports from community members about one another's performances. The head of the community would keep four registers on which the moral and immoral conduct of community members were recorded.[46] Such registers categorized people by their good deeds, evil deeds, repentances, and reconciliations.[47] While the local head observed people's daily conduct, he also solicited reports from community members. After each sermon on the Sacred Edict, he made an announcement based on the four register books and sent a review to the local administrator.[48] In some places, the names of the virtuous and the wicked were displayed on the placard of the pavilion where the Sacred Edict was preached.[49] In one early Qing illustration (fig. 2.1) of the setting in which people come to listen to the Sacred Edict, the local heads kneel in front of the table displaying incense, candles, and the tablet on which the Sacred Edict is inscribed, with those described as "the good," "the wicked," "the repentant," and "the reconciled" kneeling behind them in a row. On the two sides of the table, the community members line up to listen to the sermon. This scene is remarkably similar to the interrogation setting in Hell in *Miraculous Proofs*, where people's relationship to the proselytization of the Sacred Edict constitutes another measuring standard of morality. The community members who wrote vernacular interpretations of the Sacred Edict, who lectured on it, and who were members of the audience, all have counterparts in the vision of the netherworld represented in *Miraculous Proofs*.

---

46. Li Laizhang, "Shengyu xuanjiang xiangbao tiaoyue xiaoyin" in *Shengyu xuanjiang tiaoyue*, 5a.

47. Tadao Sakai, *Zōho Chūgoku zensho no kenkyū*, 2:24–31.

48. Li Laizhang, "Xinshi si kuan" in *Shengyu xuanjiang tiaoyue*, 1b.

49. Zhang Boxing, "Shenchi xiangyue baojia shi" 申饬鄉約保甲示, compiled in Zhou Zhenhe, *Shengyu guangxun jijie*, 544.

FIG. 2.1. Li Laizhang 李來章 (fl. 1660–1690), "Instructions on Positions of Kowtow and Prostration during the Proclamation [of the Sacred Edict] in Counties and Towns" ("Yu chengxiang xuanjiang guibai wei tu" 諭城鄉宣講跪拜位圖), in *Conditions about Explication of Sacred Edict* (*Shengyu xuanjiang tiaoyue* 聖諭宣講條約). Cishutang edition, 1705. Unpaginated.

*Miraculous Proofs* was intended to morally transform its audience. Written in alternating passages of prose and rhymed pentasyllabic lines, the text brings to mind the tradition of *baojuan* with regard to not only form but also themes, social functions, performativity, and intended audience.[50] For example, the ten kings' and sinners' revelations in Hell in *Miraculous Proofs* constitute an important theme in the *baojuan* tradition, as represented by *The Precious Scrolls of Ten Kings* (*Shi wang baojuan* 十王寶卷). Even though the text proper of *Miraculous Proofs*

50. *Baojuan* is a narrative genre characterized by alternating verse and prose; it is associated with Buddhist and Daoist preaching and popular tales of retribution.

does not strictly follow that of *baojuan*, it also "provide[s] an intimate picture of the morals and beliefs of the local population."[51] For example, one preface of *Miraculous Proofs* suggests that it would benefit a household to read this book during festivals when family members gather; the book, it was said, should also be read aloud at gatherings to bring about the desired moral transformation. This kind of linkage between performance of *Miraculous Proofs* and accumulation of moral merit resonates with popular belief in the benefit of *baojuan* performances. Though *baojuan* was mainly associated with Buddhist and Daoist preaching when it originated, by the nineteenth century it was also used to tell stories of retribution, popular legendary tales, and even contemporary news.[52] During the second half of the nineteenth century, *baojuan* texts were produced to educate "ignorant men and women" (*yufu yufu* 愚夫愚婦) and combat the threat of Christianity.[53] *Miraculous Proofs* and *baojuan* share the same kind of imaginary audience that belonged to the lower level of the social strata.

Despite some similarities to *baojuan*, *Miraculous Proofs* differs in that its rhymed lines take up only a very small portion of the text, which is largely composed of narrative prose.[54] In *Miraculous Proofs*, the transgressors' stories are told in prose and the narrator engages in conversations with the audience as a storyteller. Narrative features of vernacular stories, such as the "storyteller's manner," are frequently used.[55] In contrast, rhymed lines are used to convey transgressors' personal feelings and reflections rather than serving a narrative function

51. Idema, *The Immortal Maiden Equal to Heaven*.

52. An overview of the development and content of *baojuan* can be found in Che Xilun, *Xinyang, jiaohua, yule*, 1–42.

53. Alexander, "Conservative Confucian Values." Her discussion of an anonymous late nineteenth-century author's narrative strategy in his adaptation of a well-known *baojuan* is on p. 98.

54. Che Xilun has a comprehensive comparison between *baojuan* and *xuanjiang* (preaching) as both literary and performative forms in "Du Qingmo Jiang Yuzhen bian." However, some of the characteristics he observes that are mostly exclusively about *baojuan*—for instance, the extraordinary textual length—also apply to *Miraculous Proofs*. Therefore, I suggest that the comparison between *baojuan* and *xuanjiang* must be made on a case-by-case basis.

55. Yasuki Abe also makes this observation about *xuanjiang* activities today in Sichuan and Hubei provinces. See "Senkō seiyu," 79.

as they do in *baojuan*.[56] Today, in some regions of southwestern China, there is still a form of performance named *xuanjiang* 宣講 (preaching), whose style suggests how *Miraculous Proofs* might have been performed.[57]

## An Imagined Community of Transgressors in *Miraculous Proofs*

By integrating the regulation of daily life in the Sacred Edict and the vision of Hell inspired by the *Jade Records* through the tradition of *xuanjiang*, *Miraculous Proofs* blends individualized experiences in the human realm and the imagined netherworld on a new level. This integration comes about through the device of trial and judgment in the netherworld. The setup prompts several questions: What are the transgressions that subject people to punishment in Hell? How does the accused person's attempted rationalization of his or her transgressions challenge moralistic admonition? Also, according to what standard is the punishment meted out, and how is the punishment described? The setting in which the Sacred Edict was preached at the time is, as we have seen, very similar to the setting in which the newly dead are interrogated in *Miraculous Proofs*. The one reflects the other, but is in its turn reflected. The writer may have intended simply to draw on everyday experiences in imagining Hell, but by doing so, he attributes

56. On the example in *Miraculous Proofs*, see Li Zhi's confession and repentance in the stories illustrating the sixteenth maxim in vol. 6, 72b–78a. In *xuanjiang* performance today, rhymed lines are also sung to express the characters' emotions and concerns. See Yasuki Abe, "Senkō seiyu," 80.

57. *Xuanjiang* preaches traditional ethic values through stories. The staging involves two performers who alternate between singing and telling, engaging in dialogues with each other during the performance. Lin Yu-Ping, "'Hanchuan shanshu' de lishi bianqian," 631. *Miraculous Proofs* was also intended for private readings. Its preface assures the reader that just by reading this book, one can already erase one's moral flaws. In *Miraculous Proofs*, there is no marginal commentary, and interlinear notes are limited. However, punctuation—a form of reading aid for people of lower literacy—is used throughout the work. *Miraculous Proofs* was therefore probably also intended for those of limited literacy who could either use the book on private occasions or read the text out loud to others.

an unearthly, even hellish quality to everyday experiences, thereby testifying to a vision of dystopia in the midst of mid-nineteenth-century reality.

## The Court of Hell

The Hell scenes in *Miraculous Proofs* are rooted in Buddhist literature and traditional court case stories, the most famous examples of which feature Judge Bao, a historic figure around whom many legends have accrued. The literary trope of traveling to the netherworld appeared as early as the seventh century in the Dunhuang scroll "The Tang Emperor Taizong's Visit to Hell" ("Tang Taizong you difu" 唐太宗遊地府). In this text, the visitor to Hell witnesses a myriad of cruel punishments imposed on wrongdoers based on the cosmological principle of retribution. Spectacular representations of Hell became particularly popular in eighteenth- and nineteenth-century *baojuan* that were intended for mass consumption. These narratives focus on portraying how people are tortured in their afterlives in a dark and gruesome Hell, but do not investigate in detail what led people there in the first place. The central importance placed upon the judicial process in *Miraculous Proofs'* Hell stories derives not from these representations but from traditional popular stories about Judge Bao, an upright and wise judge who "served as the preeminent embodiment of justice in China."[58] Judge Bao sometimes also occupies the role of the king of Hell.[59] In the Judge Bao stories, the scenes of investigation are illustrated in great detail. Such descriptions demonstrate how justice, usually represented as a result of karmic retribution, is carried out after Judge Bao's scrupulous examination.[60] A large number of the Hell stories focused on divine investigations re-create the traditions of both netherworld travel and Judge Bao stories in popular literature. *Miraculous Proofs* follows this model,

58. Idema, "Introduction," ix. Ting Chao-Chin, *Suwenxue zhong de Bao gong*, and Abe Yasuki, *Hōkō densetsu no keisei* both give surveys of the development of the Judge Bao stories.
59. Li Yongping, "Fojiao wenhua dui Bao gong."
60. Hanan, "Judge Bao's Hundred Cases Reconstructed."

melding both literary traditions, and thus makes Qing ideological discourse take on a new light in the mid-nineteenth century.

The dead who come to Hell do so because of their moral transgressions; their foibles, however—just as in the earlier text, *Jade Records*—are not crimes according to law. One illustrative example is the story titled "In Discordance with One's Sister-in-Law Because of Rumors" ("Wei yanyu buhe zhouli" 為言語不合妯娌). In this narrative, a woman with the surname Lan has a quick and sour temperament. An example given of her wrongdoing is an argument she has with her sister-in-law, who has the surname Shao, over the lamp oil in the house. On the seventh day of the third month of *gengyin* year, seeing that the oil is about to run out, Shao says, "It has been less than ten days since I added oil last time. We only have so much oil. Better to be frugal in using the lamp. One should not go to bed with the lamp lighted. Otherwise, later we have to feel our way in darkness" 這罐油舀起來未上十天，就止有這點兒了。這些點兒油的。大家要減省些。莫要點起燈睡。恐怕後來摸黑. Lan replies, "You are the only one smart enough to be thrifty. We are all dumb. We just know about going to bed; we didn't know that we should blow out the lamp" 只有你聰明。曉得掙家。我們是啞巴。只曉得睡，不曉得吹燈. Shao explains that she was not criticizing Lan, but Lan resentfully returns, "How many lamps do we have in the house? To whom do your words apply? I simply have no idea. Now that mother-in-law Shao has said so, how dare I, the daughter-in-law, disobey her orders. From now on, as soon as it turns dark, I will go to bed. However, I have only one thing to say: since you want to take up the role of mother-in-law to admonish me, you have to sleep with our father-in-law tonight" 這屋有幾盞燈點油？你的話落在哪個身上？我就不曉得了。這下子邵氏婆婆說了的。媳婦兒不敢傲令。自今以後，黑了就睡。但有一種：你既要當婆婆教訓於我，今夜就要同公公去睡.[61]

First, the fictional, concrete date associated with Lan's wrongdoing conveys a sense of realism. By calling Shao her mother-in-law, Lan implies that Shao has an illicit sexual relationship with her father-in-law, a taboo in late imperial society.[62] This insult certainly places Lan

61. *SYLZ*, 3:28b, 29a.
62. On the legal consequence of incest in Qing society, see Theiss, *Disgraceful Matters*, 108–17.

in the camp of an aggressive sister-in-law and unfilial daughter-in-law. In reality, people like her, though not sent to jail, probably had a bad reputation among their neighbors and were frowned upon by moralists. In the story, the moral judgment in the human realm is converted to severe punishment in Hell: based on the number of times she transgresses, her stomach is to be set ablaze, her lips scorched and tongue cut off, thousands of times. Because of what seem to be minor moral transgressions in her lifetime, the woman suffers horrible punishment in her afterlife. With numerous examples like this, *Miraculous Proofs* strives to make people internalize moral regulations through simulated judgments in Hell.

In these carefully constructed narratives, however, the details transgressors revealed in everyday situations sometimes reflect moral conundrums in the human realm. For example, when irresponsible senior family members exhaust family fortunes, do heirs have the right to criticize them? The distinction between right and wrong seems unclear, as shown in the very first story of the book, "A Son Who Failed to Be Filial" ("Erzi buxiao" 兒子不孝), which probes into the fundamental Confucian ethical relationship: parents and son. In this story, when the transgressor is accused by the king of Hell, he defends himself by explaining: because of his parents' extravagant lifestyle, they had to sell all the land left to them by their ancestors, so there was nothing for him to inherit. Furthermore, when he worked at the household of a local landlord, the parents frequently visited him to ask for meals and money, and in doing so, tarnished his reputation as a disciplined worker. Out of anger and resentment, he refused to support his parents and began to verbally abuse them.[63] In another story, "Being Unfilial toward One's Foster Parents" ("Buxiao fuyang fumu" 不孝撫養父母), the transgressor attempts to justify his reasons for not taking care of his parents with the king of Hell: his foster father was originally his fifth uncle. Because his uncle's household had no son, they adopted him to carry on their branch in the lineage. Their relationship was good at first, but when their biological daughter married, the foster parents spent all their possessions and even borrowed money to prepare a dowry for her. When he tried to dissuade them from spending lavishly,

63. *SYLZ*, 2:4a–8b.

they cursed him for abusing their generosity in fostering him. He therefore returned to his birth parents and no longer contacted his foster parents.[64] In both cases, the unfilial sons are punished because of their violation of a fundamental Confucian moral principle. However, their defenses unexpectedly undermine the authority of their parents (foster parents included) who have failed to fulfill their responsibilities in the first place.

In response to these challenges, the king of Hell validates the authority of Confucian ethics by maintaining that the omnipresent divine force keeps the balance of karma on a general scale. In the case of the unfilial biological son, the king of Hell tells him that his parents, who are neither industrious nor thrifty, will not be pardoned. As for the foster parents, the king of Hell summons them, gives them a lesson, and then lets them return to the human realm. After his return, the foster father becomes paralyzed by a stroke; the couple then suffers mistreatment from their daughter and her husband in their remaining years. At the same time, both sons are informed that only the divine, instead of mortal beings like them, has the authority to punish those who fail to perform their roles as seniors in society. The power of divine judgment, we are to infer, prevails when moral ambiguities cannot be resolved in the human realm.

## Punishment and Retribution

*Miraculous Proofs* clearly borrows the system of punishment taking place on ten levels from the *Jade Records*. In fact, the *Jade Records* is mentioned by name in some cases where the king of Hell accuses the transgressors of not following the instructions of the text despite their possession of the book.[65] At the same time, *Miraculous Proofs* does not consistently follow the vision of Hell in the *Jade Records* and sometimes aggravates the punishment.[66]

64. *SYLZ*, 2:16b–20a.
65. *SYLZ*, 5:84b.
66. One example is that in the fifth level of Hell in *Jade Records*, people who erred by not believing in retribution, being ungrateful, or having illicit sexual affairs have their evil hearts cut out. See *Yuli zhibao chao quanshi wen*, 25a. This punishment is not commonly applied elsewhere for other infractions. In comparison, cutting out the

If *Jade Records* offers only a general picture of the netherworld, *Miraculous Proofs* portrays the process of torture and the punished person's sufferings in full detail. In the story titled "In Discordance with the Sister-in-Law Because of Rumors" ("Wei renyan buhe zhouli" 為人言不和妯娌), Woman Wen is tied to a pillar, waiting to be executed by a ghost runner (as in the human world, the beings with power have runners who act as messengers and agents). The runner says, "You, wicked woman, have ears but only listen to empty words . . . What do you do with ears like these? Let me cut them off for you" 你這惡婦有耳專聽空話 . . .這樣有耳拿來做什麼？待我與你割下.[67] The runner then "cuts her ears slice by slice" 碎碎割下來. As the woman cries nonstop, he mocks her, asking why she cannot hear her sister-in-law speaking ill of her now. He then exclaims, "Oh, you cannot hear it because blood has blocked your ears! Let me open them up for you" 你的耳心被血糊住了不聽見。待我來與你旋通.[68] Upon these words, he pierces her ears with a knife. After her ears are cut off, Woman Wen begs the ghost runner to let her go, only to be told that this is merely the beginning of her punishment: the same procedure will be applied 1,652 times based on the times she gave credence to rumors.[69] Sometimes, the sinners are first tortured to death but then brought back to consciousness by a wind of *yin*, so that they can continue to receive their remaining punishment ("Niefeng huanhun" 孽風還魂).[70]

The meticulous calculation of moments of culpability resonates within a retribution system of "ledgers of merit and demerit." In "A Wife Who Fails to Respect Her Husband" ("Bujing qifu" 不敬其夫), the king of Hell points out that in the course of the woman's forty-four-year marriage, she had scolded the husband 3,213 times, been disobedient 5,751 times, and disrespectful 398 times.[71] At the end of each transgressor's punishment session, the balance of his/her demerit and

---

heart is a common punishment for most transgressions in *Miraculous Proofs*. Such increases in the severity of punishment show that the later book takes a harsher approach toward disciplining people through their fear of supernatural judgment.

67. *SYLZ*, 2:43b.
68. *SYLZ*, 2:43b.
69. *SYLZ*, 2:44a.
70. *SYLZ*, 2:57a.
71. *SYLZ*, 2:48a.

merit is calculated again (*gongguo zhesuan* 功過折算).[72] At the same
time, their merits in this life may not be enough to redeem their accumulated demerits from previous lives, as the king of Hell explains.[73]
Thus the cause-and-effect chain in the retribution system spans several
lifetimes; individuals are denied access to the complete picture of their
fate, except that they have to be heedful of every single action and
thought, so that they are left with fewer demerits in the king of Hell's
account book.

Sometimes the agony is described from the individual's perspective, perhaps to make the moral lessons even more compelling. For
example, in "Vying for Lands and Being in Discord with His Brothers" ("Zheng tianchan buhe dixiong" 爭田產不合弟兄), the transgressor recounts that he has been nailed to a pillar in Hell for an entire
year, during which his eyes and heart have been gouged out repeatedly, day and night. If he is ever about to collapse, the *yin* wind brings
him back to life. He also remembers that he was reborn as a pig and
bitten by myriads of mosquitoes and flies; the precarious sty he lived
in threatened his life every day; when he was being slaughtered as a
pig, he was fully aware of the pain that came with each strike of the
cleaver. In another story, "Lodging a False Accusation out of Resentment" ("Xiefen wugao" 挾忿誣告), the transgressor, having been reborn as a bull for three consecutive lives, tearfully recalls the castration
he received as a one-year-old calf and the pains he endured while
being slaughtered.

In addition to its emphasis on family ethics, *Miraculous Proofs*
also furthers efforts to proselytize the Sacred Edict by mobilizing seniors, local gentry, and students studying for the civil service examinations. First, it justifies the incorporation of morality books into the
Confucian education system. Under the principle "Give weight to
colleges and schools, in order to rectify the practice of the scholar"
(the sixth maxim of the Sacred Edict), *Miraculous Proofs* requires that
teachers prioritize morality books and the Sacred Edict instead of the
Four Books and Five Classics. In the story titled "The Elementary
Tutor Who Did Not Rectify Students' Behavior" ("Mengshi buduan

72. *SYLZ*, 2:8b.
73. *SYLZ*, 4:19a.

shixi" 蒙師不端士習), the king of Hell tells the neglectful tutors that since most children from poor families do not pursue further education, the Four Books and Five Classics are not as advantageous for them as morality books. In the same tale, he also advises the teachers of more advanced students that they should first instruct students on how to be a moral person. When a *tongsheng* 童生 argues that he should be exempted from such responsibilities because he is not an official, the king of Hell admonishes him, "The matter of teaching people is commanded by the emperor, organized by officials, but it all depends on learned men to share the responsibility" 教民之事，統於君，督率於官，而分任全在士子。[74] Therefore, says the king of Hell, the student is obliged to repay imperial favors by diligently preaching the Sacred Edict. At the end of the story, like all other transgressors who fail to proselytize the Sacred Edict and other morality books, this *tongsheng* was sent down to the "Great Hell of Howling" (*jiaohuan da diyu* 叫喚大地獄). This example points to a concern that must have come close to the author's own experience; it also points to the roles expected of Confucian students from lower social strata in combating heretical ideas—which, in that period, would include the Taiping Christian ideology that spread through local communities in the southwestern provinces.

The text implies that most people either do not listen to the proselytization of Sacred Edict diligently and respectfully or do not take its messages to heart. The punishment inflicted on those who talk during lectures is to have their mouths torn and tongues bitten by a snake ("The Listeners Who Chat Nonstop" 聽者說話不休).[75] Women, it directs, have to be included in formal instruction, too: husbands should make sure their wives attend the lectures.[76] Many of the stories, as we have seen, are about women who fail to follow the Sacred Edict. In "A

74. A *tongsheng* is a student who hasn't passed any level of civil service examination, and is thus placed at the lowest rank of the system. *SYLZ*, 5:60a.

75. *SYLZ*, 5:71a–72b.

76. Both of the stories about the sinners who do not attend lectures feature women. See "A Husband Who Forbade His Wife to Listen to Preaching of the Sacred Edict" ("Fu buxu qi ting xuanjiang" 夫不許妻聽宣講) and "A Wife Who Did Not Listen to Preaching of the Sacred Edict" ("Qi buting xuanjiang" 妻不聽宣講) in *SYLZ*, 5:65a–69b.

Woman Who Aborted Her Baby or Drowned Her Daughter" ("Furen datai ninü" 婦人打胎溺女), an aunt and her niece accidentally encounter each other in Hell. After telling each other about the dreadful tortures they have witnessed, they reveal how deeply they regret not following the instructions in the Sacred Edict.[77]

The writer of *Miraculous Proofs* has counterparts in the netherworld: literate wrongdoers who are asked to compose vernacular songs (*su ge* 俗歌) to redeem their sins.[78] Having no pen, they write with the blood from their fingertips. These writers usually begin their songs by calling attention to their status as wrongdoers, and then assume a personal voice to tell their experiences.[79] The logic and rhetoric of the words delivered by the wrongdoer are just like those used by a lecturer of the Sacred Edict.[80] When the wrongdoers are illiterate, the ghost runners sometimes compose a song on their behalf.[81] This creates a presumably inadvertent parallel with the situation of *Miraculous Proofs'* author, who in this case acts very much like a ghost runner composing songs for the wrongdoers in the tales and speaking in their voices. Since the wrongdoers emulate those engaged in proselytizing the Sacred Edict in their confessions and declarations, the proselytizers too, by association, become implicated.

The modes of representation in *Miraculous Proofs* were inspired by various literary, religious, and cultural traditions. They also come from practices in the human realm, as we have seen: interrogations and punishments following the practices of a law court, and confessions following the lectures on the Sacred Edict. Conversely, the human realm imitates the imagined supernatural one in its meticulous surveillance of behavior. In real life, the way a room is set up for a lecture on the Sacred Edict reflects a court scene. Members of local communities, as they watch and report upon each other's daily conduct, both discipline others and are disciplined. This system of mutual

77. *SYLZ*, 2:71a–75a.

78. *SYLZ*, 2:61a, 61b, 67a, 67b, 84a, 85b. Some literate women authors also compose songs. *SYLZ*, 3:34b.

79. One of the examples is from "Uncles Not Being Kind to Their Nephews" ("Boshu buci zizhi" 伯叔不慈子侄).

80. *SYLZ*, 2:61a.

81. *SYLZ*, 3:11a.

surveillance creates fears that are essentially the same as those triggered by belief in an omnipresent divinity. Because every party involved in proselytizing the Sacred Edict has an imaginary counterpart
in Hell (as judge, transgressor, or ghost runner), when moral judgments
are made in public settings in the human realm, they evoke imagined
trials in the netherworld. Viewed through the lens of the *Miraculous
Proofs*, Qing society in the mid-nineteenth century, where every member was under the scrutiny of divine forces and Qing laws, could be
regarded as a literal living Hell. Nevertheless, the Taiping millenarian
vision, which embraced the ideals of Heaven and promised instant
liberation, was equally terrifying in many respects.

## Common Ground: *Miraculous Proofs* and Taiping Discourse

One of the aims of *Miraculous Proofs* is to eradicate heretical thoughts,
with Christianity as its primary target. Nevertheless, the ways that
*Miraculous Proofs* imagined and constructed divine authority suggests
that both its author and the Taiping rebels drew from a common
ground of popular beliefs. For example, in both discourses, scenes of
judgment involving supernatural elements in front of an audience constitute an essential device.

    *Miraculous Proofs* presents Christianity as a heterodox religion that
befuddles people's minds and entices them with the promise of material benefits. In the text, missionaries proselytizing Christianity in
China are described as "shameless men sneaking into China to spread
heretical teachings" 無恥之徒，偏要私入中華，傳習邪教.[82] The edition
of *Miraculous Proofs* I study was produced after the 1880s, when anti-
Christianity campaigns were waged in the Hunan area, so it is also
possible that the stories discussed in this section were inserted later in
the reprinted version. In any event, the spiritual and material benefits
that missionaries provided attracted many to join them, especially students who had spent many fruitless years trying to pass the civil service

---

82. *SYLZ*, 5:30b.

examinations. In the story "Learning Deviant Practices Out of Greed" ("Tancai xixie" 貪財習邪), a fifty-nine-year-old man, disappointed and discouraged by his failures at the civil service examinations, converts to Christianity. When he is unemployed, no friends, relatives, or people from his lineage can offer him help. He therefore follows the advice of a tutor and converts to Christianity. Within the Christian community, he is offered an annual stipend and ample opportunities to employ his skills in writing and lecturing. After hearing his explanation, the king of Hell castigates him as a "scholar of the narrow-minded" (*xiaoren ru* 小人儒), a derogatory term borrowed from the *Analects*. This criticism is based on the fact that instead of proselytizing the Sacred Edict to bring back those who were deluded by foreign thoughts, he spread Christian teachings among people for the sake of monetary gain.

This story's presence in the collection shows that the author of *Miraculous Proofs* recognized the danger of the emerging social and cultural trend: Christianity's influence had spread among the educated, who in turn made Christian messages accessible to the uneducated, thereby presenting a serious threat to imperial rule. Mid-nineteenth-century China had an excess of highly educated men and disillusioned students unable to either pass the stringent examinations or find suitable work. Among them was rebel leader Hong Xiuquan, who appropriated Christianity to establish his Heavenly Kingdom in opposition to the Qing empire. As chapters 4 and 6 will show, however, unsuccessful Confucian students continued to search for a meaningful identity in the aftermath of the Taiping Civil War, though many were no better off after the war than they were before it.

Like the Taipings, the author of *Miraculous Proofs* needed to establish the authority of an omnipotent divine being within the human realm. The common narrative device—or form of literary imagination—chosen by both sides is the scene of judgment, which simulates a theatrical space "staging" the scene of an omniscient deity presiding over trials of human beings.[83] In both scenarios, there are elements of power

83. On the representation of divine revelations in Taiping discourse, see discussions on *The Sacred Decrees of the Heavenly Brother* and *The Sacred Decrees of the Heavenly Father* in chapter 1.

and hierarchy, a code of law, confession, adjudication, and punishment. *Miraculous Proofs* also consciously emphasizes the staging of confession and the presence of an audience who authenticates the manifestation of the divine. For instance, the story titled "Returning to the Human World to Recount His Sins" ("Huanyang suzui" 還陽訴罪) describes how a Taiping follower received his punishment in Hell. The mediation of divinity in the text looks like a parody of incidents of divine interventions during the early stage of the Taiping movement. However, the story also illustrates how the very credibility of the stories in *Miraculous Proofs* relies on a rationale similar to the one the Taiping rebels employed to construct their own stories.

"Returning to the Human World to Recount His Sins" falls under the seventh maxim of the Sacred Edict: "Extirpate strange heterodox principles, in order to exalt the correct doctrine."[84] Compared with other stories directly describing the scene of judgment, this story delivers the netherworld court trial through the mouth of the dead wrongdoer as his spirit receives judgment. The story goes that a Christian devotee dies suddenly after he insults a fellow townsman who shows him a morality book titled *Precious Admonishment on Saving People from Calamity* (*Jiujie baoxun* 救劫寶訓). As the man's brothers prepare his body for burial, the body starts to voice the man's experience in Hell, assuming the voices of the ghost runners, the man himself, and the king of Hell. As the king of Hell accuses the man of spreading foreign thoughts and participating in immoral gatherings worshipping the false god, the man retorts that the Western Buddha with the name "Jesus Christ" (Yesu 耶穌) promulgated his religion in order to deliver the faithful. The man calls this religious leader the Heavenly Brother, one of the titles associated with the Taiping leader Xiao Chaogui, through whom it was claimed Jesus Christ "descended" to Earth.

As the spirit of the dead man continues voicing his trial in Hell, he describes the new religion as easy, tolerant with its followers who share food, wealth, and wives with each other. Everyone is guaranteed

---

84. In the interpretive discourse revolving around the Sacred Edict, an anti-heterodox agenda existed long before the rise of the Taiping Rebellion, as shown in Mair, "Language and Ideology in the Sacred Edict."

a place in Heaven after death. Since the religion promises the purest, supreme form of happiness—a happiness without end—people of various occupations and religious beliefs follow this path. The man attempts a threat to the king of Hell: "Don't you talk nonsense excessively. I am a small Buddha from Heaven. If you do not release me, I am afraid that Heaven will execute you" 閻君莫亂鋪。我是天堂一小佛。你再是不寬恕，恐怕天祖把你誅。[85] Immediately, however, a solemn and deep voice that belongs to the king of Hell bellows from the man's mouth to enumerate his crimes and declare the punishment he will receive. When the king of Hell finishes delivering his verdict through the dead man, the body suddenly falls to the ground. The followers witnessing this event, though astonished by what they have seen, still hesitate to abandon their religion. Nevertheless, their doubt instantly dissipates when a frightening deity appears in the sky, killing one of them, proving the validity of this divine authority and its imposition of divine punishment. At the end of the story, all the followers forsake the new religion, and from then on, no one else dares to subscribe.

The story's references to Christianity and Taiping practices make it evident that the heretical belief under attack is Taiping ideology. The wrongdoer's dramatic refusal of the morality book about the divine revelation calls to mind how the rebels started their movement by demolishing statues of Confucian figures and popular deities in family shrines and local temples. Further, the features of the new religion the wrongdoer describes are exactly what the Taiping rebels offered to new adherents at the beginning stage of their movement. A fundamental Taiping policy was to share possessions among its followers—a tenet that attracted many impoverished people to join the Taiping cause. Besides promising material prosperity, the Taiping ideology also promised euphoric states of existences; we see an abundant usage of terms such as *kuaihuo* 快活 (happiness) and *fengliu* 風流 (unrestraint).[86]

---

85. *SYLZ*, 5:44a.

86. *TPTGYS*, 1:22, 26. The idea of "being unbounded" is conveyed by the word *wu jushu* 無拘束 in *Miraculous Proofs*. This seems to be another way of saying *fengliu* and

The opposing sides of this ideological confrontation, the Qing elites and the Taipings, shared common ground in their invocation of the divine. But compared to the instances of Taiping divine interventions, the tale "Returning to the Human World to Recount His Sins" presents a more complex mechanism of mediation of the divine. Here, the wrongdoer's body serves as an empty site for a variety of supernatural forces to pass through, including the ghost runners, the wrongdoer himself, and the king of Hell. The skillful braiding of these forces, which bring about retribution and restore karmic balance, effectively demonstrates the potential power local elites derived from indigenous beliefs in their confrontation with the Taipings.

The audience in the human realm watching the progress of the court case in Hell recalls the Taiping followers who witnessed the "descending" of God and of Jesus Christ. The narrative design in some stories may in fact parody the Taiping practice of "ascending to Heaven" that involved many Taiping followers. For example, in "Returning to the Human World to Recount His Sins," one of the Christian devotees, after witnessing the strange performance of Hell's judgment, says, "This kind of thing even happens in our religion. I am afraid that someone who knows how to play magic tricks has summoned the spirit [of the dead man] to trick us. I suppose his purpose is to let us follow the unorthodox and abandon our orthodox belief that will lead us to Heaven. I still do not believe in that" 我們教內都會有這種事。只怕是哪個會使法，弄他的魂來，與我們玩耍。使我們恐怕去學他們那些邪教，把我們這上天堂的正教丟了。我還是不肯信.[87] In another story, "Instant Retribution on Learning the Heterodox" ("Xixie xianbao" 習邪顯報), the transgressor/protagonist suddenly collapses while hitting and cursing his son, who had tried to persuade him to abandon Christianity and to return to Confucianism. The dispute between the father and son takes place in the streets, where neighbors surround them and attempt to stop the father. When the father's earthly body enacts his underworld punishment, the neighbors "watch" the entire process. Like the eyewitnesses to the Heavenly Father's trials in Taiping pamphlets,

---

*weifeng* 威風, two words essentially connoting the meaning of unboundedness. In both texts cited above, these words appear together with *kuaihuo*.

87. *SYLZ*, 5:45a.

those in *Miraculous Proofs* are described as very impressed by the efficacy of instant retribution.

In both Taiping narratives and *Miraculous Proofs*, the scene of judgment reaches a dramatic climax when the judge, representing the divine, provides irrefutable evidence of the wrongdoer's deeds. In both Taiping and Qing proselytization discourses, divine authority is established through trial scenes in which the representative of omnipresent divinity discloses the offender's wrongdoings with ruthless precision. The many such stories showcasing divine revelations of the wrongdoer's behaviors in *Miraculous Proofs* include "Credulous Man on Bad Terms with His Brother." In this story, the wrongdoer attempts to elude punishment by claiming that no one instructed him on the virtues of living harmoniously with his brother. However, the king of Hell scolds him, "Bastard! Are you saying that there is no one who can expose your lie" 狗奴！說無人指破於你嗎, pointing out that the man's son-in-law had made an effort to educate him with Confucian virtues.[88] In another story, when a younger sister-in-law wants to hide her history of fomenting discord with her stepmother-in-law, the king of Hell tells his clerk to enumerate her offenses: "This wicked woman. If we don't show her the evidence, she will not admit her sins. You, bring out the register and read one or two pieces of evidence to her" 這個惡婦，不指出她的實事 . . . 全憑口問，也是不認的。爾執簿，將他實事念一二條與她聽.[89] In these examples, the tension between oral testimony given by the transgressors in vernacular Chinese, and the textual proof spoken by the king of Hell in vocabularies from classical Chinese, is also noteworthy. In both Taiping propaganda and *Miraculous Proofs*, the evidence for a person's wrongdoings comes from the private, often hidden or secret domain of life. Therefore, the revelation further proves the omnipresent and omnipotent power of divine authority.

At first glance, Taiping texts and *Miraculous Proofs* seem to stem from contesting discourses that describe polarizing visions of Heaven and Hell, utopia and dystopia. But as we have seen, they share common ground in their characterization of a wrathful deity (Shangdi and God), the notion of *jue/xing* (awakening), the trope of "divine judgment," and

88. *SYLZ*, 3:7b.
89. *SYLZ*, 2:28b.

the important role of witnesses. Underlying the simulated theater directed by divinity in both discourses is the desire for an ultimate authority.

## Defending the Authentic Will of Heaven

Both *Miraculous Proofs* and Taiping ideology imagine a supernatural authority that serves as a jurisdictional alternative to the Qing imperial authority. How does the writer of *Miraculous Proofs* construct this alternative authority and yet position this book under the rubric of imperial ideology? Authorship, which involves "a repertoire of practices, techniques and functions" on the historical and imaginary planes, is key.[90] Operating behind a mask, the author of *Miraculous Proofs* maintains anonymity and constructs various imagined authors to present his argument. All of these textual devices, however, are underpinned by the ancient Chinese idea of the Mandate of Heaven that grants legitimacy to the ruler's governance, and therefore guarantees his or her ability to rule in prosperity and peace, which are bestowed by Heaven. This reliance on the Mandate of Heaven, however, has an ironic consequence, in that it implies that prosperity is due not to the efficacy of Qing imperial governance but to supernatural forces.

*Miraculous Proofs* conceals its historical author but presents a "declarative author" who plays the role of "owner of the words" in the public sphere. As I note above, the book associates itself with Qing imperial authority by borrowing an 1805 preface. However, the identity of the main agents behind the book—the authors who wrote vernacular stories to illustrate the maxims, the editors who compiled various resources to bring the book to its current shape, and the publishers who organized the printing of the book—are unknown. The prefaces represent the composition process as contrived not by men but by the divine. Though one of *Miraculous Proofs'* prefaces suggests that a man named Jiang Lingzhong played an important role in its production, his name is likely a pseudonym, since no historical record of the man can be found, and his involvement in the supernatural revelation, as narrated, is anything

90. Love, *Attributing Authorship*, 33.

but realistic. Jiang Lingzhong's byline describes him in this way: "At the age of sixty-nine, having benefited from imperial favor but not returned the debt of gratitude, I, useless Jiang Lingzhong, kneel and bow (to the emperor) and record this piece respectfully" 六十九歲枉食皇恩毫末未報無用臣江靈中稽首頓首恭紀.[91] On the one hand, the historical author of *Miraculous Proofs* presents "Jiang Lingzhong" as an old man who has not served in any office during his lifetime; on the other hand, he also posits "Jiang Lingzhong" as someone who has discovered an alternative way to be politically engaged.

One preface represents the book as the result of transmission through multiple layers of supernatural mediation. This creates the impression that the book is entirely a product of the divine, with humankind having little impact on its formation. Entitled "An Authentic Record of the History of the Netherworld Cases Cited in the *Miraculous Proofs*" ("*Shengyu lingzheng* yin ming'an laili kaozhen ji" 聖諭靈徵引[冥案來歷考真記), this preface gives a detailed account of how divinity manifests in the human realm.

The preface begins with God's anger at people's disrespect for the Sacred Edict. He therefore inflicts punishments both on Earth and in the netherworld. Feeling an urgent need to rectify people's wrongs, the "author" Jiang Lingzhong is determined to compile the netherworld court cases to caution the living, but he becomes increasingly frustrated with people's unwillingness to share their knowledge with him. One evening, however, an old man unexpectedly visits Jiang Lingzhong, telling him that Heaven confers the task of compilation on him. Three months later, Jiang Lingzhong goes to a hall to lecture on the Sacred Edict. That night, he sleeps at the eastern porch of the hall and dreams of Lord Guan Yu, who reads out to him a series of netherworld cases, which Jiang Lingzhong subsequently compiles. The morning after his dream, Jiang Lingzhong discovers that at the western porch, an old man named Yu Yiming has experienced the very same dream. After nightfall that day, he observes Yu Yiming being possessed by a supernatural force. Jiang Lingzhong hears the king of Hell speaking through Yu

91. *SYLZ*, vol. 1. This page is paginated separately from the group of prefaces that are dated after 1855. The pagination of this text runs from the prefaces dated prior to 1855 to the main body of the text. Its page number is 7a in this pagination.

Yiming—the gist of the story being that the king allows the accused dead to explain their cases and asks the ghost runners to record and transmit the cases to Yu Yiming. After the king of Hell departs, Yu Yiming wakes up and begins to write down the cases, exactly as Jiang Lingzhong heard them. Over the next few days, Yu Yiming is possessed sixteen times and is able to record more stories; his cases, however, are only about Confucian morals. Two months later, Jiang Lingzhong has another dream. Following the revelation in that dream, he receives a book of more cases from a Buddhist monk. Putting these two books together—the stories about Confucian morality, as mediated by Yu, and those about Buddhist retribution, as mediated by Jiang—to make this collection, Jiang Lingzhong consolidates and compiles *Miraculous Proofs*.

The role of the supernatural elements in these "miraculous revelations" bears a remarkably close resemblance to the construction of divine authority in early Taiping discourse: in those narratives, Hong Xiuquan also dreamt of revelation, though in his case he ascended to Heaven and met God. The episode in which Jiang Lingzhong is able to watch Yu Yiming's possession by a supernatural power recalls incidents in which Taiping followers witnessed how Yang Xiuqing and Xiao Chaogui received divine interventions from God and Jesus Christ through similar possessions by the divine. Like Yang Xiuqing and Xiao Chaogui, Jiang Lingzhong and Yu Yiming do not possess divine dispositions as individuals on Earth. In fact, even Lord Guan Yu is merely playing his role as a "manager" of the project assigned to him by Heaven. *Miraculous Proofs* is packaged not as the validation of any human being's special powers, but rather as an authentic and conventional manifestation of the will of Heaven.

Like its Taiping counterpart, *Miraculous Proofs* refers to the will, or Mandate, of Heaven as the highest authority. The Mandate of Heaven is "arguably the single most important political concept" in early China, which assesses a ruler's political legitimacy and communicates this assessment to Earth. If Heaven is not pleased, natural disasters occur.[92] In Chinese history, both rulers and rebels used this concept of the Mandate of Heaven to argue for their political legitimacy. According

92. Zhao Dingxin, "The Mandate of Heaven," 419–20.

to one of *Miraculous Proofs'* prefaces, Heaven had already composed the Sacred Edict before sages and emperors transmitted the text to people, so the Sacred Edict issued by the Kangxi Emperor comes, in fact, from Heaven.[93] Divine revelations, the preface explains, are merely used to expound the will of Heaven to convince those who are close-minded. The preface defines the relationship between the ruler and the people in this way: "Heaven gives rise to people and then sets up the ruler for them. [The ruler] is the master who transforms the people on behalf of Heaven" 天生民而立之君。君也者，代天化民之主也.[94] The first sentence in this quotation, "Heaven gives rise to people and then sets up the ruler for them" (*Tian shengmin er li zhi jun* 天生民而立之君), comes from *The Chronicle of Zuo*, the earliest Chinese narrative history and one of the Confucian classics. In *The Chronicle of Zuo*, this statement occurs in a story about Duke Dao of Jin (586–558 BCE), who asks a subject's opinion on the Wei people who have driven out their ruler. The answer he receives is that Heaven establishes the ruler to lead people. As Heaven loves the people profoundly, it does not allow a corrupt ruler to govern them; therefore, Heaven would certainly abandon unqualified rulers.[95] In this sense, this line from *Miraculous Proofs* reminds people of the idea of popular sovereignty, which is precisely what the Taiping rebels advocated.

The next argument the preface poses is even more provocative. Since the people have corrupted the laws that have been passed onto them—namely, the Sacred Edict—another divine being has to be introduced to convey the messages from Heaven to Earth. In *Miraculous Proofs*, Lord Guan Yu serves as the important messenger for Heaven's will. Following this logic, one could say that the mid-nineteenth-century Qing government failed at its mission of properly transmitting the Mandate of Heaven to Chinese people. In fact, by ascribing the "true" authorship of *Miraculous Proofs* to Heaven, the author assigns to the text an authority as sacred as that of the Qing emperor's Sacred Edict. The intricate construction of authorship, therefore, allows the author to

93. *SYLZ*, 1:33a.
94. *SYLZ*, 1:29a.
95. Yang Bojun, *Chunqiu Zuozhuan zhu*, 3:1016.

protect himself from potential censorship and persecution as the work
he contrives signals the implosion of the tradition of Qing ideological
proselytization.

Compared with its predecessors, *Miraculous Proofs* pushes the cosmological boundaries of the Qing discourse on the Sacred Edict by introducing divine authorities from popular religion and morality books.
When ideas such as divine intervention and moral retribution are
politicized through storytelling that takes an ahistorical approach,
the religious and the political are united. Unlike the Taiping vision that
promised to bring Heaven to Earth, *Miraculous Proofs* imposed onto reality a dystopian picture in which ordinary people living in nineteenth-
century China are portrayed indirectly as analogs of the community
of transgressors in the supernatural netherworld. Although *Miraculous
Proofs* is still part of the exegetical discourse of the Sacred Edict, it
constructs a cultural infrastructure in which the Qing emperor is
not the exclusive legitimate transmitter of the Mandate of Heaven. In
doing so, this work—which is meant to oppose the Taiping ideology—
inadvertently conveys a message as unsettling as what it resists. It carries an urgent sense of the loss of stability that comes close to panic.
This work and those of the Taiping rebels, taken together, show the
extent to which writers from this period, on both sides of the political
spectrum, mourned the demise of the ideal of coherence and completeness and yet strove to resurrect such ideals. The alternative visions they
respectively presented only sped up the dissolution of an already crumbling reality.

CHAPTER THREE

# *Order in Disorder*

## Personal Accounts of War

Between Heaven and Hell, there is Earth. Instead of divine revelations like those envisioned in Taiping and Qing discourses, what individuals witnessed during the Taiping period was prolonged, devastating warfare. Vivid accounts of the war survive in private writings. One scene, recorded in *Diary of the Unperturbed Studio* (*Nengjing ju riji* 能靜居日記), is particularly bizarre and horrendous: when the Qing troops broke into Suzhou, in the Taiping homes they entered they found "what was being cooked in the boiling cauldrons were all human hands and feet. In some bowls, there were leftovers of chewed human fingers" 釜中皆煮人手足，有碗盛嚼余人指. Even against the background of ceaseless violence and countless deaths, this cannibalistic scene is nightmarish, but the language and the imagery resonate strongly with descriptions of Hell discussed in chapter 2. The diarist, Zhao Liewen 趙烈文 (1832–1894), a secretary of Zeng Guofan, continues: "[I] heard that [the Qing troops] took back the city before dawn, and did not stop

Discussions on the materiality of Shen Zi's diary manuscript and his editing strategies in this chapter have appeared in my article "Stitching Words to Suture Wounds: A Manuscript Diary from the Taiping-Qing Civil War (1851–1864)," *Late Imperial China* 40 (2019): 141–82. I thank the journal for permitting me to reuse relevant content with modification.

the slaughter until noon. By then, the city was still enveloped in darkness, and one had to walk [in the city] with a candle" 聞收城之日，五鼓攻陷，殺戮至辰巳，時城中昏昧，行路尚須用燭。[1] He ends with an anguished cry, "Alas! Who on earth brought about this boundless calamity? . . . Hearing this, what I felt was neither agony nor sorrow, but only the unbearable clamors in my chest" 嗟乎！無邊浩劫，誰實釀成，聞之非痛非悲，但覺胸中嘈雜難忍而已。[2] In Zhao Liewen's account, the continuous slaughter from daybreak to midday upended the natural order of time, as if Suzhou was "suspended" from normal time by that outrageous violence. At the hour (noon) when *yang* (life force, human activities, brightness) should peak during the day, the city was instead overwhelmed by *yin* (death, blood, darkness). The horror is further amplified when the dim light of a candle illuminates nothing but half-eaten human fingers. When violence debases humanity to such an extent, language reaches its limit in communicating one's emotional and psychological responses not only to others, but also to oneself. Zhao Liewen, like many of his contemporaries, was clearly traumatized by what he had experienced.

Writers of the Taiping period repeatedly attribute the historical trauma they experienced to an unbenevolent Heaven. After witnessing the Taiping rebels' barbaric activities in his hometown, a writer from Hefei, Anhui Province comments, "[The rebels] are [as] cruel as this. How come Heaven has the heart to watch them go on a rampage in this world?" 殘酷如此，天何忍使之橫行於世？[3] Another writer from Songjiang, a town that suffered greatly during the violent transition between the Ming and Qing dynasties, laments, "Without warning, Heaven lets disaster befall [Songjiang]. The arrival of the rebels is like ants, lice, pests, beasts feeding on their mothers, starving eagles, and insatiable wolves" 不意天降喪亂，賊匪之來，如蟻，如蝨，如蟊，如獍，如飢鷹，如貪狼。[4]

---

1. Zhao Liewen, *Nengjing ju riji*, 7:108.

2. Zhao Liewen, *Nengjing ju riji*, 7:108.

3. Though "testimony" and "witnessing" are terms with strong Judeo-Christian connotations, I use these words in the Chinese context, without their Western associations. By "testimony," I refer to the account of a personal experience of history. With "witness account," I emphasize the act of seeing an event, crime, or conflict take place. The sentence I quote is from Zhou Bangfu, *Meng nan shu chao*, 5:43.

4. Yao Hongchou, "Postface" to *Xiao cangsang ji*, 6:534.

The analogies drawn between the Taiping rebels and pests and beasts, as chapters 5 and 6 show, occur also in dramas and short stories written in the aftermath of the Taiping War. The evocation of *jie* (calamities doomed to happen by Heaven's will) in both accounts, as well as in Zhao Liewen's expression of grief and distress, is only a fraction of the collective discourse that describes the Taiping Rebellion as something allowed or even inflicted by Heaven. When Heaven, the last recourse that people call upon at a time of despair, is presented as the "author" of the calamity, people couldn't help but ask what individual existence meant in those circumstances.

Individual writings generated during the war are particularly gripping because of their immediacy in mediating personal trauma within the context of historical tragedies. Personal accounts that are "rigorously continuous, steadily serial" can "foster the textual illusion of temporal continuity," and a continuous self-construction.[5] In contrast to texts discussed in chapters 1 and 2, which move between historic time and mythic or heavenly time, most of these private writings are structured around the calendrical day, and their narrative authority stems from an "I" rather than a representative of Heaven. Focusing on private accounts from the war, especially those that may be classed as "diaries," this chapter demonstrates how writers gave powerful testimonies to everyday, extreme violence by making the statement "I was there," as they called out the collapse of Heaven.

## Personal Writings during the War

The transition from the Ming dynasty to that of the Qing, which occurred in the seventeenth century, was a traumatic, devastating precedent to the period of the Taiping Civil War. Few writings with explicit descriptions of the Manchu invasion survived the ruthless Qing censors; in contrast, a significant number of individual accounts remain from the Taiping period.[6] Personal accounts written during and immediately

5. Sherman, *Telling Time*, 33–34.
6. One notable exception to the dearth of extant accounts of the Ming-Qing transition is Wang Xiuchu's 王秀楚 short diary recounting the events of the 1645

after the war record events in both private and public realms, revealing a remarkable historical consciousness. Generally, these accounts can be divided into two categories: those that primarily document contemporary events, emulating an official history; and those, consisting mostly of personal accounts and memoirs, that describe individual experiences against the historical backdrop.[7] The titles in the second category are expressive of the writers' traumatic experiences: *Records of Pondering Pain* (*Sitong ji* 思痛記), *Records of Escapes and the Remaining Life* (*Zhuanxi yusheng ji* 轉徙餘生記), and *Accounts of Falling into Rebel Hands* (*Mengnan shuchao* 蒙難述鈔). Extant texts are preserved in manuscripts, woodblock prints, stereotype prints, and installments in serialized magazines. In comparison with the broad dissemination of proselytizing texts during the Taiping Civil War, personal writings tended to remain in manuscript form; those printed in woodblock usually were produced immediately after the war, either by the writer or his family. However, around the turn of the twentieth century, when the influence of both Taiping and Qing ideological discourses subsided, some of the printed accounts were reprinted on letterpress as self-standing publications or published in serialized magazines as installments. Few manuscripts survive. Nevertheless, the emergence and reemergence of these personal accounts in modern media reignited memories of the Taiping War as China faced recurrent political turmoil in the twentieth century.

In China since the Song dynasty (960–1279 CE), a piece of writing characterized by a day-by-day temporal structure and references to a writing self was known by various names, such as "daily accounts" (*riji* 日記), "miscellaneous notes" (*biji* 筆記), and, sometimes, simply

---

massacre at Yangzhou. It should also be noted that the titles of private accounts generated from the Taiping period are reminiscent of those from the early Qing which are preserved in catalogues (even though the texts are destroyed under Qing censorship).

7. Works in the first category include *Zei qing huizuan* and *Yuefei jishi* 粵匪紀事. Meyer-Fong discusses the former in detail in her article "To Know the Enemy." It should be noted that *Zei qing huizuan* is not exactly a chronicle. The author, who was in Zeng Guofan's entourage, meant to provide information to combat the Taipings, and he possibly also aspired to use this book to preserve raw materials for official history.

"accounts" (*ji* 記, *lu* 錄). Premodern Chinese personal daily accounts, or diaries, have been associated with "journeying," especially during the genre's formative stage. When caught in a war that "took place outside the parameters of 'normal' reality, such as causality, sequence, place, and time," authors metaphorically "journeyed" through a realm where the temporal and spatial structure of the familiar and mundane was utterly fractured.[8] Giving a witness account of the violence encountered every day bound the self, to some extent, to a natural diurnal rhythm. Therefore, the practice of writing may have created a certain sense of order amid the chaos that threatened self-continuity.[9]

Diaries, unlike memoirs and autobiographies, are not recounted from a greater historical distance. A memoir written decades after the conclusion of the Taiping Civil War could "take on its full traumatic power across the abyss of time" without being restrained by a specific time and space.[10] Instead, diaries written during the war capture an immediate, raw exposure to profound human suffering and usually exhibit poignant reflections on moral issues. At the same time, there is an inherent problem with personal records written down during political turmoil. A diary allows one to reduce the temporal and spatial scope to the day-to-day, but it risks losing sight of the large picture. As a result, if they are to make sense of causality and contingencies in the larger historical context, these daily records of the "localized" experiences often need to be reframed. In fact, this often happened: revisions—sometimes repeated and multiple—were made to diaries at later dates.

Personal daily accounts of the Taiping Civil War are often reminiscent of accounts from the Ming-Qing dynastic transition. For example, *An Account of Ten Days in Yangzhou* (*Yangzhou shiri ji* 揚州十日記) is an eyewitness narrative by a survivor of the Manchu armies'

8. Laub, "Bearing Witness or the Vicissitudes of Listening," 69.

9. On diary writing as a practice connected with a sense of self-continuity, see Wiener and Rosenwald, "A Moment's Monument." Also see Struve, "Self-Struggles of a Martyr," 343.

10. Tian, "Translator's Introduction," 9, 18. The memoir's author, Zhang Daye 張大野, witnessed the atrocities of war when he was a child. As an adult, he revisited these traumatic memories, which returned in the form of nightmarish flashbacks in his memoir that was characterized by religious concerns.

1645 massacre at Yangzhou. Allegedly written in the seventeenth century, this text was discovered only in the eighteenth century.[11] In fact, some writers from the Taiping period explicitly referenced *An Account of Ten Days of Yangzhou* when they described and reflected on what they saw and experienced during the Taiping War. In endeavoring to record and make sense of their calamitous reality, they turned to a literary tradition of private accounts that drew from firsthand experience to describe the sudden downfall of the Ming dynasty and the traumatic Manchu invasion.

Personal accounts featured intimate sensory details about one's escape from immediate violence. These concrete descriptions of complex human behaviors and emotions contrast with the historical participants and imaginary characters presented in political discourses. In *Records from within Disaster* (*Nan zhong ji* 難中紀), the author, who narrowly escaped death the day Taiping rebels took over his hometown, describes what he heard at his hideout:

> It was before dusk. Every household was still in the field, escaping [from the rebels]. They hid among dense forests and grass. [I] could only hear houses on fire collapse, [rebels] yell to capture [the villagers], and the sounds of killing, shouting, and screaming. The tragedies took multifarious forms. All I could do was weep silently and swallow my tears.
>
> 天未曉，各家仍出避。潛伏長林豐草間。但聞燒屋崩塌聲，捉人叫喊聲，殺人呼號聲，慘情萬狀，唯有吞聲飲泣而已。[12]

The sounds and descriptive details in this description (dusk, the countryside setting) make palpable the brutality of the war and the urgency of preserving one's life. The repetition of horrific sounds (*sheng* 聲) conveys a strong oppressive effect as they relentlessly assault the survivor's senses. The sound of crying needs to be suppressed, which symbolizes that the war must be endured, swallowed, and internalized as violence occurs, until those experiences are expressed on paper and in

11. For a translation, see Struve, "'Horrid Beyond Description': The Massacre of Yangzhou."

12. Zhang Erjia, *Nan zhong ji*, 6:635.

words. This account is just one among many accounts of the Taiping Civil War that unambiguously resonate with the acute sensory details found in the much older *An Account of Ten Days of Yangzhou*. In both texts, eyewitness accounts render a vivid picture of the real-time horrors individuals experienced at some of the most intense moments of the violence.

Rumors about the war, though not recorded in grand historical narratives, are integral to ordinary people's everyday reality. Transient and unreliable, these rumors communicate mistrust, anxieties, and fears. In *Wu Qingqing taishi riji* 吳清卿太史日記 (*Diary of the Historian Wu Qingqing*), Wu Dazheng 吳大澂 (1835–1902) records how quickly confusion spread on one occasion in a commercial street of Suzhou, soon enveloping the entire town:

> The business on the street was running as usual. Suddenly, rumors spread, and the street became clamorous. People hid themselves in a haste, as if chastened by someone. No one knew where these people had gone . . . Instantly, the rumors were circulated throughout the city. When things became quieter, I inquired about it, and was told nothing truly had happened.
>
> 市面照常，忽播流言，人聲鼎沸。市上行人爭先避匿，不知所往，如有人追其後者。店鋪人家同時掩門；頃刻之間，城中傳遍。及風氣稍定，詢之並無所事。[13]

Riding on fear and anxiety, rumors appear and disappear like invisible waves pushing people around. The event Wu Dazheng records seems not to have had significant political and social consequence; however, some rumors damaged people's trust in the Qing government. Pan Zhongrui 潘鐘瑞 (1823–1890), in *Records on Deer of the Gusu Terrace* (*Sutai milu ji* 蘇臺麋鹿記), writes that before Suzhou fell to the Taipings, rumors circulated that the Qing local officials considered setting the city on fire to forestall the invasion. Even after the local official denied this, people still believed that there could have been such an

---

13. Wu Dazheng, *Wu Qingqing taishi riji*, 5:327.

intention.[14] This anecdote shows Suzhou's vulnerable situation during the war, as well as people's suspicions of the Qing government and officials. We should also note that to make sense of daily contingencies and uncertainties, personal accounts and literary works from the Ming-Qing dynastic transition also demonstrate a heightened interest in rumors. For example, in the mid-seventeenth century *A Short Record to Settle My Thoughts* (*Dingsi xiaoji* 定思小記) and *Daily Jottings from the End of the Ming* (*Mingji riji* 明季日記), the writers keep keen records of how rumors spread in chaos.[15] Therefore, despite the temporal distance of centuries, Keulemans's insight holds true: rumors, though fragmentary, create a sense of contemporaneity in a community that "defines itself through a single shared imagination of time/space/action."[16]

Another recurring topic in private accounts that official history usually omits or glosses over is how ordinary people fled from military conflicts. In writings about the violent Ming-Qing dynastic transition, local elites describe how people escaped to the countryside to seek refuge.[17] However, because bandits had infiltrated the entire Jiangnan area during the prolonged Taiping War, the countryside was no longer safe. In *Brief Notes on Encountering Militaries in Zhongzhou in the Year of Guichou* (*Guichou Zhongzhou libing ji lüe* 癸丑中州罹兵紀略), Chen Shanjun 陳善鈞 (fl. 1853) records moving his whole family to a neighboring village after the rebels entered their town. However, a few days after they moved, rumors arose that rebels had entered the village. When all the villagers fled, Chen chose to stay in the village with his family. He wrote:

> Women in our family do not step out from the house. How could they walk and run on hills?[18] In addition, we are already fifty miles away from the city. It could not be said that we haven't escaped far enough, or this

---

14. Pan Zhongrui, *Sutai milu ji*, 5:271.
15. The examples can be found in *Voices from the Ming-Qing Cataclysm* on pp. 18 and 60, respectively.
16. Keulemans, "Onstage Rumor, Offstage Voices," 170.
17. Wu Renshu, "Taoli chengshi."
18. Bound feet were a major impediment to women's mobility during the war.

place of refuge is not sufficiently isolated. Who would have known that
the rebels would eventually come here, a place where we thought they
would never come? We are all people trapped in calamity [*jie*]. We could
not escape from [it] even if we flee again. In comparison with dying and
filling the ditches with our bodies, I would rather have us die together.

余家內眷，足不出戶，豈能奔走小阿，且已距城五十里矣，避之不謂不
遠，居之不謂不僻，乃料賊斷可不來之地，而竟來焉。是余等皆在劫之
人，即再避亦不能免，與其死填溝壑，莫若共死一方。[19]

Chen's dilemma in deciding whether and where to escape was common
among local gentry living in towns and cities, who had the social and
financial means to move their entire families away from the rebels'
invasion. However, if the countryside had once been a possible refuge
in the seventeenth century, fleeing to the country did not guarantee
safety and survival for those living during the Taiping War. There is a
strong sense of dismay in many nineteenth-century local elites' accounts of their experiences of escape: between Heaven and Earth, they
could find no refuge on the contested ground. The all-encompassing
nature of *jie* as a temporal category leaves no room for spatial escape.
As a result, as shown in chapter 6, writers fantasize temporal escapes
in their short stories about the Taiping War.

Despite—or precisely because of—the senseless violence, individuals strove to bring closure and rationality to what they had witnessed
during the war. For some writers, private accounts serve both as evidence of their (and others') existence in a specific historical time and
a source they could later use to make sense of personal and collective
trauma. Shen Zi's *Diary of Escape from the Rebels* (*Bikou riji* 避寇日記),
a manuscript consisting of fragments pasted into repurposed account
books, is exemplary in this respect. With its intriguing materiality
and descriptions of events in the private realm, this text showcases
how the relationships of materiality, temporality, and narrativity inter-
twine when a diarist seeks to attribute a certain narrative order to the
chaos.

19. Chen Shanjun, *Guichou Zhongzhou libing ji lüe*, 5:175.

## A Diary Manuscript

*Diary of Escape from the Rebels* (hereafter *Diary*) represents personal accounts of the Taiping War in its direct portrayal of the catastrophe.[20] Historians have used diaries and memoirs from the Taiping period as valuable resources to understand the destruction of urban space and everyday life.[21] Meyer-Fong writes that accounts of the war make "a place for individual suffering, loss, religiosity, and emotions."[22] Shen Zi's *Diary* is a case in point, providing readers an opportunity to understand a survivor's intimate, personal cognitive processes of meaning-making both during and after the war. Shen Zi's records of everyday violence on a local level are exhaustive, representing personal tragedies and expressing intense private feelings thoroughly. In addition, the physical condition of the diary yields much information about the complete mayhem (fig. 3.1): composed of paper fragments, the manuscript evinces the historical violence that deprived Shen Zi of basic resources. At the same time, the traces of multilayered editing offer insight into his struggles to negotiate the personal and the public as he seeks to come to terms with individual loss and sociopolitical chaos.

Shen Zi's account runs from March 1860 to September 1864, a period during which his hometown of Puyuan, a major market town in upper northern Zhejiang Province, endured repeated military occupations.[23] This text was never published during the Qing or Republican eras, and probably did not circulate before the modern typeset edition's 1961

20. Earlier versions of this section and the section "Reconstruct, Revise, and Restore" appeared in Huan Jin, "Stitching Words to Suture Wounds."

21. On the destruction of everyday life in Jiangnan area, see Chen Ling 陳嶺, "Zhixu bengkui." On cities in chaos, see Meyer-Fong, "Urban Space and Civil War, Hefei 1853–1854," as well as her "Gathering in a Ruined City."

22. Meyer-Fong, *What Remains*, 15.

23. With a history going back to the Yuan dynasty, Puyuan today is part of the city of Jiaxing. On June 15, 1860, Taiping forces conquered Puyuan. Their arrival marked the beginning of four years of incessant military conflicts, causing a significant decrease in population. Nevertheless, soon after the war, Puyuan's economy and education revived and developed. See Rankin, *Elite Activism and Political Transformation*, 56, 82, 138.

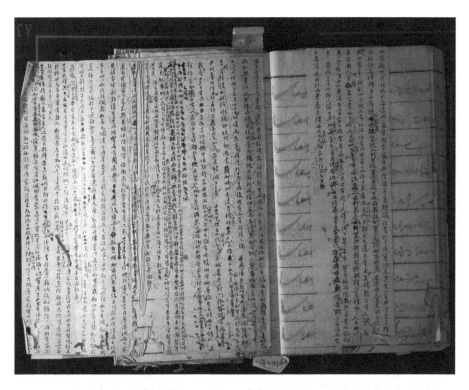

FIG. 3.1. Page spread from the manuscript of Shen Zi's *Diary*, MS 2:8, 1863. Courtesy of the Jiaxing Library.

publication under the title of *Bikou riji*.[24] Each volume's title, written by the diarist on a small paper slip, is pasted on the book cover's top left corner, suggesting that the diarist himself probably compiled the volumes. The arrangement of the content conveys a certain disorder. The entries are not chronological. The dates and content of some entries are repeated; it appears that Shen Zi did not always immediately record a given day's entry, but retrospectively reconstructed some entries

---

24. As the Chinese Communist Party established its revolutionary connection with the Taiping Rebellion, after the foundation of the People's Republic of China and before the Cultural Revolution (1967–1977), Chinese historians collected local historical documents about the war and published them as archival projects under the leadership of the Party. *Diary* is one of the texts published under such efforts.

based on memories and notes. Sometimes he also first jotted down a brief note and then returned to expand it while his memories were presumably still fresh. Every entry was subject to additional rounds of scrutiny and revision. It is likely that Shen Zi kept these accounts about the war as it occurred, with the intention of later compiling them into a history or using them as material for some kind of historical writing. This may also explain the thorough revisions and editing found in the manuscript.

The text itself is written on pieces of paper of various sizes. Because the pieces of paper usually do not fully cover the pages on which they are pasted, one can tell that the volumes are constructed from the folded pages of used accounting books.[25] Each folded page is half the size of the pages in the original accounting books. I examined three volumes of the text, conserved at the Jiaxing Library in Zhejiang Province. A few pages are simply tucked into the books, but most pages are attached to the books by one or two corners. The diary is written on one side of each sheet of paper, but sometimes fragments of prose and poetry in refined calligraphy appear on the back of pages pasted into the account books. Judging from the themes and the seals borne by the writings, it is evident that these prose pieces and poems were written in preparation for the civil service examinations before the war. Economical use of space on the sheets of paper, rather than a consistent format, is evidently the diarist's primary concern. Occasionally, handwriting crowds the marginal space surrounding the prose and poetry. The smallest piece, bearing one day's entry, is about as wide as two index fingers, but the largest pieces of paper are folded and attached to the accounting book at one of their short ends. The entries' varied

25. Details about the preservation of the diary manuscript are in Huan Jin, "Stitching Words to Suture Wounds." The manuscript comprises three volumes in all: *Beishan biji* [ca. 1860–1864], a manuscript in one volume, and *Bikou riji* [ca. 1860–1864], a manuscript in two volumes, both held at the Rare Book and Local Documents Reading Room, Jiaxing Library, Zhejiang. I cite both the page in the manuscript and the page number in the modern typeset edition; "MS 1" refers to *Beishan biji*, and "MS 2" and "MS 3" refer to the two volumes of *Bikou riji*, according to the chronological order that these volumes follow. The modern edition puts the entire manuscript under the title of *Bikou riji*.

content makes the text a rich repository of miscellaneous information and historical accounts of the war.

A biography of Shen Zi reports that he "strived to study . . . and excelled at composing examination essays."[26] His father, Shen Tao 沈濤 (?–1850s), who had run a family business before becoming a Confucian scholar, died shortly before the Taiping invasion of Puyuan.[27] Therefore, when the war broke out, twenty-eight-year-old Shen Zi became the head of a household comprising his mother, his pregnant wife, a widowed elder sister, an unmarried younger sister, and a younger brother living away from home as a business apprentice in Suzhou.[28] Around the time of the Taiping invasion of Suzhou in May 1860, Shen Zi lost connection with his brother. Shen Zi made several attempts to look for his brother before the outbreak of the war in Puyuan, but never found him. On October 10, 1860, his widowed sister committed suicide by starving herself to death. On October 16, Shen Zi married off his youngest sister. The next day, his wife, who had recently delivered a baby girl amid the chaos, passed away. A few days later, the baby also died. By the end of hostilities in 1864, only Shen Zi and his mother had survived the catastrophe. After the war, Shen was selected to study at the Imperial Academy and acquired the post of secretary in the Grand Secretariat (*Neige zhongshu* 內閣中書), from which he soon resigned under the pretext of filial responsibilities. He subsequently became an active philanthropist in Puyuan, establishing the Xiangyun Academy (Xiangyun shuyuan 翔雲書院) and creating the Baoyuan Philanthropy Hall (Baoyuan shantang 保元善堂) to distribute clothes and medicine to the poor and organize proper burials for the deceased. Shen Zi's *Miscellaneous Notes from the Studio of Cultivating Austerity* (*Yangzhuo xuan biji* 養拙軒筆記) survives in print. In this book, Shen Zi organizes accounts of the war according to individual events and figures. Though its actual content overlaps with that of *Diary*, *Miscellaneous Notes* assumes the form of an official history focused on the public realm. The generic differences between these two texts are

26. Zhu Fuqing, *Yuanhu qiu jiu lu*, 211.

27. *Puyuan zhi*, 21:1114.

28. Shen Zi also had two married sisters who lived elsewhere; one survived the war.

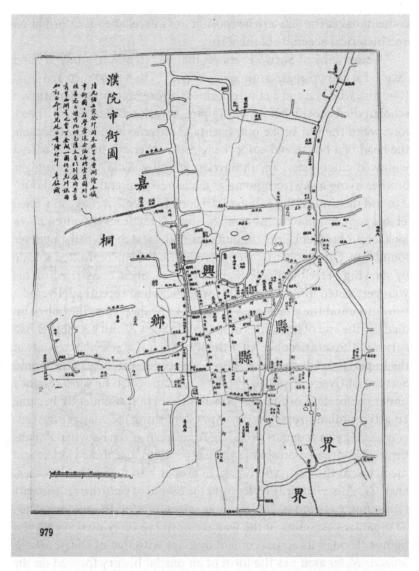

MAP 3.1. The town of Puyuan, with its dense waterway network, 1902–1903. Reproduced from *Puyuan zhi* in *Zhongguo difangzhi jicheng: xiangzhen zhi zhuanji* 中國地方誌集成：鄉鎮誌專輯 (Shanghai: Shanghai shudian, 1992), 21:979.

similar to those between *Surviving Chronicle from the [Yangzi] Cape* (*Haijiao yibian* 海角遺編) and *Record of Military Subjugation in [the land of] the Yu Hills and the Sea* (*Haiyu beibing ji* 海虞被兵記), both of which treat Changshu events during the Ming-Qing dynastic transition.[29]

Compared with other personal accounts during the war, Shen Zi's *Diary* is distinguished by its exceptional meticulousness in recording historical events, personal experiences, and intimate feelings. Shen Zi's concerns are first and foremost local, which could reflect how the war restricted his mobility. Located at the center of a triangle formed by Suzhou, Hangzhou, and what is now Shanghai (then an emerging metropolis in Songjiang Prefecture), Puyuan was characterized by a dense web of rivers, with the Grand Canal running through the town and dividing it into two parts, one of which during the Qing dynasty was under the jurisdiction of Tongxiang County and the other, of Xiushui County, the seat of Jiaxing Prefecture. On a map of Puyuan dated 1902–1903 (map 3.1), it is possible to reconstruct Shen Zi's route of escape from his house in the town's northeastern segment to the northeastern suburbs. In recording the progress of the war, Shen Zi's primary focus is on the military movements that could have a direct, major impact on Puyuan and Hangzhou. In addition, he pays close attention to the status of the war around Nanjing (the Qing prefectural seat of Jiangning), the Taiping capital. Thus, most of the cities and towns mentioned in the text were located in Zhejiang and Jiangsu Provinces, including major cities such as Hangzhou and Suzhou, as well as numerous medium-sized cities, towns, and villages. In addition, his *Diary* allows us to map out most of Puyuan's streets, riverbanks, temples, bridges, and suburbs.

With Puyuan at the center of its geographical scope, Shen Zi's *Diary* provides a comprehensive view of the Taiping Civil War, albeit on a small scale. The text, mediated through and constituted by Shen Zi's experiences and observations, touches upon personal, religious, political, economic, social, and historical issues on various levels. Unlike Wang Shiduo 汪士鐸 (1802–1889), a Nanjing elite who fled from the city

29. Translations and comparisons of excerpts from these two texts can be found in Struve, "Changshu in Chronicle, Storybook, Memoir, and Romance."

nine months after it fell into rebel hands in March 1853, Shen Zi stayed in the Taiping-occupied area until the end of the war. He seemed to have avoided being put into the Taiping camp. Wang wrote about Taiping practices, whereas Shen Zi focused primarily on local affairs.[30] The events Shen Zi recorded are many and various: the misfortunes befalling Shen Zi and others; local people's intensified adherence to religious rituals in the face of danger; the passing troops from both sides; rumors about relevant political and military changes; local gentry's futile defense efforts; Taiping customs and regulations; the social and economic inequality amid the chaos; and power struggles between the Qing government, the Taiping regime, and local armed forces— both militias and bandits. The text mentions over one hundred people by name. Among these, more than half are from Shen Zi's immediate social circle, including his friends, extended family members, classmates, and neighbors. The rest are military leaders from both sides, as well as the heads of local armed forces.

Overall, the fragmentary condition of the manuscript and the non-chronological arrangement of its entries both refer to and re-create the disjointed temporal structure modeling Shen Zi's personal experience of the Taiping War. The manuscript embodies three temporal dimensions for which the war serves as a reference point: prewar times, when the civil examinations played a paramount role in the life of an educated man; wartime, when that sociopolitical structure was dismantled and destroyed; and postwar times, when the allocation of resources and monetary transactions was registered in the account book. The text also foregrounds at least three temporal points, with Shen Zi's personal experiences as the focal reference. He was, first and foremost, an individual who encountered the war firsthand; second, he was a writer who documented witness accounts and collected information as soon as he could; and third, he was the editor who assiduously and thoroughly revised the text.

The revisions Shen Zi made to the text are also indicative of the notoriously pliant and fragile nature of memory. Shen apparently made revisions at various times: his recollection of specific details and

---

30. On Wang Shiduo and his diary, see Wooldridge, *City of Virtues*, 88–117, especially 106–10.

additions of minor events of the day suggest that he made many changes while his memories were fresh; other changes also demonstrate specific historical hindsight. Although Shen Zi did not publish these diary accounts during his lifetime, the way he compiled and revised the text suggests that he probably anticipated audience engagement. Collated as they are, the pieces from several temporal planes form a patchwork of experience where victimhood and agency, reality and memory, interlace. It is precisely through the interstices of the numerous textual layers that we can comprehend how Shen Zi could be said to have "sutured" the wounds of history to cope with individual suffering through the mediation of language.

## Different Levels of Witnessing

In comparison to descriptions of divine revelations invoking absolute truths and certainty, private accounts from the Taiping Civil War are characterized by both a sense of bewilderment and moral ambiguity. As a diary is, for the most part, written immediately after the occurrences it narrates and comments on, it is inherently a piece of retrospective writing. If it is then subjected to processes of revision, the diary is at the mercy of the vicissitudes of memory. The numerous layers of revision in Shen Zi's *Diary* convey his ceaseless struggle to accurately present testimonies in disarray. The process illustrates that "what ultimately matters in all processes of witnessing . . . is not simply the information, the establishment of the facts, but the experience itself of *living through* testimony, of giving testimony."[31] Dori Laub, in his research on testimonies of the Holocaust, recognizes three levels of witnessing: "the level of being a witness to oneself within the experience; the level of being a witness to the testimonies of others; and the level of being a witness to the process of witnessing itself."[32] We see these different levels of witnessing in Shen Zi's *Diary*, as he situates himself within various relationships; they constitute a space for him to deal with delayed

31. Laub, "An Event without a Witness," 85; emphasis is original.
32. Laub, "An Event without a Witness," 75.

traumatic responses, flashbacks, and the dynamics of different levels of witnessing.

The term "I," once spoken or even merely posited, identifies the self within existing conditions, and implies self-reflection.[33] The references to "I" found in Shen Zi's *Diary* thus signify his heightened awareness of the self within complex relationships and situations amid a war that was an imminent threat to life. The first entry in the *Diary* reads: "On the twelfth day of the second month in the tenth year of the Xianfeng reign [March 4, 1860], I was at the Gao Household in Xincheng [County]. Suddenly, I heard that the long-hair bandits had entered from the town of Si'an in Changxing County, Huzhou Prefecture" 咸豐十年二月十二日，余在新塍高氏，猝聞長毛賊於二月八日由湖州長興縣之泗安鎮入。[34] Xincheng and Puyuan are about twelve miles apart; it takes several hours, according to Shen Zi's *Diary*, to travel by water between these towns. Instead of beginning with political events on the national level—such as the 1851 creation of the Taiping regime or the establishment of its capital at Nanjing in 1853—the text begins at the moment when Shen Zi perceived the rebels as encroaching on his life. It should be noted that this kind of abrupt opening is also typical of other personal accounts of political calamities. The earliest entries of the *Diary* have room for objective facts such as geographical locations and relevant customs and practices of towns and cities, but as the rebels approached and invaded Shen Zi's hometown, his writings begin to be filled with personal experiences, feelings, and thoughts. In declaring the presence of his self in a specific time and space, Shen Zi makes an important statement: "I was there."

In the face of a devastating war, the familiar social, geographical, and temporal order that people had relied on to navigate the world in peaceful times was completely overthrown. Shen Zi's decisions, however well calculated or supposedly divinely blessed, were based on understandings of a peacetime world, and led to dire consequences that forced

33. For a systematic discussion of "utterance and the speaking subject," see Ricœur, *Oneself as Another*, 44–51. In "Stitching Words to Suture Wounds," I discuss the shifting place of "I" in the *Diary* from the beginning to the end of the war.

34. MS 1:1, *BKRJ*, 8:1. No revision. The Taipings were called "long-hairs" because they did not follow the Qing custom of shaving their foreheads but let their hair grow.

him momentarily to surrender his agency. On the morning of September 11, 1860, as the Shen family was having breakfast, the Taipings suddenly overtook Puyuan. Shen and his family members had prepared to escape to the countryside later that day, but the unexpectedly early arrival of the Taipings forced them to alter their plans. Shen Zi's mother ordered him to leave by himself to preserve the bloodline. Shen recorded their heartbreaking conversation: "I said, 'There are five in the family. I was not able to plan for this earlier. I cannot abandon you. Also, what should I do with you, my old mother?'" 一家五口，余不能早計及此，余拋撤不下，且如老母何！[35] Direct speech in this context creates drama and a feeling of immediacy for the audience. In this record, Shen Zi presents an image of the self who, torn between his attachment to his family and his filial responsibilities, is steeped in regret and self-recrimination. His speech also serves as testimony, confession, and possibly defense of his good intentions. Eventually, Shen fled because of his mother's constant and urgent insistence.

When suffering overwhelms the self, the resulting deprivation of agency suffocates hopes of survival. The next morning, Shen Zi returned to the ruined house. He found his elder sister and mother safe but his wife and younger sister missing: his mother had sent them off, to escape with the neighbors. Shen decided first to escort his mother and elder sister to the countryside, and later to look for his wife and younger sister. In a related account, he describes the process of the family's escape, "It rained heavily again. There was no shelter in our immediate surroundings, so we had nowhere to hide. The field was rather slippery. Mother fell and got up again. I cried out for Heaven and wept" 天又大雨，四面無屋，無可躲避，田塍甚滑，母跌而復起，余呼天而泣.[36] After Shen finally found his wife and younger sister, on September 23, he moved the whole family to another place in the countryside. It was again a frustrating process: "As soon as we untied the cable [of the boat], it rained again. When we arrived at Bridge Zhai, it rained heavily as dusk was falling. Extremely discouraged, I could only cry out to Heaven" 既解纜而天又雨，至翟家橋，而雨甚大，天已薄暮矣。余*恢

35. MS 1:11, left leaf; BKRJ, 8:22.
36. MS 3:27, left leaf; BKRJ, 8:25.

甚，唯呼天而已.[37] In the entire diary, these are two of the rare moments where Shen Zi records crying to Heaven. Shen Zi's elaborate
remembrances of the hostile weather and his struggles emphasize
moments of despair. However, the witness account about Shen Zi himself reveals a certain sense of agency as he recognizes external challenges
that were beyond his control.

Shen Zi's close observations of the state of his health reveal his
heightened awareness of the self as a corporal existence limited by external conditions. In the entries from September 29 to November 14,
1860, he mentions being ill about ten times; in the remaining part of the
diary, he rarely touches on his physical condition. During this one-and-
a-half-month period in 1860, several of Shen Zi's family members died
one after the other. Throughout this period, he had to keep providing for
the family. The responsibility exhausted him and exacerbated his already
poor health. For instance, on September 29, he returned to Puyuan from
the countryside to purchase essentials. In that day's entry, he writes, "I
was already greatly exhausted. This night, I stayed at the Dongs' house.
*Nüe* [intermittent fever and diarrhea] erupted again" 予力已大憊矣。是
夜宿董宅，又發瘧.[38] Two days later, Shen made another quick trip to
town to collect information about the war. While he was there, a rumor
arrived that the rebels would invade the town again, so Shen, summoning all his strength, attempted to return to the countryside. "After
walking less than half a mile," Shen wrote, "[I] had to sit on the ground.
Hot sweat oozed, and both my legs were sore and painful. I was utterly
helpless" 不半里，便坐地上，方發熱汗，且下兩腿酸楚，無如何也.[39]
His symptoms and his overall frail physical condition point to the
collapse of Shen Zi's body, the material site of the self onto which social
constructions are mapped. By juxtaposing descriptions of his physical
breakdown with these highly demanding social and moral situations,
Shen represents a self that is both frustrated by his inability to act for
his family, and apologetic for that self.

---

37. MS 1:14, right leaf; *BKRJ*, 8:30.
38. MS 1:14, left leaf; *BKRJ*, 8:30. On *nüe*, see Hanson, *Speaking of Epidemics in
Chinese Medicine*, 79–80.
39. MS 1:14, left leaf; *BKRJ*, 8:31.

Shen Zi, as we see, describes his actions and physical conditions in a matter-of-fact manner with great immediacy; his revisions expand on these straightforward accounts with emotional memories and introspection. For instance, when Shen Zi went searching for his wife and younger sister, his cousin refused to help him deliver a message of reassurance to his mother. The sentence in the first draft is short and simple: "I was on the journey by myself." In the revision, Shen elaborates: "Alas! Since the loss of my younger brother, I have been on the journey all by myself. I had absolutely no support from siblings. Things have always been this way. There has been a history of the family having conflicting opinions, and there is a reason for that to lead to disasters" 噫！自余弟既失，而余單身獨行，余絕無手足之助，往往如是。而家人意見又各不相屬以及於難，有由來也.[40] In this addition, Shen Zi highlights his loneliness and tries to rationalize the family tragedy. In a note dated February 14, 1862, he writes, "[I] bought the flags of the rebels. On my way home, the boat capsized" 辦長毛旗回家舟覆.[41] In the expanded entry, he uses more than three hundred words to delineate vividly how the boat capsized and his moment of panic in the water, as he did not know how to swim.[42] However, Shen Zi continued to write about how he remembered his mother as he was on the verge of drowning, recalling his sensations of drowning. This situation is symbolic of his helpless situation and how he took agency to survive. Another example is Shen's account of the deaths of his wife and their newborn daughter. In the revision, before his friend's description of what happened in the last moment of his wife's life, Shen inserts his emotional response to the dreadful news he received: "Hearing that, I lost my soul and spirit in astonishment. Neither did I know why things had suddenly changed as they had" 余聞之，神魂驚喪，亦不知何以變至是.[43] Shen Zi's intention, when he inserts these revisions, does not seem to be to portray himself in a more positive light. Instead, private feelings such as stress, despair, and sorrow become more intense in the revised diary.

40. MS 1:13, left leaf; *BKRJ*, 8:27.
41. *BKRJ*, 8:165.
42. *BKRJ*, 8:101.
43. MS 1:15, right leaf; *BKRJ*, 8:35.

FIG. 3.2. A left leaf of the manuscript of Shen Zi's *Diary*, MS 3: 26, September 1860, recording the female family members' disastrous encounters with the rebels. One piece of paper extending from the account book is probably an examination prose written for practice before the war. Courtesy of the Jiaxing Library.

In addition to writing down his own experiences during the war, Shen Zi also witnesses testimonies from the women in his family (see fig. 3.2). Returning from fleeing the rebels, Shen Zi only briefly records in the first draft that the women in his family are safe; he later inserts, between the lines, a full paragraph about what had happened during his absence, as told by his mother and elder sister:

> My mother and my elder sister described their encounters with the rebels in detail: at first, the rebels hit the front gate. Unable to break it, they broke the door in the back garden. My older sister, wife, and younger sister all jumped into the river. The rebels used bamboo sticks with hooks to pull them out and pressed them for money and valuables. [They] gave the rebels their jewelry, but the rebels pressed them again. Getting nothing, they hit them with the back of their broadswords. The family managed to survive. Fortunately, they threw themselves into water, so their

bodies were covered with waterweed, and their faces with mud: there-fore, they avoided being seized or humiliated by the rebels. After the rebels left, my wife and younger sister hid among the tall grasses, whereas my older sister jumped into the river once more. Some time had passed. When she was not yet completely immersed in water, a rebel leader pass-ing by saw her and saved her. He pulled her to the gate and laid her on the ground. Spitting blood and water, she woke up. At night, she attempted to hang herself, but was saved and didn't die.

母姊備言遇賊狀：賊初打大門不能破，而後園之門先破，姊與妻妹皆入河，賊以長竿之有鉤者挑而起之，逼取財物，以首飾付之，又逼財物，無所得，遂以刀背擊之，俱得無死。幸投入水，身上皆浮萍蘊草，面上皆塗泥，故得不被擄辱。賊去後，妻妹匿亂草中，姊又赴水，有頃，未沒，有賊目見而救之，舁至大門內臥地上，吐血水而醒，入夜又投繯，得救不死。[44]

This paragraph provides a rare close-up account of women's fates. In Zhejiang, to avoid "being seized or humiliated," many women chose to drown themselves; because of the dense web of waterways in the area, they chose places near their homes. In narrating the sufferings of the women in his family—events involving many people and situations when life and death were a hair's breadth apart—Shen Zi uses a sequence of plain, factual statements, conveying a sense of urgency and agony.

Shen Zi also gives an account of the death of his elder sister, Shen Fen 沈芬 (d. 1860), a woman known for her painting and calligraphy.[45] Widowed before the war and living in her parents' household, Shen Fen's fragile physical condition was exacerbated by the chaos of the war. Therefore, Shen Zi and other family members are thrust into a dilemma by the tumultuous situation: as family members they have moral and ethical obligations to care for her, and these obligations add yet more challenges to their own struggle for survival. Shen Zi's *Diary* details how he sought medical resources for Shen Fen, as well as his conversations with his sister that often revolve around Shen Zi's

44. MS 3:27, left leaf; *BKRJ*, 8:24.

45. Shen Fen came from an area known for its women writers. Puyuan lies at the intersection of Jiaxing and Tongxiang counties. In the Qing dynasty, Jiaxing had many women writers, unlike Tongxiang. Mann, *Precious Records*, 6; her discussion of possible reasons for the varied distributions of female writers is on p. 202.

determination to find her medicine despite her resistance to the idea. In Shen Zi's revisions, he strives to construct Shen Fen as a virtuous woman: she resolved to die in order to alleviate the burden on the family and especially on Shen Zi. For example, emphasizing the sister's agency in her suicide by starvation, Shen Zi adds a doctor's conclusion about her illness: "She was only delirious, but not severely ill" 姊但恍惚，無甚病也, which suggests that her death was not a result of her illness; it was brought about for a virtuous cause. Moreover, Shen Zi often revises what his sister said in order to introduce psychological depth and a rationalization for her suicide. At one point, he alters her plea "Please don't buy the medicine. I am determined to die" 慎毋買藥。余決計求死也 to "Please don't buy the medicine. I yearn to die from morning to night" 慎毋買藥。余朝夕求死也.[46] The revised version has a certain lyrical quality, effectively changing Shen Fen's impulsive resolution into a long-held feeling.

Shen Zi's revisions of his last conversations with Shen Fen demonstrate his struggles to cope with his role as the witness to both Shen Fen's account of her tragic experiences and his own experience of loss. In the first draft, Shen Zi recounts Shen Fen's words: "When there are alarms in the town, you all flee and hide. I cannot walk at all. No one in the village will stay with me except for mother. What [shall we do] if the rebels come to hurt me and hurt mother as well?" 鎮上有警，爾等皆走匿，余斷不能行，鄉惟母以伴余獨存，萬一賊至傷余而並傷母如何.[47] The revision goes, "What is the difference between living in the countryside and in the town? Upon hearing the alarms, we don't know if they are true or not. Though my sister-in-law and younger sister would both escape and hide in the grassy field, I am unable to walk. Everyone in the entire village will flee, leaving only mother who stays behind with me. What [shall we do] if the rebels come to hurt me and hurt mother as well?" 居鄉與居鎮何異。此地一聞警信，不知虛實，弟婦妹等皆走匿蕩地中，余不能行，舉鄉居民無一不走，惟母以伴余獨

---

46. MS 1:14, left leaf; *BKRJ*, 8:31. For some reason the modern editors chose to follow the original line in their transcription.

47. MS 1:14, left leaf; *BKRJ*, 8:31.

存，萬一賊至傷余而並傷母將如何。[48] Shen Zi is here speaking for his sister, putting words in her mouth about unreliable information, survival instincts, abandonment by others, and her sense of indebtedness toward their mother. In doing so, he reveals his own state of mind; the desperation he had felt in the face of the ubiquitous violence and chaos resurfaces, in retrospect— Shen Zi had left his female family members behind to the rebels and outlived Shen Fen.

Shen Zi's struggles to cope with his role as witness to Shen Fen's death continue after the war, as shown by the biography he wrote for her that was printed in a local gazetteer (fig. 3.3). In the biography, he blames the tragic end of her life on her deceased husband's family, and goes further to present her as a moral paragon. She was, he says, childless and widowed at the age of twenty-nine, and thus in a disadvantaged situation before the outbreak of the war. Though she had originally intended to die with her husband, she set aside that idea when the lineage let her adopt her brother-in-law's son to continue her husband's branch of the family. But when her father-in-law died, the brother-in-law demanded that the son be returned, so she was once again left childless. In her biography, Shen Zi rationalizes the reasons she gives for her suicidal decision:

Our mother tried to dissuade me from suicide because she wanted me to keep her company and to take care of her in her old age. At first, I thought that was right. However, I wanted to raise and educate my foster son myself, but he was snatched away by his birth parents. If they let him play as he wishes and, in the future, he ends up with the wrong friends and associates, how could he carry on my husband's legacy! Additionally, in this utterly chaotic world, I have brought a burden upon mother and younger brother. Now that I have exhausted the obligations of the "Three Obediences" [san cong], I would rather die!

老母勸我不死，欲我奉養終天耳。我初念本如是，然我嗣子長大，欲親為教育，而見奪於所生。若聽嬉戲，他日比之匪人，何以為夫後！且世亂如麻，徒貽母若弟累我。三從之義窮矣！不如死![49]

48. MS 1:14, left leaf; *BKRJ*, 8:31.
49. Shen Zi, "Jiefu Shi Jianshan qi Shen shi," in *Puyuan zhi*, 21:1131.

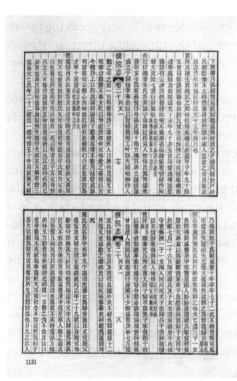

FIG. 3.3. Excerpt from Shen Zi's "A Brief Biography of the Virtuous Wife of Shi Jianshan, Shen shi (Shen Fen)" ("Jiefu Shi Jianshan qi Shen shi zhuan lüe" 節婦施兼山妻沈氏傳略), undated. Reprinted from *Puyuan Gazetteer* (*Puyuan zhi* 濮院志) in *Zhongguo difangzhi jicheng: xiangzhen zhi zhuanji* 中國地方誌集成：鄉鎮誌專輯 (Shanghai: Shanghai shudian, 1992), 21:1131.

The Confucian guideline of the "Three Obediences" specifies: "[A woman should] obey the Father when unmarried, obey the Husband when married, and obey the Son after the husband's death."[50] By letting Shen Fen prioritize her obligations and moralize her actions in reference to her deceased husband, Shen Zi conformed her image to the Qing moral expectations of a widow. This image is echoed by Shen Fen's own poems, preserved in the same local gazetteer. Dated 1855, the poems express deep anguish over the consecutive deaths of her husband and father within a span of two years. Taken together, the biography and the poems allow Shen Fen to be commemorated in the local history

---

50. Li Jinglin, ed., *Yili yizhu*, 308. In the original context, this line prescribes the funeral rituals woman should follow to commemorate the deaths of family members, but it was interpreted later by Neo-Confucian scholars to require women's unconditional obedience to their direct male relatives.

that formed a part of the basis for moral reconstruction in the postwar context.

In *Diary*, as we have seen, the writer tries to accommodate different levels of witnessing: physical and emotional trauma surface; the testimonies of others emerge, retrospectively; the continuous telling and retelling of Shen Fen's death demonstrate Shen Zi's attempts to make sense of the trauma he and others experienced. We can see the effort he made to report those personal and private experiences. In engaging with the affairs of the public domain, it seems easier for Shen Zi to achieve a reflective distance on events. As we shall see in the next section, the process of "being a witness to the process of witnessing itself" may be most recognizable in the numerous layers of Shen Zi's revisions of accounts associated with the public domain.

## Reconstruct, Revise, and Restore

In his revisions to *Diary*, Shen Zi uses a variety of means, including various narrative devices, adding and removing information, and rearranging syntax and changing words to reconstruct "what happened" based on the calendrical structure of the text.

Many entries in the diary manuscript are reconstructed with the aid of notes that functioned as mnemonics: one or two sentences with minimal information about a few key events of a given day. A note of ten characters could be expanded to hundreds of words with additional information. For instance, the note dated February 12, 1862, reads, "[I] visited Yan's tomb. [I] came across Shen Huanqing and Shen Qiweng. We shed many tears" 至嚴墓，遇沈桓卿，沈憩翁。大哭。[51] The corresponding expanded entry adds the following elements: Shen Zi's accidental encounter with a villager who informs him that both the Qing general and the Taiping rebels are making announcements to pacify residents in nearby villages; a friend who accompanies Shen Zi to Yan's tomb; information about the rebels' movements in Shuanglin, a town northwest of Puyuan in Huzhou Prefecture; the narrow escape of

---

51. *BKRJ*, 8:165. Yan is a friend of Shen Zi who appears in some earlier entries of the diary.

Shuanglin's local defense force leader from the rebels; and the deep
sorrow of Shen Zi and Shen Qiweng, whose hair suddenly turned gray
after he lost a boat full of family members.[52] Another note, dated November 27, 1863, reads, "[I] received Wu Langao's letter." Shen Zi elaborates
with two entries, both marked with the same date.[53] In the first, he
summarizes the content of the letter in one sentence; in the second, he
gives it more context: Wu, his nephew-in-law, was a resident of Huzhou
Prefecture, then under Taiping control. He was sent by the local defense
force to Shanghai to seek collaboration with Qing troops to resist the
rebels. Shen Zi knew this Qing military force was incompetent and tried
to dissuade Wu from taking this trip, advice Wu did not take. In the
letter, Wu told Shen of his setbacks on this mission. Together, the letter
and the comments add up to thousands of words. For public situations
like these, Shen Zi expanded on his original brief notes by introducing
other relevant events, contextualizing and elaborating on details, and
articulating his historical and moral judgment.

Some revisions reflect a heightened political sensitivity —and occasional self-censorship, especially in Shen Zi's representation of his
contact with Taiping rebels. In a note dated February 14, 1862, he revises "[I] bought the flags of the rebels" to "[I] went to the Bureau to
buy two yellow flags for Shen Qiweng, on which are the stamps of the
Xincheng military commander" 赴局中為沈憩翁辦黃旗二，蓋新睦軍
帥印.[54] These flags were probably for Shen Qiweng to use to go and
fetch his family.[55] The references to the yellow color and to the stamps
of "the military commander" do not identify the political significance
of these flags. By writing in this manner, Shen Zi avoids specifying his
contact with the Taipings. Another example that demonstrates certain
political sensitivity is the entry of January 5, 1862, in which Shen Zi
records that he witnessed hundreds of low-ranking Taiping soldiers

52. MS 2:27, left leaf; *BKRJ*, 8:101.

53. *BKRJ*, 8:222, 223.

54. The note: *BKRJ*, 8:165; the expanded entry: *BKRJ*, 8:101. The Taiping rebels'
flags with the official stamp served as permits allowing boats to pass Taiping customs
stations on rivers. For an example of how local bandits used these flags to pass customs
stations freely, see *BKRJ*, 8:169.

55. In the entry from February 14, 1860, Shen Zi records that someone reported
in the evening that they saw the boat of Shen Qiweng's family in another town.

entering the town. When he asked some soldiers about the silver medals hanging from their waists, he was told, "This is the award we won after capturing Hangzhou" 此番破杭之功故，得賞也.[56] In the first version, he recorded the four characters on the Taiping soldiers' medals as "The Manchu fled and the Blessed triumphed" (*Man zou Fu sheng* 滿走福勝). "The Blessed" (*fu* 福, a homophone of "father" [*fu* 父]) is often used to refer to God, the "Heavenly Father" in Taiping ideology; so, "The Manchu fled and the Blessed triumphed" implies that the Taipings were acting for God when they routed the Manchu, thus celebrating the victory was celebrating God.[57] Given that the Taipings conquered Hangzhou on December 10, 1861, it is likely that what Shen Zi wrote at first was the actual inscription, which expresses hatred of the Manchu as an ethnicity and glorifies the Taiping troops and their alternative ideology.[58] In the later version, he crossed out all four of those characters and replaced them with just two: "urgent affairs" (*ji gong* 急公), which do not have the strong, specific connotations of the originals.[59] Shen may have removed the original phrase because in the post-Taiping context, references to the conflict between the Taipings and the Manchu rulers could have political repercussions.

Shen Zi often first jotted down records of events in the manner of "annals"—that is, unsorted and comprehensive.[60] However, the reconstructions and revisions added to the manuscript demonstrate his efforts to organize the events of "annals" into a "chronicle" with greater narrative coherence. The insertions of time markers assert multiple "beginnings," indicative of an intention to historicize the events in the revisions. For instance, Shen Zi at first described the rebels' arrival in Puyuan in this way: "On this day, a few rebels came to the outside of the barriers" 是日，有零碎長毛到柵外, but he later revised it to "On this day, a few rebels began to scurry right up to the barriers" 是日，始

56. MS 2:53, right leaf; *BKRJ*, 8:76.

57. *Taiping tianguo da cidian*, 273.

58. On the Hangzhou battle, see Guo Tingyi, *Taiping tianguo shishi rizhi*, 2:833–40. On collective memories of Hangzhou, see Hu Hsiao-chen, "Liluan Hangzhou."

59. MS 2:53, right leaf; *BKRJ*, 8:76.

60. See White on the difference between "annals" and "chronicles": White, "The Value of Narrativity," 8, 16–22.

有零碎長毛竄到柵外.[61] This change recognizes the duration of time with the marker word "began."[62] In the entry for October 30, 1861, Shen describes the situation of the refugees on a lake adjacent to Puyuan. He first wrote: "On the twenty-fifth and twenty-sixth, some refugee boats from Huzhou began to return to Xincheng" 廿五、六，湖州逃難船在 新塍始有歸者. He then changed it to: "At the beginning, five to six hundred refugee boats from Huzhou docked at Xincheng" 先是湖州 逃難船在新塍者幾五六百.[63] Despite the explicit, numerous statements of "beginnings," however, the diary stops without a clear ending, even after local order was fully reestablished after the Taipings lost the war. This is characteristic of the "chronicle," which promises yet does not provide closure.

Many inserted entries fill the gaps between events of political, social, and personal significance that "interrupt" the continuity of the calendar. A date mentioned in an entry often serves as the point of departure for Shen Zi's recollections. For instance, in the first draft, Shen records nothing from May 7 through May 12, 1860; however, in the entry for May 13, he records that he heard that on May 8, Qing troops had passed by Wuzhen, a town close to Puyuan. In the revision, which is literally inserted between the lines, Shen adds not only the title of the Qing general leading the passing troops on May 8, but also two brief entries for May 9 and May 11 that relate to rumors Shen had heard about military affairs. He now has entries for May 9, May 11, and May 13, by back-filling from the one he wrote first (from physical evidence on the page we know the entry for May 13 was written before the other two). In the inserted entry for the twenty-first day, Shen notes that he heard the siege's gunfire, which seems to echo the march of the Qing troops he noticed on May 8 and recorded on May 13.[64] The sound of gunfire is enigmatic and meaningless without retrospection. As Paize Keulemans points out, acoustic elements in narrative texts can map out abstract

---

61. MS 1:12; *BKRJ*, 8:22.

62. Another change in this example is "scurry" (*cuan* 竄), a negative term usually used to describe the movements of animals and despicable people. This change not only highlights the unexpected appearance of the rebels but also conveys Shen Zi's scorn for the enemy.

63. MS 2:51, left leaf; *BKRJ*, 8:69.

64. MS 1:4, right leaf; *BKRJ*, 8:9.

values in concrete, spatial terms.[65] In another example, between the entries of December 13 and December 18, 1861, Shen Zi inserts an entry for December 16 in which he records a placard he saw that announces the opening of a Taiping academy for local children.[66] Without direct impact on Shen's personal life, this inserted entry seems to be solely for "record-keeping," but it also provides a glimpse of how the Taiping regime gradually institutionalized its governance in various aspects of life in Puyuan. In addition, by directly quoting the Taiping announcement, Shen Zi domesticates a fragment of the Taiping discourse into his own text. This practice of "filling in the blanks" between consecutive entries a few days apart demonstrates Shen's desire for a version/vision of reality characterized by the continuity and "completeness" promised by the diurnal structure of the calendar.

In addition to offering an overarching historical view in his revisions, Shen Zi tries to be more precise about the people, scope of events, and exact locations that he observed, even though sometimes the revision seems to be based on general impressions. One example is his record of the number of boats docking at Xincheng ("some" becomes "five to six hundred"), in the entry for October 30, 1861, cited above. A similar example is the entry for May 9, 1863; here, Shen describes the sudden arrival of the Taiping rebels. He first wrote, "a large troop," but then inserted "[a large troop] of four to five thousand soldiers."[67] Some revisions were made to alter the earlier records with subsequently acquired information. One of the numerous examples of this kind of revision is the entry for November 24, 1863, in which Shen writes about how a local bandit leader and his armed followers seized a boat loaded with goods and passengers. The first draft gives a general description of the event. In the revision, Shen specifies the number of passengers as twenty, of whom fifteen were killed. He also describes the crime in more detail: the bandits coerced the boatman to sail to a remote cove, where they killed fifteen passengers, sank the bodies in water, and sailed the boat away.[68] In adding the exact number of victims and more details

---

65. Keulemans, *Sound Rising from the Paper*, 239.
66. MS 1:49, left leaf; *BKRJ*, 8:73.
67. MS 2:5, right leaf; *BKRJ*, 8:194.
68. MS 2:11, right leaf; *BKRJ*, 8:222.

about what happened, Shen delineates more clearly the local gangster's criminal activities amid the local disorder. These meticulous additions to events that did not have direct impact on Shen Zi's own life show how important it was to him to assume the role of a historian.

Minor changes to characters and words address aesthetic concerns: they bring euphony, clarity, and precision to subsequent drafts. For instance, during his homecoming journey on September 12, 1860, the day after his escape from the Taiping invasion, Shen Zi arrived at the end of the Wang Plank Bridge. There, he saw a dismembered female body. In the first draft, Shen describes the body in graphic detail: "On the stone-covered southern bank of the river near the Wang Plank Bridge, I saw a woman's body covered by a straw mat. Her feet were cut off, and fresh blood covered the ground" 見王板橋南岸階沿石上，以席掩一婦人，足已斷，鮮血淋滿地.[69] In the revision, he changes "fresh blood covered the ground" 鮮血淋滿地 to "blood covered the ground" 血淋滿地 to make it a phrase of four characters that better abides by the aesthetic tradition of classical Chinese. This change, however, reduces the vivid sense of horror and astonishment in the original version. In another entry, Shen at first writes, "Our family of five were all sick and lying in bed, unable to rise" 一家五口均病臥，不能興, then edits it to read "Our family of five were all lying in bed, sick, not able to rise" 一家五口均臥病，不能興.[70] Even though the meaning of the sentence remains unchanged, the revised version makes "sick" (*bing* 病) rhyme with "rise" (*xing* 興). Occasional stylistic changes like this demonstrate Shen Zi's efforts to polish the text aesthetically, evidence of his search for order on a linguistic level.

With the revisions, causal relationships are implied and built through additional information acquired in hindsight. In August 1860, when the Taipings defeated Qing troops and began to approach Puyuan, the prevailing sociopolitical order of the town was completely

---

69. MS 3:27, left leaf; *BKRJ*, 8:24. It is uncertain whether this torture imposed on the woman is due to the Taipings' policy against bound feet. However, the striking image Shen Zi observes here bizarrely resonates with rumors that the Taiping rebels took a cannibalistic interest in women's bound feet. A literary manifestation of this rumor is seen in the play *Snow on the Pear Blossom* (*Lihua xue* 梨花雪), which I will discuss in chapter 5.

70. MS 1:14, left leaf; *BKRJ*, 8:31.

disrupted. Shen Zi at first wrote, "[I] saw villagers and townsmen rob packages from the pawn shops" 見鄉人及鎮人搶包裹.[71] In the revision, he added, "[Those people] used spears as carrying poles and held broadswords in their hands. Previously, they were members of the Defense Bureau" 以長槍作扁擔，而手執腰刀，蓋即向者保衛局之團勇也.[72] In reporting that the local militia soldiers had turned into looters, Shen Zi makes sense of the ultimate deterioration of order in the town.[73] Another illustrative example is the account of September 1, 1863. In this entry, Shen gives a fuller explanation of the Taiping troops' movements with additional knowledge about the conflicts of interest between different Taiping cliques. He relates that the Taiping military commander, surnamed Zhong 鐘, who had been stationed in Tongxiang, received an order to march to Hangzhou. Unsatisfied with the amount of revenue gathered from levying the people of Tongxiang, Zhong postponed his departure; however, another Taiping commander succeeding him arrived at the town and took control of all the Taiping offices. As a result, Zhong could take little of the money he had collected. Forced to leave Tongxiang, Zhong headed for Jiashan, a county in Jiaxing, northeast of the prefectural seat, instead of going to Hangzhou, to the southwest. In between the lines, Shen Zi inserts text explaining that "at the time, the rebel Ting King [Ting Wang] was in Jiashan, and Zhong was the nephew of the Ting King's wife" 時偽聽王在嘉善，鐘故聽王之妻侄也.[74] The Ting King was Chen Bingwen 陳炳文 (fl. 1860–1864).[75] Implicitly, this detail explains the reason for Zhong's movement by revealing the nepotism and power struggles within the Taiping leadership.

Furthermore, inserting the names of neighboring towns establishes not only spatial relationships but also causal linkages. For instance, the original draft of the entry for October 2, 1860, reads: "[I] heard the Qing troops came. A general wearing a blue stone on his

71. MS 1:13, left leaf; *BKRJ*, 8:24.

72. MS 1:13, left leaf; *BKRJ*, 8:24.

73. The Taiping War did not involve only the Qing government and the Taiping rebels; the political milieu on the local level was complex, and there were conflicts among many parties. See Zheng Xiaowei, "Loyalty, Anxiety, and Opportunism."

74. MS 2:12, right leaf; *BKRJ*, 8:210.

75. See Chien Yu-wen, *Taiping tianguo dianzhi tongkao*, 1:38.

official cap first arrived. . . . Wherever they showed up, it became empty. I think that at this moment, the Qing troops do not dare to come to the town. It was probably the rebels pretending to be the official troops." The revised entry elaborates:

> Chaos ensued as there was a rumor that the long-hairs [Taipings] had arrived at the town. People all fled. Immediately afterward, I heard they were Qing troops from Tongxiang. A general wearing a blue stone on his official cap first arrived at the Temple of Guan Yu. . . . Wherever they showed up, it became empty. I think that at this moment, Hangzhou troops do not dare hope to recover Jiaxing. How could they dare to come to the town? It was probably the rebels pretending to be the official troops so that they could attack the capital of the province.
>
> 嘩傳長毛至鎮，人皆逃，既而聞系官兵自桐鄉來，有藍頂領兵官，先至關帝廟，而兵勇遂打大街各店屋，入而居之，所至為空。余謂此刻杭州官兵斷不敢作恢復嘉郡之想，安敢來鎮？恐是長毛假扮官兵往攻省城，亦未可定。[76]

The revision begins with a change of perspective: the insertion of his fellow townsmen's reactions to the rumor (fleeing what they thought were bandits) makes the subsequent hearsay (that they were not bandits but, apparently, Qing troops) a piece of information not only relevant to Shen Zi but also shared by all residents of the town. The names of places such as Tongxiang, Jiaxing, and Hangzhou (the capital of the province) mark the supposed route of the troops, which leads Shen to infer that what people took to be Qing troops were in fact rebels in disguise, since the Qing would not be headed to Jiaxing, in Taiping territory.[77] The picture emerging from these revisions reflects Shen Zi's attempts to connect disjointed temporal and spatial experiences to establish links between his limited knowledge and the unfolding of greater historical events.

76. MS 1:14, left leaf; *BKRJ*, 8:30. The differently colored precious stones that Qing officials wore on their caps indicated their official ranks. A *lan ding* 藍頂 (blue button made of precious stone or glass on a Qing official's cap) indicated the general was of middle rank. See Li Li, *Qingdai guanzhi yu fushi*, 186–87.

77. For a similar example about anxiety over disguise, see Meyer-Fong, *What Remains*, 69–70.

Another of Shen Zi's concerns, as he set about revising and amplifying his initial accounts, was to set straight the moral record. His revisions of accounts about his family members are replete with moral judgments, as he contrasts the courageous self-sacrifice of some with the apathy and selfishness of others. When all the family members remaining in Puyuan except for Shen Zi and his mother had died, his mother insisted on staying in their own house in town rather than escaping to the countryside: she wanted to protect the house while Shen Zi hid to avoid being drafted by the Taipings. Shen Zi first laments, "My mother was already in her fifties. With her house broken and family dead, she lived here alone. Fierce and brutal bandits came frequently. How much did she suffer from fear, worry, and frustration?" 我母已花甲，家破人亡，煢煢獨居，恐懼憂憤，苦何如哉.[78] In the revisions, Shen inserts: "Already a victim of the disaster . . . [she was] too weak to escape, so she stayed in this broken house [to guard it]. Every day, she dealt with fierce and brutal bandits" 既罹禍難 . . . 力不能避，守此蔽盧，日與此兇暴盜賊相接.[79] The first draft portrays the mother as someone who decided to stay behind to guard the house and perhaps to safeguard the fleeing family members. She was ready to sacrifice herself to keep both intact. In the revisions, the mother is redrawn as resilient and brave despite her victimhood.

In contrast to his praise for his mother, Shen Zi's retrospective edits do not hide grudges he held against certain family members. A case in point is the entry for October 15, 1863, when Shen visited the graveyard where his youngest sister was buried. After she married into the Chen family in 1860, her in-laws had sent her to live with her married sister; she later lived with her mother and died in the Shen house.[80] By the date of the 1863 diary entry, her husband, who had once been captured by the Taiping rebels, had died. When visiting the graveyard, Shen Zi noticed that the Chen tombs were facing in an inauspicious direction. He concluded that if nothing were done about the positions of the tombs, they would foreshadow the extinction of the Chen clan. But

78. MS 118, left leaf; *BKRJ*, 8:42.

79. MS 118, left leaf; *BKRJ*, 8:42.

80. On the development of the youngest sister's story, see *BKRJ*, 8:102, 103, 131, 201, 203, 213.

none of the Chens listened to him. Shen first wrote, "The auspicious land awaits the burial of the blessed people" 吉人獲吉壤也 but changed it to "A piece of [auspicious] burial ground is not comparable to a [good] heart" 陰地不若心地也. In the following sentence, which remains unchanged, he makes this comment: "The Chens have no integrity, so they deserve to be buried inauspiciously even in this auspicious ground" 陳氏人品不軌，其獲吉壤而不得葬，宜哉.[81] Shen Zi's judgment of the Chen family is extremely harsh, given the cultural significance placed on ancestral tombs and family graveyards in late imperial Chinese society. The revised sentence, a strong moral generalization about "the good heart," escalates Shen's condemnation of the Chens' dishonesty.

Many inserted lines reflect Shen Zi's inferences and deductions as a historian when he tried to evaluate the information he was receiving. The best illustration of this is his changing record of the Taiping capture of Hangzhou on December 10, 1861. For about two months, Shen Zi diligently and anxiously gathered scraps of information on how the battle in Hangzhou was proceeding. He also inserted comments retrospectively. At first, he interpreted the information as implying that Qing armies were resisting Taiping incursions. On hearing that the Qing troops had left Huzhou, the seat of the adjacent prefecture north of Hangzhou, on January 7, 1862, Shen Zi supposed they were marching toward Hangzhou, and told his friends, "This means Hangzhou has certainly not been lost" 此則杭州必不失也.[82] When he learned that local gangsters in the neighboring town had tried to occupy the Taiping headquarters, he reasoned, "In that case, not only is Hangzhou not lost, probably the Long Hairs [Taipings] have been defeated" 如此，則杭州非但不失，大約長毛敗也.[83] Both lines were inserted into the text: Shen Zi apparently sought to convince himself of a favorable outcome of the war for the Qing government as he reviewed the assembled information. The entry for the following day even records a complete story circulating at the time about the Taipings' defeat.[84] It was not until

81. MS 2:15, right leaf; *BKRJ*, 8:214.
82. MS 2:52, left leaf; *BKRJ*, 8:78.
83. MS 2:52, left leaf; *BKRJ*, 8:78.
84. MS 2:52, left leaf; *BKRJ*, 8:78.

January 10 that Shen Zi finally confirmed in his *Diary* the Taiping takeover of Hangzhou, and his description of the process is close to what we know today.[85] Shen Zi's assiduous record-keeping activities and his reflections show how an individual with heightened historical awareness continuously tried to make sense of the history on a larger scale amid all the confusion and disorder, revising his narrative as new information came in.

In these revisions, Shen Zi also makes retrospective judgments on what he observed in the public realm. Some of these are moral comments. In the entry for November 27, 1861, he records how he witnessed bandits on gunboats abducting women from wealthy families. Perplexed, he inserts, "Is this because of their [the women's] guilt in previous life? Or is it the retribution for the [sins] of their fathers or husbands? Why didn't the rich families think about previous examples before their eyes rather than indulge themselves in brothels" 其前身冤業耶？抑乃父乃夫孽報耶？於是而富家人不思眼前榜樣，而猶往往沈溺銷金窩者何哉?[86] His attempts to apply the rule of moral retribution to a chaotic reality resonate with early Qing discourse that blamed the exuberant commercial culture of the late Ming for the fall of that dynasty, and his particular focus on the role of women in social disorder is reflective of the familiar trope associating decadence and sensual pleasures with political corruption and social disorder.[87] The moral logic in early Qing short stories and novels that says "If I don't sleep with someone else's wife, no one will sleep with my wife" 我不淫人婦，人不淫我妻 may also be relevant: the abducted women were forced to serve the bandits in the same fashion as courtesans serving wealthy men subject to moral retribution.[88]

85. *BKRJ*, 8:82; Guo Tingyi, *Taiping tianguo shishi rizhi*, 834.

86. MS 2:52, right leaf; *BKRJ*, 8:72.

87. For an early Qing literati's repentance of the exuberant lifestyle in late Ming society, see Wang Fansen, *Wan Ming Qing chu sixiang shilun*, 91–92, 194. On women as metaphorical sites where literati pass moral and political judgment, see Wai-yee Li, *Women and National Trauma*, chap. 1. On people's sense of retribution, common during the Taiping War, see Meyer-Fong's discussion of Yu Zhi in *What Remains*.

88. This moral logic is shown in late Ming short stories such as "Jiang Xingge chonghui zhenzhu shan" 蔣興哥重會珍珠衫 from the early seventeenth-century

Others of Shen Zi's retrospective judgments reflect on the causes behind historical events. An example is the revision he made to the entry for October 21, 1863. In the original draft, he describes a famine in the Qing-controlled region after a natural disaster, where saltwater flooding farmland made many people sick and caused many to die of starvation; he then contrasts this situation with the good harvest in the Taiping-controlled area unaffected by this disaster. In the revision, he inserts this elaborate comment:

> Seeing the disaster of salty water and the large number of deaths from sudden intestinal turmoil [*huoluan*], I know that Heaven let disaster befall people. Seeing the harvest of rice in paddies fill the rebels' stomachs, I know that Heaven is assisting the rebels. I suspect that the poisonousness of the rebels is not exhausted yet. Otherwise, how could Heaven favor [the rebels] in this way?
>
> 觀鹹水為災，霍亂餓死之多，知天之降災于民；觀田稻豐熟，適飽賊腹，知天之資助于賊。意者賊之流毒未有窮也，不然，何天意之眷佑若是耶?[89]

The original draft records the disparity between regions controlled by Qing troops and Taiping rebels, respectively; the insertion interprets this disparity as a reflection of Heaven's will. The former literally observes the Earth, the here and now; but the latter extends this observation to make sense of the Heaven, the whole realm of China and its future. The ultimate point of reference Shen Zi uses to make sense of the calamity, therefore, is Heaven. Nevertheless, in this case Heaven is hardly an arbiter of morality.

Comparisons between Shen's first notes and their corresponding expanded diary entries demonstrate that there were numerous ways to

---

collection *Yu shi ming yan* 喻世明言 and in seventeenth-century novels such as *Rou pu tuan* 肉蒲團.

89. MS 2:16, right leaf; *BKRJ*, 8:217. The term that Shen uses for the illness, *huoluan*, is found in classical medical texts and "referred to distinctive clinical cases characterized by their sudden onset and simultaneous vomiting and exhaustive diarrhea." These symptoms can stem from cholera, and in fact a cholera epidemic occurred in Shanghai in 1862. Hanson, *Speaking of Epidemics*, 136, 141–42.

construct "what had happened." In the revisions, Shen Zi expresses his private and intimate feelings more intensely, but also demonstrates a degree of self-censorship when representing his political stance. On the linguistic level, his search for order is evinced by stylistic changes. On the narrative level, this search manifests itself in an attempt to claim beginnings, to "fill in" the calendrical structure, to construct causal relationships, and to moralize or historicize the phenomena recorded. On a moral level, he changes the language of female family members to fit into the family structure he imagines. In all, these attempts stitch together "what had happened" and the memories associated with the disorienting occurrences.

For most people who lived through the Taiping Civil War, what they saw was not Heaven but a shattered Earth, about which individual writers assiduously kept witness accounts. After the war, private diaries and memoirs were published in various print media and read widely. The many editorial changes they underwent were, of course, effaced in the final printed versions. But the processes of revision, reconstruction, and restoration of personal and historical memories—by either the author or the editor—are, as we have seen, preserved in manuscripts and other ephemeral texts, themselves witnesses to the time and the sufferings of the people. Revisions and edits made to and based on individual memories are found not only in personal accounts but also in fiction written during the war, as the next chapter shows.

PART II

*Making Sense of the Past
and the Future*

PART II

Making Sense of the Past
and the Future

CHAPTER FOUR

# Traces of History

## A Literati Novel and Its Precedents

### Writing from within the War

When concerning contemporary events, both Taiping texts, such as *The Taiping Heavenly Chronicle*, and private writings, as represented by Shen Zi's *Diary*, aim for the effect of a "chronicle" that promises completion and morality—with mixed results. By contrast, such promises seem easy to fulfill in full-length fiction and drama, because the conventions of those genres traditionally include narrative closure. However, in making sense of history, the imageries and adaptations of tropes in fiction and plays addressing the Taiping Civil War provide a vision just as contingent and fragmentary as the one we find in writings such as Shen Zi's manuscript. We can see this illustrated in the work of the novelist Wei Xiuren.

Wei's life, like the lives of most people during his time, was turned upside down by the war. From a gentry family in Fujian Province, Wei Xiuren had followed his father's advice and embarked on the journey north to Beijing to take the civil examination one more time in 1855.[1]

---

1. Wei Xiuren, *WXRZZ*, 2:1278. On his previous examination trip, in 1851, Wei Xiuren never made it to the capital: he was forced to return home halfway because of the rise of the Taiping Rebellion.

Wei Xiuren failed the examination once again and, on his way back to his hometown Tingzhou, was stranded in Taiyuan in Shanxi Province, a place far from the war zone but also far from home.[2] He took a temporary position as a tutor there and developed a relationship with a courtesan. While he was in Taiyuan, his hometown fell to the Taiping rebels. His younger brother committed suicide during the chaos; several months later, his father, already ill, died too.[3] When Wei Xiuren received the tragic news, he embarked on a journey homeward as soon as he could, but ended up spending the next six years in various places before reaching home. During that time, he sojourned along the way, mostly Shaanxi and Sichuan Provinces. In an attempt to come to terms with what happened, he wrote *Traces of Flowers and the Moon*, a literati novel (*wenren xiaoshuo* 文人小說) with strong autobiographical echoes, notable also for its lyricism and fantasy.[4]

*Traces of Flowers and the Moon* uses the conventions of the literati novel to work through personal and national trauma. Wei Xiuren had not been appointed to any official position; nor had he been able to protect his family from misfortune. In other words, the most meaningful roles for a man in Confucian society were closed to him. Therefore, the novel was Wei Xiuren's creative adaptive response to a lack of opportunities. In the novel, he transforms himself into a metonymic representative of the traditional world underpinned by Confucian values that had been lost. The transformation is also anchored in the Chinese lyrical tradition that has always been a significant component of novels and drama written by literati. The novel draws heavily on Wei Xiuren's personal experiences, especially his romantic relationship with a courtesan between 1857–1858.[5] The male protagonist of the

2. Wei Xiuren, *WXRZZ*, 2:1279.

3. Wei Xiuren, *WXRZZ*, 2:1285, 1287.

4. Literati novels are full-length novels of the late imperial period written by "literati," who studied Confucian classics in preparation for civil examinations but also engaged in various artistic activities.

5. Pan Jianguo, "Wei Xiuren *Hua yue hen* xiaoshuo," 160. Xie Zhangting 謝章鋌 (1820–1903) was the first to link the novel to Wei Xiuren's life experiences; he considers the composition of the novel a significant event in Wei's life. Xie's "Wei Zi'an muzhi ming" 魏子安墓誌銘, now collected in *Duqi shanzhuang wenji* 賭棋山莊文集, are also major sources for information about Wei Xiuren's life. Lu Xun follows Xie when

novel is named Wei Chizhu, one of the many sobriquets the writer used in his youth.[6] The novel concerns two couples forced apart to escape the violence ravaging the nation: the Taiping Rebellion in the south, the Muslim rebellion in the north, and foreign invasions in the coastal regions. Because the Taiping rebels blocked his way home, Chizhu was stranded in Shanxi Province. There, as a traveler with limited means, Chizhu pursues a hopeless romance with a courtesan, Liu Qiuhen. They befriend another couple, Han Hesheng and Du Caiqiu (also a courtesan), who also met in Shanxi. Han and Du's story has what seems to be a happier outcome, since both are more competent in coping with an unsettling reality, but their successes are illusory and based on wishful thinking—in reality, at the end of the Taiping-Qing conflict, the Qing empire, though it had vanquished the Taiping movement, is wrecked by the war.

*Traces of Flowers and the Moon* consists of fifty-six chapters, chapters 2 through 44 of which were likely finished by 1858, with the remaining chapters being written by the author after the war concluded in 1864.[7] Chapters 2 through 44, created during the war, center on the romance of the two couples, especially that of Chizhu and Qiuhen. Chapters 45 to 56 cover the untimely deaths of Chizhu and Qiuhen, and transform the war into a fantasy where ghosts and supernatural beings prevail to triumph over the rebels, in accordance with Chizhu's political insights.

---

commenting on *Hua yue hen*. "Wei Zi'an muzhi ming," in Xie Zhangting, *Duqi shanzhuang wenji, juan* 5:6a–8b. Lu Xun, *Zhongguo xiaoshuo shi lüe*, 206. Since the 1980s, more studies of *Hua yue hen* have appeared; they generally consider the autobiographical elements merely the background of the novel.

6. Wei Xiuren, *WXRZZ*, 1:154. The author's surname, Wei 魏, is a homonym of his protagonist's surname, 韋. However, the autobiographical implication is clear. The literal meaning of Chizhu 癡珠 is "crazy pearl," which could be read as an echo to Baoyu 寶玉 (precious jade) in *Dream of the Red Chamber*.

7. The two prefaces of the novel are dated 1858. In chapter 30, the narrator says that the beginning of the next spring is on the twenty-first day in the last month of the present year, based on the sexagenary cycle. This date reflects the peculiarity of the transition between the year *bingchen* and the year *wuwu* in Chinese calendar, which in the nineteenth century corresponds to 1856 and 1858, respectively. See Du Weimo, "Jiaodian houji," 449.

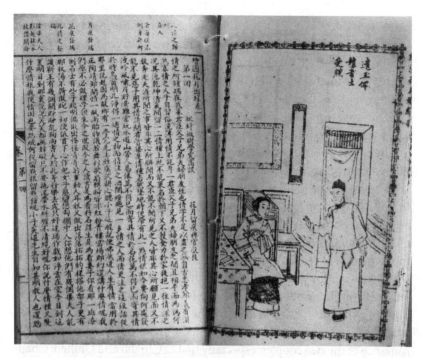

FIG. 4.1. Page spread from *Traces of Flowers and the Moon* (*Hua yue hen*), publisher unknown, 1908.

When *Traces of Flowers and the Moon* was published in 1888, it was an immediate success in the burgeoning literary market. Its popularity lasted for decades, and it signaled a new trend in Chinese fiction (fig. 4.1). At the beginning of the twentieth century, men of traditional education became increasingly disillusioned with the civil exam system and started to write for a general audience in magazines and newspapers to make a living. They emulated *Traces of Flowers and the Moon* by writing ill-fated romances between couples, especially courtesans and their customers, during times of political turbulence.[8] David Der-wei Wang

8. Fu Zhaolun thought Wei Xiuren wrote the novel to display his poetic talent. See Kong Lingjing, *Zhongguo xiaoshuo shiliao*, 233. Ye Chucang (1887–1946), who once served as a minister in the Nationalist Party's propaganda department during the Republican era, praises the use of classical language in the novel. See Ye Chucang, *Xiaoshuo zazhu*, 113. Zheng Zhenduo praises the novel in *Wenxue dagang*, 606.

suggests that Wei's novel is a critical transition point between older Chinese literary conventions and Chinese literary modernity.[9] Keith McMahon points out that "prior to the 1890s, *Traces of the Flowery Moon* [his translation of the title] is the novel that most explicitly equates the destiny of love and the destiny of China as a historically symbolic whole."[10] I agree with both these observations, but my close examination of the numerous aesthetic and literary experiments in the novel shows that the writer's attempts to transcend personal trauma through narrative and lyricism reinvent not only the genre of the literati novel but also imaginings of the Taiping Civil War and its relationship to previous dynastic transitions.

## Between Reality and Fictionality

In his novel, Wei Xiuren, like the diarists, revisits and re-creates his memories of personal experiences during the war. But unlike the revisions that left visible traces in Shen Zi's manuscript, Wei's re-creations of memories are invisible in the printed edition. We have to infer them by studying the variances between the poems in the novel and their analogues in Wei Xiuren's own poetry collection; the correspondences make *Traces of Flowers and the Moon* a kind of secret repository of memories embedded in a semifictional context.

In the narrative, two temporal axes extend in different directions: one is the fictional time experienced by the characters, which continues forward; the other is the time experienced by the writer as he looks backward to the past. This temporal structure resonates with that of *The Peach Blossom Fan*, an early Qing southern play from the seventeenth century ascribing historical significance to personal tragedies against the backdrop of dynastic change. The story of *The Peach Blossom Fan* takes place during the Ming-Qing transition: two historical figures, the scholar Hou Fangyu 侯方域 (1618–1654) and the courtesan

9. David Der-wei Wang writes, "Wei Zi'an's novel points to an integral element of Chinese literary modernity." See his *Fin-de-Siècle Splendor*, 81.

10. McMahon, *Polygamy and Sublime Passion*, 77. McMahon also points to instances in *Traces of Flowers and the Moon* that show an awareness of the harm of opium smoking, in his *The Fall of the God of Money*, 156.

Li Xiangjun 李香君 (fl. 1640), fall in love but are soon separated. In the aftermath of Ming collapse, Hou and Li are reunited, but decide to part to pursue Daoist enlightenment instead of personal fulfillment. The play's author, Kong Shangren 孔尚任 (1648–1718), gave voice to the experience of the generation preceding his, when the effect of historical trauma was beginning to subside. Wei Xiuren, however, was still experiencing the tectonic shift brought about by the Taiping Rebellion at the time of writing. His work poses the question of whether the dramatic imagination can rationalize and transcend the violence of history as it occurs.

The short temporal distance in *Traces of Flowers and the Moon* between the writer who is creating the novel and the novel's autobiographical self is bridged by what I call "anticipatory nostalgia": the characters' feelings in the fiction's present are colored by their anticipation of a nostalgia they will feel in the future, a future corresponding to the time when the novel is composed. With markers of specific time and space, Wei Xiuren points to the gaps between the real and the fictional, where we can find traces of the emotional reality he once lived in. At the same time, his efforts to search for and cope with that reality involve much manipulation and reconstruction of that past. This nostalgic position appears not only in the plot design but also in prefaces, epilogues, and poems embedded in the novel.

The main story of the novel begins, Wei tells us, in the summer of the year of *bingshen* 丙申, in the suburb of the ancient capital Xi'an.[11] Without specifying the date and year, he uses a literary, traditional way of marking events and thus injects a timelessness into events that occur in historical time in the fictional world he constructs. The protagonist Chizhu is on a journey that takes him by Ba Bridge (Ba qiao 灞橋) and the Tong Pass (Tong guan 潼關), both locations known for having endured numerous rounds of destruction and restoration since the Six

11. Wei uses the traditional sexagenary cycle way of marking time, rather than the common calendar year. In the sexagenary cycle, the *bingshen* year repeats every sixty years; that is, 1656, 1716, 1776, 1836, 1896, etc. If the story is read as an autobiography, this *bingshen* year is presumably 1836, as Wei participated in the civil examination that year. Overall, though the writer is reflecting on a real war, in a real time and place, the novel shifts events into literary time and possibilities.

Dynasties period (220–589 CE).[12] As generations of writers inscribed multiple layers of memories and projection onto these sites, they also transformed them into cultural icons associated with the vicissitudes of historical change. Symbolizing separation and departure in the Chinese literary tradition, Ba Bridge evokes feelings of yearning, melancholy, and sadness. The Tong Pass has been a key military site on the route from the western frontier to the central plain; it appears frequently in "frontier poetry" (*biansai shi* 邊塞詩), a poetic subgenre that takes warfare and frontier scenarios as its themes. By beginning with the Ba Bridge and the Tong Pass, the story of *Traces of Flowers and the Moon* opens into places permeated with historical memories and literary imagination.

The Ba Bridge and the Tong Pass are permeated also with the writer's personal remembrances and sorrows. When Wei Xiuren tried to return home from Beijing, after failing the civil examinations for the fourth and last time, he found his way was blocked by the fighting and had to go instead to Sichuan, by a route that took him past the bridge and the pass. In the novel, Chizhu is represented as a pensive, solitary traveler, much as Wei must have been:

In a single carriage, Chizhu arrived at the Tong Pass after a few days. . . . [He] appreciated the view and thought of the bygone years. Happiness and sadness alternated to occupy his heart. He sat in the carriage for an entire day without a word. In fact, even with pages and pages, his feelings could not be elucidated.

癡珠單車趲行，不日已抵潼關。 . . . 一路流連風景，追溯年華，忽然而喜，忽然而悲。雖終日兀坐車中，不發一語，其實連編累牘，也寫不了他胸中情緒。[13]

Those obscure feelings, however, are given voice in a quatrain Chizhu subsequently composes:

12. Wei Xiuren made his first trip to the Ba Bridge and the Tong Pass in 1847. See Wei Xiuren, *WXRZZ*, 1:124.

13. Wei Xiuren, *HYH*, 10. I use the modern typeset reprint of the first edition of *Hua yue hen* that was published in 1888.

蒼茫仙掌秋，              Boundless is the autumn at the
                            Immortal's Palm,[14]
搖落灞橋柳。              Wither and fall—the willows' leaves
                            along the Ba Bridge.[15]
錦瑟惜華年，              On the beautifully patterned zither
                            one laments bygone youthful years,[16]
欲語碑在口。              About to speak, I feel a stone tablet
                            in my mouth.[17]

The start of this poem suggests a longing for the land of immortals, but immediately, the second line draws one's attention back to the human realm, where people feel deep attachments to friends and family. The last two lines lament the transience of life and the intense sorrow the autobiographical hero experiences. Through Chizhu's poem at the opening of the novel, Wei Xiuren mediates emotions evoked by his personal tragedy: a failed romance, lack of success in his career, and family misfortune.

The violence that overtook Wei Xiuren's hometown during the war is referred to in chapter 11 of the novel. Chizhu receives a letter (summarized in the storyteller's voice) describing the fates of his family, who fled their home in order to avoid the rebels but were separated by local

14. "The Immortal's Palm" may refer to Mountain Hua, known also as the Mountain of the Immortal's Palm, or to Hua Prefecture in Shaanxi, where Mountain Hua is located.

15. The Ba Bridge is east of Chang'an. When people parted at this bridge, the one to stay would break a willow branch to express a wish for the other person to stay too. "Willow" and "to stay" are homophonous in Chinese. A line in a poem by the Tang poet Li Bo, "Seeing [someone] off at Ba Ling" ("Ba Ling xing songbie" 灞陵行送別), reads, "Sending you, my friend, off at the Pavilion of Ba Ling, where the immensely flowing Ba River resembles my sadness" 送君灞陵亭，灞水流浩浩. Li Bo 李白 (701–762), *Li Bo quanji jiaozhu*, 5:2374.

16. The allusion to the zither, *jinse*, comes from Li Shangyin's 李商隱 (813–858) poem "Jinse" 錦瑟. The first couplet of the poem reads: "For no reason, the beautifully patterned zither has fifty strings, / each and every string and pillar is in reminiscence of the youthful days" 錦瑟無端五十弦，一弦一柱思華年. Li Shangyin, *LSYSG*, 3:1420.

17. The stone tablet, or stele, *bei* 碑 is a homophone of *bei* 悲, which means sadness. These homophones form a commonly used play on words in *yuefu* poems.

bandits in chaos.[18] Chizhu's concubine, Qianwen, has committed suicide; the family's house, lands, properties, and possessions have all been destroyed. Chizhu's mother and a few other family members have, nonetheless, managed to survive. His mother tells Chizhu in the same letter to stay in the north for his safety and protection. Chizhu is overwhelmed by helplessness and despair.

Chizhu's distress is represented through not only the narrative of events and the accompanying storyteller's commentary and description, but also his quotations from poetic works. Here, Chizhu's emotional reactions may very well find resonances in readers versed in traditional learning. The plot goes that a friend of Chizhu comes to visit him and hears him speaking in his delirium: "If you have no family to part from in life / how can you be even one of the common folks!" 人生無家別，何以為蒸黎.[19] He goes on, more softly, "I want to rise and fly off there, but I lie sick in bed" 身欲奮飛病在床.[20] Chizhu calls out Qianwen's (his concubine at home) name and says, "Since then I heard that all there had suffered calamity / the massacre extending to the chickens and dogs" 比聞同罹禍，殺戮到雞狗.[21] The last sentence the friend hears is "Wild grass creeps to wrap the remains of bones; tall trees of arching branches gather the souls" 蔓草縈骨，拱木斂魂.[22]

This is a dually mediated episode, where the author writes about a character's delirious dream as voiced through ancient poetry lines. What Chizhu utters in his delirium is a composite of lines from ancient poetry that speak to his own situation. Though the quotations are from the past, these fragmentary expressions acquire a sense of wholeness in the context of the novel. The first three quotations are from Du Fu's

---

18. This episode brings to mind the seventeenth-century play *Wanli yuan* 萬里圓 (*Reunion across Millions of Miles*) written by Li Yu 李玉 (fl. seventeenth century). *Wanli yuan* centers on the journey undertaken by a filial son, Huang Xiangjian 黃向堅, who endured many hardships to look for his father after the fall of the Ming dynasty. In this play, the father hears about the destruction and war in his hometown from a soldier sojourning at an inn on the southwestern frontier.

19. Du Fu, *Du Fu quanji jiaozhu*, 3:1316–23; Owen, *The Poetry of Du Fu*, 2:97.

20. Du Fu, *Du Fu quanji jiaozhu*, 8:4822–34; Owen, *The Poetry of Du Fu*, 4:366.

21. Du Fu, *Du Fu quanji jiaozhu*, 1:841–48; Owen, *The Poetry of Du Fu*, 1:297.

22. Jiang Yan, "Hen fu," 2:744; *Wen xuan, or, Selections of Refined Literature*, 1:193.

杜甫 (712–770) poems; the last is from Jiang Yan's 江淹 (444–505) "Rhapsody on Resentment" ("Hen fu" 恨賦). Du Fu's words refer to the destruction of his family and homeland, his own ill health, and the inhumanity of war during the An Lushan Rebellion (755–763), which sent the prosperous Tang dynasty into decline. In the third quotation from Du Fu, the poet describes waiting for—and dreading—a letter from home. The final quotation, from Jiang Yan who also lived in a warring era, is a bleak, prophetic image of wild grass and trees. In the original poem these lines are followed by a disturbing question: "When human life reaches this point, why bother to discourse on the Way of Heaven?" 人生到此，天道寧論.[23] Wei Xiuren may be suggesting in that last quotation that Heaven is of no help in the face of the war raging around him, too. This whole episode demonstrates at least two ways in which Chizhu reworks his personal traumatic experiences through fictional construction. First, he models the protagonist's situation on his own. Second, he uses literary allusion to characterize the protagonist's deeply troubled psyche—both to imply what was happening in the man's mind, and also to imbue it with cultural associations that would have held deep meaning for his readers.

Wei Xiuren quoted not only from ancient and famous poets; he also quoted his own work. *Traces of Flowers and the Moon* uses more than seventy of Wei's poems, which constitute a quarter of his entire poetry corpus and almost half of all poems in the novel.[24] The variations between the poems in his collection, "Sixteen Poems Based on Real Events in the Courtyard of Autumn Heart, Matching the Rhyme of Huang Zhongze's 'Thoughts of Longing'" ("Qiuxin yuan benshi shi shiliu shou yong Huang Zhongze 'Qihuai' shiyun" 秋心院本事詩十六首用黃仲則綺懷詩韻),[25] and those in the novel show that in the novel, the writer disrupted the original chronological order of composition and revised some of the poems to fit their new context. At several

23. Jiang Yan, "Hen fu," 2:744; *Wen xuan, or, Selections of Refined Literature*, 1:193.

24. Pan Jianguo identifies sixty-eight poems occurring in both the novel and the author's poetry collections. Pan Jianguo, "Wei Xiuren *Hua yue hen* xiaoshuo," 157.

25. Huang Zhongze 黃仲則 (1749–1783), a poet known for his intense emotions and mournful diction; "Thoughts of Longing" (comprising sixteen poems) is representative of his style. See *Zhongguo wenxue tongshi*, 6:153.

points in the novel, specific dates are given for moments of departure and separation, which don't appear in the originals; phrases indicating hope and good cheer that appear in the poetry collection are omitted in the novel. Furthermore, the author injects memories of later events into the poems composed earlier. Examples of these alterations occur in chapter 25, where Han Hesheng reads some of Chizhu's poems.

The novel emphasizes that the poems are "authentic accounts" of events in Chizhu's life; they are not, however, "authentic accounts" of Wei's life, since the writer has made changes from his originals in order to fit them into the novel. For example, the first line of the poem as it appears in the collection ("Sixteen Poems") reads: "Still, I remember the beginning, when the horse with a white nose stops" 猶憶騧停白鼻初; in the novel, it has been changed to: "Still, I remember the beginning, when we got to know each other in the third month of autumn" 猶憶三秋識面初.[26] The image of the horse stems from Li Bo's 李白 (701–762) "Horse with a White Nose" ("Bai bi gua" 白鼻騧), in which the poet on a white-nosed horse rides to a (female) wine vendor's shop to drink.[27] With this allusion, the line in Wei's "Sixteen Poems" idealizes and poeticizes the relationship between the author and his courtesan lover. In contrast, the corresponding line in the novel's poem tells us instead the season of their first meeting, possibly denoting the time when the romance between Wei and his lover began.[28] In addition, though the line in the "Sixteen Poems" recalls an initial encounter both gallant and refreshing, the line in the novel reminiscences on the lapse of time and hence heightens a nostalgic feeling.

Revisions made to a poem in chapter 15, when compared to its counterpart in the poetry collection, also shed light on feelings coming together from different temporal points. The context in the novel is Chizhu's visit to his friend Han Hesheng; finding him not at home, Chizhu leaves a poem:

26. Wei Xiuren, *WXRZZ*, 2:1066; *HYH*, 207.

27. Li Bo, *Li Bo quanji jiaozhu*, 5:881.

28. Chizhu and Qiuhen meet in the tenth month of the year *dingsi* 丁巳; their relationship lasts for seven months. See *HYH*, chap. 39. This may mirror the length of Wei Xiuren's romance with the courtesan.

月帳星河又渺茫，      Vague and vast again is the curtain made
                          by the moon and the river of stars,
年年別緒惱人腸。      Year after year the feeling brought on
                          by separation stokes frustration.
三更涼夢回徐榻，      At the third watch, a cold dream returns
                          to the mat of Xu,[29]
一夜西風瘦沈郎。      A night of west wind makes the Shen
                          lad slender.[30]
好景君偏愁裏過，      The scenes are lovely, yet you experience
                          them in sorrow,
佳期我轉客中忘。      For my part I as sojourner have
                          forgotten about the good old days.
洗車灑淚紛紛雨，      Rain washes the carriage like
                          copious tears,
兒女情牽乃尔長。      The threads of attachment binding us
                          are so long.[31]

Chizhu's poem reproduces, in part, one of Wei's: "Mocking the Recluse of the Wood of Red Leaves on the Seventh Day of the Seventh Month" ("Qixi chao Lindan jushi" 七夕嘲林丹居士), dated 1857. The date in Wei's poem title would carry connotations for his audience: the seventh day of the seventh month is the date of a traditional festival marking the yearly reunion of the Weaver Maid and her lover, who are separated by the Milky Way. This festival celebrates a reunion of great bliss, but it is colored by the anticipated sorrow of their imminent parting. The first three couplets of Wei's poem are reproduced in the novel. The last couplet, "Mocking the Recluse," however, is not; it reads: "For this moment, let's focus on getting a dipper of wine to extend our enjoyment of autumn; / we should live up to the candlelight reflected on the silver

---

29. The "mat of Xu" is the mat Chen Fan 陳蕃 (?–168) set out for Xu Chi 徐穉 (fl. 160) whenever Xu visited him. In Chinese literary tradition, this special courtesy shows one's appreciation of the person's talent. On Chen Fan's story, see "Xu Chi zhuan" 徐穉傳, in *Hou Han shu*, 1:574.

30. Shen Yue 沈約 (441–513) in his later years wrote to his friend that he had become thinner due to illness and had to tighten his belt each month. See Shen Yue, "Yu Xu Mian shu," 3:1403.

31. *HYH*, 109.

screen" 且謀斗酒延秋爽，莫負銀屏畫燭光.[32] Wei probably composed the original poem on the occasion of a meeting with a friend. His revision, which fits the poem into the novel by replacing the "happy couplet" with a more melancholic one, sets the elegiac tone for Chizhu's story.

The retrospective construction of nostalgic feelings applies not only to the poems but also to the way characters are drawn and to the autumnal mood that governs the entire novel. Chizhu and Qiuhen both treat the present as something they will lose in the near future, already experiencing it with regret and longing. In chapter 19, at the beginning of their relationship, Qiuhen asks, "Do you know what my fate will be?" 你曉得我這個人，怎樣結果. Chizhu replies, "I don't even know my own fate; how could I know yours? Haven't you heard from Hesheng today about the situation in Jiangnan? As far as I see it, no one under Heaven knows what the future will hold, let alone you and I" 我自己結果也不知道，那裏曉得你？你今日不聽荷生說那江南光景。給我看來普天下的人，也不知如何結果，何況我與你呢.[33] Qiuhen, as well as the reader, may perceive a sense of distance in Chizhu's reply about "you" and "me" instead of "us" when he reckons "their" future as a couple. This distance is created by uncertainties shared not only by them but also "all under Heaven." In the rest of the novel, their conversations consistently end with Qiuhen's anxious inquiries about the future and Chizhu's despondent replies, leaving the impression that individuals have little agency over their fate. The loss of vitality and hope unmistakably evokes the metaphor of autumn. In fact, Qiuhen's name means "autumn traces," and her place is named "Courtyard of Autumn Heart" (*Qiu xin yuan* 秋心院), with the characters *qiu* and *xin* making up the word "sorrow" (*chou* 愁).

Time and season are not simply metaphorical in this novel. Wei Xiuren emphasizes dates and locations to make for a solidly structured, coherent narrative. Some of the places, events, and spans of time are, as we have seen, patterned after his own life and adapted to fit the exigencies of the novel and the time period of its setting. Wei Xiuren also uses and adapts his own poetic work, attributing them to his alter ego, Chizhu. These strategies have the effect of blurring the distinction

32. Wei Xiuren, *WXRZZ*, 2:1060.
33. *HYH*, 148–49.

between the real and the fictional, the past and the present. As a result, though fragmentary and episodic, traces of the collective and personal past remain in the fictional frame the writer composes.

## Fragments of the Illusory World

The Chinese full-length novel was already well developed by the sixteenth century.[34] Novel-writing was one among various artistic pursuits of the literati, who were (supposedly) shaped by their study of Neo-Confucianism and sense of responsibility for the public good.[35] By the seventeenth century, although novel writing was still considered secondary to classical genres such as prose and poetry, it "was a respected vehicle for serious artistic experimentation and intellectual expression."[36] During the eighteenth century, fiction turned increasingly autobiographical.[37] Many eighteenth-century writers, as Martin Huang points out, adopted various strategies of appropriating "others" in these novels to write indirectly about the self; those "others" are metaphors for the self, but they also limit the expression of the self.[38] At the same time, novelists of the period, who had become increasingly specialized and professionalized, implicitly undermined the Neo-Confucian orthodoxy, which centers on self-cultivation and moral progress.[39]

It is within this tradition of the literati novel that Wei Xiuren began his *Traces of Flowers and the Moon*. When the first forty-four chapters of the novel were finished in 1858, Wei was in full existential crisis, as he found himself failing all the moral and political goals expected of a

34. Plaks, *Four Masterworks of the Ming Novel*. Plaks discusses the dating of the four Ming novels, *The Plum in the Golden Vase* (*Jin Ping Mei* 金瓶梅), *Water Margin*, *Journey to the West* (*Xiyou ji* 西遊記), and *Romance of the Three Kingdoms*, on 59, 189, 280, and 362, respectively.

35. Roddy, *Literati Identity and Its Fictional Representations*, 9–10.

36. Hegel, *The Novel in Seventeenth-Century China*, 5.

37. Plaks, "Towards a Critical Theory of Chinese Narrative," 329. Plaks mentions *Dream of the Red Chamber, Unofficial History of the Scholars* (*Rulin waishi* 儒林外史), *Six Records of a Floating Life* (*Fu sheng liu ji* 浮生六記), and others.

38. Huang, *Literati and Self-Re/Presentation*.

39. Roddy, *Literati Identity and Its Fictional Representations*, 6.

member of the educated elite in traditional society. He could, however, still draw on his associations with the literati class and his literary education. Scholars point out that the romance between Chizhu and Qiuhen in *Traces of Flowers and the Moon* is modeled after a similar one between the couple of Jia Bayou and Lin Daiyu in *Dream of the Red Chamber*, the mid-eighteenth-century novel by Cao Xueqin 曹雪芹 (1715?–1763?).[40] The connections, I would argue, go deeper than mere similarity of plot and tone. Both works are premised on the loss of a cohesive, coherent world that guarantees eternity and completeness. We see this in Chizhu's chaotic world, and in Jia Baoyu's journey to the illusory realm in *Dream of the Red Chamber*.[41]

The dream world emerges in chapter 5 of *Dream of the Red Chamber*: "Jia Baoyu visits the Land of Illusion, and the fairy Disenchantment performs the 'Dream of Golden Days.'" The realm of illusion and the human realm connect with each other, and the dialectic relationship between them plays out in the experience of the character Vanitas (*Kong kong daoren* 空空道人): "Vanitas, starting off in the Void (which is Truth) came to the contemplation of Form (which is Illusion); and from Form engendered Passion; and by communicating Passion, entered again into Form; and from Form awoke to the Void (which is Truth)" 因空見色, 由色生情, 傳情入色, 自色悟空.[42] In the illusory realm, Jia Baoyu's feelings become fully aroused by the sensual pleasures he experiences, but waking suddenly from the dream, he plunges into a fleeting moment of disenchantment. The same fascination with illusions seems to motivate Wei Xiuren. However, the

40. C. T. Hsia has pointed out that the romance between Chizhu and Qiuhen resembles that of Jia Baoyu and Lin Daiyu in its pathos; David Der-wei Wang, instead of viewing the romance in *Traces of Flowers and the Moon* as a recapitulation of older love stories, suggests that the story "preempts the pathetic consequence of *Story of the Stone [Dream of the Red Chamber]* . . . and makes it the motivation of all narrative acts." David Der-wei Wang, *Fin-de-Siècle Splendor*, 76.

41. Du Zhijun, "*Honglou meng* yu *Hua yue hen*." Du Zhijun does not, however, point to specific plot elements in *Traces of Flowers and the Moon* that might show the influence of *Dream of the Red Chamber*.

42. Hawkes and Minford, *The Story of the Stone*, 1:51. I use the more common translation of the novel's title, *Dream of the Red Chamber*, but for terms and usages from the novel, I mostly follow Hawkes's translation.

illusory realm he creates does not offer a comprehensive, universal framework allegorizing the totality of human experience, as does the one in *Dream of the Red Chamber*. For Cao Xueqin, imagining or remembering the ideal world that had been lost was still possible, but a century later, Wei Xiuren experienced a more devastating loss in the sense that there was no "lost world" for him to return to. His relationship with that unitary, complete world is expressed only through fragmentary recollections.

In chapter 5 of *Traces of Flowers and the Moon*, Chizhu spends a night at a temple and has a dream about enlightenment that he can recollect only partially the next day. He recalls seeing a couplet on a temple door: "Autumn moon and spring wind, how pitiful the way things are. / Azure Heaven and blue ocean, in vain is the cry 'what is to be done?'" 秋月春風，可憐如此; 青天碧海，徒喚奈何. In *Dream of the Red Chamber*, Baoyu sees a comparable couplet before he enters the Land of Illusion: "Ancient earth and sky, marvel that love's passion should outlast all time; / star-crossed men and maids, groan that love's debts should be so hard to pay" 厚地高天，堪嘆古今情不盡; 痴男怨女，可憐風月債難償.[43] Chizhu recalls other details: he sees a stele with a lengthy inscription and starts to read it out loud, whereupon the stele falls on him and he wakes up. There is a stele, too, in *Dream of the Red Chamber*, inscribed with the story of Baoyu and the Jia family. Stone steles traditionally are taken to reveal, as Jing Wang notes, "the divine order through the medium of written words."[44] So the stele that crashes down on Chizhu in the dream implies a catastrophe that goes well beyond an unfortunate personal accident.

Chizhu attempts to write down what he remembers of the writing on the stele, but is interrupted by pauses and fails to remember. The omniscient narrator notes: "He felt that he could fully recall the beginning and concluding sections. As for the middle part with two sections, he had forgotten about half of it" 覺得首尾二段，是全記得，中

43. Hawkes and Minford, *The Story of the Stone*, 1:130. The character *qing* 青 is homophonous of *qing* 情, which means feelings and emotions. Therefore, the second line can also be translated as "Heaven of feelings and seas of emotions, in vain is the cry 'what is to be done.'"

44. Jing Wang, *The Story of Stone*, 74.

間兩段，什忘四五. As Chizhu continues recalling the dream experience, he comments: "Strange indeed. This is like a story of my own family" 怪呀，竟是我家的故事了. Chizhu sometimes fills in the blank space of the forgotten characters with circles,[45] but he manages to reconstruct a few lines: "Clad in a light fur coat and riding a swift horse, I arrive at Yuzao Pass when the frost is deep. / Amid the sounds of the cold horn and pure fife, the moon chills the foot of the Rouge Mountain. Seeing millet of uneven height, I lament the former palace after its devastation by barbarians. / Listening to clear tunes of *Yi* and *Liang*,[46] I feel the frustration and grief conveyed by plucked strings" 輕裘快馬，霜嚴榆棗關前。寒角清笳，月冷胭脂山下。弔故宮于劉石，禾黍高低，聆冷調于伊凉，箏琶激楚.[47] Writing down these couplets, Chizhu comments that they could serve as his epitaph.[48] He also notes the pathos of the speaker's situation and the formal eloquence of the phrasing, all the more reason he should recall the words that he has forgotten. Composition, he notes, is easier than recall.

The formal style of writing that Chizhu notices on the stele is known as "parallel prose," which employs conceptually contrasting or complementary images to describe a world that embodies the cosmic principle of harmony and balance.[49] The form fits a world where all things fall into properly delineated categories, so Chizhu's failure to reconstruct this prose implies a disjunction between that ideal world and his experience in the chaotic present. The disjunction has three components: the dream, Chizhu's incomplete recollection of that dream, and Wei Xiuren's construction of an autobiographical self

45. *HYH*, 30.

46. *Yi* and *Liang* are two elegiac pieces of music named after Yi Zhou and Liang Zhou, two frontier administrative areas formed after the Tang dynasty.

47. Liu and Shi were the barbarian (*Xiongnu*) leaders Liu Yuan 劉淵 (252–310) and Shi Le 石勒 (274–333) who came from the northwest and drove the Jin dynasty (266–420 CE) south of the Yangzi River, ending the rule of what was later called Western Jin (265–316 CE). See *Zhongguo tongshi*, 2:900–905. "Millet" alludes to the poem "The Millet" ("Shu li" 黍離) in *The Book of Odes* (*Shijing* 詩經). An early commentary of *The Book of Odes*, the Mao commentary (an influential Confucian text) interprets this poem as an aristocrat's lament of Zhou decline. See *Shijing zhuxi*, 194–97.

48. *HYH*, 30.

49. Ching-I Tu, "The Chinese Examination Essay." Also see Plaks, "Where the Lines Meet," 49.

through the event. The slippages and gaps are intriguing, for they give us a glimpse of what Wei Xiuren considered difficult to express at the time of composition—a difficulty very much induced by the generic expectations and constraints of parallel prose. For example, Chizhu could not remember what comes after this line: "At the time when autumn wind spreads the fragrance of sweet osmanthus, his name is inscribed on the list of successful examination candidates" 名題蕊榜，秋風高掇桂香.[50] The counterpart of these lines (the other half of the couplet) should probably describe heroic exploits or joyful marriage. However, given Wei Xiuren's situation in 1857 and 1858, even though he might still cherish hope of succeeding in the civil service examination, heroic exploits or joyful marriage must have seemed unimaginable. His protagonist is blocked in exactly the same way, in both Chizhu's recollection of the dream and the character design. The tension between writing and not writing, between revelation and hiddenness, highlights Wei's struggle between hope and despair as he faced an uncertain future. The tragedy for Chizhu, unlike Baoyu's disillusion in *Dream of the Red Chamber*, is not about failing to remember the divine message. Instead, his plight lies in remembering only enough to sense what he has lost.

Wei Xiuren, like many of his contemporaries, reflected on and expressed the self through words in an extraordinary historical moment. Compared with others, he conveys his most private experiences and feelings under the cloak of fictionality by exploring the dialectic between illusion and disillusionment, a dialectic we've seen already, in a very different age, in *Dream of the Red Chamber*. In both Wei's and Cao Xueqin's works, "what is most intensely private can become public . . . through the ironic distance the writer sets up between himself and his fictional illusion."[51] Wei Xiuren attempts to make sense of his world by constructing a coherent realm of illusion in his tale of Chizhu, and in the process lays bare the disjunction between the ideals informing the classic Chinese literary tradition and his unsettling reality.

50. *HYH*, 30.
51. Wai-yee Li, *Enchantment and Disenchantment*, 177.

## Romance in the Metatheater

Even though the loss of the golden world of *Dream of the Red Chamber* proves to be permanent for its hero, not all is lost in *Traces of Flowers and the Moon*. Wei Xiuren justifies writing a personal romance by casting it as historically significant, and linking it to the tradition exemplified in the seventeenth-century play *The Peach Blossom Fan*. In making the autobiographical character Chizhu the "male lead" in the novel, Wei draws from the genres of fiction, autobiography, and drama. Nevertheless, his invocation of *The Peach Blossom Fan* is as fragmentary as his appropriation of the tropes and elements from *Dream of the Red Chamber*.

Autobiographical writings in late imperial China feature a range of narrative devices and overlap with many literary genres, such as poetry, biography, and elegy. Although documenting one's own life is arguably "authentic," there has always been an interest in the dialectics between fiction and reality in autobiographical writings.[52] During the late Ming era, autobiography reached its golden age: "The Buddhist view of human existence, the syncretic emphasis on sin and punishment, the reality of social and economic disintegration, corrupt administrations under some of the worst emperors, the decline in moral behavior of the gentry and literati, and the brutal persecution and martyrdom of Neo-Confucian officials all played a part."[53] Writers' self-portrayals feature the desire for self-invention, as we see in the writings of Mao Qiling 毛奇齡 (1623–1716) and Wang Zhi 王直 (1379–1462), who presented themselves as heroes fulfilling Confucian moral ideals.[54]

After the Ming-Qing transition, the explicit, playful, and celebratory tones of late Ming autobiographical writings gradually faded; under Qing political and cultural pressure, more indirect, somber reflections on the self became essential tools in writers' self-representation as they searched for the cause of the dynastic fall. The most illustrative

---

52. Liao Cho-cheng surveys autobiographical writings in China from ancient to modern times. See "Zizhuan wen yanjiu," 68–77.

53. Wu Pei-yi, *The Confucian's Progress*, 233.

54. Wu Pei-yi, *The Confucian's Progress*, 233.

examples may be plays by writers such as Wu Weiye 吳偉業 (1609–1671) and You Tong 尤侗 (1618–1704). Their writings give voice indirectly, through role play and staging, to the most private feelings.[55] In fact, some of their role-playing could also happen offstage. For instance, Wu Weiye, one of the most prominent poets of his time, is famous for giving these last words on his deathbed: "When I die, dress me in a monk's garb . . . and erect a rounded rock before my tomb with the inscription: 'Here lies the poet Wu Meicun [Wu Mei-ts'un].'"[56] As he faced death, Wu wanted to assert control over his posthumous reputation and acknowledge the controversial positions he had taken, deliberately choosing the role of poet-monk.

*Traces of Flowers and the Moon* picks up this late Ming tradition of autobiography and develops it in the early Qing literary mode, which sets a distance between the subject and the feelings/objects under representation. Wei Xiuren's continuation and adaptation of those traditions is first seen in the simulated theatrical space of the novel: his metatheatrical representation of reality. The way the novel frames its main story recalls a seventeenth-century short story collection, *Idle Tales from the Bean Arbor* (*Doupeng xian hua* 豆棚閒話), as well as Kong Shangren's *The Peach Blossom Fan*, both of which reflect on the Ming-Qing transition.[57] Like *Idle Tales from the Bean Arbor*, *Traces of Flowers and the Moon* employs a framing device. In the frame story, an anonymous storyteller, "I" (*xiaozi* 小子), discovers the book of *Traces of Flowers and the Moon* by chance as he plows a field. Several years later, his hometown is afflicted with a drought. He then flees his hometown, telling the story of "Traces of Flowers and the Moon" to make a living and support his old mother. Before introducing himself, the narrator draws an analogy between life and performance, asserting

55. Tschanz, "Wu Weiye's Dramatic Works," 427–54. See his discussion of the autobiographical sentiment in Wu Weiye's *Tongtian tai*, 449–50. Zeitlin, "Spirit Writing and Performance," 127. Liao Yan wrote three plays (*Zui huatu* 醉畫圖, *Su pipa* 訴琵琶, and *Jinghua ting* 鏡花亭), casting himself as the leading male role in each; he frequently reflects on his identity as an author and the meaning of writing. See Liao Yan, *Liao Yan quanji*, 2:588–610.

56. Kang-i Sun Chang, "The Idea of Mask in Wu Wei-yeh," 289.

57. On *Idle Tales from the Bean Arbor*, see Hanan, *The Chinese Vernacular Story*, 195–98.

that people hide themselves behind masks to fulfill the expectations and obligations of social roles. In saying this, he signposts the dialectical relationship between reality and fiction that the main story explores. Chapter 1 ends thusly: "The weather today is clear and bright; if you have nothing else to attend to, why don't you come to the teashop at the entrance of Willow Alley and listen to my telling of *Traces of Flowers and the Moon*" 今日天氣晴明，諸君閒暇無事，何不往柳巷口一味涼茶肆聽小子講《花月痕》去也.[58] This setup is similar to the opening of *Idle Tales from the Bean Arbor*, where men and women share stories with one another as they rest in the shade. It also brings to mind *The Peach Blossom Fan*, which opens when the protagonist Hou Fangyu joins friends to watch a performance by Liu Jingting, a famous storyteller whose surname means "willow." In that scene, Liu Jingting sings about musicians who fled political disorder during the Spring and Autumn Period (770–476 BCE), a chaotic time that echoes the background against which the main story of *The Peach Blossom Fan* is situated. In framing the narrative in the way it does, chapter 1 of *Traces of Flowers and the Moon* explains how the story to be told has been recovered from the ruins of history, therefore representing history as an object of reflection from the perspective of the present.

If chapter 1 of the novel frames the main plot as a storytelling performance, the "fourth wall" of this performance is frequently broken by the intrusion of the storyteller, a distinct rhetorical device in Chinese vernacular fiction.[59] By acknowledging the existence of an imagined audience, the writer gives the impression that his autobiographical self—and other characters—are engaged in role-playing in an illusory world. In *Traces of Flowers and the Moon*, the phrase *kanguan* 看官, meaning "readers," appears more than fifty times, far exceeding the frequency

58. *HYH*, 5.

59. On how this rhetorical device creates a dialogical engagement between the narrator and the imagined audience, see Hanan, *The Chinese Vernacular Story*, and Idema, *Chinese Vernacular Fiction*. Idema writes: "The storyteller's manner provided a convenient means to present the *Leitatikel* (the editor) and to draw conclusions, besides providing a convenient and lively way to link up the individual stories that form one *hua-pen*" (40).

in other major literati novels.[60] In Wei's usage, the rhetorical device usually precedes a description of a character's psychology and of plot elements that represent real historical figures and events. He addresses *kanguan* to justify the representations of feelings and situations that are difficult to describe. For instance, in chapter 11, when Chizhu bursts into tears after receiving a letter from home about the tragedies that happened to his family, the narrator asks: "*Kanguan*, what do you think this is about?" 看官，你道為甚麼呢. The simulated storyteller then relates the content of this letter.[61] As I have shown, based on what we know about Wei Xiuren's life, in reality misfortunes befell his family when he was traveling. Hence, disturbing news and strong sentiments drawn from life are transposed into this fictional world. In another scene, when the novel introduces Doggy Head, the character based on the Taiping rebel leader Chen Yucheng 陳玉成 (1837–1862), whose distinctive physiognomy earned him the nickname of "Four-eyed Dog," the writer/narrator asks a rhetorical question: "*Kanguan*, who do you think the Four-eyed Dog is?" 看官，你道這四眼狗是誰.[62] During moments such as these, the writer deliberately creates a performative effect and thereby evokes the illusion of direct address. A similar effect is achieved in *The Peach Blossom Fan*, which reflects on history through the conventions of theater.[63]

The backdrop of *Traces of Flowers and the Moon* is the ubiquitous and persistent mid-nineteenth-century political turmoil that included both domestic rebellions and foreign invasions: "For years, the bandit rebels had devastated the coastal provinces via sea routes: in the north, they were active in Tianjin, Dengzhou, and Laizhou; in the south, they

60. In Chinese fiction from the sixteenth to the eighteenth century, *kanguan* is used at critical moments when authorial presence or an important comment is inserted into fictional narrative, for example, *The Plum in the Golden Vase*, *Water Margin*, and *A Romance to Awaken the World* (*Xing shi yinyuan zhuan* 醒世姻緣傳).

61. *HYH*, 71.

62. *HYH*, 365. There is a mole under each of Chen Yucheng's eyes, so he was given the nickname of "Four-eyed Dog" (*Siyan gou* 四眼狗). The appellation "Four-eyed Dog" is used by many Qing writings to refer to Chen Yucheng: for example, in one of the home letters of Zeng Guofan, *Zeng Wenzheng gong jiashu quanji*, 331.

63. On the use of theatrical convention in *The Peach Blossom Fan*, see Struve, "History and *The Peach Blossom Fan*."

brought troubles to Zhejiang from Ningbo, and to the Three Rivers from Guazhou" 逆倭連年由海道蹂躪各省、北天津、登、萊，南則由寧波滋擾浙江，由瓜州滋擾三江.[64] Casting himself as a tragic character (Chizhu) performing on the stage of history, Wei Xiuren "us[es] the feelings of union and separation to depict the pathos of the rise and fall of dynasties" 借兒女之情，寫興亡之感 as was done in *The Peach Blossom Fan*.[65]

*Traces of Flowers and the Moon* borrows allusions and expressions from *The Peach Blossom Fan* to establish a connection to the latter's elegiac reflections on dynastic change. A case in point is its evocation of *qing* 情 (emotions, feelings, attachments). An important concept in late Ming discourse, *qing* is also expounded upon in other post-Taiping writings, as the following chapters will show. At various points in the book, Wei Xiuren is tempted to follow the example of Kong Shangren's Hou Fangyu and Li Xiangjun in choosing Daoist renunciation. In chapter 16, for example, the titles of the last two scenes in *The Peach Blossom Fan*—"Finding Refuge in Temples" (*qi zhen* 棲真) and "Entering the Way" (*wu dao* 悟道)—are recalled at a drinking party where Wei's main characters gather. Another example comes in chapter 1 of the novel, where an interlocutor argues with the storyteller: "You talk such nonsense about the 'seeds of feeling' and the 'root of feeling.' Even if there is a field of feelings, I am going to tramp it down to nothing, so how can the 'seed of feeling' and the 'root of feeling' be preserved?" 你說什麼情種，又是什麼情根，我便情田也要踏破，何從留點根留點種呢.[66] His statement paraphrases something that the Daoist Zhang says to Hou Fangyu and Li Xiangjun as they rejoice in their reunion after suffering many adversities: "What are you babbling about? What are you saying? At this moment when earth crumbles and heaven is overturned, you still cling to the roots of love and the seeds of desire. Is that not ludicrous!" 你們絮絮叨叨，說的俱是那裏話。當此地覆天翻，還

64. The Three Rivers area is where the Song 松江, the Qiantang 錢塘江, and the Puyang Rivers 浦陽江 meet, in southeastern China. *HYH*, 18. The bandits, possibly referring to the invaders during the Second Opium War (1856–1860), are called *wo* 倭, like the Japanese pirates of the Ming dynasty.

65. Kong Shangren, *Taohua shan*, 1; Wai-yee Li, *The Peach Blossom Fan*, unpublished manuscript.

66. *HYH*, 2.

戀情根欲種，豈不可笑.[67] As Hou Fangyu responds that it is natural for man and woman to desire each other, Zhang castigates him and wins the argument by asking: "Where is your country? Where are your homes? Where is your ruler? Where is your father? Can this bit of romantic love not be cut off?" 看國在那裏，家在那裏，君在那裏，父在那裏，偏是這點花月情根，割他不斷麼.[68] In Wei's novel, however, the storyteller continues to affirm the value of feelings and attachment in the main story that follows. Wei Xiuren draws back just when he is on the verge of directly addressing the topic of dynastic fall. In addition, the Daoist Zhang's remarks about "root of feelings" appear at the conclusion of *The Peach Blossom Fan*, but *Traces of Flowers and the Moon* refers to this plot element in the very first chapter, so it gestures to the author's explicit engagement with the literary tradition as one of the major themes of the novel. At the end of the novel, Chizhu and Qiuhen, like Kong's lovers, become Daoist immortals who reunite in the land of eternity—but *Traces of Flowers and the Moon* is more about Chizhu's escape from his personal dilemma than about finding a solution for the national trauma.

Wei Xiuren gives some degree of historical significance to his alter ego's life and failed romance before constructing a personal escape. One way he does this is by evoking two famous early Qing courtesans represented as moral paragons in the literary imagination. In one preface, Wei Xiuren describes Chizhu as a talented man whose worth is not recognized and asks: "How could Li Xiang and Fang Zhi slight him merely because he is lowly and poor?" 李香、方芷，烏得以微賤而少之.[69] Both Li Xiang and Fang Zhi were courtesans who lived through the Ming-Qing transition; they are remembered as literary and cultural icons who protested against corrupt late Ming officials and the violence

---

67. Kong Shangren, *Taohua shan*, 257; Wai-yee Li, *The Peach Blossom Fan*, unpublished manuscript.

68. Kong Shangren, *Taohua shan*, 257; Wai-yee Li, *The Peach Blossom Fan*, unpublished manuscript. In this context, "root of feelings" (*qing gen* 情根) unambiguously harks back to the tradition of *The Peach Blossom Fan*, but it should also be noted that *qing gen* is a generic term that appears often in individual collections, vernacular fictions, and religious texts.

69. *HYH*, 421.

of the Qing conquest.[70] This particular statement in the preface implicitly compares Qiuhen to the women remembered in history for their loyalty to the fallen dynasty. However, in the novel, Qiuhen is dedicated to Chizhu, not the disintegrating empire. If the writer's "murder" of his autobiographical self in chapter 43 is the pinnacle of the sentiment of self-denial and abasement expressed in previous chapters, Qiuhen's suicide (she "follows him in death") seems only to retrospectively affirm Chizhu's life and provide it with meaning. The object of female loyalty thus shifts from empire to an individual man. From the way their story ends we see how far the literary ideals have fallen by the wayside: Daoist enlightenment and female virtues symbolic of political integrity in *The Peach Blossom Fan* appear only as residual fragments in *Traces of Flowers and the Moon*.

Wei's final attempt to cling to the illusory realm is shown in a story element of chapter 52, where he re-creates the romance of the main characters through dream and performance. An old friend of Chizhu, who lodges at a house where the main characters used to meet, dreams that the two couples, Chizhu and Qiuhen, and Han Hesheng and Du Caiqiu (whose romance is more successful), come together at the annual Double Ninth Festival and perform their roles on a theater stage that simulates the coherent world of a southern play. The derivation of this particular scene in the novel is open to interpretation: it might draw on Wei's own experience of the Double Ninth Festival in 1857, early in his relationship with his lover, therefore a happy occasion; or it may be a reworking of memories of a mournful and sad Double Ninth Festival in 1858, when Wei Xiuren left Shaanxi. Whichever memory is evoked or reworked here, the theatrically mediated Double Ninth Festival in chapter 52 (like the festival Wei alludes to in his poem that adapts "Mocking the Recluse of the Wood of Red Leaves on the Seventh Day of the Seventh Month") simultaneously looks back to a blissful past, anticipates the nostalgia he will feel at future occurrences of the festival, and sets up a wishful construction of eternal happiness in an illusory

70. The story about Fang Zhi can be found in Shen Qifeng, *Xie duo*, 143. On how Li Xiangjun and Fang Zhi became the epitome of loyalty in early and late Qing memory of the Ming-Qing transition, see Wai-yee Li, *Women and National Trauma*, 304, 389. Fang Zhi's story became popular only in the late Qing.

realm. The scene collapses past, present, and future through the literary manipulation of personal memories. This moment of eternity, however, is also fleeting, as it can only take the form of a momentary event, a brief scene in a theater.

## A Tapestry of Traces

To point to the gaps between fiction and reality, as well as to bring together fragments borrowed from various lyrical traditions, Wei Xiuren develops a metaphor of "traces." The background and unfolding of the metaphor are explained in the preface and epilogue of the novel. However, before approaching this theme of "traces" more directly, Wei Xiuren invokes other categories to frame his novel. In the preface, he discusses two pairs of dialectical concepts: right and wrong (shi 是 and fei 非), separation and union (li 離 and he 合):

> Things under Heaven will not go beyond the two categories of right and wrong; trends under Heaven will not go beyond the two categories of separation and reunion. If one wants to make things right, it is acceptable to compromise for the sake of the right. If one wants the trend of reunion/union, it is acceptable to take the trouble to achieve reunion. However, for the things caught between right and wrong, and the trends lingering between separation and reunion, is there anyone else who is like these four persons: Han and Du, Wei and Liu?
>
> 夫天下之事，是與非二者而已；天下之勢，離與合二者而已。其事而是焉者，委曲以求其是可也；其勢而合焉者，輾轉以求其合可也。若夫事介在是非之間，勢介在離合之際，孰有如韓杜、韋劉之四人者乎？[71]

The opening sentence, following an ontological or structural convention in traditional Chinese drama and fiction, frames the novel within a world governed by moral order and fate. The characters are carefully designed to represent and manifest this worldview of the universe. The peculiarity of the characters, however, is that they are caught in limbo between right and wrong, separation and reunion. The narrative tension,

71. HYH, 421.

therefore, results from the way the characters fall outside the existing philosophical scheme that explains the world. As the preface elucidates, the couples' separation and reunion largely depend on historical contingency. But the statement that purports to reconcile opposites in fact casts into question eternal and universal binaries in the human condition, such as right and wrong, separation and reunion. The preface ends on an elegiac note: "[For those] whose encounters somehow resemble his [Wei/Chizhu's], we certainly know his white bones buried in yellow dust will move people to visit his tomb and mourn for him" 略同此日之遭逢，定知白骨黃塵，更動後人之憑弔. The tragic deaths of Chizhu and Qiuhen (notwithstanding their subsequent apotheosis) apparently contrast with the "grand reunion" (da tuanyuan 大團圓) kind of ending, a common literary trope in "scholar-and-beauty" romances where the male protagonist succeeds in the civil examination and marries the female protagonist with whom he is in love.

In the epilogue, dated a few months after the preface, the writer asks what the implications these stories of the four lovers are: "Are these traces of tears? Traces of blood? Traces of wine? Or, traces of flowers and the moon? I am about to surrender all of them to the Great Emptiness, and would like to have flowers and the moon in my heart to keep me company to the end of history" 淚之痕耶？血之痕耶？酒之痕耶？花月之痕耶？余方將盡付之太空，而願與此意中之花月相終古也.[72] Wei Xiuren muses on the meaning of "trace":

So-called "trace": a flower has it, the absence of a flower has it; the moon has it, the absence of the moon has it. What does it mean to say "the absence has it"? It is the property of a flower to blossom and fall, but since people have the intention of not letting it fall, the trace of flowers endures; it is the nature of the moon to wax and wane, but since people have the intention of not letting it wane, the trace of the moon endures.

夫所謂痕者，花有之，花不得而有之，月有之，月不得而有之者也。何謂不得而有之也？開而必落者，花之質固然也，自人有不欲落之之心，而花之痕遂長在矣；圓而必缺者，月之體亦固然也，自人有不欲缺之之心，而月之痕遂長在矣。[73]

72. HYH, 423.
73. HYH, 422.

How, he asks, can one retain possession of desirable objects when they are absent? His answer is that one retains a "trace" of them, a concept pointing to a range of psychological states: attachment, memory, and nostalgia, for example. Despite the differences between these states, they all occur as responses to the absence of beautiful but transient things, which now have become an absence, a past, and a history. Therefore, looming large behind the romantic images of flowers and the moon, the unspoken motif is the temporal gap between the delicate past and the unfulfilled present, generating "a sense of belatedness."[74] Moreover, as objects of the natural world, flowers and the moon follow cyclical seasons and patterns of waxing and waning. Unlike words such as "dream" and "shadow," which evoke the Buddhist idea of emptiness, the word "trace" implies a strong attachment to both the present and the past. Through his attachment, Wei Xiuren makes sense of his present existence in the ruins of history. *Hen* (trace), the last word in the title of his novel in Chinese, *Hua yue hen*, also means "scar," a physical mark of pain experienced and a wound inflicted: it denotes the violence of the past with ever-present disfigurement.[75] This permanent scar of the self, at the same time, is projected on the poetic imageries characterized by eternal cycles of traces.

## Writing after the War

Three days after he composed the epilogue, on his way back south, Wei Xiuren wrote in a poem that he had "exhausted all sorrowful songs in the world" 唱盡人間可哀曲.[76] However, the war that devastated Wei Xiuren's life would transform into a source of meaning for his last decades. After returning to his hometown in 1862 and until his death a decade later, Wei Xiuren continued writing both prose and poetry about recent history, published for the first time only in modern times

---

74. David Der-wei Wang, *Fin-de-Siècle Splendor*, 77–78. He reads the superiority given to "trace" as based on "derivative aesthetics," which aestheticizes the deprivation of the actual object as the fulfillment of desires and yearnings in imagination.

75. "Trace" may also have tragic undertone, as in "traces" of tears, blood, or wounds.

76. *WXRZZ*, 2:1083.

under the titles *Useless Words Written in Exasperation* (*Duoduo lu* 咄咄錄) and *Poetry Notes from the Gainan Mountain Studio* (*Gainan shanguan shihua* 陔南山館詩話).[77] He also added eight more chapters to the part of *Traces of Flowers and the Moon* that he had already completed. In these chapters, he transformed the war into a fantasy vindicating Chizhu's foresight. Once he started engaging with the history of the Taiping Civil War in *Useless Words*, Wei Xiuren himself became identified with traces of that war.

## Courtesans in a Surreal War

A comparison between Wei's representations of nineteenth-century history in *Useless Words* and the transposed echoes, or traces, of this history in *Traces of Flowers and the Moon* suggests that the monstrous nature of the Taiping War was too alien to be accommodated straightforwardly through fictional manipulation of historical facts. The novel's framing and plot turns are not history; instead, the author represents the war to be fundamentally based on supernatural power and magical tricks. Discharging his anger and exasperation into the rich historical details he amassed about the recent trauma, Wei paints a horrific picture. This picture is especially grotesque given the fluid boundary between imagination and historical witnessing: the real is as fantastic as the surreal.

Wei portrays the Taipings as enactors of sexual abuses to accuse them of lacking political morality. For example, he gives this scene: "As people searched the mansions of the rebel leaders, they cleaned up the kitchens and found more than ten piles of male members and dismembered female genital parts" 後來掃蕩偽王府，每府廚房，掃出男人陽物，女人陰戶，約有十余擔. After listing three courtiers in the rebel government who were famous for abducting women, ingratiating themselves with the rebel kings, and inventing grotesque methods of

---

77. "Useless Words" alludes to the phrase *duoduo shu kong* 咄咄書空. After being banished by the emperor, Yin Hao 殷浩(?– 356) spent days writing four characters in the air: *duoduo guaishi* 咄咄怪事 (lit. "a strange thing indeed"). See *Jin shu, ce 7, juan* 77:2047. The phrase was later used to refer to political discontent and frustration. The title *Poetry Notes from the Gainan Mountain Studio* refers to Wei's studio. *Useless Words* and *Poetry Notes* are both in *WXRZZ*. *Duoduo* also appears in Li Yu's 李漁 (1611–1680) poem written after the Ming-Qing dynastic transition. See Kile, *Towers in the Void*, 88.

torture (respectively), the writer asks, "Readers, materials like this do not even make true rebels. How could you expect them to guard cities? . . . Even if they occupy the entire southeastern region, given how they disregard human norms and the big picture, how could they hold the city for even one day?" 你道這個材料，做個鼠賊還算不得一個好漢，哪裡能守城池呢？. . . 就使東南各道，都占據完了，這不順人情，不顧大局，也怎樣守得一日呢.[78] These representations of the rebels, citing their depraved sexual practices, convey the writer's deep disdain for their moral and political identity.

In the last chapters of the novel, Wei allegorizes historical reality through fantastic warfare involving courtesans with supernatural power, nuns employing dark Daoist magic, and a vengeful female ghost. This is his counterfactual representation of an actual battle from the Taiping Civil War, the battle at the Terrace of Raining Flowers Mountain (Yuhua tai 雨花台) outside of Nanjing. In his historical writing, *Useless Words*, Wei gives an account that more or less agrees with what we know today about that battle, in which the Qing army broke through the Taiping guard. The battle began when the Qing general Zeng Guoquan stationed his troops at the Terrace of Raining Flowers in May 1862. It was a risky step because at that time, Zeng Guoquan had penetrated deep into the zone controlled by the Taipings. However, using smart military strategy and ample supplies from the Qing government, his troops conquered Nanjing on July 19, 1864, and thereby achieved the final victory of the war.[79]

Chapter 48 of the novel is titled "At the Ferry of Peach Leaf, Xiao Sanniang Arranges the Battle Formation / On the Terrace of Raining Flowers, Zhu Jiumei Manifests Her Numinous Power" ("Taoye du Xiao Sanniang paizhen, Yuhua tai Zhu Jiumei xianling" 桃葉渡蕭三娘排陣，雨花台朱九妹顯靈). In this chapter, Wei turns the weighty matter of the pivotal battle into a farcical and grotesque competition of supernatural skills between the courtesans (representing the Qing government) and Xiao Sanniang, the third daughter of Emperor Yuan of Liang (r. 552–555)—now a Daoist immortal, who sides with the rebels. In their

---

78. *HYH*, 393.

79. On the specific details of this war, see *Taiping tianguo zhanzheng quanshi*, 4:2435–553.

battle, the scene described in greatest detail is one in which Caiqiu leads the female troops to break through the enemy's "false *yin* troop formation" on water.[80] The *yin* troop formation was one of the main military tactics used in ancient China and was associated with water. The word *yin* in the name derives from the Daoist concept of *yin/yang*, but the formation itself did not necessarily take an explicitly gendered form. However, the novel's description of the battle suggests that in this fictional battle it assumed a female form: the *yin* troop formation here resembles female reproductive organs, and the process of breaking this formation simulates a penetration; the courtesan warriors representing the Qing force first break down the exterior defense walls made of iron and bronze, then enter a gradually enlarging passage. This *yin* troop formation was created by black magic, so the courtesan warriors do not see an enemy, but have to resist the weakening effects of sweet-toned music and sweet-smelling scent. The final victory comes when the ships of the formation scatter and disperse.

The Qing government to an extent is characterized by *yang* (it is politically orthodox; the character Han Hesheng is male and a Qing official). Nevertheless, the battle at the Terrace of Raining Flowers Mountain, a crucial battle during the Taiping Civil War, is associated with quintessential *yin* power in fictional imagination: both sides are represented by women. The *yin* power is reinforced by the subsequent appearance of the spirit of Zhu Jiumei, a beautiful and talented young woman killed by the Taiping rebels. Keith McMahon reads the episode as "an allegory . . . in which Chinese victory is linked with native sexual . . . energy pitted against a demonic enemy characterized by base sexuality."[81] I would take that a step further to argue that Wei Xiuren uses gender, especially the female gender, as a metaphor that captures

80. The origin of the *yin* troop formation can be traced to "Diagrams of Eight Troop Formations by Master Sun" 孫子八陣圖. The *yin* formation corresponds to the *yang* troop formation. The *yin* formation is associated with water, but the *yang* formation was used on land, and was especially useful on sloping terrain. A detailed exploration of military strategy in ancient China can be found in Lin Fan, "Knowledge, Power, and Technology." In *Traces of Flowers and the Moon*, the writer's addition of the derogatory adjective "false" to "*yin* formation" is in line with how the Qing elites typically referred to the Taiping regime and its practices, in order to show disapproval.

81. McMahon, *Polygamy and Sublime Passion*, 69.

the nature of the war, as evinced by the conquest of the rebels' "false *yin* troop formation." His configuration of the war as oversexed, animalistic, and absurd finds resonances in post-Taiping plays, too, and in short stories contemporaneous of *Traces of Flowers and the Moon*, as shown in the following chapters.

Wei's use of fantasy, magic, myth—"fiction of gods and demons" (*shenmo xiaoshuo* 神魔小說)—to capture the chaos and the absurdity of history appropriates a model best exemplified by *An Unofficial History of a Female Immortal* (*Nüxian waishi* 女仙外史). Written and published by Lü Xiong 呂熊 (fl. 1674) in 1711, this early Qing novel reconstructs the 1402 usurpation of the Ming dynasty in supernatural terms. Around the time of the Ming-Qing transition, such fictions were often employed to negotiate national trauma.[82] *An Unofficial History of a Female Immortal* concerns the earthly adventures of the moon goddess, Chang'e, when she is born in the human realm as the leader of a rebellion against the Ming Yongle Emperor (r. 1403–1425). Based on a real historical rebellion led by a peasant woman in 1429, the political connotation of this novel is significant, since the Yongle Emperor's usurpation of the throne jeopardizes the legitimacy of the entire lineage of the Ming emperors after him. Written in the aftermath of the Ming-Qing dynastic transition, *An Unofficial History of a Female Immortal* is characterized by "the fantastic mode [that] enables Lü Xiong to create an imagined alternative to heal the wounds in history. At the same time, he is only too aware that the power he has projected onto the female immortals and Māras (demons) is but a constructed fantasy."[83] In *Traces of Flowers and the Moon*, Wei comes to a similar conclusion.

Despite its closeness to *An Unofficial History of a Female Immortal*, the heroines in *Traces of Flowers and the Moon* are not as elevated as those in its early Qing predecessor. The women of *Traces of Flowers and the Moon* are courtesans, not female knights-errant. We see this clearly

---

82. Hu Sheng, *Ming Qing shenmo xiaoshuo yanjiu*, 91–95. Hu considers several early Qing novels to be allegories attempting to come to terms with the dynastic change. Though it is arguable whether or not these novels should be read as political allegories, after the fall of the Ming, the literary interest in "fiction of gods and demons" increased exponentially. In early Qing Nanjing, novels in this vein were popular. See Han Chunping, "Liudu Nanjing dui Ming dai."

83. Liu Chiung-Yun, "Ren, tian, mo," 44.

in Wei's description of the great battle in chapter 48, which shares characteristics with Lü's chapter "One Hundred Thousand Barbarian *Wo* Are Killed / A Couple of Beauties Establish Wondrous Merit" ("Shiwan woyi zao shajie, liangsan meinü jian qixun" 十萬倭夷遭殺劫，兩三美女建奇勳). In *An Unofficial History of a Female Immortal*, Lü offers a fantastic description of how fierce Japanese pirates (*wo* 倭) are instantly cut in half by two female knights from the Tang dynasty. The parallels between the two chapters are obvious: both feature female leaders who triumph over the evil forces; both similarly describe the deployment of vast armies and the massive slaughter of soldiers. Nevertheless, unlike *An Unofficial History of a Female Immortal,* where the battling forces play roles predestined by Heaven, *Traces of Flowers and the Moon* connects neither party with Heaven. Neither is there any suggestion that the courtesans are destined to develop supernatural power and vanquish their enemies by carrying out the demonic war. In short, whereas *An Unofficial History of a Female Immortal* has an overarching framework that allegorizes and thereby justifies earthly political turmoil, there is no such framework in *Traces of Flowers and the Moon.*

Another significant difference between the two works is in the status of the figure of the moon goddess, Chang'e, whom the courtesans of Wei's novel point out had a love affair (just as they had) that transgressed Confucian moral and social order. They refer to the legend in which Emperor Taizong of Tang (r. 626–649) visits Chang'e at the Moon Palace, which has been adapted in many versions in drama and fiction.[84] In traditional culture, Chang'e has always been portrayed as an embodiment of purity and chastity.[85] However, in literary works created after the Ming-Qing dynastic transition, Chang'e is also associated with dynastic upheaval, as shown in *An Unofficial History of a Female Immortal* and the *chuanqi* play *The Palace of Eternal Life* (*Changsheng dian* 長生殿) written by Hong Sheng 洪昇 (1645–1704). In *Traces of Flowers and the Moon,* the portrayal of Chang'e is not only

84. On the various versions of this legend, see Li Chunyan, "Tang Minghuang you yuegong."

85. For instance, *Tianbao yishi zhugong diao* 天寶遺事諸宮調 from the Yuan dynasty. See Li Chunyan, "Tang Minghuang you yuegong," 23.

disrespectful: it is profane and obscene, symbolizing the loss of order and hierarchy in the time of the novel. Through the courtesans' mouths, the writer expresses his disillusionment in a literary ideal once held dear in traditional Chinese culture.

Wei's novel may emulate the model of *An Unofficial History of a Female Immortal*, but it does so in as broken and fragmented a way as its emulation of the models of *Dream of the Red Chamber* and *The Peach Blossom Fan*. The rebels are so alien that their practices seem to be fantastic and surreal; in the war, humans are reduced to their sexual organs; the moon goddess has been degraded. Wei has severed himself from what writers in the past identified with in their effort to find order in chaos. Nevertheless, something new emerges from the wreck, as Wei tentatively introduces a redemptive power to confront such darkness: the spirits of a female victim of the war and of the autobiographical hero, two characters respectively embodying virtue and political insights.

## The Vengeful Female Ghost

Jacques Derrida spoke of ghosts as an important tool for conceptualizing historical justice: "It is necessary to speak of the ghost, indeed to the ghost and with it. . . . No justice . . . seems possible or thinkable without the principle of some responsibility, beyond all living present, within that which disjoins the living present, before the ghosts of those who are not born or who are already dead, be they victims of wars, political or other kinds of violence."[86] Ghosts—or at least, what they represent—raise troubling questions about the present when they expose the uncertainties and indeterminacies of the temporal continuum. In both early Qing and modern times, as Judith Zeitlin and David Der-wei Wang separately point out, a returning ghost causes traumatic memories to surface.[87] In *Stories about the Strange from Liaozhai Studio*, several stories about ghosts of late Ming palace ladies "enable the threatening memory of the old dynasty to surface, to be tamed and

86. Derrida, *Specters of Marx*, xix.
87. Zeitlin, *The Phantom Heroine*; David Der-wei Wang, *The Monster That Is History*.

rehabilitated, and finally put to rest and purged."[88] Among the ghosts that haunt post-Taiping literature, we have the spirit of Zhu Jiumei in *Traces of Flowers and the Moon*.

Zhu Jiumei, whose spirit comes to the rescue of Caiqiu and Hesheng during the battle of the Terrace of Flowers and Rain, is a woman who died following her capture by the Taipings in historical reality. Among the numerous female figures that emerged after the Taiping War, Zhu Jiumei perhaps is the most famous because she embodies the conflation of female education and sexuality in both historical accounts and literary imaginations.[89] Her figure undergoes a metamorphosis over time, which can be traced in genres ranging from history, memoir, and miscellaneous notes to short story collections. In many ways, the representation of Zhu Jiumei in these accounts calls to mind how early Qing writers formed a literary space commanded by the metaphor of woman to come to terms with the fall of the Ming.[90] None of the accounts, including the one in Wei Xiuren's *Poetry Notes from the Gainan Mountain Studio*, represents Zhu Jiumei as a spirit or a ghost. In addition, among the numerous post-Taiping short stories about female ghosts (discussed in chapter 6), none of them features Zhu Jiumei as a specter. Therefore, the transformation of Zhu Jiumei into a vengeful ghost in the novel is probably Wei Xiuren's invention.

Zhu Jiumei in the novel is in some ways very similar to the Zhu Jiumei of Wei's *Poetry Notes*. In the novel, after asking the rhetorical question—"Readers, who do you think this Zhu Jiumei is?"—the narrator introduces her as a beautiful and talented woman who, after being abducted by the rebels, seeks protection from a Taiping official to avoid being drafted by the rebels to become a copy clerk (*nü bushu* 女簿書). An entry in *Poetry Notes* seems to be the source of this episode:

---

88. Zeitlin, *The Phantom Heroine*, 88.

89. In late imperial China, especially starting from the late Ming era, there was a heightened desire for learned mothers in gentry families, as shown by Dorothy Ko in *Teachers of the Inner Chambers*, 128, 157. The Taiping rebel's desire for a woman with education may reflect this cultural phenomenon in late imperial society.

90. Wai-yee Li, *Women and National Trauma*, 3.

There was Zhu Jiumei from Wuchang. Twenty years old, she was beautiful and good at composing poetry and prose. After she was abducted
by the Taiping rebels, she sought the protection of a Guangxi female
Taiping official. Each time when the female official was required to
report a possible candidate for a female copy clerk, she did not list her
name.... After their secret was disclosed, the female official was decap-
itated. Jiumei thus was assigned to serve in the palace of the Eastern King
rebel. She was then conferred [the position of] imperial concubine. As
she was conspiring to poison [Yang] Xiuqing [the Eastern King], a palace
lady discovered her scheme. [Jiumei was] burned to death.

有朱九妹者。武昌人。年二十。有姿色。能詩文。自為賊攜，依廣西偽女
官某。凡選女簿書，皆不列其名 . . . 後事泄，女官環首。九妹遂入偽東
府。結為妃。將酖秀清，為同伴者發覺。焚死。[91]

In the official histories compiled by both the Taipings and late Qing
historians, Zhu Jiumei's name stands out. In *The Edicts of the Divine
Will Made during the Heavenly Father's Descent to Earth*, there is an
incident in which the Heavenly Father descends to Earth to rebuke
Hong Xiuquan for treating his son and the female officials in the Heavenly Palace too harshly, including Zhu Jiumei. An interesting twist in
this record is that the Heavenly Father, apparently on second thought,
decided to have these female officials sent to his own palace.[92] This
record suggests that Zhu Jiumei, a talented beauty, was an object of

91. *WXRZZ*, 1:691–2. *Nü bushu*: female copy clerk, an official position invented
by the Taipings. The Taiping regime is known for its employment of female officials
in political, cultural, and military fronts of state affairs. Women could also participate
in the civil examination set up in the Taiping Heavenly Kingdom. As shown in chapter 1, women played an important role in Yang Xiuqing's episodes of "trances." The
uneducated Taiping leaders seemed to take particular interest in well-educated
women. A female copy clerk probably worked as a secretary, and might also have been
an object of the Taiping leaders' sexual desires. A well-known female clerk from the
Taiping Kingdom is Fu Shanxiang, who will be introduced in more detail in chapter 6.
In any event, Zhu Jiumei's resistance to being a female copy clerk may be interpreted
as both her unwillingness to participate in the Taiping regime and determination
to preserve her chastity. The power of Zhu Jiumei's specter derives from her spirit of
resistance.

92. *TPTGYS*, 2:472.

Yang Xiuqing's desire. The other Taiping account about Zhu Jiumei is a placard announcing her execution because of her attempt to poison Yang Xiuqing.[93] In *Draft History of Qing* (*Qing shi gao* 清史稿) compiled in the 1920s, she is found in the listings of "Biographies of Notable Women" ("Lie nü zhuan" 列女傳). According to the account, she was originally from Wuchang, and was dismembered after Yang Xiuqing discovered that she served him wine containing poison.[94]

Aside from these official histories, Zhu Jiumei's name also appears in poems, memoirs, poetry notes, and plays written around the time of the Taiping War. A survey of the materials that survive suggests that stories about her circulated primarily in southern China. Of all the resources, *Brief Accounts in Jinling During the Guijia Years* (*Jinling guijia jishi lüe* 金陵癸甲紀事略) is considered the most historically accurate.[95] It was written by Xie Jiehe 謝介鶴 (fl. 1853–1856), who was captured by the Taipings and forced to work for them. Xie introduces the Taiping official from whom Zhu Jiumei sought protection. He presents a dramatic scene in which Yang Xiuqing, who, while receiving the divine intervention of the Heavenly Father, disclosed the secret and brought these two women to trial in front of a large congregation. Zhu Jiumei insisted on denying her literacy; for this, she received three hundred lashes. The female official was executed in front of Zhu Jiumei—the Taipings gouged out her eyes, cut off her breasts, cut out her heart, and beheaded her, to frighten onlookers. At the time, the weather suddenly turned violent, so other people who were involved in this incident were exempted from punishment. At the end of this very detailed entry, Xie concludes: "Zhu Jiumei sacrificed her life to plot against the rebels. [Though] her regret will last for thousands of years, how could there be any difference between her and the heroic man?" 朱九妹捐軀圖逆，遺憾千秋。媲烈丈夫何以異.[96]

93. Baiyun Shanren 白雲山人, *Dangping fani tu ji*, 290:417. Li Bin, *Zhongxing bieji*, 2:225.

94. Zhao Erxun, *Qing shi gao liezhuan*, 14133.

95. *Guijia* years: the first two years after the Taipings established their capital in Nanjing.

96. Xie Jiehe, *Jinling guijia jishi lüe*, 4:663.

Other accounts show how Zhu Jiumei's story transmuted as it traveled through different regions and time periods. Most accounts associate Zhu Jiumei with Hubei or Wuchang, but a few identify her hometown as Yangzhou or Nanjing (Jinling); both cities suffered severely in the seventeenth-century Manchu invasion and the nineteenth-century Taiping Civil War.[97] In all accounts, she is twenty years old and beautiful; in the versions that are dated relatively earlier, she is often said to be good at composing poetry and prose.[98] All versions except one say she was put to death because she attempted to poison Yang Xiuqing. The one exception, by Wang Pijiang 汪辟疆 (1887–1966), a Jiangxi scholar, has her jump from a boat into a river to commit suicide after being abducted; he claims that Zhu Jiumei hailed from Nanchang, the capital of Jiangxi. This account, however, is not backed up by any other source,[99] though it does suggest that there may have been stories about other chaste women known for their virtuous deaths during the Taiping period. *Traces of Flowers and the Moon*, a *chuanqi* play titled *Snow on the Pear Blossom* (*Lihua xue* 梨花雪), and the short story "Zhu Huixian" by Wang Tao all imagine that Zhu Jiumei's resistance takes place on a river.[100]

Among all the historical accounts and the short stories, Wang Tao's "Zhu Huixian" stands out because of how it synthesizes information from multiple sources. It fleshes out a background story for Zhu Jiumei,

97. For instance, Ding Rouke identifies Zhu Jiumei as being from Nanjing. Ding Rouke, *Liu hu*, 282. Ding is from Jiangsu Province.

98. As is seen in *Jinling guijia jishi lüe, Huannan yijia yan,* and *Liu hu.* The writers of these works were well aware of the importance of literacy in the Taiping-controlled region.

99. The story was originally published in 1915 in the magazine *Xiaoshuo hai* 小說海. Wang Pijiang, *Wang Pijiang shixue lunji,* 2:489.

100. *Lihua xue* was a *chuanqi* play by Xu E 徐鄂 (1844–1903). See Huntington, "The Captive's Revenge." Wang Tao's story appeared in his short story collection *Dunku lanyan,* first published in 1875 by *Shenbao.* According to Wang Tao's preface to this collection, all the stories had been written years before. If this is true, "Zhu Huixian" would have been written during or immediately after the Taiping Civil War. In the early Republican Era, individual stories from Wang Tao's collection *Dunku lanyan* were reprinted by editors and anthologists. For instance, "Zhu Huixian" also appears in Yifen Nüshi's 挹芬女史 *Minggui qiyuan ji* 名閨奇媛集, a collection of stories about virtuous women and their marvelous deeds, published in 1917.

a brilliant woman betrothed to a young man of good family, when the Taiping rebels conquered Wuchang. Among other abductees, she was captured and put on a boat to be sent down the Yangzi River to the Heavenly Capital. She tried to commit suicide by jumping into the water, but was saved by a female Taiping official. The official, who protected her and tried to hide her when Yang Xiuqing was searching for literate women, suffered a cruel death because of her actions.[101] Wang tells us how Zhu Huixian came to renounce suicide and instead to plot to kill Yang Xiuqing "for the sake of the people": she remembered a precedent, the late Ming palace Lady Fei, who murdered a rebel.[102] Collaborating with one of Yang Xiuqing's concubines, she poisoned Yang's wine; though he did not die, her plot was discovered, and she was executed.

As Wang Tao describes Zhu Jiumei's thinking, he harks back to literary imaginations of a late Ming palace lady, Lady Fei. She offers to take the place of the Princess Changping when Li Zicheng 李自成 (1606–1645) led his rebel troops into Beijing and occupied the imperial palace.[103] Lady Fei's righteous aura prevents Li Zicheng from even approaching her. He therefore gives her to a rebel general. On the night she is to marry him, she assassinates the general and commits suicide. Believing her to be Princess Changping, Li Zicheng does not search for the princess, so Lady Fei effectively protects the Ming imperial descendant through her heroic deeds.

Once again, a nineteenth-century author turns to the literary legacy of the Ming-Qing transition to conceptualize and represent the contemporary upheaval. Wang ends his story extolling the Taiping female official: "As for this woman who perished for the sake of

101. The scene in which Zhu Jiumei and the female official are sentenced matches that in *Jinling guijia jishi lüe*.

102. Wang Tao, *DKLY*, 1: *juan* 3, 2a–3b.

103. The story about Lady Fei is found in *Yu chu xu zhi* 虞初續志, a short story collection. Though *Yu chu xu zhi* was not published until 1802, Lady Fei's story had been circulating since the early Qing. Chen Weisong 陳維崧 (1625–1682), for example, has a poem praising Lady Fei in his *Furen ji* 婦人集 which had been circulated in manuscript form since the seventeenth century. (One of the earliest manuscript copies was dated 1791.) Lady Fei's story was also appropriated by many late Qing writers who extolled her as the paragon of morality and resistance who brought hope to the crumbling Ming dynasty. On her story and discussions of it, see Wai-yee Li, *Women and National Trauma*, 316.

protecting Jiumei, even scholars and officials would have found it difficult to act in that way!" 至某女以庇九妹之故而殞其軀，則尤士大夫之所難也.[104] It is interesting that Wang bases his judgment of this nameless woman from Guangxi on her motive and the outcome of her deeds, completely bypassing issues such as her education and whether she was beautiful or not, not to mention ideological constraints and political categories. Wang Tao's inclination to go beyond absolute moral and political boundaries will be further explored in chapter 6.

Among all the writings about Zhu Jiumei, Wei Xiuren's invention of her ghost identity is unique. He showcases her resolute courage and the sense of tragic sacrifice in her actions by casting her as a fierce ghost-spirit. In doing so, he evokes the literary and figurative connotations of ghosts in Chinese culture, particularly recalling seventeenth-century literary works that mediate traumatic memories of dynastic transition through returning female ghosts.[105] The description of Zhu Jiumei's death in the novel is different from the death he describes in his *Poetry Notes*. In the novel, magic enters the story: the unnamed rebel official assigns Zhu Jiumei to her disciple, who changes gender identity every half month. Determined to escape rape by this hermaphrodite, Zhu Jiumei commits suicide on a boat by stabbing herself with a dagger, and her corpse is discarded by the rebels under the Terrace of Raining Flowers. But that is not the end of her, in this story.

Returning female ghosts in the early Qing are represented mostly as delicate, elegantly dressed palace ladies from the fallen Ming dynasty. In comparison to those, the image of Zhu Jiumei's ghost in *Traces of Flowers and the Moon* exhibits a kind of imagination that exoticizes violent shocks of recent trauma through female nudity freshly marked by the war. In the novel, the scene in which Caiqiu and Hesheng are saved by Zhu Jiumei is sensational: the couple first feel a whiff of *yin* wind and smell blood in the air, and then see a ghost in the form of a naked woman's body covered in blood. The ghost announces that she is Zhu Jiumei. The emphasis on blood overtaking the visual and olfactory senses calls to mind the ubiquitous dead bodies of war; female nudity connotes woman's victimhood from sexual violation during the war or

---

104. Wang Tao, *DKLY*, 1: *juan* 3, 3b.
105. Zeitlin, *The Phantom Heroine*, 87–130.

the writer's eroticization of inexplicable violence. As chapter 6 shows, this kind of association between explicit female sexuality and wounds from violence also appears in Wang Tao's works: in the post-Taiping context, a new kind of imagination about gender and violence is born.

Zhu Jiumei's ghost symbolizes the resilient spirit that redeems not only herself but also others who perished in war. On the one hand, the painful memories are still fresh; on the other hand, the hope of rising from the ruins of history resides in collective resilience. Respectively, those sentiments are conveyed by the blood-soaked image of Zhu Jiumei's ghost and the poem attributed to her in the novel. In contrast to the prose description in this episode about Zhu Jiumei's spirit, this poem conveys not a sense of horror but a fighting spirit. This juxtaposition of opposites may be a result of the varied functions poetry and prose serve in traditional Chinese novels: poetry does not necessarily reflect or advance the overall narrative flow. The poem attributed to Zhu Jiumei begins in wistfulness:

| | |
|---|---|
| 晨光隱約上檐端， | Morning twilight touches the top of the roof, |
| 絳幘雞人促曉餐。 | The guards in red caps call for a morning meal.[106] |
| 顧影自憐風側側， | Standing in the wind, she sorrowfully takes pity on her shadow. |
| 回頭應惜步姍姍。 | Moving her delicate steps slowly, she looks back, reluctant to leave. |
| 蝦蟆堆上聽新法， | On the Toad Mound the "New Law" is announced, |
| 蟋蟀堂前憶舊歡。 | In front of the Cricket Hall the old joy is remembered. |
| 明日鴻溝還有約， | Tomorrow we still meet at the Hong Canal, |
| 大家努力莫偷安。 | We should try our best and not seek temporary ease. [107] |

106. *Jiren* 雞人 (literarily, chicken man) refers to ritual masters who are responsible for animal sacrifices and announcing the morning hours. *Zhou li zhengyi*, vol. 3, *juan* 32, 4b.

107. *HYH*, 390.

In this poem, the blood-soaked ghost-spirit is transformed into the ghost of a palace lady. As morning breaks, she must withdraw from the human realm, and yet she lingers; the dawning of the new day symbolizes, however, the imperial victory over the rebels, and the victory will avenge her wronged soul. The image of this ghost calls to mind Chen Weisong's "The Song of Lin Siniang" ("Lin Siniang ge" 林四娘歌), in which the spirit of a late Ming palace lady returns to cause trouble among the Qing, but later retreats from the human world where only her sorrowful songs linger.

The tone of the second half of Zhu Jiumei's poem changes from sadness to valor to hope, ending with a resolution of heroic endeavor. The fifth line of the poem draws a connection between the heroic action of a general of the Jin dynasty (1115–1234 CE) with the Qing army's fight for Nanjing. The line alludes to Guo Hama 郭虾蟆 (1192–1236), the general who guarded the last city of the Jin dynasty from Mongols after Emperor Aizong (r. 1224–1234) died and the capital had fallen into the enemy's hands. In the last battle, when it was impossible to repel the attacks any longer, Guo Hama summoned all his female relatives together with those of his officers to one room. He told his female relatives to burn themselves to death. His soldiers, upon exhausting their arrows and weapons, also walked into the fire. Guo Hama shot hundreds of enemies. Having depleted his arrows, he threw himself, with his bow and sword, into the blaze.[108] By linking this valiant and resolute figure with the "New Law," Wei Xiuren/Zhu Jiumei is signaling great admiration for heroic striving and suicide. "Cricket Hall" may allude to a story about the corrupt Song minister Jia Sidao 賈似道 (1213–1275), who watched crickets fighting at his "Hall of the Half-Immortal" (*Banxian tang* 半仙堂). Such frivolity may indeed have been the cause of the empire's subsequent military setbacks. Hence, the anticipation of action and resoluteness in the last two lines of the poem: tomorrow, a critical treaty is to be signed; its importance is equal to the Treaty of the Hong Canal, agreed to by the two rivals Xiang Yu 項羽 (232–202 BCE) and Liu Bang 劉邦 (247–195 BCE) as they struggled for supremacy. The treaty demarcated the north and the south of the territory of the old Qin

108. Tuotuo 脫脫 (1314–1356), *Jin shi*, 8:2708.

empire (221–207 BCE); it did not last long: the conflict reemerged and eventually ended with Liu Bang's victory and the establishment of the Han dynasty (202 BCE–220 CE). In the context of the 1860s, the treaty to be signed is one between the Qing government and representatives of Western interests. Thus, the speaker of the poem implies that more battles will be fought in the future. Overall, the speaker rises from the ruins of the past to confront the urgency of the present.

## The Hero in Liminal Space

Wei Xiuren adapts the literary tradition of the heroic Zhu Jiumei to validate hope and unyielding resolve. To do this for his story, he makes her a specter with magical powers. Wei also assigns otherworldly qualities to his autobiographical hero, Chizhu, so that his character also can embody traditional ideals and transcendental values. Imagining a range of possibilities for Chizhu's posthumous identity, Wei invokes the magical power of fantasy to transcend a wretched reality. Nevertheless, it seems that the hero ultimately fails to find a way to insert himself into the liminal space commanded by spiritual beings.

Chizhu has a divinely inspired dream before his death (see fig. 4.2). The sequence of the events, the specific scenarios, and the character's psychological activities all resonate uncannily with Hong Xiuquan's visionary journey. Both heavenly journeys begin with the subjects seeing a flash of light. Upon their arrival in Heaven, both Chizhu and Hong Xiuquan are invited to change their garments. They are both greeted by a celestial male figure before being introduced to their wife/lover. As in *The Taiping Heavenly Chronicle*, specific temporal markers play an important role in connecting the realms of Heaven and Earth in Chizhu's experience. He learns that in his life as a Daoist immortal, he had jurisdiction to handle a case but had misjudged it; this miscarriage of justice has caused endless sorrows to men and women of deep feeling. Therefore in the Heaven of Parting Sorrow (*li hen tian* 離恨天), the Jade Emperor removes him from his post. Chizhu and the female immortals who were his assistants are banished from Heaven in order to personally experience the anguish of emotional attachment. As with Hong Xiuquan, Chizhu's heavenly journey marks his change of identity: he has endured the sufferings of his earthly life and is about to resume his previous celestial position. Hong Xiuquan and Wei Xiuren shared similar yearnings to transcend this world, as evinced by their construction of the self as celestial being. The crucial difference, of course, is that Wei Xiuren stayed within the boundary of fiction, whereas Hong Xiuquan turned his vision into a sacred, religious scripture demanding collective political action.

The trope of "banished immortal" (*zhe xian* 謫仙) employed in the episode about Chizhu originates in Daoism and occurs frequently in writings from 1840s to 1880s. In this trope, an immortal makes a three-stage journey through the divine realm, the human realm, and the divine realm again (*shen jing, ren jing, shen jing* 神境，人境，神境).[109] The process is usually described in this way: an immortal is banished from Heaven for a mistake committed during their life in the human realm, goes through ordeals to compensate for the mistake, and is eventually restored to Heaven after repaying the karmic debt.[110] Bookending the realm of disorder (life in the human realm) with that governed by eternal order, this trope serves to justify individual and collective suffering on Earth. *An Unofficial History of a Female Immortal* uses this framework to rationalize early Ming political conflict. Hong Xiuquan's re-creation of this literary tradition may be the most influential in history: from Earth he travels to the Heavenly Realm, and he does not return to Heaven until all Chinese have been delivered to Heaven. The Taiping ambition was for everyone to ascend to Heaven; Wei Xiuren merely attempts to redeem his autobiographical self from his sorrowful and frustrating experiences.

Though stories of banished immortals conventionally end with the protagonist's return to Heaven, Chizhu in a sense remains in the human realm because he is commemorated as the embodiment of Confucian ideals. The writer has Han Hesheng collect Chizhu's poetry and put it into print, and thus has his autobiographical self fulfill the

---

109. Zhang Jinchi, "Lun *Shuihu zhuan* he *Xiyou ji*," 72. Even though *Shuihu zhuan* and *Xiyou ji* were formed in the late Ming era, the perennial theme of the "banished immortal" is salient in literary works from the 1840s to the 1880s.

110. Lee Fong-mao, "Chushen yu xiuxing," 72.

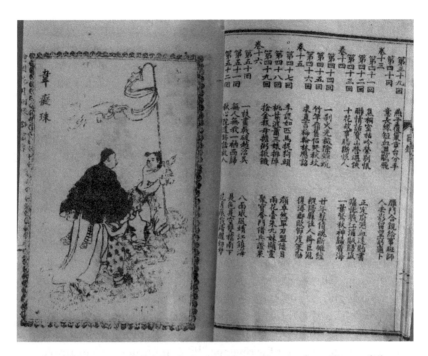

FIG. 4.2. Illustration of Wei Chizhu's ascension to Heaven, from *Traces of Flowers and the Moon* (*Hua yue hen*), publisher unknown, 1908.

Confucian ideal of "establishing words" (*li yan* 立言).[111] At the same time, the worldly accomplishments of Chizhu's son make good the major regrets that Chizhu, and by implication the writer, has had throughout his life: Xiaozhu transports his father's coffin back to the south to bury him properly, succeeds in the civil examinations and

111. Wei Xiuren was a prolific writer; among the works already noted he also wrote an exegesis on the classics. However, in the nineteenth and twentieth centuries only *Traces of Flowers and the Moon* was printed. It was not until the twenty-first century that his poetry collection, notes on poetry, and some historical accounts were printed. A detailed publishing history of Wei Xiuren's writings is found in Chen Qingyuan, "Wei Xiuren jiqi zazhu," in *WXRZZ*, 1:5–7. In addition, Wei Chizhu's illustrious posthumous career discussed here resonates with what Shang Wei observes about *Rulin waishi*'s representation of literati's struggles when their "prescribed roles in family, lineage, and local community cease to be fulfilling." Shang Wei, *Rulin waishi and Cultural Transformation*, 285.

wins imperial favor, marries a military general's daughter, and together this couple return to the south. Chizhu is also publicly commemorated through the epitaph Han Hesheng writes for him and by the shrine erected in his memory.[112] Not only all this, but Chizhu also "engages" with political affairs posthumously, through the military victories in the remainder of the novel, which prove his wisdom and foresight.

Chizhu also has an active afterlife as a ghost-spirit. His ghost allegedly haunts the house he previously lived in, making it uninhabitable, though his frustration and sadness never transform into outbursts of vehemence, as sometimes happened with other ghosts. The etymological origin of the Chinese character for "ghost" (*gui* 鬼) connotes return.[113] In the *Chronicle of Zuo*, a ghost of no proper return appears in the human realm in an inauspicious manner (meddling, troublesome).[114] "Ghost" has become a metaphor common to both traditional and modern Chinese literature, where there are abundant examples of reluctant ghosts lingering in the human realm because they are anchored by unfinished business, emotional attachments, and sentiments of the past.[115] Female ghosts tend to return "as much or more for love and desire as for a thirst for revenge."[116] Zhu Jiumei is an example, but Chizhu's ghost seems to be harmless and peripheral. As a ghost, he is inconspicuous and subdued, as if his spirit was not strong enough to make an appearance. This lack of power adds more ambiguity to the idealization of order in the novel's last few chapters.

112. There are three types of shrines (*citang*) in Chinese history. The first is the family shrine in which deceased ancestors are worshipped, popular especially during late imperial times. The second type is established to worship nature and divine beings. The third is a temple or shrine dedicated to a famous, heroic figure to allow the general public to offer sacrifices to them. Wang Heming and Wang Deng, *Zhongguo citang tonglun*. The shrine commemorating Wei Chizhu seems to serve the function of worship; his spirit becomes part of the divine world after his death, and the frequent references to his military insight implies that he is respected as a hero.

113. For example, in one of the early China classics, *Liezi*, there is "Ghost means returning" (*Gui, gui ye* 鬼，歸也). See *Liezi jishi*, 20.

114. See "Gui you suo gui, nai bu wei li" 鬼有所歸，乃不為厲, in *Chunqiu zuozhuan*, 4:1292.

115. David Der-wei Wang, *The Monster That Is History*, 266.

116. Zeitlin, *The Phantom Heroine*, 138. She also points out that, compared with female ghosts, male ghosts are usually represented as sheepish characters.

It could be argued that Chizhu's ghostly presence is redeemed by his identity as an eternal writer in Heaven. In the novel, about forty years after Chizhu's death, lines of his poetry appear, uncannily, on a planchette used for divination: "The fine eyebrows in the mirror are as remote as the sky" 鏡裏蛾眉天樣遠 and "I ruminate on all that has happened in the old dusty world" 前塵後事思量遍.[117] The first of these lines suggests Chizhu's romantic tribulations have become a distant past; the second implies a lingering, though tenuous, attachment to the earthly realm. At the end of the divination, more lines appear: "I am Wei Chizhu. Following the celestial order, I am going to the Palace of Illusion to compose essays. I cannot linger long here, and will leave now" 吾韋癡珠也。奉敕赴飄渺宮撰文,不能久留,去矣![118] After evoking and dismissing his worldly attachments, his spirit leaves for his greater work in Heaven.

Despite all the frames of order and posthumous identities that Wei has invented for his autobiographical self, he still needs to use the Daoist trope of the banished immortal at the novel's conclusion: restored to his celestial status, Chizhu thus manages to escape the ruins of history. The escape has a specific geographical location: an island in the "Fragrant Ocean." Taking a modern steamship from Xiangshan, Chizhu's son, Xiaozhu, and his wife arrive at the island and meet Chizhu and Qiuhen, who have become immortals. This episode recalls the tale of the Peach Blossom Spring, where a fisherman chances upon a village that has somehow been bypassed by history.[119] Wei connects this utopian place with Xiangshan, which is located in the Canton area including Guangzhou, the only seaport open to foreign trade since 1757. In doing so, Wei brings the West into his story, and a vision of an open and vast world inviting future exploration. There was considerable interest and excitement—and anxiety—about the ocean at the time, as serialized literature in major newspapers and magazines from the 1870s to the 1890s demonstrates.[120] Late Qing stories tend to emphasize the strangeness of the ocean, but *Traces of Flowers and the Moon*

117. *HYH*, 415.
118. *HYH*, 416.
119. This story appears in an essay by Tao Qian 陶潛 (365–427), *Tao Yuanming ji*, 100.
120. Huntington, "The Weird in Newspaper."

romanticizes it, and uses the concepts of Daoism to transform it into a desirable place. Thus, after constructing and dismantling various systems of order, the ultimate possible idyllic place the writer summons is one that points to the new global order with which China is on the verge of engaging. The struggle the writer experiences in exorcising his haunting memories, therefore, is dubiously resolved with the acknowledgment of foreignness.

To make sense of his historical existence as an educated man who had little influence on contemporary political affairs, the writer searched between Heaven and Earth in the fictional world for an identity that might render his existence relevant in history. His invention of the autobiographical self as a banished immortal, a perfect Confucian, living on through the people's memory and as a returning ghost constitutes a rather ambivalent way of engaging with history. On this site of the fictional self, many issues intersect, such as communicating divinity, Confucian morality, literati identity, and memories and ghosts of historical violence. Wei Xiuren's evocation of various tropes and traditions in attempting to conclude the story and restore a certain familiar order bring to mind the suspended ending of *The Taiping Heavenly Chronicle*: both texts attempt to moralize but find it difficult to conclude their narratives. Hong Xiuquan fights, literally, for a return to Heaven, which in the end doesn't materialize; Wei Xiuren struggles with his protagonist's fictional return to Heaven, which leads to a rather quiescent, anticlimactic ending to the novel.

## Returning to *Traces of Flowers and the Moon*

In 1873, as Wei Xiuren neared the end of his life, he reflected on *Traces of Flowers and the Moon*. His reflections are shown in his poem "On *Traces of Flowers and the Moon*" ("*Hua yue hen* tici" 花月痕題詞), which is composed of lines taken from the poems of Li Shangyin 李商隱(813–858). Li's times clearly parallel Wei's own. Li had witnessed the continuing decline of the Tang dynasty, which had started with the An Lushan Rebellion and worsened as a result of a series of peasant rebellions led by figures such as Wang Xianzhi 王仙芝 (?–878) and Huang Chao 黃巢 (?–884).

| | |
|---|---|
| 東山事往妓樓空， | Xie An's stories are no more; the brothel is empty of entertainers,[121] |
| 朱邸方酬力戰功。 | At the vermilion mansion, military excellence has just been rewarded.[122] |
| 欄藥日高紅髮鬆， | The sun shines high over the shimmering red of the balustrade of peonies,[123] |
| 斷無消息石榴紅。 | Cut off from all news, the pomegranate is still red.[124] |
| 生兒古有孫徵虜， | In the old days, a boy would become General Sun,[125] |
| 煙幌自應憐白紵。 | The thin smoke curtain is moved by the song "White Silk."[126] |
| 赤簫吹罷好相攜， | After playing the coral flute, we can now walk hand in hand,[127] |
| 嬛娥搗藥無時已。 | The Moon goddess pounds medicine, without ever letting up.[128] |
| 凍壁霜華交隱起， | Slowly in succession, flowers of frost appear and disappear on the frozen wall,[129] |

121. Quoting from Li Shangyin, "Zeng Zhao Xielü Xi" 贈趙協律晳, *LSYSG*, 1:51–55. Xie An 謝安 (320–385) was known for traveling with female entertainers. Xie An also went by the name Dongshan, or "Eastern Mountain."

122. Quoting from Li Shangyin, "Guo Yin Puyi jiu zhai" 過尹僕射舊宅, in *LSYSG*, 3:948–54. Yin Shen 尹慎 (744–811) was an accomplished late Tang general commended by the emperor. Li's poem begins with this line ("At the vermilion mansion"), which is followed by a line lamenting that only ruins remain. Li's original line is heroic, but in Wei's use of it, it conveys nostalgia.

123. Quoting from Li Shangyin, "Ri gao" 日高, in *LSYSG*, 5:1733–36. Li was imagining an inaccessible lady locked inside a palace; some scholars interpret the poem as political lament.

124. Quoting from Li Shangyin, "Wu ti" 無題, in *LSYSG*, 4:1451–60.

125. Quoting from Li Shangyin, "Man cheng" 漫成, in *LSYSG*, 3:912–28.

126. Quoting from Li Shangyin, "Bianshang song Li Ying zhi Suzhou" 汴上送李郢之蘇州, in *LSYSG*, 3:1009–14. The image is of a lonely poet yearning for like-minded friends. The song "White Silk" was popular in the Tang dynasty.

127. Quoting from Li Shangyin, "Yu shan," 玉山 in *LSYSG*, 1:318–22. The speaker imagines himself in the company of immortals.

128. Quoting from Li Shangyin, "Ji yuan," 寄遠 in *LSYSG*, 5:1777–79. The first two lines in Li's poem use two legendary figures to represent permanent rulers in the universe, and the last two describe drastic changes in history.

129. Quoting the last line in the last poem in Li's "Yantai si shou" 燕臺四首. See Li Shangyin, *LSYSG*, 1:79–98.

| 老耄曾孫更不來。 | Old men and young children will never come again.[130] |
| 空留暗記如蠶紙。 | Secret marks left in vain, like paper dotted with silkworm eggs.[131] |

Some readers fault Li's poetry for its ornate diction; others defend it as political allegory.[132] Since the mid-seventeenth century, as the Ming-Qing dynastic transition reshaped intellectual discourse, the argument supporting allegorical readings has gained ground.[133] Since it was written within the context of Qing commentary tradition, it is possible that Wei Xiuren's "re-creation" and adaptation of Li's literary legacy follows the trend of Qing exegesis that seeks deeper political meanings in the poems. But Wei clearly was also drawn by their aesthetic qualities. Wei Xiuren should have found Li's obsession with beautiful, but also fragile and transitory poetic images as appealing as the sentiments of nostalgia and lament in Li's poetry, since he employed this aesthetic mode in *Traces of Flowers and the Moon*. Neither Li Shangyin nor Wei Xiuren could have foreseen that about half a century after their deaths, their empires—empires that had enjoyed prosperity for hundreds of years—would collapse. Nevertheless, both were fascinated by the transience of beauty and human attachment, as well as the ephemerality of heroic achievement. Many traditional literary critics morally judged the "aesthetics of decadence," sometimes even blaming it for dynastic decline. Instead of drawing a causal relationship between this aesthetic mode and political upheavals, it may be more relevant to ask why this kind of aestheticism generated such resonance at the moments that precede the fall of dynasties.

130. Quoting from Li Shangyin, "Wuyi shan" 武夷山, in *LSYSG*, 5:1949–51. Li's poem is about a mountain that used to connect with the Heavenly Realm in ancient times, but it has now become a place no one visits.

131. Quoting from Li Shangyin, "Wu chou guo you chou qu: Bei Qi ge" 無愁果有愁曲北齊歌, in *LSYSG*, 1:15–21. Li's poem has a "ghostly" feel to it, especially the last four lines (which includes this line). In the edition *WXRZZ*, the last character is missing.

132. Owen, *The Late Tang*, 338.

133. See Rouzer, *Writing Another's Dream*, 30.

Wei Xiuren did not merely collect Li Shangyin's lines of poetry. He shapes the lines into a specific succession of images and scenes, therefore transforming the meaning and implications the lines carry in their original context. These selected images and scenes might have triggered memories, onto which the writer imposed an order to form a new narrative. As in *Traces of Flowers and the Moon*, the two instruments Wei Xiuren uses to understand and represent the world are the lyrical—which indirectly describes things through imagination and allusion—and the historical, which documents and defines the existence of things. Ultimately, Wei Xiuren uses Li Shangyin's rich poetic imagery to describe a journey of his own, blending together memory and imagination.

The first line of the poem "On *Traces of Flowers and the Moon*," with its measured, nostalgic tone, would remind readers of the romance between Wei Chizhu and Liu Qiuhen in *Traces of Flowers and the Moon*. The vermilion mansion suggests success, both social and financial, and its tie to "military excellence" echoes the wars and battles described in the novel. Life's achievements, however, are now bygone glories in this time of reflection. The next two lines shift attention to nature—the sun, peonies, a pomegranate—each of which in their own way supersedes transient human affairs. We may wonder whose attention, whose eye and mind, is drawn by these sights? The lines create a mild anxiety: what is implied by this absolutely still image of the sun over the balustrade? By the (red?) peonies, and the pomegranate, also red? Could redness be both literally descriptive and also metonymic for the beloved, as the red pavilion is a metonymy for worldly achievement? The phrase "absolutely no message from outside" suggests as much. The writer, then, borrows Li's lines and the implications of their original contexts to lament his own losses. There used to be heroes, such as Sun Quan 孫權 (182–252), but Chizhu—or the author—will always be the failed student. In the poem by Li Shangyin, "Random Composition" ("Man cheng" 漫成), which Wei quotes from here, Li first compares the refined life of the literati to the heroic one: "Let me ask: to spend a whole life with flutes and books— / How does that compare to looking up at banners during the Three Kingdoms?" 借問琴書終一世，何如旗蓋仰三分. However, with the line that follows, "The thin smoke curtain is moved by the song 'White Silk,'" Wei Xiuren makes a melancholic, rather self-pitying comment about life as a writer. In the last lines of the poem, Wei first evokes an image of the friends and company found in the realm of immortals, but immediately follows it with two chilling lines: the unceasing sound of medicine being pounded in a mortar, and the imaginary world freezing over; the only flowers now are flowers of frost. The closing lines withdraw from this realm and its illusions—all that passion, valor, and excitement came to nothing but ink dots on paper, in the end. The writer, having survived a horrendous war and its aftermath, finds in the poetic world that Li Shangyin created one thousand years before a way to understand and come to terms with the world he lives in and the life he now lives, but it is a very different vision from Li's.

The ambiguous rendition of heroism and glory in Wei's poem recalls the works of renowned early Qing poets such as Wu Weiye and Chen Zilong 陳子龍 (1608–1647), who uses mythological terms and illusions to describe historical personages and the members of imperial family, as well as those who witnessed, fought, and survived the Ming-Qing dynastic transition.[134] Fu Zhaolun 符兆綸 (fl. 1860s) used the phrase "melancholy beauty and mournful sentimentality" (*ai gan wan yan* 哀感頑豔) to describe the style of *Traces of Flowers and the Moon*, terms also used by literary critics to describe Wu Weiye's poetic style.[135] The style may be similar, but (as with Li Shangyin) the values are different. Early Qing poets transformed loyal generals and imperial family members into heroes and immortals; Wei Xiuren imagines himself as a hero and immortal—though in his work, the quality of that apotheosis is muted.

At possibly the most painful moment in his life, Wei Xiuren found a creative way to express his autobiographical impulse in fictional terms. Sifting through various literary and cultural conventions to contrive a means for a transcendence of the war-torn self, Wei constructs a metatheatrical world for his autobiographical hero to dwell in. But it

134. See, for instance, Wu Weiye's "Xiaoshi qingmen qu" 蕭史青門曲, discussed in Wai-yee Li, "History and Memory in Wu Weiye's Poetry," 117.

135. Fu Xueqiao [Zhaolun], "Ping yu" 評語, in *HYH*, 426.

is a world both fragmented and worn out. The various devices Wei employs prove inadequate for voicing the war's outrageous violence. With the scraps left from the collapse of Heaven, he projects a cynical vision of recent history, but at the very end of his novel allows that the future, and the world beyond China's shores, could serve as a possible escape. Toward the end of his life, as Wei Xiuren reflected on his traumatic encounters for one last time, he recalled in lyrical terms the two most critical moments of dynastic change in Chinese history: the late Tang and the Ming-Qing transitions. In doing so, he reconfigured the Taiping Civil War as yet another catastrophic moment in Chinese history, almost equivalent to dynastic fall.

CHAPTER FIVE

# *Violence in Drama*

## The Reinvention of Community

Many plays emerged during and after the Taiping Civil War, ranging from those that directly represent the war to those that evoke traumatic historical moments. They drew on stories and theatrical traditions from the past, but at the same time displayed new characteristics that diverged from conventional Chinese dramatic practices. These plays respond to an acute need to represent and mediate the violence occurring both in their own time and at critical comparable junctures in history.

Theater, perhaps more than any other cultural genre, allows a spectrum of emotions to arise and circulate among an audience, exhibiting various views during tumultuous times.[1] At the same time, structures, styles, staging, and character development can all be adapted rapidly to fit new circumstances. We see this experimentation happening in different ways among various playwrights following the war. *Chuanqi* plays, for example, known for their exceptional length (they often exceed forty scenes), were very popular among literati between the sixteenth and eighteenth centuries. However, after the Taiping Civil War, many writers chose to write shorter *zaju* 雜劇 plays. These plays could presumably be written and produced more rapidly, providing a faster and

---

1. Idema, "Drama after the Conquest," 377.

more direct medium for people to express themselves and record the history they had witnessed.

In comparison to diaries and fiction, neither of which circulated widely either during or immediately after the war, postwar plays often found an audience as soon as they were published, on both page and stage. The large amount of paratext surrounding the plays, including prefaces and commentaries penned by the playwrights' friends, indicates the extent of this community, as well as the role played by theater among survivors of the catastrophe. All these interconnections were an important part of the theater scene of the time. As Lam Ling Hon reminds us, theater is not confined to a particular space of performance: it extends outward from the stage as what he calls "theatricality": "a notion of intermediation that is beside and beyond theater."[2]

## The Plays and the Playwrights

In the postwar community generally, feelings and emotions associated with the war were still raw, and everyday life was not secure. The continuing political turbulence both endangered playwrights' lives and made the plays vulnerable. In the preface to his *The Calamity of the Red Ram*, a play that centers on the Taiping War, Zhu Shaoyi 朱紹頤 (1833–1880) wrote: "In the autumn of *jiayin* year, hearing the alert from the government, I left hastily to move to a distant place. The original copy of *The Calamity of the Red Ram* has been lost. Thus I record it based on what I remember" 甲寅秋，朱門告警，余匆匆遠徙。《紅羊劫》原本已經遺失 ... 因就記憶所及為錄出之。[3] In contrast, another playwright, Wei Xiyuan 魏熙元 (1830–1888) gave up trying to rescue his works after the war, which had claimed the lives of his whole family. In the epilogue of *Bitter "Blessings" for a Pedantic Scholar* (*Ru suan fu* 儒酸福), dated 1880, he writes: "In the old days, I composed four *chuanqi* plays. . . . As soon as I put them into print, they were destroyed in the war. After that, I fled both south and north, but I have not played the tunes for

2. Lam, *The Spatiality of Emotion*, 11.
3. Preface to *Hong yang jie*, 1. The play was first published in 1862. Also quoted in Cheng Huaping, *Ming Qing chuanqi biannian*, 526.

more than twenty years" 曩余撰傳奇四種 . . . 付梓初竣，頓遭劫灰。
嗣後南北奔馳，不彈此調者，二十余年.[4] The play *Bitter "Blessings"*
depicts the life of a destitute scholar, and thus may be based on Wei
Xiyuan's own experiences. When Wei Xiyuan took up playwriting
again after hostilities ended, he did not choose war as his subject;
instead, he wrote about postwar life, which he viewed with cynicism.

Just as in the aftermath of the Ming-Qing transition, after the Taiping Civil War the changes and conflicts that had occurred (and were
still occurring) became vehicles for playwrights to explore contemporary issues such as order and disorder, political morality and ambiguity, as well as personal existential dilemmas. In the mid-nineteenth
century in particular, ethics and feelings were mediated through cultural memories and imaginations associated with the Ming-Qing
dynastic transition. Historical figures, especially legendary late Ming
heroines, were frequently evoked in plays examining ethics during
times of political turbulence. Examples are *The Winsome General* (*Gui
hua feng* 媯嬪封) and *Hemp Beach Post Station* (*Matan yi* 麻灘驛) by
Yang Enshou 楊恩壽 (1835–1891), a prolific playwright and theater
critic.[5] *The Winsome General*, which I will discuss in more detail later,
summons the legendary late Ming figure of Lin Siniang 林四娘 to celebrate female chastity and heroism during political chaos. *Hemp Beach
Post Station* dramatizes a story based on historical accounts of three
women's resistance against late Ming bandits, which Yang adapts to
commemorate a Qing military couple who died in a battle against the
Taiping rebels.[6] In early Qing plays, the writers had accepted Manchu
rule, turning the seventeenth-century trauma into an object of aesthetic contemplation, but in the nineteenth century, following the end

---

4. Wei Xiyuan, *Ru suan fu*, 2a. Also quoted in Cheng Huaping, *Ming Qing chuanqi biannian*, 529.

5. *Gui hua feng, tanyuan* 坦園 edition; one of the prefaces dated to 1870. *Matan yi, tanyuan* edition, one of the prefaces dated to 1875.

6. Yang Enshou explains the connection between the play and his contemporary times in a preface. The other two prefaces of the play are a complete biography of Shen Yunying 沈雲英 (1624–1660) written by Mao Qiling, and an account of two courtesans who tried to poison the late Ming rebel leader Zhang Xianzhong 張獻忠 (1606–1647). The play centers on the stories of Shen Yunying and the two courtesans.

of the Taiping Civil War, memories of the Ming's violent fall are evoked as vivid anticipations of the recent catastrophe.

Explicit portrayals of the Taiping War also abound among late nineteenth-century plays. Many of these plays show the lives of ordinary men and women during the war, giving form to the writers' reflections upon the impact of brutal violence on a personal level. Xu Shanchang's 許善長 (1823–1889?) *The Cliff for Burying Clouds* (*Yi yun yan* 瘞雲巖) is said to be based on the lives of a young scholar and a woman who was forced into prostitution during the war.[7] The plot echoes some elements of Wei Xiuren's novel, *Traces of Flowers and the Moon*, and the numerous prefaces (twenty-nine in total, including the author's) appended to it suggest how the artistic transformation of people's tragic encounters during the war elicited strong responses from contemporary readers. Another example is Xu E's 徐鄂 (1844–1903) *Snow on the Pear Blossom* (*Lihua xue* 梨花雪), completed in 1886 and published in 1887 to commemorate a woman named Huang Shuhua 黃淑華 (1847–1864), who killed her abductors before committing suicide.[8] Several plays have strong autobiographical associations, notably Zheng Youxi's 鄭由熙 (?–1898) *The Person in the Mist* (*Wu zhong ren* 霧中人) and *Karmic Ties in a Dream* (*Meng zhong yuan* 夢中緣), which was written under a pseudonym. Both plays, like Wei Xiuren's novel *Traces of Flowers and the Moon*, examine people's personal experiences of large-scale historical events.

Taken together, these plays were part and parcel of the literati's collective endeavors to rebuild social and ideological order in the postwar context. Many writers believed that Confucian ethical codes would be an effective cure for sociopolitical chaos, and advocated for drama as a means to morally transform the audience. Their support to some

7. The earliest extant edition published by *Bi sheng yin guan* 碧聲吟館 is dated 1877.

8. Xu E, *Lihua xue*. The story about Huang Shuhua in the local gazetteer is discussed in Meyer-Fong, *What Remains*, 150–51; Platt, *Autumn in the Heavenly Kingdom*, 351–52. Her abductors were Xiang Army soldiers who may have been former Taipings. Rania Huntington has an in-depth discussion of this play in "The Captive's Revenge."

extent elevated the status of drama.[9] Yang Enshou equates drama with poetry, the most respected genre in Chinese literary tradition.[10] Quoting the late Ming thinkers Wang Yangming and Liu Zongzhou 劉宗周 (1578–1645), Yang Enshou argues for the efficacy of dramatic works in influencing the audience's morality. He also adheres to this principle in his own dramatic creations.[11]

Another example is Yu Zhi 余治 (1809–1874), a local gentleman who actively resisted Taiping ideology by writing plays about moral retribution, in addition to printing and distributing popular religious tracts.[12] Like the author of *Miraculous Proofs of the Sacred Edict*, he promotes Qing ideology but senses that traditional ways of preaching the Sacred Edict are limited. He explains his efforts to use drama as a medium to proselytize Confucian morals in the preface to his collection of plays, *Contemporary Music of the Shuji Studio* (*Shuji tang jin yue* 庶幾堂今樂): "The disaster under Heaven is extremely urgent. The teachings of Confucian teachers are unsuccessful, and the village compact bores people over time. Only contemporary plays appeal to human feelings in the best way. In this resides the way to transform custom" 天下之禍亟矣。師儒之化導既不見為功；鄉約之奉行又歷久生厭。惟茲新戲，最洽人情，易俗移風，於是乎在。[13] Comprising sixty-eight plays, all of which center on filial piety, loyalty, and righteousness, *Contemporary Music of the Shuji Studio* is proof of Yu Zhi's determination to put his dramatic theory into practice.[14] To reach a large audience, Yu Zhi also chose the genre of *pihuang* 皮黃, a theatrical form that evolved into the Peking opera of today and drew a broad audience from

9. Late Qing scholars held that dramatic performance should have a moral function. Zhang Xiaolan, *Qingdai jingxue yu xiqu*, 432–34.

10. Yang Enshou, *Yang Enshou ji*, 308.

11. Yang Enshou, *Yang Enshou ji*, 320–21.

12. Yu Zhi explicitly mentions the Sacred Edicts at several places in *De yi lu*, one of the morality books he compiled.

13. Yu Zhi, "Preface" to *Shuji tang jin yue*, 532.

14. As Rania Huntington points out, Yu Zhi measures individual conduct according to a scale of moral retribution that rationalizes the sufferings not only of commoners but also of the Taiping rebels. In doing so, he shows little sympathy toward ordinary people, whose actions brought them to the state of pain and distress. See her "Singing Punishment and Redemption."

those having low or no literacy during the nineteenth century.[15] The popular appeal of drama led to a shift from the elite *kunqu* to the Peking opera in the late nineteenth to early twentieth centuries, a process very much catalyzed by the Taiping War.[16] In the twentieth century, as Hsiao-t'i Li points out, this trend of using drama as a vehicle for *jiaohua* (teaching and transforming) continued and reincarnated as a means to mobilize the masses.[17]

Some playwrights sought to go beyond the binary opposition of right and wrong. The answers they offer from a religious cosmological perspective make no clear demarcation between the hero and the villain. One of the most frequently used frameworks in nineteenth-century drama is the "deliverance play" (*dutuo ju* 度脫劇), which constructs stories around the "banished immortal" motif in dramatic form. The deliverance plays produced during the Yuan dynasty (1271–1368 CE) featured Daoist immortals; those from the seventeenth century, in response to the Ming-Qing dynastic transition, featured renowned historical figures who progressed toward enlightenment. In the nineteenth century, in post-Taiping plays such as *Snow on the Pear Blossom* and *Karmic Ties in a Dream*, ordinary men and women feature as the protagonists, and their sufferings are justified as necessary for the restitution of Heavenly order.[18]

In post-Taiping plays, the religious significance of the "deliverance play" is also seen in discourse about *jie*, the cyclical return (and resolution) of catastrophes through historic time. Zhu Shaoyi premises *The Calamity of the Red Ram* on this concept. It begins with a scene titled "The Calamity Begins" ("Kai jie" 開劫) and ends with "The Calamity Comes Full Circle" ("Jie yuan" 劫圓), a structure both representing the war and providing its resolution at the end. The play was written just

15. Goldman, *Opera and the City*, 4, 5, 13.

16. On the culture of Peking opera in the nineteenth century, see Wu Cuncun, *Xi wai zhi xi*.

17. Hsiao-t'i Li, *Opera, Society, and Politics*, 45–46. Chapter 2 discusses the concept of *jiaohua* extensively.

18. On Daoist literature, see Yang Jianbo, *Daojiao wenxue shi lungao*, 404. A discussion of how plays respond to the Ming-Qing dynastic transition can be found in Idema, "'Crossing the Sea in a Leaking Boat'" and Tschanz, "Wu Weiye's Dramatic Works."

one year after Zhu Shaoyi and his wife tried to commit suicide as the Taiping rebels took over Nanjing. Only Zhu Shaoyi survived the war. For those like him who were burdened with traumatic memories from the war, drama became an essential medium to collectively commemorate and mediate the recent past.

## Staging Ferocity

The concept of *qing* (emotions, feelings, attachments) characterizes late imperial Chinese literature and culture. As Haiyan Lee puts it, before the late imperial period, "Confucian sentimentality [*qing*] sanctifies . . . the bonds between lord and subject and between parent and child."[19] However, the discourse of *qing* shifted during the late Ming era with the celebration of subjectivity. In *Anatomy of Qing* (*Qing shi* 情史), a collection consisting mostly of romantic love stories, Feng Menglong 馮夢龍 (1574–1646) proposes a religion of *qing* grounded on sincerity and faithfulness (*qing jiao* 情教). The transformative power of *qing* is epitomized in the late Ming classic *The Peony Pavilion* (*Mudan ting* 牡丹亭) by Tang Xianzu 湯顯祖 (1550–1616), which famously pronounces, "The origin of love is unknown, yet it runs deep. The living can die for it, and through it the dead can come back to life" 情不知所起，一往而深。生可以死，死可以生.[20] In this play, *qing* causes Du Liniang, the young and beautiful daughter of an important and stern official, to awaken to love and desire, thereby crossing the boundary between life and death. In comparison to *The Peony Pavilion*'s passions for the discovery of the self and *The Peach Blossom Fan*'s lamentations for irrevocable historical tides, post-Taiping plays feature animosity toward the Taiping rebels and a thirst for revenge.

Post-Taiping plays romanticize violent sacrifices made by those fighting on the Qing side. A case in point is Yang Enshou's *Shadows of the Paired Purities* (*Shuang qingying* 雙清影), a *chuanqi* play based on

19. Haiyan Lee, *Revolution of the Heart*, 26.
20. Tang Xianzu, "*Mudan ting* tici," 8; translation from Wai-yee Li, *Enchantment and Disenchantment*, 51, with my modification.

a historical event from the Taiping Civil War. In this play, the Qing governor Chen Daiyun 陳岱雲 (fl. 1850) hanged himself when the Taiping army attacked his city. The governor's suicide was not the first instance of self-harm in the play; before his death, his wife cut flesh from her arm to cure her husband of an illness. These lines glorify the wife's sacrifice, aestheticizing the self-mutilation graphically indicated in the play: "In Heaven, immortal companionship was formed / On Earth, the root of feelings is firmly held / The blood and flesh on the blade carry traces of spring / This is precisely the miraculous medicine that brings recovery" 天上結來仙伴，人間拿定情根。刀頭血肉帶春痕，恰是回生妙品.[21] Spring traditionally connotes romantic and idyllic feelings, so the unusual juxtaposition of tropes—blood, flesh, and springtime—creates especially unsettling effects. In contrast to the "righteous" violence of the Qing, the Taiping rebels' violence is represented as unjust and unruly. This lopsided re-creation of a history of violence differs from the perspective in private accounts, which recorded how the destruction of the war was brought about not only by the Taiping rebels but also by the Qing troops and local bandits.

To further vilify the Taipings, postwar theatrical representations of violence draw extensive analogies between the rebels and animals both literal and figurative. The rebels are repeatedly portrayed as beastly Others outside the bounds of humanity. In this, the plays echo contemporary stereotyping, which we see also in some private accounts (see near the start of chapter 3). There are many examples in the theater. Zheng Youxi, in *The Person in the Mist,* uses the images of tigers in the scene of the Taiping invasion: "Numerous, disturbing, unrestrained, and greedy, [the Taipings] are as cruel as tigers and leopards" 紛擾肆貪，殘同虎豹.[22] Describing the Taiping troops' preparation for battle, the stage direction tells the actors to "turn around and put on the fur coats of fox and lamb" 將狐羊各裘，翻轉披戴介.[23] The specific instruction for the actors to put on costumes of animals implies disappearing

21. I am quoting this example from Liang Shu'an, *Zhongguo jindai chuanqi*, 55. For unknown reasons, Yang Enshou did not incorporate the play into his *Tanyuan liuzhong qu* 坦園六種曲, a collection of his *chuanqi* plays.

22. Zheng Youxi, *Wu zhong ren*, 2b.

23. Zheng Youxi, *Wu zhong ren*, 40a.

boundaries between humans and animals, as costuming is often "a means of negotiating disrupted personhood at a time when the world and the state were simultaneously entangled and detangled."[24] The rebels invading villages are "densely packed as the net capturing fish, / overpowering as serpents devouring humans, / chaotic as the homeless dogs, / ferocious as the ruthless King of Hell. / Extremely savage, they extract tributes, pacify the residents, and post unauthorized announcements" 密層層好似求魚的罾網，勢洶洶好似吞人的蛇蟒，亂紛紛好似喪家的吠尨，燄騰騰好似無情的閻羅狀。忒猖狂。納貢安民張偽榜。[25] The metaphors cover a range of associations, from ferocity (leopard and serpent) to selfishness, slyness, and cowardliness (foxes, sheep, and mice). A similar example occurs in Zheng Youxi's *Fragrant Osmanthus* (*Muxi xiang* 木樨香). This play is based on an 1855 event in which the honest local magistrate of the She County in Anhui Province commits suicide because he can find no support from corrupt officials to counter the Taiping invasion of the town. Zheng Youxi writes: "Chaotic are the merciless knives and saws; / crowded and hustling are the fleeing foxes and mice. / Weeping are the orphans deprived of milk; / pitiful are the legions of men and women" 亂紛紛是些無情的刀鋸，急攘攘是些狂奔的狐鼠。苦哀哀是些失乳的孤兒，凄慘慘是些結隊的男和女。[26] Here, the deployment of animal imagery intensifies the pathos of the violence and disorder brought about by Taiping actions.

In some plays, the intense emotional state of the writer-survivors brings violence onto the stage when the characters express mournfulness, trepidation, and despondency as both evidence and result of the fragility of human existence. These descriptions strongly parallel those found in private accounts. Examples of how these responses are enacted and given form onstage and on the page occur in *Karmic Ties in a Dream*, which follows the actions of a band of five men during a violent war modeled on the Taiping War. In one scene, after the main protagonist's mother dies of illness during the war, he vents his sorrow, guilt, and frustration via twelve arias, a prose soliloquy, and profuse

24. Wang Guojun, *Staging Personhood*, 4.
25. Zheng Youxi, *Wu zhong ren*, 40a.
26. Zheng Youxi, *Muxi xiang*, 21a.

tears. The emotions expressed in his monologue—which may voice the playwright's devotion to his own mother—call to mind the narrative devices used by Wei Xiuren to express agony and despair through his alter ego Chizhu in *Traces of Flowers and the Moon* as Wei mourned his father's death while he was stranded in the north. In another scene in *Karmic Ties in a Dream*, the protagonist witnesses soldiers looting households and raping women. His strong emotional response finds form in an aria:

How pitiful are those women who are raped. / How tragic those young and old wounded by the sword. / Corpses are strewn on streets and fresh blood is splattered, / crows and dogs find themselves a feast. / Warfare and beacon-fire saturate the land. / How am I to escape from this!

可憐那婦女逼姦, 可慘那老幼遭劍。這屍骨沿途鮮血濺。受用殺鴉餐犬嚼。干戈偏到處烽煙。叫俺怎生逃殿![27]

The protagonist finds refuge in a temple, where he continues his lament:

At present, I lie on a prayer mat made of hay. / My body is tired and my feet worn out. / It is as if there are arrows piercing my back. / In chilly coldness, my startled heart trembles with fear. / In desolation and loneliness, I am short of breath and my eyes are clouded. / In complete darkness, I could not see the moonlight.

權倒在草蒲團，身疲足軟。猶如背穿箭，寒兢兢心驚膽戰。冷清清神昏目倦。黑濃濃月光不見。[28]

Through the passionately sung arias, staging, and movement implied in the lines, the playwright vividly theatricalizes ordinary people's remembrances of private feelings and intimate experiences amid chaos. This kind of staging and delivery is a common feature of such plays: the close juxtaposition of (spoken) prose and (sung) lyric heightens the expressivity of language in representations of violence.

27. *MZY*, 2:48b.
28. *MZY*, 2:49a–b.

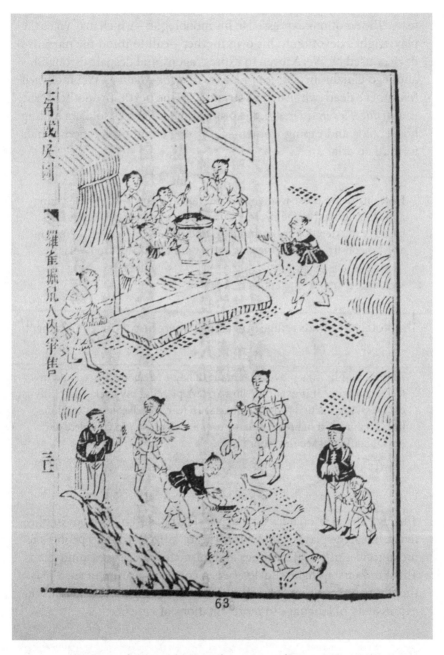

FIG. 5.1.  Illustration from Yu Zhi, *Tears from a Man of Iron in Jiangnan* (*Jiangnan tie lei tu* 江南鐵淚圖), 1864. Reprint, Taipei: Guangwen shuju, 1974, 63.

In addition to intense emotions, in post-Taiping plays we are also given direct descriptions of physical wounds and dismemberment, which are symptomatic of the psychic dislocation of the aftermath of the war. The horrific sight of human hands and feet boiled up in cauldrons to be eaten, recorded in *Diary of the Unperturbed Studio* (see chapter 3), is echoed in the play *Snow on the Pear Blossom*, where the Taiping antagonist carries around dried "beauty's feet" as his favorite dish to accompany wine.[29] Here, sexual desire and monstrous brutality are strangely blended together, as they are in the magical battle in *Traces of Flowers and the Moon*. In general, these visceral images are produced across genres: Yu Zhi's morality book *Tears from a Man of Iron in Jiangnan* (*Jiangnan tie lei tu* 江南鐵淚圖) also features images of armed rebels, tearful commoners, damaged figures, and body parts scattered on the ground, which collectively convey a sense of the overwhelming violence experienced during the war (fig. 5.1). These images also clearly echo traditional portrayals of the torments of Hell (see chapter 2).

Violence in private accounts and illustrations is vivid but two-dimensional—it lies immobile on the page; but in post-Taiping plays, the killing, disemboweling, and severing of body parts is narrated to the audience in real time.[30] This kind of direct representation would reignite the audience's traumatic memories of the war; at the same time, by inflicting violence upon the Taiping rebels in a theatrical imaginary setting, the representation could also provide the survivors (writers, readers, and spectators) some sort of catharsis. The explicit and gruesome details of human bodies being torn apart are presented in both *The Liling Mountain* (*Liling po* 理靈坡) and *Snow on the Pear Blossom*. These descriptions betray the writers' strong and urgent desire to grapple with the psychological wounds caused by mutilation and killing, whether those wounds are inflicted on the heroic and righteous or on the cruel and vicious. Yang Enshou's *The Liling Mountain* is about a late Ming martyr's resistance to the rebel leader Zhang Xianzhong 張獻忠 (1606–1647). Yang gives explicit descriptions of violent tortures

29. Xu E, *Lihua xue*, 1:sc. 4, 3a.

30. Based on existing materials, we are uncertain about how violence is enacted on stage.

imposed on the martyr: the rebels first chop off his feet and tongue, then thrust a sword into his chest and kill him off slowly in a "death by a thousand cuts."[31] After each laceration, the martyr declares his righteousness, so the stark contrast between the rebels' cruelty and the hero's virtue heightens the dramatic effect of each torment. Stage directions that instruct the actor to follow (or accompany) a verbal expression with an action—a characteristic also of late Ming "contemporary plays" (*shishi ju* 時事劇)—serve to intensify this dramatic effect.[32]

Graphic theatricalization of violence also appears in *Snow on the Pear Blossom*: the female protagonist carries out her full revenge upon her abductors with poison and disemboweling, singing out each of her moves:

(The rebel moving again, so the heroine quickly stabs his abdomen) I cut the lamb stomach of yours and let blood splash, (taking out the liver) take the chicken liver of yours and throw it away, (plucking the heart) pluck the wolf heart of yours for sacrifice, (taking the intestines) cut the fish intestines of yours by inches, (chopping the limbs) cut the boar feet of yours off completely, (cutting the neck) cut the eagle neck of yours to avenge old wrongs.

「副淨復動，且急剖其腹介」把你剖羊腔血飛濺，「出肝介」把你出雞肝棄捐，「摘心介」把你摘狼心供祭筵，「抽腸介」把你冒魚腸條條寸剪，「剁足介」把你截損了野豬蹄不連，「截頸介」把你絕鷹吭報夙冤。[33]

The rhythmic, repetitive lines of the song create a feeling of intensity magnified by their content. In the song, each of the heroine's actions on stage is accompanied by a line that not only describes the actions but also characterizes the Taiping villain as a monster assembled from the body parts of different animals. The vicious imagery vindicates her

31. Yang Enshou, *Liling po*.

32. On the characteristics of *shishi ju* in the seventeenth century, see Wang Ayling, *Xiqu zhi shenmei gousi*, 205–42. On the development of *shishi ju* in the nineteenth and early twentieth centuries, see Tian Gensheng, *Jindai xiju de chuancheng*, 160–68. This topic is also discussed in Zhang Xiaolan, *Qingdai jingxue yu xiqu*, 120–25.

33. Xu E, *Lihua xue*, 3:sc. 11, 11a, b.

violent revenge, justifying the disembowelment of another human being who is merely a composite of various animal parts. The bearers of cruel violence in *The Liling Mountain* and *Snow on the Pear Blossom* are from opposing camps: an imperial official, on the one hand, and a rebel, on the other. In one play, the violence is presented as a horrific event evoking sympathy; in the other, as justified revenge. Thus each play stakes out a different ethical perspective on violence.

The plays we have been considering do not reserve violent acts only for men; as we see, the character enacting violence is often an avenging woman. Many of the post-Taiping plays follow the early Qing tradition where women constitute a metaphoric site for mediating thoughts and feelings in response to national trauma, but with this difference: more often, post-Taiping plays portray women as the military leaders, assassins, and butchers of the Taiping rebels. An example is *The Winsome General*, a post-Taiping theatrical adaptation of the popular early Qing story about Lin Siniang. In almost all early Qing stories, Lin Siniang is a pale, delicate, and dainty creature.[34] Her image starts to change in *Dream of the Red Chamber*, which gives her the identity of a loyal warrior fighting and dancing for the Ming prince. *The Winsome General* follows *Dream of the Red Chamber*, but recasts Lin Siniang's dance as a hunting game and military drill: she shoots a pheasant and breaks through a simulated formation. In the scene titled "The Flower Formation" (*hua zhen* 花陣), which alternates between Lin Siniang's martial dance moves and the prince describing them in a song, reveals how female-gendered violence becomes an object of desire and appreciation under the male gaze.

The male playwrights appropriate heroines' voices to declare and act out animosity against the Taiping rebels. They do this through imagery that visualizes the heroines combating and avenging the dehumanized Other. Like their counterparts among the male characters, the female leading roles refer to their foes as animals. In *The Winsome*

---

34. The only exceptions are stories about her in Lin Yunming's 林雲銘 (fl. 1658) *Sunzhai fenyu* 損齋焚餘 and *Yikuilou xuangao* 挹奎樓選稿, as well as Chen Yixi's 陳奕禧 (1648–1709) *Yuzhou ji* 虞州集. Wai-yee Li has an extensive discussion of the various early Qing accounts about Lin Siniang in *Women and National Trauma*, 269–93.

*General,* Lin Siniang claims that she can defeat the enemy effortlessly, as "[The rebels are] reckless as troops of ants, / chaotic as legions of wolves. / A light knock of my delicate hand would defeat the rebels' base, / which is like a beehive" 紛紛螻蟻師，擾擾豺狼輩。禁不起玉手輕敲，打破蜂窠壘.[35] At the end of *The Calamity of the Red Ram,* the female assassin of Yang Xiuqing, a sword in her hand, comes on stage and sings: "My chest is filled with anger. / Pressing my sword and raising my eyebrows, my fury is not pacified.... / Displaying female power, I am infuriated. / For all the people under Heaven, I stab the ferocious tiger, stab the ferocious tiger.... / Tonight, I dare to emulate the dog butcher; / taking the head [of the rebel king], I watch the blood splatter" 氣塞胸脯，按劍揚眉恨未舒 ... 俺且逞蛾眉，一怒替天下刺將猛虎，刺將猛虎 ... 俺拼得今宵學狗屠，更看取紅濺頭顱.[36] The imagined figures of these daring and revengeful female protagonists in post-Taiping plays anticipate the new martial women of the early twentieth century.

By representing violence and negotiating with traumatic memories, post-Taiping plays exhibit new dimensions in the discourse of *qing.* We see a peculiar romanticization of violence in theatrical celebrations of Qing military actions. These plays dehumanize the Taiping rebels. At the same time, in the fanciful world of revenge conjured up by the male writers, virtuous women and female immortals become enactors of violence against the Taiping rebels in a new gender dynamic.

## Righteous War in *Karmic Ties in a Dream*

Among extant post-Taiping plays, *Karmic Ties in a Dream* (hereafter *Karmic Ties*) stands out because of its unusual length and its ambition to comprehensively configure the recent war through existing literary models. Most post-Taiping plays have fewer than twenty scenes, but *Karmic Ties* has forty. The play is attributed to "The Handan man awakened from his dream" (*Handan mengxing ren* 邯鄲夢醒人), a pseudonym yielding little information about the writer. My research on

35. Yang Enshou, *Gui hua feng,* 14a.
36. *Hong yang jie,* 54.

materials connected to the play leads me to identify the playwright as Pu Wenbin 濮文彬, born during the 1830s–40s in Anhui Province.[37] "Handan meng" (a dream in Handan), which is also referred to by writers of prefatory pieces, may allude to the story tradition that dates back to the Tang *chuanqi* story, "The World within a Pillow" ("Zhen zhong ji" 枕中記). The protagonist of this story falls asleep and has a vivid dream; upon waking, he realizes that the millet porridge someone began to cook before he fell asleep is not yet ready. By virtue of his dreamed experiences, he achieves enlightenment. During the Yuan and Ming dynasties, this story was adapted into two plays, one by Ma Zhi-yuan 馬致遠 (fl. 1251–1321) and the other by Tang Xianzu.[38] The message of the Tang story is about detachment, but Tang Xianzu's play ends with a grand fantasy of escape in the name of Daoist enlightenment. Evoking the dramatic tradition of *Records of Handan*, the playwright emphasizes the illusory quality of the play and the transitoriness of his life experience through theatrical representation.

37. Modern scholars who have discussed the play show interest in the writer's identity, but thus far, no one has been able to identify him convincingly. Yan Dunyi points out that the play seems autobiographical; he proposes that, since the protagonist He Hua's name is a homonym of lotus (*hehua* 荷花), the playwright should have the surname of Zhou, like Zhou Dunyi 周敦頤 (1017–1073), author of the well-known essay "On Loving Lotus" (*Ai lian shuo* 愛蓮說). Liang Shu'an and Yao Kefu suggest the approximate time the playwright lived, but present no evidence. Zuo Pengjun notes that some prefaces suggest an autobiographical dimension to the play, but unpersuasively infers that the playwright's surname is He. For his reading and summary of the discussion, see Zuo Pengjun, *Wan Qing Minguo chuanqi*, 154–55. I based my identification of Pu Wenbin as author of this play on what is known about his social network and the names associated with the prefatory materials of the play.

38. On the early development of the trope, see Li Ji, "Huangliang meng gushi ticai." One of the earliest versions of this story appears in the fourth-century short story collection *In Search of the Supernatural* (*Sou shen ji* 搜神記). In *Extensive Records of the Taiping Era* (*Taiping guangji* 太平廣記), the tenth-century imperial compilation of short narratives, this literary trope is developed into a full-fledged story. In the sixteenth century, the famous late Ming literati Tang Xianzu adapted the story into a *chuanqi* play. This *chuanqi* play, together with the other three *chuanqi* plays written by Tang Xianzu that feature the motif of dream, are known as "Linchuan's (Tang Xianzu's courtesy name) four dreams" (*Linchuan si meng* 臨川四夢). By the nineteenth century, the literary trope of dreaming at Handan is well established.

Pu Wenbin's friends saw elements in this play as having strong biographical overlap with Pu's life. The protagonist, He Hua, and Pu Wenbin are alike in terms of birthplace, travels, involvement in the Taiping War, and their long wait for a civil appointment after the war. In addition, some unusual plot elements have direct counterparts in Pu Wenbin's private life experiences. For example, in the play, He Hua's mother experiences waves of pain while carrying her unborn child. This parallels the great difficulties that the playwright's mother had during his birth. Pu was known as a devout Buddhist who, because of his mother's ordeal, vowed to refrain from killing living beings throughout his lifetime.[39] Pu's religious background could be seen reflected in the "deliverance play" framework employed in *Karmic Ties*. The Taiping Rebellion would have marked a sharp turn in Pu Wenbin's life: like other families of his class, they likely fled the disaster when rebels conquered his hometown Anhui in 1853. For several years, Pu must have relied on the kindness of strangers to survive, like the protagonist in the play, as his poems and prefatory writings to the play show.

The details of Pu Wenbin's life and the circumstances surrounding the play's writing are insufficient to prove a solid connection between members of Pu Wenbin's social circle and other characters in the play. Many characters and events, however, appear to be the writer's artistic re-creation of actual experiences. In one of the prefaces, he suggests that certain plot elements were fictional (dreams) but that the feelings or affective consequences (*yuan*, karmic ties) are real: "As for the sworn brotherhood formed at the Temple of Guandi, the armed force organized on the South of the Yangtze River, the visit paid to the prison to collect remains, and the tears shed to commemorate the dead—all are examples illustrating that though dreams are false, the karmic ties are true" 觀夫關廟結拜，江左起兵，探監背骨，洒淚祭亡，此夢假而緣真.[40] Those dramatic moments may be complete and deliberate fabrications;

---

39. Kang Zhaobin's prefatory poem in Pu Wenbin, *Huangzhou huanyou cao*, 7a.
40. *MZY*, 1:4b. *Yuan* carries various meanings in *Karmic Ties*. In the Buddhist context, *yuan* refers to the "conditions" that underlie causes and their effects.

or they may be based on a mixture of reality and imagination, especially regarding the main characters. Whatever their precise relation to actual events, the playwright finds a way to represent true *yuan* through an innovative aesthetic lens.

The plot of *Karmic Ties* concerns the activities of five friends who, sharing similar aspirations, take an oath to band together as "sworn brothers" during the Taiping War. They organize their own militia, independent of but working in tandem with official government forces, to combat rebel troops and eradicate the rebel kings one by one. After the government has reestablished order, this self-organized militia has to dissolve so that it does not turn into another potential source of violence threatening the central government. At the end of the play, this band of brothers is disillusioned by the political corruption they encounter and the unfair recognition of military merit in the central government. Seeking to reconcile a general view of history with an individual's experiences, *Karmic Ties* is a serious attempt to emulate *The Peach Blossom Fan,* which revolves around a couple's tragic romance and the fall of the Ming dynasty. However, in place of the romance plot of *The Peach Blossom Fan,* the writer of *Karmic Ties* constructs a story of fraternity to bring meaning and order to the political chaos.

*Karmic Ties* sets up an antithesis between the rebels and the brothers using metaphors to represent the savagery of the rebels, on one side, and the virtue of the brothers, on the other. The four Taiping kings have animal names: Leopard (Ai Yebao 艾葉豹, homophonic with "Suffering Karmic Retribution"), Ignorant Deer (Lu Mu 鹿木), Poisonous Wolf (Lang Du 狼毒), and Rhino (Xi Luo 犀洛, homophonic with "Ridiculing"). The traitor is named Prying Tiger (Hu Ci 虎刺). The sworn brothers, on the other hand, are named for plants: Lotus Flower (He Hua 何華), Orchid (Zhu Lan 朱蘭), Bamboo (Feng Zhu 風竹), Chrysanthemum (Jin Qianju 金錢菊), and Plum Blossom (Mei Zhankui 梅占魁). In Chinese culture, the lotus flower is often compared to a righteous man who strives against difficult conditions; in Buddhism, it is a symbol of enlightenment. At the same time, the images of orchid, bamboo, plum blossom, and chrysanthemum form the pattern of a popular subject of traditional painting that symbolizes the virtues of endurance, purity, and resilience in the four seasons. These images are also referred to as "the Four Gentlemen" (si junzi 四君子) in traditional Chinese visual arts. To associate flower spirits with male characters is a relatively unusual literary practice, but the choice is effective in the context of the play and is justified by a constructed back-story. Following the genre convention of the "deliverance play," the rebel kings are revealed to be celestial animals who have left Heaven surreptitiously to come down to Earth; the brothers, meanwhile, are revealed to have been flower goddesses in their previous lives. The images of the plants—elegant, pure, and calm—contrast with those of the wild animals, figuring the difference between refined literati culture and unconstrained, rebellious energy.

The account of the rebellion in *Karmic Ties* generally follows the course of the Taiping Rebellion. The rebel king, Leopard, describes how it progressed:

> Looking back to the time when I staged the uprising in Jintian, we had no more than three thousand men, counting the troops headed by Second Brother Ignorant Deer, Third Brother Poisonous Wolf, and Fourth Brother Rhino. Who could have known that the civil servants are afraid of death, and the military officials cling to their lives? Everywhere we went, the officials welcomed us and surrendered. Now we have taken over the entire province. After sending Second Brother Ignorant Deer to take southern Hunan, I arrived in the Chu region with Third Brother and Fourth Brother. Coming to Xunyang, I commanded my Third Brother to conquer Yuzhang. Going straight down to Anhui, I sent my Fourth Brother to attack northern Anhui. Now I myself lead the major division and sail down to Jiangnan.

> 想俺在金田起義之時，同二弟鹿木三弟狼毒四弟犀洛不過三千人馬。誰知文官怕死，武官貪生。到處迎降，已得全省。派二弟鹿木取湘南，遂同三弟四弟到楚。行至潯陽，已命三弟親取豫章。徑行到皖，又派四弟取皖北。此時親督大軍直下江南。[41]

Clear historical references are made here: the Taipings officially declared war against the Qing regime in Jintian, and the Jintian uprising is deemed by historians to be the beginning of the Taiping Rebellion.

41. *MZY*, 2:42b.

The description of the strategic route the rebels plan to take in the play also agrees with reality: After leaving Guangxi, where the rebellion started, the Taipings first entered Hunan Province. Setbacks in Changsha, however, made them send the army in the direction of southern Hunan. Having taken Wuhan in Hubei Province, Jiujiang in Jiangxi Province, and Anqing in Anhui Province, the Taipings marched down to Nanjing, where they founded the Taiping Heavenly Kingdom. Facing the arrival of the Taiping army, Qing officials either quickly abandoned their cities to preserve their lives, or obsequiously surrendered to the rebels. In the play, the cowardly Qing officials are represented through the character of Prying Tiger, who submits his letter of surrender, together with a boatload of treasure, to the rebels in advance of their arrival.

The pride Leopard takes in his military success is undermined by an internal political struggle that simulates the Tianjing Incident of 1856, which is represented in the scene titled "Eradicating the Rebels" ("Jiao zei" 剿賊). After being defeated by Lotus's troops in Hunan, Poisonous Wolf manages to escape and joins Rhino's army in northern Anhui. However, observing Lotus's successive victories, Poisonous Wolf decides to surrender, albeit not directly. Pretending that he supports Rhino's strategic plans, Poisonous Wolf wins his trust; once this trust is established, he murders Rhino and takes control of his army. The play does not strictly follow historical facts here, but it echoes some features of the conflict's history. The relatively sensible Rhino calls to mind the tragic story of the Wing King, Shi Dakai. As one of the earliest followers of Hong Xiuquan, Shi did not actively seek political power through divine revelation in the way that Yang Xiuqing and Wei Changhui did. Instead, he led many successful military campaigns to establish and expand the Taiping Kingdom. When the Tianjing Incident took place, Shi Dakai was away from the Heavenly Capital on another military campaign. Upon receiving the news of the incident, he returned only to find that Wei Changhui had killed his entire family. The scene in *Karmic Ties* mirrors the plotting and treachery among the Taiping leaders. Its central focus is not so much the savagery as the unstable structure of the rebel leadership.

The playwright uses Lotus's official declaration of war to denounce the rebels, in a scene titled "The Rise of the Righteous Army" ("Qiyi" 起義). This is the point in the play when the sworn brothers assemble a military force to combat the rebels. The phrase *qiyi* is, oddly, the same phrase that Leopard uses to refer to his military advance in an earlier scene. By putting both forces under the same rubric, the armed force organized by the brothers ironically mirrors the very rebellion they are trying to put down. Thus the question arises, how far are the righteous brothers from the rebels in the view of the central government?

On one level at least, Lotus's declaration of the war is meant to be legitimate: the playwright himself sets it up as such by imitating Zeng Guofan's "Denunciation of the Yue Rebels" ("Tao Yue fei xi" 討粵匪檄), issued in 1854.[42] In this proclamation, Zeng denounces the Taiping rebels for driving men to the frontline to build fortifications, and for forcing women to transport rice and coal and keep vigil during the night. They have turned family relationships upside down by calling fathers "brothers" and mothers "sisters." Zeng Guofan asks how anyone who is literate can watch the rebels destroy thousands of years' worth of rituals, cultural norms, human relationships, and the Confucian canons, such as the *Book of Songs* and the *Book of Documents*. He predicts that the deities will soon let disaster befall the rebels. Lotus's declaration adopts a tone that by and large follows the content and logic of Zeng Guofan's proclamation; both conclude by urging people to join the Qing side. There are some differences: Zeng Guofan "respectfully receives the commission from the Son of Heaven" 奉天子命, whereas Lotus acts out of gratitude for imperial favors and in honor of his family: "Aristocratic families like mine in this dynasty have been wearing noble caps and ornaments for generations. How can we not repay the imperial favor? The tragic loss of fortune and home is too painful to speak about" 華等熙朝舊族，世席簪纓，食毛踐土之恩，何堪不報; 絕產喪家之慘，痛苦難言.[43] The author of *Karmic Ties* imbues political rhetoric in Qing history with an individual voice, so in the theatrical world, the protagonist's unofficial military action is as justified as an official military campaign. In sum, the playwright takes revenge in the imaginary realm and injects a personal dimension into his portrayal of this grand history.

42. A section of Zeng Guofan's denunciation is quoted in the introduction (n. 5) as an example of a Qing proclamation.

43. *MZY*, 3:45b.

Despite its references to the specific historical context, the theatrical representation of the war in this play is mostly melodramatic and stereotypical. As the playwright portrays the rebels, he parodies famous historical figures traditionally celebrated for heroism, nobility, and sacrifice, and turns their well-known episodes in literature and history into scenes bordering on the absurd. One scene in particular, titled "Achieving the Merit of Victory" ("De gong" 得功), stages the downfall of the rebel king, Leopard, as imagined through his interactions with his concubine and daughter. The first thing this scene does is to deconstruct the literary convention of using female virtue to symbolize political loyalty. When the rebel king learns that his city is besieged by Lotus, he sighs, "I have not faced such a crushing defeat since I staged the uprising. What am I supposed to do?" 孤家自起兵以來，未有如此大敗。如何是好.[44] Leopard sings to his concubine, Jin Yuling,

(Sings:) Hurry up, defend the city! Hurry up, defend the city! / With three thousand soldiers left, / how am I supposed to resist [the enemy]? / This is precisely, precisely, karma of my own making, / and Heaven is sending me to die. (Speaks:) Beauty, hurry up, fetch the wine. Get yourself drunk and prepare yourself to receive this fatal blow.

快些守城池，快些守城池。殘卒三千，如何撐持？這才是，這才是，自作孽, 天教死。美人，快取酒來，吃醉了好受這一刀。[45]

In the moment when his city and fate are at stake, Leopard's solution is to capitulate, and get Jin Yuling drunk before decapitating her. Leopard's downfall in some ways resembles that of an ancient king, Xiang Yu 項羽, known not only for his lack of political acumen but also for his bravery. At the last moment of his life, like Leopard, he sees his tragic destiny. In *Records of the Grand Historian* (*Shi ji* 史記), Xiang Yu sings to Lady Yu, his favorite concubine: "My strength plucked the hills. My might shadowed the world. But the times were against me. And Dapple runs no more. When Dapple runs no more, what then can

44. *MZY*, 3:45b.
45. *MZY*, 3:45b–46a.

I do? Ah, Yu, my Yu, What will your fate be?" 力拔山兮氣蓋世，時不利兮騅不逝。騅不逝兮可奈何，虞兮虞兮奈若何。[46] Lady Yu commits suicide so her loyalty and virtue remain pure. By the late Ming, Lady Yu's suicide had become a popular motif in literary imagination, a tragic parting, a "farewell my concubine" (*bawang bie ji* 霸王別姬).[47] In *Karmic Ties in a Dream*, however, the heroic aura associated with Xiang Yu is replaced by the rebel king's dispiritedness and abjectness.

As Leopard urges Jin Yuling to end her life to avoid being taken away by the enemy, her reaction turns this scene into a parody of "farewell my concubine":

(Sings:) I urge my King not to worry. / I urge my King not to worry. / Put up placards and recruit soldiers. / Wipe out the evil foxes. / In a moment, immediately, / Heaven will send down the divine one [to help you]. (Speaks:) Please drink, my King.

勸大王休疑，勸大王休疑。掛榜招兵，斬盡妖狸。霎時間，霎時間，天降神人至。大王飲酒哩。[48]

The mention of placards in this line is a direct allusion to Taiping proclamations, in which the Taipings vilified the Manchu rulers as the offspring of a white fox and a red dog.[49] If Lady Yu's death adds to the pathos generated by the king's failure, Jin Yuling's manipulativeness and self-interest halt the tragic momentum of the scene. Her refusal to do the traditionally approved action, to commit suicide, insinuates the moral corruption associated with the rebels. In that case, her immoral qualities would place her in the category of evil women who befuddle rulers and cause dynastic failure. This interpretation suggests that the Taiping rebels' failure was at least in part a result of political errors rather than illegitimacy, a suggestion that would make the issue of political righteousness and its claiming even more ambiguous.

46. Sima Qian, *Shiji*, 2504; translation from Watson, ed., *Records of the Grand Historian*, 145.

47. For instance, "Yu meiren" 虞美人, in Feng Menglong, *Qing shi*, 1:44–46. The beginning of the late Ming novel *Jin Ping Mei* also summarizes the story of Lady Yu.

48. *MZY*, 3:46a.

49. *TPTGYS*, 1:109.

The negative portrayal of a woman associated with the Taiping rebels, however, is complicated by Leopard's daughter, who is also present in this scene. The rebel Princess Nanxiang, unlike the concubine, is resolved to commit suicide to protect her integrity. She sings,

> Presently, the crisis is coming; / presently, the crisis is coming. / I hope for help, and yet no one comes to my rescue. / I foresee myself being dismembered soon, tragically, tragically. / With one cut of the sword, / I leave this dusty world. (Speaks:) Let it be. Let it be. Things have come to this. I will exempt myself from disgrace and shame.
>
> 頃刻在顛危，頃刻在顛危。望救無人。眼見分屍慘淒淒，慘淒淒。一劍紅塵棄。罷，罷，罷。勢已如此，免受其辱也。[50]

And so, she dies. King Leopard's response, however, dissipates the solemn and tragic aura that should be associated with her death. Upon hearing the news, he replies, "Who cares about her? I do not even know what will happen to my own life. Hurry up, fetch me wine!" 不要問他。我命不知如何。快取酒來。[51] Such a blatant refusal to attribute meaning to the princess's political sacrifice parodies another well-known episode featuring the young Ming princess Changping. Many stories and plays present the heroine as a symbol of political virtue. *The History of Ming* (*Ming shi* 明史) records that when rebels took the capital, Princess Changping—who had just been betrothed—grasps her father's robe and weeps. Her father, the Chongzhen Emperor, lets out a sigh of profound anguish, "Why were you born into our house!" 汝何故生我家. Having uttered these words, he lifts his sword and cuts off her left arm.[52] Traditionally, the last Ming emperor's tragic choice of mutilating one of his favorite daughters is read as his effort to preserve imperial honor. However, *Karmic Ties in a Dream* parodies this reading: Princess Nanxiang's death is a senseless sacrifice made for a cause that is already doomed. In doing so, the playwright questions the

---

50. *MZY*, 3:46a.
51. *MZY*, 3:46a.
52. Zhang Tingyu, *Ming shi*, 12:3677.

validity of inscribing meaning onto the collapse of an empire through the image of a virtuous woman.

## A Romance of History and Fraternity

For people who had just endured the Taiping War, the kind of "deliverance" offered in the traditional deliverance plays could not satisfactorily account for the catastrophe. To engage the complex polemics of history and representation, the playwright of *Karmic Ties in a Dream* adopts *The Peach Blossom Fan* as a model. This earlier play influences *Karmic Ties* in many formal aspects, as we see in the elements the playwright adopts from two of Kong Shangren's prefaces: "Categorical Principles" ("Fanli" 凡例) and "The Principle Guidelines of *The Peach Blossom Fan*" ("*Taohua shan* gangling" 桃花扇綱領), where Kong explains his choices in the staging, composition, and character design of his play. *Karmic Ties* also has a preface, titled "Categorical Principles," which explains the structural, linguistic, and aesthetic design of the play. Like his predecessor, the playwright stresses that he is including detailed stage directions to prevent the performers from making impromptu changes on stage. In several places, he quotes verbatim from *The Peach Blossom Fan*'s "Categorical Principles." Examples include "uses [illusions] at ease, without making the impression of assemblage" 信手拈來，不露餖飣堆砌之痕, and "the characters thus are divided into the categories of noble man and petty man. As for the major characters, sometimes I put them into the categories of *jing* and *chou*" 腳色所以分別君子小人，至於正色，借用淨醜.[53]

Despite such overlaps, *Karmic Ties in a Dream* departs from *The Peach Blossom Fan* greatly in its language, aims, and character design. Kong Shangren explains his use of language and its appeals to the taste of literati: "I did not write the songs and lyrics carelessly. When it comes to the feelings in my chest that I cannot articulate, and the visions in my mind that I cannot reveal, I convey them with songs and lyrics . . .

---

53. Kong Shangren, "*Taohua shan* fanli" 桃花扇凡例, in Kong Shangren, *Taohua shan*, 2. "Fanli" 凡例, in *MZY*, 1:17a.

there is always meaning in the songs I compose. Each aria is a composition; each sentence is also a composition" 詞曲皆非浪填。凡胸中情不可說，眼前景色不能見者，則借詞曲以詠之 ... 製曲必有旨趣，一首成一首之文章，一句成一句之文章.[54] He here emphasizes using the features of poetry to convey meaning indirectly, rather than articulating it in a way that can be directly understood. *Karmic Ties in a Dream*, however, adopts a different linguistic approach to make the text comprehensible to readers outside the literati circle. The author says that he aims "to make the singing and dancing accessible even to women, so that when people hear the songs, they will understand them in their hearts and their feelings will be aroused" 歌之排場，即婦人女子盈於耳，了於心，當亦有所興感.[55] His intention to transmit a powerful, clear message to the masses resonates with many other nineteenth-century dramatists' agendas.

*Karmic Ties* also differs from *The Peach Blossom Fan* in its emphasis on moral admonishment, rather than on lyrically expressed sentiments. Both plays begin with an aria. In *The Peach Blossom Fan*, it is sung by the Old Master of Ceremonies:

An antique gentleman nonpareil: who can be my equal? / This vessel, neither jade nor bronze, / is wrapped in the luster of appreciation. / A remnant spirit, a friendless survivor— / Why bother to hide from the modern scoffers? / With one stroke the brush erases old regrets that fill my heart. / Encounter the drinking and the singing, / and any place becomes fit for tarrying. / Sons are filial; subjects, loyal: everything's cordial— / Don't pine for what is impossible.

古董先生誰似我？非玉非銅，滿面包漿裹。剩魄殘魂無伴夥，時人指笑何須躲。舊恨填胸一筆抹，遇酒逢歌，隨處留皆可。子孝臣忠萬事妥，休思更吃人參果。[56]

54. Kong Shangren, "*Taohua shan* fanli" 桃花扇凡例, in *Taohua shan*, 2.
55. *MZY*, 1:6b.
56. Kong Shangren, *Taohua shan*, 1; Wai-yee Li, *The Peach Blossom Fan*, unpublished manuscript.

The Old Master of Ceremonies has witnessed historical change, but his time has passed. His way of existence brings to mind the early Qing "remnant subject" (*yimin* 遺民), who imagined themselves to have been "left behind" in the abyss of time formed by the transition into the new dynasty. Claiming to have neither attachment nor feelings, the Old Master of Ceremonies indulges himself in song and wine. The evocation of "old sorrows," however, cues readers to contemplate the pain behind the lighthearted tone.

In *Karmic Ties*, the first aria is sung by the Ritual Master at a celestial palace:

> A crippled old man in charge of the Jade Palace, / Success, failure, rise and fall: I have watched them all. / Refilling water and burning incense, I have no company. / Unoccupied, I sit among flowers and the shadows of trees. / Ceaseless, human affairs are like the turning axle of a cart. / Bronze camel among thistles and thorns: how many wars have they witnessed? / If filial duty and loyalty reign, the universe will thrive. / Reward for good and retribution for evil are all decided by karma.
>
> 監管瓊宮一老跛，成敗興亡，閱盡無非我。換水燒香無伴夥，閒來無事花陰坐。人事忙忙如轉輠，荊棘銅駝，幾見遭兵火？子孝臣忠萬事妥，善彰惡報皆因果。[57]

The Ritual Master here clearly parallels the Old Master of Ceremonies in *The Peach Blossom Fan*. Some phrases in *Karmic Ties*, such as "no company" 無伴夥 and "if filial duty and loyalty reign, the universe will thrive" 子孝臣忠萬事妥 are verbatim quotations. The Ritual Master is also an old man who has witnessed the vicissitudes of history. However, he speaks of being "crippled," which may suggest that he is a war survivor; as such, his performance of obliviousness and carefreeness could be read as a form of survivor's emotional escape. Both authors, through these arias, express indifference toward public life and sensual pleasure, but of the two, only the writer of *Karmic Ties* visualizes

57. *MZY*, 1:1a. During the Jin dynasty (266–420 CE), Suo Jing 索靖 (239–303) foresaw the coming political crisis. He once pointed to the bronze camel in front of the Luoyang Palace and commented, "I see you will be buried in thistles and thorns." People later used this image in descriptions of war. See *Jin shu, ce* 5, *juan* 60:1648.

the destruction caused by war, bringing memories of the war to the fore. The Old Master of Ceremonies ends his song with a yearning for immortality, but the Ritual Master keeps his focus in the human realm, ending on a reductive, moralistic note: rewards and punishment will be meted out according to the karmic rule of retribution.

The way characters are drawn in *Karmic Ties* may be influenced by "The Principal Guidelines of *The Peach Blossom Fan*," but it does not accord with the principle of cosmic balance on which Kong Shangren bases his characters. *The Peach Blossom Fan* divides its characters into the categories "left" (*zuo* 左), "right" (*you* 右), "odd" (*ji* 奇), "even" (*ou* 偶), and "general" (*zong* 總); these categories complement one another, demonstrating the *yin* and *yang* balance of the cosmos.[58] The author of *Karmic Ties* defines the categories a little differently, keeping "left" and "right," and adding the category "additional" (*fu* 附). Under the "additional," the playwright groups together political and military figures—the kind of figures that are categorized as "odd" and "even" in *The Peach Blossom Fan*. *Karmic Ties* leaves out the "general" category of *The Peach Blossom Fan*, which includes two characters symbolic of the transcendental order promised by Daoist enlightenment and Confucian rituals. Kong Shangren's design reflects his attempt to provide a rational understanding of events in his theatrical representation;[59] in the case of *Karmic Ties*, we see no such attempt to offer an all-encompassing rationalizing structure.

In *Karmic Ties*, even the "left" and "right" categories that supposedly stand for the cosmic balance of the play do not fulfill that capacity completely, as a comparison between this play and *The Peach Blossom Fan* shows. In "The Principle Guidelines of *The Peach Blossom Fan*," the category "left" comprises the main male characters, who are members of the Restoration Society (Fu she 復社) fighting against corrupt administrators; "right," on the other hand, includes mostly female characters from the courtesan quarter. This design suggests a balance between male and female, as well as the political and the romantic. *Karmic Ties*, at the first glance, seems to follow this design by designating the main male characters as "left" and the deities as "right." However,

58. C. H. Wang, "The Double Plot of *T'ao-Hua Shan*," 10.
59. Wai-yee Li, "The Representation of History," 424.

since the deities are the celestial forms of the male characters, the complementary relationship between the "left" and "right" is unsubstantiated: the deities may as well be the empty reflections of the male characters.

*Karmic Ties* seeks to adopt the structural design of *The Peach Blossom Fan* to represent history in a meaningful way, but the plot turns on the bond of brotherhood, which in this case is formed through familial relations and fortuitous encounters. Confucian virtues such as righteousness and loyalty formed the idealistic basis for such bonds. In an early scene of the play, at a Daoist temple, the four main characters vow to pay back imperial favors through loyalty and righteousness. The brothers model themselves on a similar sworn brotherhood, whose members swear an "oath at the Peach Garden" (*taoyuan san jieyi* 桃園三結義) in a novel, *Romance of Three Kingdoms*. As part of a shared repertoire of Chinese dramatic and storytelling traditions, the trope of this "Oath at the Peach Garden" circulated also among the Taiping rebels (quoted in chapter 1) to depict their "brotherhood." In this overlap, we see how, by using the same trope, both the Taipings and the Qing elites represented themselves to be righteous executors of violence.

However, whether brotherhood is meaningful enough to salvage or compensate for political disorder remains a question. Though Lotus and his brothers harbor ambitions in the political domain and eventually find their cause by joining together to fight the rebels, their first actions are unfocused and ineffective. First, their brotherhood is tested. When the rebels come down the Yangtze River and take over the town, Lotus, Orchid, and Chrysanthemum gather their families and flee. On the outskirts of the town, Orchid sees Chrysanthemum hustling his family to his cousin's house in the countryside. Having prepared a boat, Orchid asks whether Chrysanthemum would like to wait for Lotus so all three families can leave together. Without giving it a thought, Chrysanthemum says, "Survival is the most important thing right now, and you want to wait for others?!?" 此時性命要緊，還等人哩 as he "dashes off" 飛跑下.[60] Orchid, however, waits for Lotus and their families. Friendship between men is always problematic in Confucian tradition,

60. *MZY*, 2:43a.

because it may hinder male family members from fulfilling their familial obligation.[61] During the late Ming, some Neo-Confucian thinkers supported the notion of the fraternal bond, since "brothers" may share an understanding of familial responsibilities and support each other in fulfilling the demands.[62] Nevertheless, these understandings could break down under the contingencies of war. To what extent should one risk one's own family for the sake of a friend and his family? More important, if the bonds of brotherhood are conditional, how can such a relationship continue to symbolize absolute order?

The uncertainties that stem from the conflicting needs of the brothers in *Karmic Ties*, however, are soon brushed aside by their collective political cause of quelling the rebels. The political aspirations the brothers share also empower them to transcend private concerns about family, and this move provides the brotherhood with a higher cause that redeems them from moral disorientation. This political ambition, however, is not realized through the channel of the Qing government, though the three men do attempt to enlist. Though Lotus's brothers are assigned positions, Lotus himself does not win the favor of the Qing general. In protest, Lotus's brothers refuse to continue serving. Seeing their predicament, other flower deities descend from Heaven to help.[63]

The cause of quelling the rebels justifies the brothers' formation of their own militia that is independent of the central government. This theme has precedents in late imperial Chinese history and literature, where private militias were justified as a means to repress subversive elements that threatened to destroy society. What the sworn brothers do, and the way they do it, is similar to the plotting in a novel written just before the Taiping Rebellion by Yu Wanchun 俞萬春 (1794–1849). Yu's novel, *Quell the Bandits*, is a sequel to *Water Margin*, a sixteenth-century novel set in the twelfth century. Yu Wanchun had participated in putting down a peasant rebellion in Guangdong Province and contributed to military action during the British invasion of Guangdong.

61. Huang, "Male Friendship in Ming China," 2.

62. McDermott, "Friendship and Its Friends in the Late Ming."

63. The deities assume the forms of a Buddhist monk and a Daoist priest in the human realm. Such transformations call to mind the liminal figures of a Buddhist monk and Daoist priest who bring messages of enlightenment to other characters in *Dream of the Red Chamber*.

In *Quell the Bandits*, the Daoist priest Chen Xizhen and his daughter, Chen Liqing, organize a local military force to pacify the bandits. They are rewarded by the central government after the military campaign, but they refuse to join officialdom. Instead, they ascend to Heaven as Daoist immortals. *Quell the Bandits* clearly follows an agenda of eradicating outlaws to reinstate the central government. However, the story also involves the disintegration of central power, thus deliberately invoking the anachronism of independent militias to comment on contemporary politics. If *Quell the Bandits* re-creates the literary past of *Water Margin* "to prescribe a historical future," *Karmic Ties* echoes that same literary past to register recent memories.[64] It is bitterly ironic that the memories in *Karmic Ties* are realizations of the future that *Quell the Bandits* foretold. If *Water Margin* and *Quell the Bandits* explicitly repress the wish for subversion, the Taiping Rebellion is the moment when repressed wishes were unleashed in their most violent forms. When *Karmic Ties* was written, the destruction caused by the war was still ubiquitous. As writers of the Taiping era articulated the different needs of the individual and the polis, they became acutely aware of the irreconcilable needs of the center and the local. The brotherhood and its military campaign in *Karmic Ties* are therefore simultaneously a reinforcement of imperial governance and an expression of anarchy, in its deployment of an unofficial, unsanctioned militia. By spontaneously banding together and taking up arms to pursue a military cause, the brothers in *Karmic Ties* parallel the rebels they aim to pacify.

This political dimension is amplified when the brothers successfully quell the rebellion. In this scene, the central government awards Orchid, Plum Blossom, and Lotus with official posts, and Lotus also marries a virtuous woman. This plot element resembles the conventional "grand reunion" closing scene in *chuanqi* drama. This kind of traditional ending represents the convergence of order in the public and private realms.[65] However, rather than domestic felicity and political

---

64. David Der-wei Wang, *Fin-de-siècle Splendor*, 129.
65. Ming and Qing *chuanqi* usually end with the marriage of the scholar and the beauty (*da tuanyuan*). The marriage is premised upon the scholar's success in the civil examination and a brilliant official career.

contentment, the "reunion" scene of *Karmic Ties* shows dissatisfaction: the government that the brothers fought to support is corrupt, and the brothers' futures are far from content. In addition, it isn't even the final, culminating scene of *Karmic Ties*, as would be typical in traditional plays. In *Karmic Ties*, Lotus's father sings,

> Alas, one should not be vainly optimistic. / Those who have fought courageously, / and did not hesitate to sacrifice their lives on the battlefield are not blessed with imperial favor. / Is anyone aware that those who enjoy high rank and sit in the imperial palace actually have benefited from nepotism? / On behalf of others, I vent my discontent. / I cannot help pouring forth this mournful song.
> 嘆人生何須妄想，看那沙場戰將，拼死不顧命的英雄受不到皇恩蕩蕩。可知那靠姻眷的功名高坐在朝堂。代人恨，不覺悲聲放。[66]

Lotus and his brothers are forced to part so each can take a post in a different region. In this way, the bureaucratic system breaks the fraternal bond apart in geographical terms. In other words, even though the bond between the sworn brothers constitutes a kind of alternative order that gives meaning to wartime disorder, the restoration of absolute imperial authority undermines that order symbolized by fraternal bonding.

Tragedies follow the separation of the brothers. Orchid, now a governor in the capital, submits a memorial to the throne to oppose the policy allowing foreigners to enter China's interior along the Yangtze River. This act offends those in power, who send Orchid to prison, where he commits suicide. Plum Blossom, after learning about Orchid's death, leaves his post as a military officer out of fear and disappointment. Lotus, meanwhile, has endured a long, lonely, and financially ruinous delay waiting for an official position to open up.[67] Once appointed, he uses public money for disaster relief following a flood, but is faulted for wasting funds from the state treasury. Confronted by this

---

66. *MZY*, 4:2b.

67. In the late Qing, due to the large number of civil-examination degree holders, a degree holder had to wait in a long queue for a position to open up. To keep their position in the queue, degree holders had to pay a regular remittance (*juan na* 捐納) to the central government. See Lawrence Wang, "Legacy of Success."

ungrounded and unreasonable accusation, Lotus resigns. Taken together, the experiences of Orchid, Plum Blossom, and Lotus illustrate the hopeless struggles waged by upright officials against the corrupt imperial system: neither civil and military officers nor local governors could escape its grip.

As *Karmic Ties* extends the temporal dimension of the plot into postwar society, we see the brotherhood break apart. The thwarted spirit of fraternity and the dispersal of the sworn brothers hark back to *Water Margin*, which centers on the question of whether rebellion is a legitimate means to fight against evil in the government. Should one support a political entity because of its legitimacy, or its morality? Once the bandits are quelled, is there an alternative for the heroes to survive the corrupt political situation?

*Karmic Ties* picks up a topic left unaddressed in *Quell the Bandits*, namely, the fate of the heroes who pacify the rebellion. The play's answer echoes what happens to the heroes of *Water Margin*; after the rebels in the novel submit to imperial power, the heroes are eradicated one by one when they enter the government. All three texts discussed here justify local use of military forces serving in absolute loyalty to the emperor; however, all the heroes in these texts, whether rebels or their oppressors, have to disband their military forces sooner or later to safeguard imperial order. In this sense, these forces are all deemed "unruly." The question then arises: When those who pacify rebels for the state are destined to share the same fate as their enemies, why should anyone uphold loyalty to such a ruling power? The plot turn in *Karmic Ties*, in which the brothers are treated so unjustly, implies the playwright's discontent with the political realm; in effect, he may have unexpectedly acknowledged the cause of rebellions. If *Quell the Bandits* only obliquely suggests the conflict between the center and the local, *Karmic Ties* makes the irreconcilability of the two starkly obvious: brotherhood threatens imperial authority because it emphasizes horizontal bonds over vertical hierarchy. Written to mark the end of the Taiping Civil War, *Karmic Ties* in effect foreshadows yet another political uprising. Having experienced the traumatic war and still living in its aftermath, the writer was not yet able to transcend the past; the disappointing present might have urged him to reevaluate the end of the war and his political environment.

## Playwriting as the Reinvention of Community

When *Karmic Ties* was written, memories of suffering and horror at war destruction still haunted the survivors; as political order was restored in postwar society, injustice and power struggles resulted in even greater disappointment.[68] Plays, as a means of coming to terms with not only the traumatic past but also the defective present, were written and circulated within literati communities, and some were likely also performed onstage. The practice of playwriting ran parallel with a series of postwar community-directed projects undertaken by Zeng Guofan and local elites like Shen Zi, such as compiling gazetteers and building temples and shrines. The sheer number of the prefatory materials attached to the plays reveals the extent to which the communities were involved in post-Taiping dramatic projects. *Karmic Ties* has sixteen prefatory pieces; another play of the period, *The Cliff for Burying Clouds*, has twenty-nine. Some writers of the prefaces use courtesy names or pseudonyms, but some sign their real names. The regional identities indicated by these writers suggest that the geographical scope of the prefatory material extends as far as Beijing and Hainan, even though the playwrights were primarily based in the Jiangsu, Anhui, Hubei, and Hunan Provinces. Some playwrights, such as Xu Shanchang and Zheng Youxi, formed friendships and wrote prefaces for each other's plays. They also shared antagonism for the Taiping rebels and lamented the catastrophic consequences of the war.[69] The large number of these paratextual materials—commentaries, prefaces, and personal accounts—contribute to the collective discourse commemorating the war dead.[70]

68. On how postwar constructions are politically charged, see Wooldridge, "Building and State Building in Nanjing."

69. For instance, Zheng Youxi wrote the prefaces for Xu Shanchang's three plays: *Lingwa shi* 靈媧石, *Fuling xian* 茯苓仙, and *Shenxian yin* 神仙引. Xu wrote a preface for Zheng's play titled *Yan shuang ming* 雁霜鳴. See Chao Song, "Wan Qing qujia Xu Shanchang yanjiu," 19.

70. Huntington, "The Captive's Revenge," illustrates this point with the example of *Lihua xue*. On collective efforts to commemorate the deceased and making sense of the war, see Meyer-Fong, *What Remains*. The contributors of the prefatory writings for *Karmic Ties* hail from regions all over China, making the discourse a national

*Karmic Ties* both reinvents and enacts memories of the Taiping Civil War to create an opportunity for collective remembrance of the past; at the same time, it is also an attempt to transcend those traumatic moments. These effects are strengthened and extended by the paratextual materials that accompany the printed text. These materials form a discursive space for sentiments ranging from frustration and unresolved angst to an appreciation of peace and reconciliation. Written to be shared with the writer's friends, *Karmic Ties* serves, in effect, as a medium to hold the group together. It is unclear whether *Karmic Ties* was ever performed, but the writer's preface suggests that it probably was. Even if it was not performed, the work was certainly read and shared within the writer's social circle.

The writers of prefaces to *Karmic Ties* shared a weariness with perpetual military violence. They reflected on the war through the lens of the literary tradition that portrays battle and ruin, thereby locating the war within the landscape of a shared cultural tradition and attributing a historical depth to the present chaos. For instance, a writer who went by the pseudonym "Old Man of Colorful Clouds in a Well" (Jing ni laoren 井霓老人) writes, "Banners and flags advance along the Chu River. / Everywhere, I see graveyards and sorrow" 旌旗直下楚江頭, 滿目黃沙遍地愁.[71] The anguished feeling is a result of the absence of a hero: "The thunderous sound of military drums shakes the ground with its sorrow. / Deer roam over the Phoenix Terrace. / No one is willing to use their power to salvage the desperate situation. / In vain comes the report that the iron lock of the Yangtze River is opened" 鼕鼓聲喧動地哀，鹿麋頻上鳳凰台。無人肯使回天力，空報長江鐵鎖開.[72] Alluding to Bai Juyi's 白居易 (772–846) "Song of Lasting Regret" ("Chang hen ge" 長恨歌) written after the An Lushan Rebellion that initiated the decline of the Tang dynasty, the first line casts the present war in the light of one of the darkest moments in Chinese history. The ground shaken by sorrow (*dong di ai* 動地哀) alludes at the same time

---

instead of local one. Military and political power in Hunan Province that arose during the Taiping Civil War and expanded to other regions is discussed in Platt, *Provincial Patriots*, 23, 25.

71. *MZY*, 1:10a. *Huangsha* 黃沙 is a standard allusion to graveyards.

72. *MZY*, 1:10a.

to Li Shangyin's line: "The singing of 'The Song of Huangzhu' shakes the ground with its sorrow" 黃竹歌聲動地哀 from "The Immortal Pool" (*Yao chi* 瑤池), a poem about King Mu of Zhou (r. ?–922 BCE). In one of his travels, King Mu saw a commoner who had frozen to death, and was moved to write "The Song of Huangzhu" to express his sorrow. By using this allusion, the author highlights the pains inflicted by the war on the people. The image that follows, in the second line— the Terrace of Phoenix that has become wilderness—is one commonly associated with devastation. In the postwar context, it would evoke in its readers the memory that the ancient city of Nanjing, the location of the Phoenix Terrace, once served as the capital for the rebels. In a poem by the early Qing poet Zhou Qiong 周瓊 (ca. mid-seventeenth century), a similar image is used to express feelings "linked to mourning for the fallen dynasty."[73] The reference to the Yangtze River alludes to Liu Yuxi's 劉禹錫 (772–842) "Meditation on the Past at Xisai Mountain" ("Xisai shan huai gu" 西塞山懷古), in which Liu expresses nostalgia triggered by the landscape in front of him. The breaking of the iron lock on the river may refer to either the Taiping rebels or the Western invasion that had reached the interior of China along the river by the 1880s. The conclusion, however, is that in both cases, no hero was present to reverse the situation.

In the absence of salvation, pain and sorrow persist as traumatic memories haunt all survivors. *Karmic Ties* becomes a site for its audience to connect with one another as they lament the tragic events that they have collectively experienced. "How many families could find each other after separation? / In the second month, the cuckoo stands on the tree branch, weeping and singing" 亂離人後幾重圓，二月枝頭泣杜鵑.[74] Another writer echoes this: "Feelings are stirred up in my bosom. / Occurrences bring to mind the time of chaos and separation" 感慨驚懷抱，遭逢憶亂離.[75] As the past is literally replayed, it triggers intimate feelings and personal memories: "Those performing on stage

---

73. Wai-yee Li, *Women and National Trauma*, 171.

74. *MZY*, 1:10a.

75. *MZY*, 1:13a.

sing with deep sorrow. / Those sitting in seats have tears running down their faces" 臺上高歌悲且切，座中人泣淚成行.[76]

For many writers, the metaphor of a dream provides various ways to keep a safe distance between the present and the past. Zhou Wenzao 周雯藻 (fl. 1860) compares dreaming to a past full of ruin: "From the distinctive traces of war, I become aware of reasons for previous occurrences. / Distant and illusory is Zhuangzi's dream, who could wake up from it?" 劫灰歷歷悟前由，迷離莊夢憑誰覺.[77] At the same time, dream as a realm of escape contrasts with the violence and ruin warfare imposed. This distinction is made in Liu Huankui's 劉煥奎 (fl. 1879) lines, "A butterfly does not know the pain of war; / it delivers dreams of spring to people living in Jiangnan" 蝴蝶不知爭戰恨，送人春夢入江南.[78] A similar yearning for recovery from the war is seen in another poem by the same writer: "There is also the time when a dream comes true in one's hometown" 家园也有梦圆时.[79]

Accompanying awareness of the war's end, however, are lamentations of the transience of life. The past everyone shared was traumatic; it changed everything. But it is behind them all now, and all they have left is the present moment, and their awareness of the impermanence of life. The Old Man of Colorful Clouds in a Well says, "Sixty years pass in a blink. / Endless are the great changes that transform seas and lands. / How can I bear retelling things that had happened. / Quietly I lean against the window and listen to the cuckoo" 六十年來一瞬時，桑田滄海變無期。何堪再道從前事，閒倚窗櫺聽子規.[80] A similar line of his goes, "An aged man is not the same as a blossoming flower. / Every round of flourishing is a spring dream" 人老不如春尚好，一年春夢一繁華.[81] Such regret on the ephemerality of human life echoes the playwright's analogy: "Like flowers that blossom in the morning and perish in the evening, the span of life is quite short" 朝榮暮落，為時無幾.[82]

76. *MZY*, 1:11a.
77. *MZY*, 1:14b.
78. *MZY*, 1:12a.
79. *MZY*, 1:12a.
80. *MZY*, 1:12a.
81. *MZY*, 1:12a.
82. *MZY*, 1:5b.

The preface writers turn to their friends to confirm their collective witnessing of the past; now, they reach the moment of enlightenment together. Liu Huankui writes:

| | |
|---|---|
| 風送袈裟月滿地， | In the luminous moonlight, wind touches his cassock, |
| 菩提休笑客來遲。 | The Buddha should not laugh at the guest for coming late. |
| 卅年走熟邯鄲道， | I have been walking on the Handan Road for thirty years, |
| 才到黃粱夢醒時。 | Only now have I awakened from the dream of yellow millet.[83] |

An even clearer example of such awakening is a poem in which Zhou Wenzao reminisces:

| | |
|---|---|
| 年來心跡等沙鷗， | The traces of my heart over these years resemble that of a sand gull, |
| 悔對痴人說舊遊。 | I regret having talked about my past to those who do not understand it. |
| 百代光陰如轉瞬， | Hundreds of generations slipped by in a blink, |
| 三生浩劫話從頭。 | From the start, let's talk about the calamity of past, present, and future. |
| 君盟白水心何皎， | With your pure heart, you take a vow by limpid water, |
| 我蹋紅塵生自浮。 | Walking in the world of red dust, I let my life drift freely. |
| 為問邯鄲欹枕客， | Thus I ask the guest leaning against the pillow at Handan, |
| 今吾還似故吾不。 | Am I still like the old me?[84] |

Zhou and his fellow literati would have been very familiar with the line by the Tang poet Du Fu, "Wind-tossed, what is my likeness? / Between

83. *MZY*, 1:12b.
84. *MZY*, 1:14b.

Heaven and Earth, a single sand gull" 飄飄何所似，天地一沙鷗.[85]
Zhou compares himself to the wandering bird, but the vast openness
of Du Fu's line is replaced by an introspective gaze. Such a reflection
must be shared with those who witnessed the traumatic history with
him. He asks his friend directly, "Am I still like the old me?" Through
friends' eyes, Zhou Wenzao hopes to find confirmation of his existence's meaning after the calamity.

The moment of collective awakening from the dreamlike past
comes when the playwright presents the play to his friends. Xu Junde
徐駿德 (fl. 1880s) writes,

| | |
|---|---|
| 古今同是一梨園， | The past and the present are both a theater, |
| 演就詞源筆底翻。 | Where words stemming from the tip of the brush are performed. |
| 悲喜無端傾肺腑， | Endlessly, sadness and joy pour out from my chest, |
| 忠奸何事苦仇冤。 | Why do the faithful and the wicked hate each other? |
| 借他紫府虛空影， | I will borrow the empty shadow from the purple mansion of the immortals. |
| 快我黃粱夢裏魂。 | To please my soul in the dream of yellow millet.[86] |

In Xu Junde's poem, as in Liu Huankui's earlier-quoted poem, the
dream of yellow millet clearly echoes how the playwright evokes the
tradition of *Records of Handan*. Liu Huankui writes, "I sigh for temporary prosperity and those performing in it. / It has been always easy
to wake up from sweet dreams" 浮雲富貴慨優伶，好夢由來最易醒.[87]
Another writer, using the pseudonym of The Woodcutter under the
Plantain Tree (Jiaolu woxin zi 蕉鹿臥薪子), writes, "In one dream, one

85. Du Fu, "Lü ye shu huai" 旅夜書懷 (translated as "Writing of My Feelings
Traveling by Night"), in *The Poetry of Du Fu*, 4:76.

86. *MZY*, 1:9b.

87. *MZY*, 1:13a.

talks about another dream. However, both contexts remain the same. In what year will we be able to tell the causes and consequences of our dreams?" 夢中說夢，境依然，後果前因相識，又何年.[88] He compares the present to another dream, pointing out that this "dream" itself may be subjected to examination through a different lens in the future. The moment of awakening itself, as an ongoing reality, is part of yet another dream. The final enlightenment is again delayed, the ultimate attainment of "awakening" always evading the writer and his audience.

In his own preface, the writer of *Karmic Ties* imbues the metaphor of a dream with a variety of meanings that convey a range of literary and historical sensibilities, all of which would have struck a familiar note with his audience. Nebulous and indefinite, a dream is comparable to one's memories of life, the writer suggests. He states that "the large world under Heaven and the vast land of nine continents constitute the realm of dream" 天下之大，九州之廣，夢境也, attributing an illusory quality to reality—again, a trope that would have been familiar for his audience.[89] Ironically, the analogy of China as the realm of dream is precisely what Hong Xiuquan saw: his vision to transform the entirety of China was an attempt to realize a millenarian dream. However, the dream in *Karmic Ties* evokes a past that has disappeared and reflects on the impermanence of life. In addition, *Karmic Ties* does not just dramatize and reenact dream imagery; it balances this imagery with *yuan*, "the karmic tie," something concrete that the author uses to describe human connections that generates and manifests through a multitude of emotional and moral instances. On the conclusion of the nightmarish Taiping War—the war itself as a "bad dream"—the only graspable things are the small particles of *yuan* signifying specific and concrete human relationships. In this sense, *yuan* in *Karmic Ties* is reminiscent of the "traces" in Wei Xiuren's novel *Traces of Flowers and*

88. *MZY*, 1:14b. This allusion is from *Liezi* 列子, an early text of uncertain date, considered one of the Daoist classics. In the story, a man who has hunted and killed a deer hides its body under the leaves of a tree. When he returns later to retrieve the body, but cannot find it, he thinks what he experienced was merely a dream. *Liezi jishi*, 107–8. Also see chapter 2 of *Zhuangzi*, "When they were dreaming, they did not know it was a dream" 方其夢也，不知其夢也. *Zhuangzi*, 185.

89. *MZY*, 1:4a.

*the Moon*; both works configure the world as fragmented residue, but residue that is nonetheless tangible. Through writing and commenting on the post-Taiping plays, the generation that survived the war collects these particles to commemorate the past and anticipate an uncertain—even bleak—future.

# CHAPTER SIX

# *Fantasies*

## Transcendence and Defiance

In the aftermath of the Taiping War, a young student found work as a secretary for the government in Hangzhou. In the middle of the night, he was visited by a beautiful woman. She introduced herself as the ghost of an official's daughter who used to live in the house where the student was staying. When the Taiping rebels approached Hangzhou, the father had decided to move the whole family. To lighten her parents' burden, the daughter committed suicide. Her filial piety moved the king of Hell, who promised that she could return to human life. When the student asked her when she would return, she said, "It is not time yet. I have karmic connections with you from our previous lives; I am here to fulfill what Heaven predestined." She spent the night with the student, and they lived as a couple for the next two years until he was assigned a new post in a neighboring county. She was distraught that he had to leave and, assuming he would abandon her, she decided to leave him preemptively, asking the student, "How could a ghost be a wife for a lifetime?" He insisted, however, that their companionship transcended the boundary between life and death and declared that she must stay with him forever. With joyful tears, she revealed her true identity: After her parents died in the war, her uncle sold her into a rich household as a concubine. As the daughter of a respected official, she refused to accept this arrangement and ran away. On the night of her escape, she passed the student's spacious but empty house and thought she might find shelter there. As a form of self-protection, she pretended to be a ghost. However, impressed by the student's courage, she decided to stay with him. Now, moved by his sincerity, she revealed her true story. Praising the wisdom of her self-preservation amid chaos, the student married her, and they spent a lifetime together.

Titled "Jia Yunsheng" 賈芸生, this story is from *Fanciful Stories from My Hideaway* (*Dunku lanyan* 遁窟讕言), a short story collection by Wang Tao.[1] Touching upon issues such as identity, gender, morality, and traumatic memories, the tale reinvents the trope of a ghost with ties to the historical past to engage the polemics of violence and the uninhabitable world in the aftermath of the Taiping Civil War. In this chapter, I show that in the 1870s–1880s, stories of the strange became a critical medium for negotiating such issues. These stories configure a multitude of experiences through a supernatural lens, revealing and augmenting a reality of emotional disorientations, moral ambiguities, and historical anarchism. The use of fantasy has a long history in Chinese literary tradition. Among the many texts that were well-known during the nineteenth century was *Stories about the Strange from Liaozhai Studio* (*Liaozhai zhiyi* 聊齋誌異), a seventeenth-century collection of fantastic stories by Pu Songling 蒲松齡 (1640–1715). Emulating the style of *Stories about the Strange from Liaozhai Studio*, Xuan Ding and Wang Tao enjoyed much popularity among their nineteenth-century contemporaries.[2] Published by means of modern print technologies, their collections were widely circulated and marketed with

1. Wang Tao, *DKLY*, 2: *juan* 8, 5b–6b.

2. Other short story collections created around the time of the Taiping War include Wu Chichang 吳熾昌 (fl. 1850s), *Kechuang xianhua* 客窗閒話; Mao Xianglin 毛祥麟 (fl. 1850s), *Mo yu lu* 墨餘錄; etc. For an overview of the Qing emulation of *Stories about the Strange from Liaozhai Studio*, see Wang Haiyang, *Qingdai fang Liaozhai zhiyi*. Rania Huntington introduces the general conditions and structures of several *biji* 筆記 (miscellaneous notes) collections written after the Taiping War in her article, "Chaos, Memory, and Genre." Stories about the strange in traditional China can be categorized into two subgenres: *zhiguai* 志怪 stories that are often found in *biji* collections, and those following the *Liaozhai* style. *Zhiguai* stories are characterized by succinct language and brevity. Xuan Ding's and Wang Tao's works align more with the tradition of *Stories about the Strange from Liaozhai Studio*, though Wang Tao's *Fanciful Stories from My Hideaway* may be deemed more of a traditional

references to their seventeenth-century predecessor.[3] The stories referencing the Taiping Civil War make up about one-tenth of Xuan Ding's
collections; in Wang Tao's, they make up almost one-fifth.[4] Even
though most of the stories I discuss in this chapter are directly linked
to the Taiping Civil War, some that do not specifically refer to the war
still indicate concerns about violence and disorder; I therefore include
them here as expressions of trauma. Through their reworkings of the
tropes and topoi of family separation and reunion, returning ghosts,
"peach blossom spring," and dreams of yellow millet, the stories by
Xuan Ding and Wang Tao convey a surreal vision of the war and its
aftermath through a strange mixture of the real and the fantastic. Their
dominant emotions are disillusionment and despair, and they summon
an apocalyptic vision of history. Their fictions respond to and reinforce
the sense of "the collapse of Heaven."

These stories could be viewed as "fabulations" oriented toward the
future, in the sense defined by Robert Scholes, who uses the term "fabulation" to discuss novels that subvert familiar narrative forms and temporal structures to include elements of the fantastic, mythical, and
nightmarish.[5] The first philosophical use of "fabulation" is found in
Henri Bergson's *The Two Sources of Morality and Religion*, where the
term denotes the process of "creating the myths of forces, spirits, and
deities that foster social cohesion and individual contentment" for

---

biji collection. In the post-Taiping context, *biji* collections of *zhiguai* stories were
mostly disseminated via the more traditional woodblock printing method.

3. From 1894 onward, Wang Tao's short story collections were published with
the phrase "*Liaozhai zhiyi*" ("the continuation of *Liaozhai zhiyi*") in their titles. See
Wang Tao, *Sanxu Liaozhai zhiyi* 三續聊齋誌異 (Shanghai: Wenyun shuju, 1894),
and Wang Tao, *Zhengxu hou Liaozhai zhiyi* 正續後聊齋誌異 (Shanghai: Shanghai
shuju, 1896). In 1911, the *Shenbao* newspaper advertised Xuan Ding's short story
collections as "the only masterpiece after *Liaozhai zhiyi*." Advertisement in *Shenbao*,
July 26, 1911. The publication of their stories should also be viewed in the post-Taiping
context when interests in fiction and stories grew among a new generation of writers
and readers. See Widmer, *Fiction's Family*, 5.

4. Between Wang Tao's first collection of short stories and his last one, the
proportion of stories about the Taiping Civil War decreases. Scholars have noted the
Taiping War theme in Wang Tao's stories. See Dai Shunli, "Dui Wang Tao Taiping
tianguo."

5. Scholes, *The Fabulators*.

religion in closed societies.[6] Gilles Deleuze, developing Bergson's discussion, uses "fabulation" to designate the process of rendering the suppressed visible through genuine creativity. According to Deleuze, fabulations offer open, liberating, and dynamic visions, but their possibilities cannot be precisely defined. Collectively, these visions "break the continuities of received stories and deterministic histories . . . and open up to an elaboration in the construction of a new mode of collective agency."[7] In the context of China at the end of the nineteenth century and the beginning of the twentieth, I would call this collective agency "reform" and "revolution."

## The Authors and Their Texts

### Xuan Ding

Xuan Ding was born into a well-to-do family in Tianchang County, Anhui Province. As a young boy, he received a good Confucian education. Under his mother's care and influence, Xuan Ding became particularly interested in Buddhism, Daoism, and stories of the supernatural and strange. When he was twenty, Xuan Ding lost both his parents and his family fortune was expropriated by greedy clansmen. After that, this newly-poor young man led a precarious life, eking out a living through his knowledge of calligraphy, painting, and literature. When he was twenty-seven years old, he was forced to flee his hometown because of the Taiping invasion. He subsequently joined one of the important late Qing military forces, the Huai army, under the command of Li Hongzhang 李鴻章 (1823–1901) to fight the rebels. Xuan Ding was never rewarded for his military service, even though some recognition was due to him as a Taiping War veteran. When the war ended, he went to Shanghai to make a living selling his artwork and calligraphy. In his thirties, Xuan Ding occasionally undertook secretarial (*muliao* 幕僚) positions for officials in Shandong and

---

6. Bergson, *The Two Sources of Morality and Religion*, 198–99.

7. See Bogue's summary of Deleuze's argument in his "Fabulation, Narration and the People to Come," 221.

Jiangsu.[8] His employment was unstable, and he constantly faced financial destitution. In one of the pieces he wrote on commission (an epilogue for an art catalog), he spoke dismissively of himself: "In both reading books and learning military skills, I accomplish nothing. Dependent upon others, my efforts only better other people's lives while everyone laughs at my rags and tattered cap" 鼎讀書不成，學劍不成，依人作嫁，殘衫破帽，人皆譏笑.[9]

In the preface to his collection of short stories, *Records under the Autumn Lamp on Rainy Nights* (*Yeyu qiudeng lu* 夜雨秋燈錄), Xuan Ding identifies four extraordinary moments in life. At the age of nineteen, he almost died of an illness, but was miraculously cured after he began to recite the *Tract on Divine Action and Response* (*Taishang ganying pian* 太上感應篇), a morality book that was widely circulated during the Qing dynasty. The next year, when on the verge of starvation at an abandoned temple, he revived after chanting *The Lotus Sutra* and *The Diamond Sutra*. On his fortieth birthday, he had an existential crisis that prompted him to begin writing *Records under the Autumn Lamp on Rainy Nights*. He recalls an autumn day when he was unexpectedly overcome with emotion while walking with a friend along a path completely carpeted by yellow flowers. Despondently, Xuan Ding asked his friend what day it was. Upon hearing the response, Xuan Ding was "taken by great surprise, and then yielded to great lamentation" 大驚, 繼而大慟.[10] It was his birthday. He wrote,

I was unaware, as if in a daze, that I was about to turn forty. And yet, I still remain adrift? After returning home, I lay on the bed like a stiff piece of wood, neither speaking nor crying. The following day, I became sick and almost died. My spirit was confused, and I did not understand what other people were saying. I was sick for fifteen days.

8. On Xuan Ding's life and his social network, see Yu Shihao, "Wan Qing xiaoshuo xiqu zuojia."

9. Xuan Ding, "Ti zeng Li Dudu huace hou," 12:11. A brief biography of Xuan Ding is in Heng He, "Qian yan," 1:1. In this book I follow the 1987 reprint of *Records under the Autumn Lamp on Rainy Nights* (1877) and its sequel (1880) edited by Heng He.

10. Xuan Ding, *YYQDL*, 1:3.

忽忽焉行年已四十矣。而淪落猶是乎？歸則僵臥。不語，亦不哭。明日
遂病且殆。精神惝恍，不知所云。病十五日。[11]

On the sixteenth day, however, Xuan Ding rose from his bed and began
to write down what he had seen, heard, and remembered throughout
his life. He continued to compose one or two stories each day, and after
several days, he recovered from his illness.

Xuan Ding's breakdown is reminiscent of Hong Xiuquan's mental
illness, which eventually led to the millenarian vision Hong attempted
to realize on Earth. In the preface to his book, Xuan Ding presents
himself as someone who finds solace in the world of the fantastic. His
book concludes with a story about a "divine revelation" he received that
was formative for his literary career. According to this revelation, in
his previous life Xuan Ding was a Daoist from famous Luofu Mountain
who was punished for his passion for writing. In his current life, the
revelation went on to say, Xuan Ding maintained this passion, but he
was spared punishment because his works were free of moral corruption. Portraying himself as someone deeply connected to the world of
the fantastic, Xuan Ding blurs the boundaries between reality and illusion, and this cancellation of differences sets a foundational tone for
subsequent stories of the strange.

## Wang Tao

The second highly popular writer was Wang Tao. Hailing from Suzhou,
he too received a good traditional education.[12] His mother introduced
him to legends and fantastic stories; his father, who spent most of his life
as a tutor, taught him how to write "eight-legged" exam essays and compose prose in the ancient style. Despite Wang Tao's initial success in the
county-level examination, he failed his first attempt at the provincial-
level examination. After this failure, he quit the conventional path of
examinations altogether and gravitated toward more practical

11. Xuan Ding, *YYQDL*, 1:3.
12. On Wang Tao's life experience and his political activities, see Cohen, *Between
Tradition and Modernity*; Zhang Hailin, *Wang Tao pingzhuan*; Xin Ping, *Wang Tao
pingzhuan*.

knowledge through work and self-directed study, including philology, geography, and military affairs. When his father died in 1849, Wang Tao left his hometown for Shanghai, where he worked with Walter Henry Medhurst (1796–1857), one of the earliest Western missionaries in China and a key founder of the London Missionary Society Press. During the thirteen years he worked with Medhurst, Wang Tao encountered modern print technology and Western intellectual discourse. In addition, he established close connections with Chinese intellectuals who were enthusiastic about Western science and culture. His knowledge of and interest in Western technology and civilization constituted an important aspect of Wang Tao's identity that sets him apart from many of his contemporaries.

During the Taiping Civil War, Wang Tao submitted many letters to the Qing governors of Shanghai and Jiangsu Provinces, in which he recommended that the government prioritize resisting foreign invasions over pacifying Taiping rebels. Wary of Wang Tao's connections with the West, the Qing government neither followed his suggestions nor gave him any political or military recognition. As Wang Tao accompanied missionaries and English generals in their immediate contacts with the Taiping rebels, the Qing government became even more suspicious of his motives. When the Qing troops broke into the camp of the Taiping leader Li Xiucheng 李秀成 (1823–1864) in 1862, they found a letter penned by a certain Huang Wan. This letter analyzed the military position along the Yangtze River in detail and provided strategies that, if they had been followed, would have led the Taipings to victory.[13] It didn't take the Qing government long to identify Wang Tao as the author of the letter and dispatch a search warrant for him. In October 1862, with the help of the missionaries and the British consulate, Wang Tao escaped to Hong Kong. There he formed a close relationship with James Legge (1815–1897), who he helped with the English translation of the Confucian classics. He was based in Hong Kong for the next two decades. During this time, he journeyed to Japan and several European countries. Two decades after the war, with the Qing government's tacit permission, Wang Tao returned to Shanghai and

13. Wang Tao, "Wang Tao shangshu," 186–211. See this letter in *Taiping tianguo wenshu*.

FIG. 6.1. Xuan Ding, "Seeking Reclusion in an Ink Stone" ("Yan yin tu" 研隱圖), 1866. Reprinted from *Huizhou rongxiang yishu* 徽州容像藝術 (Hefei: Anhui meishu chubanshe, 2001), 60.

began writing for the *Shenbao* newspaper, one of the earliest and most influential modern newspapers in China.

The contrast between the worldviews of Wang Tao and Xuan Ding is illustrated by two portraits (figs. 6.1 and 6.2). In a self-portrait, "Seeking Reclusion in an Ink Stone" ("Yan yin tu" 研隱圖) (fig. 6.1), Xuan Ding portrays himself as a scholar sitting within an ink stone, a visual representation that suggests the author's retreat into a dark, cave-like space where ink, the medium with which he writes and paints, will be his redemption. The portrait of Wang Tao, however, is produced using modern photographic technology (fig. 6.2). His clothes are of a style commonly adopted by late Qing social and cultural elites, so his identity as a professional writer is not immediately discernible.[14] The

14. Catherine Yeh discusses Wang Tao's identity as a major professional writer in Shanghai in *Shanghai Love*, 185–90.

FIG. 6.2. Portrait of Wang
Tao, 1868. Reproduced from
Xin Ping, *Wang Tao pingzhuan*
(Shanghai: Huadong shifan
daxue chubanshe, 1990), 2.

contrast between the traditional painting and the modern photograph
indicates the different cultural paths that literati adopted in the late
nineteenth century. If Xuan Ding represents the "antique" school,
Wang Tao embodies modernity.

## Fanciful Stories for a War-Torn Populace

Both Wang Tao and Xuan Ding wrote books in the early 1870s in response to the *Shenbao* publisher's solicitation of "innovative, marvelous, erotic, strange, secluded, and splendorous" material (*xinqi yanyi
youpi guiwei* 新奇豔異幽僻瑰瑋).[15] Modern print technology played
an important role in the production and reception of their short-story
collections. In 1877, Shenbaoguan 申報館 printed Xuan Ding's *Records*

15. "Benguan gaobai," *Shenbao*, November 13, 1874.

*under the Autumn Lamp on Rainy Nights,* which readers enthusiasti-
cally welcomed. Three years later, *The Sequel to Records under the Autumn Lamp on Rainy Nights* (*Yeyu qiudeng xu lu* 夜雨秋燈續錄) was
printed.[16] With the popularity of these books came forgeries and
bootleg copies: other publishers not only plagiarized their titles but also
incorporated stories written by others into forged works.[17] The forged
editions at first competed with the originals in the literary market and
then seemed to supersede them.[18]

In comparison to Xuan Ding, whose premature death made it
easier to exploit his authorship, Wang Tao's reputation in the late Qing
cultural milieu was probably what protected his works from being
misused. His *Fanciful Stories from My Hideaway* was published in
1875. Stories in his other two collections, *Random Jottings of a Wusong
Recluse* (*Songyin manlu* 淞隱漫錄) and *Tales of Trivia from the Banks
of the Wusong* (*Songbin suohua* 淞濱瑣話), were first serialized in the
*Dianshi zhai Pictorial* (*Dianshi zhai huabao* 點石齋畫報), then published in 1887 and 1893 collections, respectively.[19]

16. Scholars are only now beginning to study Xuan Ding and his works. Woman's
image in Xuan Ding's stories is explored in Chang Ningwen, "'*Yeyu qiudeng lu*' suo
zhanshi de"; see also Zhang Fan, "'*Yeyu qiudeng lu*' yu '*Liaozhai zhiyi*.'" For a comprehensive study of Xuan Ding's life experiences and social circles, see Sheng Yang,
*Rushi yu chushi.*

17. Some major forged editions include those printed by Wenming shuju 文明
書局 in *Qingdai biji congkan* 清代筆記叢刊 (1912) and by Jinbu shuju 進步書局 in *Biji
xiaoshuo daguan* 筆記小說大觀 (1913), as well as the punctuated Guangyi shuju 廣益
書局 edition (1915). Research on editions of *Records under the Autumn Lamp on Rainy
Nights* include Song Xin and Yang Pu, "'*Yeyu qiudeng lu*'"; and Ling Shuowei, "'*Yeyu qiudeng lu*' yanben." From *Shenbao* advertisements, we learn that Shenbaoguan sold the
original editions from 1877 to 1939, interrupting publication only between March 19,
1905, and July 26, 1911. On December 18, 1895, *Shenbao* claimed that the edition they
published was authentic, in contrast to other editions on the market.

18. The most famous example is that in *Zhongguo xiaoshuo shilüe*, written in 1925,
Lu Xun describes *Records under the Autumn Lamp on Rainy Nights* as characterized
by stories about courtesans and prostitutes. His description, however, is based on the
forged edition, suggesting that by the 1920s, the forged editions were widely circulated.
Lu Xun, *Zhongguo xiaoshuo shilüe*, 171.

19. Scholarship on Wang Tao's short stories focuses on his use of new media and
his descriptions of foreign encounters. For instance, Jiang Yubin, "Zhongguo gudai
xiaoshuo"; Dang Yueyi, "Lüelun Wang Tao wenxue guannian" and "Cong 'hou *Liaozhai*.'" Some studies look at war and violence in Wang Tao's stories. For *Tales of Trivia*

These stories originally appeared in media of different formats and content. When they were collected in books, both authors aligned themselves with the *Liaozhai* tradition by assuming an authorial persona that makes comments after the stories.[20] Xuan Ding identified himself as the Man of Frustrations (Ao nong shi 懊儂氏), and Wang Tao adopted the persona of the Historian of What Was Lost (Yi shi shi 逸史氏). In both *Records* and *The Sequel*, Xuan Ding includes his commentary after most stories. However, Wang Tao added authorial comments only to his earliest collection, *Fanciful Stories from My Hideaway*. This is because the stories in Wang Tao's later collections were originally serialized in *Shenbao*, where space constraints left no room for the author's comments. In addition, unlike other collections in the style of Pu Songling's *Stories about the Strange from Liaozhai Studio* that include stories of varying lengths, those in Wang Tao's later collections share a relatively consistent length, again due to the requirements of newspaper serialization. These features yield a glimpse into how new publication methods influenced the nineteenth-century continuation of the *Liaozhai* tradition.[21]

With the rise of modern newspapers and the introduction of Western technology, Xuan Ding and Wang Tao, from the same generation of Taiping War survivors, both reimagined the recent trauma. Their engagements with the real and the fantastic may reflect their different life experiences: Xuan Ding looked at reality through the lens of the fantastic, as evinced by his construction of an identity that includes many supernatural elements, whereas Wang Tao maintained a certain distance between these two realms. This is shown by the story at the beginning of the chapter, where his reversal of the trope of "a female ghost that returns from history" ironizes the tradition about the fantastic.

---

*from the Banks of the Wusong* I use the 1893 edition (of twelve *juan*, four *ce*) by Taipei Guangwen shuju, reprinted 1991.

20. Pu Songling, the author of *Stories about the Strange from Liaozhai Studio*, refers to himself as "Historian of the Strange," crafting an authorial image of a frustrated scholar who vents his discontentment with political corruption and social ills through stories about the strange. See Zeitlin, *Historian of the Strange*, esp. 43–61.

21. For more on how newspapers influenced the form and content of Wang Tao's literary work, see Zhang Yuanyue, "Cong baokan meiti yingxiang," and Ling Shuowei, "Shenbaoguan yu Wang Tao."

# A Moral Solution?

Morality is advocated as a remedy for war-torn, disordered reality in post-Taiping drama, but could it serve the same function in the realm of the strange and fantastic? Both authors experiment with this possibility in their stories. Xuan Ding seeks recourse in the late Ming celebration of *qing* to buttress the power of morality, whereas Wang Tao adopts the early Qing tradition extolling woman as a symbol of virtue amid catastrophic times. Their apparently opposite approaches are nevertheless connected on a deeper level. The discourse of *qing* is maintained in Pu Songling's *Stories about the Strange from Liaozhai Studio*, where attachments and desires, primarily in the forms of romantic love and friendship, are projected onto the realm of the strange. Nevertheless, in the stories composed after the Manchus consolidated their power, Pu Songling shows a strong tendency to subsume an often-transgressive "strangeness" under moral laws.[22] In eighteenth-century *zhiguai* 志怪 stories, praise for *qing* is replaced by an emphasis on moral retribution carried out by supernatural powers.

## Qing *at the Service of Morality*

Xuan Ding deems *qing*, especially *qing* manifested through sexual desire, dangerous because of its potential to transgress moral boundaries. An example of this danger can be found in the story titled "Qin Erguan" 秦二官.[23] This story begins with a young couple's budding romance, but when the parents on both sides oppose the relationship, it soon develops in an uncontrollable direction: Qin Erguan's insatiable sexual desire for her lover turns her into a sadist, criminal, and murderer, and her desire does not vanish even after she is put to death. Xuan Ding comments after this story: "Fondness in one's nature brings out *qing*, the manifestation of *qing* forms desire, the entanglements of desire become evil karma, and what is most destructive in evil karma leads to disaster" 性之暱者為情，情之發者為慾，慾之結者為孽，孽之

22. Barr, "A Comparative Study."
23. Xuan Ding, *YYQDL*, 2:584–92.

凶者為禍.[24] The narrative progression rhetorically captured in this line mirrors that in the story. Excessive *qing* and desire, therefore, could be sinful, disastrous, and destructive to human existence. Xuan Ding recognizes the transcendental power of *qing*, but approves only if it is contained within moral boundaries:

> When it comes to *qing*, parents and teachers cannot stop it; Heaven, Earth, ghosts and gods cannot forbid it; mountains, rivers, and oceans cannot separate it. . . . Isn't it truly profound *qing* when one does not harm the lover with excessive *qing* and alerts those infatuated with illusions? For those who engage in sexual intercourse all day without a pause until their bodies and minds are exhausted, and those who keep their purity but make the other person's mind and heart entangled and linger [on them], it is indeed enmity and evil karma. How could [such attitudes] be called *qing*?
>
> 情之所在，父母師保不能止。天地鬼神不能禁，山川河海不能隔 . . . 不以餘情害情人，復能以幻相警癡子，是非真深於情者乎？否則朝伐夕戕，非髓竭神枯而不已。又或潔身而退，令人魂銷氣結不能忘，直冤且孽矣，尚得謂之情乎？[25]

"Alerting those infatuated with illusions" brings to mind the Goddess of Disenchantment and the Illusory Realm of the Great Void in *Dream of the Red Chamber*, where *qing* serves as a means of achieving enlightenment. However, as Xuan Ding adapts the relationship between illusion and *qing*, he defines true *qing* as embodying Confucian moral propriety.

The trope of illusion and enlightenment takes an unlikely form in Xuan Ding's story "Mrs. Pigs" ("Hai shi furen" 亥氏夫人) to convey the horror of the complete mayhem of the Taiping War. In this story, a monk gets lost in deep mountain areas. He comes across a reclusive house with a beautiful and seductive woman in her thirties and many extraordinarily attractive young girls. Upon invitation, the monk stays with them and engages in a series of sexual adventures until one day,

---

24. Xuan Ding, *YYQDL*, 2:592.
25. Xuan Ding, *YYQDL*, 1:147.

a huge serpent suddenly appears and devours everything. Only then did the true form of the beauties manifest as they fled: they were all wild boars. The monk managed to escape and return to his village, but contracted leprosy from this experience and became grossly ill. However, he was proud of this encounter and kept boasting about his sexual rendezvous.

Here the author reverses the topos of a man's accidental visit to the illusory realm, where he relishes sensual pleasures with deities and may even achieve enlightenment.[26] In "Mrs. Pigs," Xuan Ding turns the man, the deities, and the spiritual enlightenment within literary tradition into a lascivious monk, anthropomorphized pigs, and physical corruption that manifests as sexual dysfunction and leprosy. In the comment attached to the story, Xuan Ding recounts that when the war reached his hometown, the domestic pigs returned to their wild state. Their skin turned thick and impenetrable, and they made their own lairs. Eating dead human bodies turned their eyes bright blood-red. "The monk," Xuan Ding writes, "is fortunate not to be chewed up by the wild boars" 其不為剛鬣大嚼亦僥倖矣哉.[27] On its surface, "Mrs. Pigs" refashions the trope of illusory transcendence into an allegory about the debasement of an immoral person whose uncontrolled sexual desire turns him into an animal-like being. On a deeper level, however, this re-creation employs sex as a metaphor to convey inexplicable violence, a narrative design reminiscent of chapter 48 in *Traces of Flowers and the Moon* (see chapter 4). Its bleak moral vision hints at the terror that arises in confrontation with the vanishing boundary between humanity and animality in the context of death and chaos, reminding us of the association between rebels and beasts in post-Taiping drama. If the anthropomorphized wild pigs are a metaphor for savage war, the

26. One of the earliest narratives using this topos is the fifth-century story about the trip of Liu Chen and Ruan Zhao to Tiantai Mountain in *You ming lu* 幽明錄. Stephen Owen traces the tenth-century development of this topos in Tang *chuanqi* stories as represented by "Liwa zhuan" and "Yingying zhuan." See Owen, *The End of the Chinese "Middle Ages,"* 130–78. One of the best-known examples of this topos is Jia Baoyu's visit to the Illusory Realm of the Great Void in chap. 5 of the eighteenth-century masterpiece *Honglou meng*, where he is situated among the deities but fails to achieve enlightenment in the end.

27. Xuan Ding, *YYQDL*, 2:761.

monk's infection with leprosy—an incurable and appalling disease in the mid-nineteenth century—may symbolize the wounds inflicted by the war as a result of man's moral failure, which will forever fester.

The tentative cure Xuan Ding proposes is the synthesis of *qing* and morality as manifested through sincere and passionate engagement with moral ideals. In one comment, he writes: "The more marvelous the event is, the more distressed the heart; the more distressed the heart is, the more devoted the *qing*; the more devoted the *qing* is, the greater the blessings. The fundamental idea is only one word: virtue" 事愈奇者心愈苦，心愈苦者情愈专，情愈专者福愈广。要其所根者，仍惟一字，曰德.[28] Part of this statement continues to connect marvelousness and *qing* in the late Ming tradition, but Xuan Ding extends his logic to complicate the familiar rhetoric with suffering, tenacity, and divine blessing. At the end of this chain, he transforms the tradition in *Stories about the Strange from Liaozhai Studio*, which often uses morality to "tame" the strangeness that is a manifestation of the transgressive *qing*. Both marvelousness and *qing*, Xuan Ding argues, are established upon the foundation of virtue, so true *qing* does not transgress but vindicates moral norms.

Under this premise, Xuan Ding extols filial piety, the fundamental Confucian moral principle propagated by the Qing government (see chapter 2), as the omnipotent *qing* that prevails over violence and disorder. For instance, in his story "The Heroic Young Martyr Fulfilling Her Filial Piety" ("Lie shang jinxiao" 烈殇盡孝), set in the aftermath of the Taiping War, a girl commits suicide to keep her virtue intact after being cheated and sold into a brothel, but her spirit returns home to take care of her sick and widowed mother as if she were alive.[29] Whereas Du Liniang's phantasmal reunion in the sixteenth-century *chuanqi* play *The Peony Pavilion* was premised on romantic love, the daughter's return to the human realm is enabled only by her unwavering filial piety. "By the early nineteenth century," as Epstein points out, "many authors responded to the perceived threat of romantic love to the intergenerational family by reclaiming *qing* as an aspect of filial piety."[30] To contain the exemplary *qing* within the proper boundaries, Xuan

28. Xuan Ding, *YYQDL*, 1:160.
29. Xuan Ding, *YYQDL*, 1:111–16.
30. Epstein, *Orthodox Passions*, 25.

Ding does not allow the returning female ghost to carry out justice, but lets the universe exercise moral retribution on the antagonists.

To continue the important literary theme of family dispersion and reunion in early Qing literature, the stories that Xuan Ding wrote are set in the aftermath of the Taiping War, and take a more directly moralizing stand than the early Qing stories do.[31] Harking back to Li Yu's 李漁 (1611–1680) "The Father and the Son" ("Sheng wo lou" 生我樓), which shows how political chaos allows a series of happy coincidences to bring together a broken family, Xuan Ding's story, "The Jar of Silver under the Pagoda Tree" ("Huai gen yinweng" 槐根銀甕), attributes the happy ending to Heaven's blessing: a virtuous young man is rewarded with a family reunion and wealth because of his filial piety.[32] Xuan Ding's story "The Virtuous and Heroic Woman" ("Zhenlie nü" 貞烈女) brings to mind another story by Li Yu, "The Male Heir" ("Feng xian lou" 奉先樓). In both stories, a wife separated from her husband is taken up by a military leader of the invading force during the war. In the seventeenth-century story, the wife's tainted honor is redeemed by her mission to preserve the male heir of the family. In addition, her attempts to commit suicide—even though they fail—show her virtue. In contrast, in Xuan Ding's story, the woman maintains her purity and her resolution impresses a rebel king, with whose help she is able to reunite with her husband, her virtue intact.[33] The morally balanced universe in Xuan Ding's vision is further reinforced in another story, titled "Just Like the Man from Qi" ("Yanran Qi ren" 儼然齊人), where he shows that a man's unscrupulous behavior amid chaos may lead to instant moral retribution costing him his life.[34] Just as Huntington observes of post-Taiping plays, in Xuan Ding's stories the Taipings are not demonized but put in a position that makes them serve as a source of justice that rewards moral integrity and punishes degeneration.[35]

31. On family dispersion and reunion in early Qing, see Tina Lu, "Fictional Reunions," 312.

32. Li Yu, "Sheng wo lou," 11:1a–33b. Xuan Ding, *YYQDL*, 2:28–31.

33. Xuan Ding, *YYQDL*, 1:121.

34. Xuan Ding, *YYQDL*, 1:85.

35. See Huntington, "Singing Punishment and Redemption."

## Pragmatic Morality

Xuan Ding insists on the efficacy of moral retribution, but his contemporary Wang Tao is skeptical of traditional moral parameters. In "The Wife of Liu" ("Liu shi fu" 劉氏婦) from his collection *Fanciful Stories from My Hideaway*, Wang Tao shows sympathy and understanding for a remarried woman who refuses to return to her first husband, who she believed had died after being abducted by the Taipings.[36] According to traditional moral standards, a remarried woman is unchaste; however, in this story, because everyone believed the first husband was dead, she had the opportunity to redeem herself by returning to him, as the woman does in Xuan Ding's "The Virtuous and Heroic Woman." The wife's decision to turn down the first husband's offer does not accord with conventional moral norms, but Wang Tao understands and approves of this unconventionality. In "Jiang Yuanxiang" 江遠香, Wang Tao writes about the accidental encounter of a husband forced to work for the Taipings with his wife, who was sold as a concubine after their separation during the war.[37] Following the wife's plan, the couple escapes from the rebel-controlled city. Stating that "little is left of the husband's moral integrity" 其節已無可稱 and "one cannot consider the woman chaste" 稱之曰貞，則亦未也, Wang Tao nevertheless continues to show sympathy for those forced to compromise their morality in extreme circumstances. In doing so, he reevaluates moral absolutes such as loyalty and chastity with practical wisdom to arrive at an endorsement of moral relativity. This sentiment, again, resonates with Li Yu's short stories such as "The Male Heir." At the same time, it foreshadows Wu Jianren's 吳趼人 (1866–1910) *Sea of Regret* (*Hen hai* 恨海), published at the beginning of the twentieth century, which lays bare the irretrievability of traditional moral ideals through the tragic romances of two young couples during the Boxer Rebellion (1899–1901).[38]

---

36. Wang Tao, *DKLY*, 2: *juan* 6, 10b–12b.

37. Wang Tao, *DKLY*, 1: *juan* 1, 16b–18a.

38. On *The Sea of Regret*, see Tang Xiaobing, *Chinese Modern*, 11–49. See also Huters, "Creating Subjectivity."

Despite the moral relativism illustrated in the above stories, Wang Tao follows the early Qing tradition of using women as a metaphorical site for the virtue of resistance amid chaos and violence. One example is his story "Zhu Huixian" 朱慧仙 (see chapter 4). In addition to this story, the other two stories (like "Zhu Huixian," also named for their protagonists), "Yuejiao" 月嬌 and "Zhao Biniang" 趙碧孃, feature virtuous heroines who either assassinate or attempt to assassinate the rebel leaders.[39] Yue Jiao poisons a rebel leader; Zhao Biniang secretly puts two strips of cloth tainted with blood into the Eastern King's headwear to cast spells on him. At the end of each story, the woman commits suicide. Placing Yue Jiao and Zhao Biniang on a par with Zhu Jiumei, Wang Tao calls these women "virtuous and defiant" (*jie lie* 節烈).[40] As chapter 4 shows, during and after the Taiping Civil War, numerous memories and fantasies of women's victimhood and resistance circulated among the survivors. Wang Tao's characterizations of these women and their stories as "virtuous and defiant" is equivalent to the moral framework in Xuan Ding's stories: by making women embody virtuous and loyal spirits, the writers attempt to impose a certain order on a chaotic reality.

Nevertheless, resistance from a virtuous woman is not enough to disrupt the tides of historical violence. In Wang Tao's story "Yao Yunxian" 姚雲仙, the eponymous heroine Yao learns supernatural skills from a Daoist teacher after her parents are killed by the rebels.[41] She cross-dresses as a man to work in the rebels' palace, seeking an opportunity to exact her revenge. One day, she dresses up as a palace lady to perform the *pipa* (a music instrument) for the king and hides a dagger in the instrument. During the performance, Yunxian smashes the *pipa* and hurls the dagger at the rebel chief. However, because of the distance between them, Yunxian misses her target—but manages to escape. One day, her Daoist teacher appears and says, "How abrupt your undertaking was! It is Heaven's will to let the people suffer from this atrocity. Weren't you going against Heaven by trying to throw the dagger at the rebel chief?" 子舉事一何鹵莽乃爾！下民遭此大劫，乃天數也。子

---

39. Wang Tao, *DKLY*, 1: *juan* 2, 9b–10b; Wang Tao, *DKLY*, 1: *juan* 3, 17b–18b.
40. Wang Tao, *DKLY*, 1: *juan* 3, 18b.
41. Wang Tao, *SYML*, 7:9b–10b.

欲推刃於巨酋，毋乃逆天。[42] While wandering around at the end of the story, she befriends a young student, whom she ultimately weds.

The multilayered gender performance in this story raises the question of how to represent an individual's resistance against the mighty Taiping power. Yunxian cross-dresses as a man to gain access to the palace, and yet she must dress as a woman to execute her plan of revenge. In a similar vein, Yunxian is eventually subsumed into the domestic order through her marriage, which may again suggest the author's desire to return to traditional gender and social norms. The convergence of the personal and the political is most pronounced when the heroine throws the dagger at the king, a scene that harks back to a scene in *The Peach Blossom Fan*, when the courtesan Li Xiangjun accuses the corrupt southern Ming prime minister of sensual indulgence and political opportunism. The heroine's unsuccessful assassination attempt on the Taiping king may also recall the assassin Jing Ke 荊軻 (?–277 BCE), who throws a dagger at the first Qin emperor but fails at his mission. Whereas *The Peach Blossom Fan* concludes by offering a Daoist solution to both Li Xianjun's personal tragedy and the fall of the Ming dynasty, in Wang Tao's story "Yao Yunxian" the Daoist teacher says the disaster is Heaven's will, offering the notion of fate to explain the inevitability of the Taiping War. Taken together, though excellent cross-dressing skills may greatly enhance one's ability to navigate difficult conditions and maximize one's agency, all efforts are meaningless when they conflict with Heaven's will.

Synthesizing seventeenth- and eighteenth-century traditions, Xuan Ding seeks to create a world where the ideal of *qing* is synonymous with impassioned morality, and family dispersion and reunion strictly follow the rule of moral retribution. Despite the tremendous significance he attributes to morality, the moral rules he invokes are also a part of the supernatural realm of the fantastic, just as the author's life is marked by apparently supernatural events in his self-introduction. In contrast, Wang Tao makes no attempt to conjure a world governed by moral consistency. Following the early Qing tradition of commemorating women who defy oppression and violence as virtuous paragons, Wang Tao, like the writer of *Karmic Ties in a*

42. Wang Tao, *SYML*, 7:9b–10b.

*Dream*, nonetheless refuses to suggest the illusion that a virtuous woman's resistance can heal national trauma.

## Ghost Matters

Although Xuan Ding and Wang Tao exhibit divergent views of the grounds and consequences of morality in a postwar reconstruction effort, they both deem the ghost of a historical personage important in making sense of the recent political turbulence. In their stories, the taxonomy of historical ghosts expands to include spectral communities, the unreliable spirits of Ming loyalists, and eerie headless ghosts as the authors attempt to come to terms with the massive death toll of the Taiping Civil War and renegotiate the legacy of the Ming-Qing dynastic transition.

### Female Ghosts Old and New

The absence of any explanation about the connection between ghosts who lived centuries apart suggests Wang Tao assumes a natural parallel between the Ming-Qing transition and the Taiping Civil War. "Yan Exian" 嚴萼仙 (named after its female protagonist) and "Random Notes of Divine Revelation on the Planchette" ("Jixian yishi" 乩仙逸事) demonstrate this observation. In "Yan Exian," a young man accidentally encounters the ghost of a late Ming palace lady and a girl, Yan Exian, who lived during the Taiping War but was put into a death-like trance by a Daoist to avoid the calamity.[43] In comparison, the other story, "Random Notes of Divine Revelation on the Planchette," invokes the issue of historical justice through spirit writings. This story juxtaposes the accounts of the spirits of two women victims who fall into the margins of history in the aftermath of the Ming-Qing transition and the Taiping Civil War.[44] The first woman is a palace lady in the short-lived Hongguang court, and her spirit writes on the planchette: "As an imperial palace lady disgraced by a slave, by the statutes of the

43. Wang Tao, *SYML*, 8:9a–11a.
44. Wang Tao, *SYML*, 4:19a–20b.

state, I did not deserve to die; as a virtuous lady of distinction who
died a violent death, I do not have my name recorded in history books.
My heart is honest, and my feelings linger endlessly" 以帝王之宮嬪，而
受辱於人奴，國法未誅；以節烈之名媛，而屈死於非命，史冊不載。一
心耿耿，此意茫茫。[45] The author then makes a smooth transition to
the second account with this comment: "About two hundred years
later . . . Their stories are alike and evoke similar grief" 前後兩百年，事
若相類，有同悲焉。[46] In this account, a girl, though she has survived
the Taiping War, is forced to commit suicide after being abducted by
a soldier in the Qing army. Her fate recalls that of the archetypal heroine in the play *Snow on the Pear Blossom,* discussed in chapter 5. In
the Ming palace lady's story, the various political forces that inscribed
violence and violation on her body are exempt from historical judgment because her death goes unrecognized. Similarly, violence and
chaos continue to ripple outward after the Taiping War with no closure. In commemorating these women's virtuous deaths that transcend dynastic and temporal dimensions, Wang Tao seeks to bring
back the righteousness and truth neglected by history and the law. In
fact, because both history and law are state institutions, in referencing
the fall of the Ming dynasty, Wang Tao arguably ascribes a similar fate
to the Qing dynasty.

In Wang Tao's stories, the trope of ghostly communities of women
who have died violently recurs several times. This recurring device
allows the author to conceptualize the scale of the violence caused by
political catastrophes, and to evoke traumatic memories of both the
Ming-Qing dynastic transition and the Taiping Civil War. A typical story
line describes a man's accidental encounter with a party of young and
beautiful women at midnight sometime after the Taiping War. Instead
of joining the party, he eavesdrops on their conversation, only to realize
that they are ghosts. The story continues with the male protagonist
interacting with one of the ghosts the next day.

An example of this trope occurs in "Feng Peibo" 馮佩伯 (named for
its male protagonist).[47] After the Taiping War, the eponymous hero of

45. Wang Tao, *SYML*, 4:19b.
46. Wang Tao, *SYML*, 4:19b.
47. Wang Tao, *SYML*, 5:13a–14b.

the story accidentally witnesses several female ghosts having a party one night. He hears the main lady ask everyone to speak from their heart. In response, one ghost wonders where the energy of the war would be channeled. Following her comment, the party shares stories about the Eastern King's decadent lifestyle and how some women indulge themselves in his palace. Women like Zhu Huixian (Zhu Jiumei) are praised by all, but the party almost breaks into argument when Fu Shanxiang is mentioned—Fu Shanxiang being a historical figure known for her success in the women's civil examination organized by the Taipings and her active involvement in Taiping political affairs. At this juncture, Feng accidentally coughs. Startled, the party disperses. Later that night, Feng is called upon by a female ghost named Lu Xuexiang, originally from Nanjing, who committed suicide when being summoned to the rebel's palace. According to her, she and Feng are destined to have a relationship, and she would return to life if Feng could take her home. Feng brings her back to his hometown as an old relative. No one doubts their relationship. One autumn night, as they appreciate the moon on a lake, they are approached by a boat carrying other female ghosts from the party. It turns out to be a celebratory gathering: the lady sitting in the principal seat is about to be reborn, so her friends gather to send her off. Only then does Feng learn that every one of them died virtuously during the Taiping War. At the end of the story, when a friend persuades Feng to take an official post, Xuexiang stops him to ask the rhetorical question, "How could this be a time to serve?" 此豈可仕時哉. Instead, she suggests he seek reclusion in the mountain.

In this story, rather than having the specters lament their own deaths, Wang Tao creates an imaginary community to pass moral and historical judgment on the beautiful and talented women abducted by the rebels. Zhu Jiumei receives unanimous acclaim, but not the controversial Fu Shanxiang. The reference to Fu Shanxiang in "Feng Peibo" contrasts with her representation in Wang Tao's other story, "Fu Luanshi" 傅鸞史, where Fu is a talented beauty from Nanjing destined to be involved in a calamity.[48] In "Fu Luanshi," the moral ambiguities associated with Fu Shanxiang are contained within religious boundaries

48. Wang Tao, DKLY, 1: juan 1, 13a–15a.

because her destiny is spelled out at the beginning of the narrative. In "Feng Peibo," however, such ambiguities appear less tolerable under the scrutiny of other female victims of the war. On the whole, the multiple and sometimes conflicting perspectives voiced by the ghosts betray the author's ambivalence about the role of the individual in the context of a historical calamity.

In "Li Yangeng," another story by Wang Tao, a community of specters from the traumatic Ming-Qing transition appears. Li Yangeng, the eponymous hero, accidentally overhears a party of female ghosts unfettered from time and space who were family members of the Ming princess Rui'an 瑞安公主 (1569–1629).[49] Historically, Rui'an's husband, the imperial son-in-law Wan Wei 萬煒 (?–1644), was in charge of the seal of the imperial pedigree, so he played a role symbolizing the sacredness and authority of the Ming imperial family. Both Wan Wei and his eldest son, Wan Changzuo 萬長祚 (?–1644), were killed by Li Zicheng's army when the capital fell. At the end of Wang's story, the hero Li Yangeng expresses his wish to become the lover of a ghost girl in the group he eavesdrops on. She, however, firmly refuses him, quoting a philosophical treatise on the various forms of existence, and then disappears. Her rejection of Li both prevents moral transgression and defends imperial respectability. Their unrealized relationship signifies the impossibility of reconstituting the Ming imperial order, echoing the evanescent quality of the relatively remote memories of the Ming fall.

## The Emasculated, the Headless, and the Rebellious

In comparison to the female ghosts in Wang Tao's stories, the male ghosts in Xuan Ding's stories imply a desire for a masculine return of political ideals and virtues, recalling Wei Xiuren's alter ego ghost in *Traces of Flowers and the Moon*, who lingers, still full of nostalgia, in the human realm. In these cases, the phantom form of the loyalist weakens even further the tentatively constructed masculinity. A good example is "The Loyal Spirit Enters a Dream" ("Zhonghun rumeng"

49. Wang Tao, *SBSH*, 1: *juan* 1, 5b–7b. I use the 1991 reprint of the 1893 edition of *SBSH*.

忠魂入夢), where Xuan Ding records a nebulous encounter with an anonymous Ming loyalist in a dream.[50] After waking up, he is told that the Ming loyalist's divine power once manifested through the melodramatic punishment of an uninhibited Qing concubine in the garden where he may also have been buried. The narrative ends with a deep sense of yearning as Xuan Ding expresses his hope to travel to the loyalist's hometown to acquire more information from his offspring. Xuan Ding's encounter with the loyalist's spirit indicates his attempt to connect with the ideal of Ming loyalism. Nevertheless, the spirit of the unidentified Ming loyalist can only regulate the unruly concubine and trivial domestic affairs, suggesting attenuated masculinity in the public realm. This story also suggests that Xuan Ding's belief in the restoration or efficacy of Ming loyalism in the post-Taiping context is waning.

A somewhat different story is "Three Strange Occurrences in the Law Office of Guilin" ("Guilin nieshu sanyi" 桂林臬署三異), in which Xuan Ding challenges and disproves the identity of a ghost whom people think is a Ming loyalist.[51] Xuan Ding explains that he heard about this ghost from a friend, who reports that in the law office of Guilin, the capital of Guangxi Province, a headless specter often appeared at midnight, holding a pot near a hill covered by luxuriant plants. The headless specter was said to be the returning spirit of a Daoist Ming loyalist. Xuan Ding refutes this claim, saying that the Daoist concerned died in Zhejiang, not in Guilin. The southeastern frontier, especially Zhejiang Province, is known for its loyalist resistance to the Manchus even after the establishment of the Qing. Given the Taipings' rise from Guangxi and their anti-Manchu political rhetoric (so reminiscent of the Ming loyalists' animosity for the Qing), Xuan Ding records a legend suggesting that southwestern frontier might carry on anti-Manchu feeling generated since the fall of the Ming. However, Xuan Ding, in proving the ghost not to be the Ming loyalist people supposed him to be, also casts doubt on the region's presumed link to anti-Manchu feeling. In effect, though the circulating legend may hint at a potential link between the Taiping Rebellion and the historical model of the Ming-Qing dynastic transition, the author refuses to recognize this possibility.

50. Xuan Ding, *YYQDL*, 1:42–44.
51. Xuan Ding, *YYQDL*, 1:39–41.

In both Xuan Ding's and Wang Tao's stories, the headless ghost is a prominent image epitomizing the confluence of traumatic memories of brutal violence with the desire for justice and revenge. The genealogy of the fierce, headless human figure may be traced to Xingtian 刑天, the mythical hero found in the fourth-century BCE compilation *The Classic of Mountains and Seas* (*Shan hai jing* 山海經). Though Xingtian's head is chopped off in battle, he continues fighting, with his nipples serving as his eyes and his navel as his mouth. His persistence has been exalted by Chinese poets.[52] In "Jia Yong" 賈雍 from the fourth-century short story collection *In Search of the Supernatural* (*Sou shen ji* 搜神記), the general loses his head on the battlefield but manages to ride his horse back to his own camp before dying.[53] Although in most cases, the headless figure has died a violent death and is not a ferocious spirit, it exhibits the signs of decapitation, demands that justice be executed, and sometimes calls for revenge upon its foes.[54] One of the earliest examples of the headless ghost is the spirit of Xiahou Xuan 夏侯玄 (209–254) in *Garden of the Strange* (*Yi yuan* 異苑) from the fifth century.[55] In this story, the spirit appears during a family sacrifice made in his name. Xiahou Xuan's spirit removes his head, and announces that God has ruled that the Sima family that killed him should not bear any offspring. In the thirteenth-century drama *The Melodious Golden Pavilion* (*Sheng jin ge* 生金閣), the headless ghost of the victim, with head in hand, chases his murderer in the street

52. For instance, see the poet Tao Qian's famous line, "Waving his axe and shield, Xingtian's vigor always exists" 刑天舞干戚，猛志固常在. Tao Qian, *Tao Yuanming ji*, 40.

53. Gan Bao, *Sou shen ji*, 11:3a–b.

54. A story is told about people in the south whose heads leave their bodies to fly around at night and return before daybreak. Gan Bao, *Sou shen ji*, 12:5a–b. In a few stories, an ugly head is supernaturally exchanged for a beautiful one, as in "Judge Lu" 陸判 in *Liaozhai zhiyi*. Headless ghosts are not necessarily associated with the battlefield, although they are usually male. Sometimes the headless ghosts only make an appearance to scare the living: see "Ye Laotuo" 葉老脫, in Yuan Mei, *Zi bu yu*, 31–32. A headless ghost often carries the head by the hair. He may treat his head with care, wiping the eyes and brows before carefully putting it back on the neck, as in "Pengtou Sima" 捧頭司馬, from *Zi bu yu*, 337–38.

55. Liu Jingshu, *Yi yuan*, 6:1a–b.

during the Lantern Festival.[56] Yuan Mei 袁枚 (1716–1798), the author of *What the Master Would Not Discuss* (*Zi bu yu* 子不語), seems especially interested in the image of the vengeful headless ghost.[57] In "Wenxin King" 文信王, he describes a grotesque scene where the heads of five hundred soldiers sentenced to execution by a fickle general roll and jump on the floor. They plead not guilty to the human official and ask to be pardoned from punishment in Hell.[58] In sum, except for very few cases, the image of the headless ghost in Chinese literary tradition is associated with uncompromising resistance, violent death, and vengeful demands for justice.

As an intuitive mediation of recent traumatic memories, the headless ghost became especially popular in the aftermath of the Taiping War. In Wang Tao's stories, these ghosts are mostly female, possibly synthesizing the image of the headless ghost and the trope of female ghosts carrying historical memories. "Zhixian" 芝仙, a story full of ambiguity and unsolved mysteries, may be Wang Tao's early experiment with the trope of the headless female ghost.[59] After the Qing recovery of Hangzhou, there were many vacant houses but very few residents in the city. During the summer, a student passing by Hangzhou decides to live in an abandoned house despite his friends' objection. On the night of his move-in day, he organizes a party with his friends in the courtyard. As they are enjoying themselves, the student and his friends see a young and beautiful woman appear in the western tower. Smiling, she looks down at the gathering and puts her head on the corner of the tower's railings close to her hand. As she starts to brush her hair, blood flows from her neck and showers down like a fine rain. The blood drops fall upon the skin of the men, and everyone feels

56. Wu Hanchen, *Bao daizhi zhizhuan shengjin ge zaju* 包待製智賺生金閣雜劇.

57. Yuan Mei, "Yuanhun suoming" 冤魂索命, in *Zi bu yu*, 421–22. In this story, the headless ghosts of executed criminals appeal to the judge to punish their fellow criminals who were spared death. Also see Yuan Mei, "Qidao suoming" 七盜索命, in *Zi bu yu*, 80–82. In this story, seven headless ghosts executed for banditry take the life of a student who was the corrupt official who sentenced them to death in his previous life.

58. Yuan Mei, *Zi bu yu*, 95–97.

59. Wang Tao, *DKLY*, 2: *juan* 4, 1a–3a.

a bone-piercing cold. Frightened, all immediately flee the yard except for the student, who continues to sip his wine.

After waiting outside for a while, the friends grow worried about the student. Summoning all their courage, they gather together hundreds of strong young men armed with weapons and ascend the tower. There they find a well-decorated inner chamber. On the books and paintings that are piled there, they find a seal bearing the name "Talented Woman Zhixian." On the bed behind a big mirror lies a naked female body. A trace of red encircles her neck, making the body seem disconnected. The color of her skin, however, is as fresh as that of a living person. In the end, the student, having lost consciousness, is found by a toilet. The next day, the party buries the woman, and burns the paintings and the objects in the chamber as sacrifices to her. However, they decide to keep the precious Song editions found in the chamber. People suspect that the woman must have come from a large and wealthy household. Unable to escape when the rebels broke into the house, they conclude, she committed suicide to preserve her reputation and chastity.

In the story, when the specter makes her first appearance, her youth and beauty resonate with the conventional image of a female ghost or an immortal.[60] This convention is immediately subverted, however, when she takes off her own head, an action that conveys inexplicable horror. As the specter "relives" and "re-presents" the violence that may have been inflicted upon her in front of a living audience, the haunting of the past is doubly intensified by her appearance and performance. Many war survivors witnessed and recorded the unsettling presence of dead bodies in the landscape. In "Zhixian," the author re-creates the process of witnessing by means of spectral images. In addition, the spatial relationship between the ghost and the party resembles that of a theater. The rain of blood is arresting: evoking visceral reactions, the blood is synonymous with the horror of the war, affecting the human realm with substantial, penetrative power.

Even though people are inclined to interpret the girl's death as the result of suicide, the red circle around her neck and the action of taking off her head suggest a violent death caused by others. The naked body

60. On the image of female ghosts, see Zeitlin, *The Phantom Heroine*, 13–52.

is also unsettling: could there have been a sexual violation? If so, did it happen before or after her death? The fresh skin color may have been supernaturally preserved because of the woman's virtue; alternatively, it may suggest that the death was recent, which points to the ongoing violence in the aftermath of the war. No account is given of what the student sees and experiences in the chamber where he is debilitated. No explanation is provided for the girl's death, and the readers are not informed of the reasons behind the naked body. Masculinity, symbolic of the power of narrative in reasoning and ordering chaos, is not potent enough to contain the recent traumatic memories as represented by the feminine phantom bearing a fresh mark of a wound. The only clue to the girl's identity is her name: "Talented Woman Zhixian." With her burial and the sacrifice, people mourn the deceased and pacify the haunting spirit. Nevertheless, the rare books they choose to preserve may imply that history has value, at least insofar as these books, symbolic of cultural legacies, would be preserved for posterity.

The bone-chilling cold and the unresolved mysteries in "Zhixian" are subsumed under a certain order in two more tales by Wang Tao, in which the ghost is physically restrained or subdued after the Taiping War: "The Loyal and Virtuous Woman" ("Yilie nüzi" 義烈女子) and "The Headless Female Ghost" ("Wutou nügui" 無頭女鬼). In "The Loyal and Virtuous Woman," when the ghost puts her head on a table, the male protagonist seizes it and will only return it after she pleads with him.[61] In "The Headless Female Ghost," the ghost had once been a mischievous teenage girl, whose body, after her death, was properly buried by the family in their garden.[62] In both stories, the bodies of the heroines are buried in the proper way, literally "laid to rest." The development of the image of the headless specter in "Zhixian," "The Loyal and Virtuous Woman," and "The Headless Female Ghost" showcases the process through which Wang Tao tames the strangeness that embodies historical memories of violence. His "taming" is done in the sense that he reveals the female ghosts' identities and moralizes their stories, a kind of domestication or "unwilding." These ghosts become increasingly harmless and agreeable. The author's self-conscious

61. Wang Tao, *DKLY*, 3:7a–8b.
62. Wang Tao, *DKLY*, 3:20a–21b.

manipulation of the trope is reflected in the development of the titles: "Zhixian" is named after an individual, whereas "The Headless Female Ghost" simply references a subcategory in the literary tradition of ghosts. In "Zhixian," the striking image of the ghost and the graphic representation of violence mediate the raw memories of the recent catastrophe. In "The Loyal and Virtuous Woman" a gendered power dynamic brings the returning ghost under control. "The Headless Female Ghost" alleviates the horror associated with the image, implying that a certain sense of order has returned in the postwar society.

Xuan Ding's tale "Silver Transformed into Toads" ("Yin bian hama" 銀變蛤蟆) presents a grotesque and carnivalesque vision with a rebellious spirit. It brings together two themes: first, the spectral community that commemorates the massive number of deaths that occurred during political turbulence; and second, the headless ghost that returns to reenact historical violence.[63] The story begins with a man walking cautiously in the dark after escaping from the Taiping camp. When crossing a river, he feels something in the water. Upon examining the item in the bright moonlight, he finds it to be silver. At the time, many people are abandoning their money and treasures while escaping, so the man has no doubt about what he has found. Delighted, he fishes in the water for more, putting his findings into his bag. After wrapping the filled bag around his waist, he continues to walk. Soon, he feels something moving around his waist, and discovers that all the silver has transformed into toads. He has a strange feeling about the experience, but lets go of the toads and keeps walking. He then comes across several men and women sitting on the ground, having a party. The man at first hides behind a rock, but upon hearing the people speak in his hometown's dialect, he comes forward to greet them. With a warm welcome, the party guests pass him a cup of wine as red as blood, which he finds exceptionally tasty. After hearing the man's story about the silver that transformed into toads, one of the party laughs and says that the windfall in this man's life will be only three strings of coins. This conversation is immediately interrupted by another party guest. After delighting in their festivities awhile, someone proposes that they take advantage of the moonlight and dance like Xingtian, the headless

63. Xuan Ding, *YYQDL*, 1:502–4.

ancient hero, to end the night. Everyone takes off their heads as if they were melons. Holding their heads by the hair, they swing them around and move their bodies, pausing and turning in rhythm. Horrified, the man sprints away as fast as he can. While running into town, he trips on several strings of coins, just as he was told.

The blurred boundary between the realms of the fantastic and the real is characteristic of many of Xuan Ding's stories. The transformation of desirable silver into repulsive toads evokes the aesthetic effect of the uncanny: a feeling of anxiety that arises when something familiar unexpectedly turns into something strange. The uncanny transformation of the silver is "related to what is frightening—to what arouses dread and horror."[64] This transformation is created by the protagonist's greed and corruption, and foreshadows another moment of terror. Hearing his hometown dialect convinces the protagonist to join the party: while speaking the same language and enjoying the same wine, the man and the specters seem to be of the same kind. Does their use of this dialect imply that the ghosts are originally from the man's hometown, but have been abducted and killed in adjacent areas? Or is the dialect merely the man's illusion, reflecting his yearning to hold onto a group identity important to his survival amid chaos? In any event, this belief in shared origins leads to the story's most unsettling moment, when the specters remove their heads with ease. Even though the headless female ghosts in Wang Tao's stories act as individuals, this eerie scene is a collective enactment of decapitation, and the dance of the headless bodies symbolizes a celebration of resistance in the spirit of the ancient hero Xingtian. If the misty rain of blood in "Zhixian" can be understood as the affective residue of violence and resentment, we can interpret the grotesquerie of "Silver Transformed into Toads" as an unfettered expression of the utopian ideals of community and freedom in a most unlikely form. Above all, the image of the ghosts taking off their heads in nineteenth-century stories anticipates the critical trope of beheading in modern Chinese literature, as represented by the numerous stories written by Lu Xun 魯迅 (1881–1936) and Shen Congwen 沈從文 (1902–1988), where we can interpret decapitation as

64. Freud's description of "the uncanny," as quoted in Masschelein, *The Uncon-cept*, 42.

both revenge and "a decadent sport . . . in search of sadomasochistic pain and pleasure."[65] Those scenes of witnessing beheading in modern Chinese literature, as Anderson points out, also embody the horror of communal violence.[66]

Memories of both Taiping trauma and Ming-Qing dynastic transition reverberate through the ghost's mediation in the works of Wang Tao and Xuan Ding. Their stories express the inexplicable horrors of massive violence and death and a deep yearning to put the traumatic memories to rest. The question then arises: Is escape from political calamities truly possible?

## Escape and Its Renunciation

Writers in various genres sometimes imagined (or reimagined) fanciful ways of escaping the trauma of war and its aftermath. They envisaged alternate worlds to which one could travel: celestial or terrestrial, traditional or brand-new. One such world, conceived in traditional terms, is called "uprooting the household and becoming immortal" (*ba zhai fei xian* 拔宅飛仙). This route out of trauma can be traced to a Tang *chuanqi* story about a Daoist surnamed Xu who lived at the end of the fourth century, a time of war and conflict. After Xu achieved immortality, his entire forty-two-member family ascended to Heaven. Before the nineteenth century, writers often saw this kind of transformation as an ideal merging of worldly desire for an intact family and a wish for religious transcendence. In the aftermath of the Taiping War, however, reinventions of this vision emphasize the possibility of physically saving one's family from chaos and war, almost to the exclusion of reaching Heaven. During the war, the limits of human agency, confined as it was by time and space, were keenly felt, intensifying the yearning for release even more. As Xuan Ding said: "When disaster befalls, one is completely constrained by one's conditions. One even admires the creatures flying in the sky and swimming in the water.

65. David Der-wei Wang, "Invitation to a Beheading," in *The Monster That Is History*, 15–40.
66. Anderson, *The Limits of Realism*, 79–80.

Let alone those pulling up their households and rising aloft to become immortals!" 禍患之來，滿身桎縛。即寥空之翔，淵溪之躍，且羨之，況明明為拔宅飛仙耶。[67]

Wang Tao gives detailed accounts of the war's historical development in order to map out the trajectories of these escapes. An example is Wang Tao's story "Biheng" 碧衡. Born in Wuchang, Biheng grows up practicing Daoist self-cultivation and supernatural skills.[68] When the rebels conquer her hometown, she has already moved her parents away. However, her male cousin, a Confucian student who is contemptuous of her studies, is abducted by the rebels and taken to Nanjing. Exercising her magical power, Biheng relocates her desperate cousin to Changshu, Zhejiang Province, and keeps her family in Suzhou, Jiangsu Province. However, when the cousin comes to Suzhou to visit Biheng and her family, they have already fled, but she leaves him a note telling him to go to Sichuan. Soon both Zhejiang and Jiangsu Provinces fall into the rebel hands. In another of Wang's stories titled "Summoning Souls" ("Shehun" 攝魂), a Daoist with the supernatural power to summon people's souls urges his neighbor to leave Songjiang because it is about to become a battlefield. According to the Daoist, the only safe place is Shanghai.[69]

Both stories imagine an alternative wartime experience for individuals, aided by divinity. The "prophecies" and magical escapes are possible because the author bases them on his retrospective knowledge of the real-life prosecution and unfolding of the war. In 1853, the Taiping rebels took over Wuchang and went upstream along the Yangtze River to conquer Nanjing. In 1860, Li Xiucheng led his army to seize Suzhou and Changzhou, taking control of most of the Jiangnan region. This history explains why Biheng and her family moved from Wuhan to the Jiangnan region, and again to southwestern China. In 1862, the Taipings took Songjiang. However, their attack on Shanghai failed because of foreign assistance to the Qing government—hence the Daoist's statement that Shanghai was a safe place. In both stories,

67. Xuan Ding, *YYQDL*, 1:330.
68. Wang Tao, *DKLY*, 1: *juan* 2, 12b–14a.
69. Wang Tao, *DKLY*, 2: *juan* 4, 11a–13a.

the specific historical details, and the course of the war, are "foreseen" as inevitable.

Xuan Ding's application of this kind of "prophecy in retrospect" conceptualizes the Taiping War and the Ming-Qing transition as parallel calamities. In his story "The Match of Kalaviṅka" ("Jialing pei" 迦陵配), a husband's ability to become an official despite starting life as an orphan is less marvelous than his wife's ability to predict the Taiping catastrophe.[70] In "The Inspector of the Offerings for the Five Mountains and the Four Rivers" ("Jicha tianxia wuyue duxianghuo shi" 稽查天下五岳瀆香火使), a similar story is set against the backdrop of the Ming-Qing transition, but with more temporal complexity.[71] At the end of the Ming dynasty, a celestial official's daughter is brought up by the righteous Lu. One night, startled by the patterns of the stars, the girl concludes that the stars' alignment is a manifestation of "the Red Ram and the Red Horse: a calamity is coming soon." With the help of the celestial official, the entire household escapes deep into the mountains. During the Yongzheng reign (1722–1735), some fishermen escape a hurricane with help from Lu, who by this time had become immortal. Upon learning that it is Yongzheng's reign, he says, "When the Sage rules, all the beings under Heaven are blessed" 聖人在位，蒼生有福.[72] With the phrase "the Red Ram and the Red Horse," Xuan Ding unmistakably likens the fall of the Ming to the Taiping War. On the temporal axis, Xuan stands in the nineteenth century, rewrites a seventeenth-century catastrophe, and feels nostalgic for the eighteenth century's sociopolitical stability. These positions illustrate doubts about the possible kinds of protections in the post-Taiping era. Xuan Ding's writings, disguised as a literary interest in the past, seem to yearn for another reign of a resolute and strong-handed imperial ruler in the post-Taiping era, demonstrating his conservative political position.

Xuan Ding fabricates other kinds of magical solutions to wartime dangers, too. Some are mediated by objects—specifically, relics from the remote past made to serve as protection during the Taiping War. In these stories, ancient objects embody the redeeming power of

70. Xuan Ding, *YYQDL*, 1:30–36.
71. Xuan Ding, *YYQDL*, 1:325–30.
72. Xuan Ding, *YYQDL*, 1:327.

antiquity, but on a limited scale. The story "The Ancient Spearhead" ("Gu jiantou" 古劍頭) centers on a piece of rusty iron recognized by a student to be an ancient spearhead, which helps him escape when the Taiping rebels conquer Yangzhou in 1853.[73] The possibility of finding refuge through ancient relics is more cautiously evaluated in "Liu Jianxiang's Stone Coffin" ("Liu Jianxiong shiguo" 柳建雄石椁).[74] In this story, a Ming official comes across a pre-Qin general's stone coffin while leading a work party of townsmen to secure the riverbank. The blurry ancient inscription on the coffin indicates that it should be moved into the mountains, so the official organizes people to do that, and pays it due respect. Many years later, when the Taiping rebels overrun this region, a young man, who was the official in his previous life, travels alone in the deep mountains to visit relatives. After night falls, a servant unexpectedly appears, inviting the student to his master's house—a majestic stone mansion, where the student is warmly welcomed by the host. During the banquet, both the host and the guest look up at the sky and see a gleaming star. The host tells the student that its appearance means violence, war, and widespread death. As the host takes out an arrow to shoot the star, the arrow shaft suddenly breaks in half "like rotten wood," and the host laughs at himself for his attempt to reverse the will of Heaven. Nevertheless, he gives the student seven ancient coins and sends him off. When the young man arrives at his relatives' house, he finds the family captured by the rebels. The coins, however, have the power to make them all invisible, so the whole family escapes.

This story implies a desire to retrieve the past, to return to a point when the tides of history might still be turned away from catastrophe. But this turns out to be an illusion, a wish that cannot be fulfilled on such a large scale. The images carrying the story—the general's coffin and the host's rotted arrow shaft, with their associations of decay and martial skill that comes to nothing— are not promising. However, this wish might be realized on a small scale, as shown by the rescue of the student and his family. Xuan Ding comments that the local people all believe that this story is true. However, he proceeds to challenge the

73. Xuan Ding, YYQDL, 1:250–52.
74. Xuan Ding, YYQDL, 2:545–48.

authenticity of the story point by point, and concludes saying that he wishes he could meet this ancient general and find out the truth.[75] Xuan Ding as a commentator shows that the story, as well as the fantastic escape he creates, are merely fables.

Unlike the rusty spearhead and the coffin from antiquity that have lost their magical power, silver remains valuable and is a common object of desire in both stories and in history. Nevertheless, far from being a means of escape and salvation, it is often associated with illicitly accumulated fortunes that grow out of vicious seeds planted in the past. During the war, these fortunes aided the Taiping rebels. Xuan Ding's "Blood-Drenched Torches Illuminate Silver" ("Xue ju zhao yin" 血炬 照銀) is set in Hangzhou in 1860, when the city has been taken over by the Taipings.[76] The rebel leader is living in the mansion that had been the residence of a late Ming prime minister, Qian Kun, and he despises the board bearing Confucian inscriptions that hangs in the hall. When the board is removed, a small bronze box hidden behind it falls to the floor. Inside the box is a tiny accounting book that serves as a map to the wealth buried in the house. The instructions are clear and specific, including the amount of silver, the rooms the silver is buried in, and even how far underground it's buried. Following these clues, the rebel leader finds the silver, which helps sustain their reign of savagery. Xuan Ding comments, "Alas! Didn't Prime Minister Qian contribute to the rebels' military expenses two hundred years after his death? During the Chongzhen reign, warfare was raging everywhere, the treasury of the Ming was empty. [Qian] didn't consider contributing this [his wealth] to the emperor, but hid it to pass on to his offspring. He had the heart to watch the Incident of Jiashen. From this [we know] the kind of prime minister Qian was!" 噫！錢相國 . . . 二百年後為賊助餉 乎？當崇禎朝，烽煙四起，國帑空虛，不思以此獻君上，而藏之遺子 孫，忍視有甲申之變，則錢之為宰相者可知矣。[77] Xuan Ding then relates that his hometown, Anhui, suffered more than other provinces during the Taiping War. The rebels were especially good at finding cellars hidden for thousands of years, unknown to the original owners'

75. Xuan Ding, *YYQDL*, 2:547–48.
76. Xuan Ding, *YYQDL*, 1:392–93.
77. Xuan Ding, *YYQDL*, 1:393.

offspring and the buyers of the houses. The reason for this, as the author is told by an escapee from the rebel camp, was that the rebels used twisted reeds drenched in human blood as torches to illuminate the houses. Should they near an underground cellar filled with silver, the flame of the torch would bend as if it were drilling into the ground. This eerie sign always led the rebels to hidden pools of wealth, the author was told, as it is human nature to desire money.[78]

This multilayered story has rich implications that together convey an ambivalent moral and historical judgment. The most striking image in the story is the torches drenched in human blood. This could easily be read as a metaphor for the bloodthirsty Taiping rebels, who mercilessly committed mass murder in their search for wealth. At the same time, it could be seen as a criticism of those dishonest officials who by their acts enabled the slaughter and suffering. A case in point is the late Ming high official Qian Xiangkun 錢象坤 (1569–1640), who accumulated wealth in order to benefit his family. In official history, Qian is portrayed positively as a cautious administrator who avoided the center of late Ming political struggles and received imperial honors when he died.[79] Qian was not even an egregious example of a corrupt official. However, his legacy and that of other officials like him not only failed to secure the well-being of their offspring, but also fueled the savage Taipings, who slaughtered their children, destroyed their land, and revealed their history of corruption in the name of holy war. Meanwhile, Xuan Ding shows little empathy for those killed and abused by the Taipings: their deaths can be read as retribution for their greed. More bleakly, human greed is shown to prevail from beyond the grave; it directs the rebels to the wealth that assists them. Inadvertently, the rebels also expose the grounds for passing moral judgment upon the immoral, both in the past and in the present. Overall, from the despicable late Ming prime minister to the guide "drawn" by human blood, the author establishes an uncanny connection between the Taiping Rebellion and the fall of the Ming dynasty, implying that the violence and destruction wrought by the Taipings were caused by a fundamental moral defect.

78. Xuan Ding, YYQDL, 1:393.
79. Zhang Tingyu, Ming shi, 21:6492.

The desire to escape from catastrophe is expressed through fantasies that transcend time and space. However, as we have seen, the stories under discussion soon disrupt these fantasies. In "The Inspector of the Offerings for the Five Mountains and the Four Rivers," a successful escape from the Ming-Qing transition can be confidently and yet nostalgically envisioned. In contrast, the future after the Taiping Civil War is beyond the capacity of the imagination. In these circumstances, Xuan Ding turns back to the past, but only to create a fantasy in which ancient relics might provide some limited protection; or, worse, to show that past wrongs enabled and exacerbated the catastrophic Taiping War.

## An Antifantasy

In his fiction, Wang Tao presents a vision that provides fantastic sequences of cause and effect to explain the inevitable violence on a grand scale. His vision takes the form of repressed desires for rebellion, unleashed in unlikely forms. Although these desires are punished and contained within supernatural frameworks, the story "A Reversed Yellow Millet Dream" ("Fan Huangliang" 反黃粱) anticipates a future of more insurgencies.

This story begins with a main character and plot elements that model the rise of the Taiping Rebellion.[80] The protagonist, Xu Qimeng, was born in Guilin, Guangxi Province. He inherits his father's military title and becomes known for his outstanding archery skills. While celebrating one particularly successful defense against bandits, Xu gets drunk and loudly recounts his adventures and accomplishments. A Daoist challenges him about his ambition. Xu replies that he would like to "clean up the realm under Heaven," but "the people in power haven't put [me] to use."[81]

---

80. Wang Tao, *SBSH*, 12a–14b. Scholars debate the authorship of this piece. Some think that Wang Tao took this work from Zou Tao 邹弢 (1850–1931), his friend and student, and added it into his own collection. See Zhang Zhenguo, "Wang Tao xiaoshuoji zhong," and Duan Huaiqing, *Wang Tao yu xiandai wenxue*, 327–32.

81. Wang Tao, *SBSH*, 12b.

Upon hearing this, the Daoist feeds Xu two large dates that plunge him into a dream-like state. Xu finds himself visiting the celestial realm under the guidance of another Daoist. After bidding farewell to the Daoist, Xu finds himself lost in a deep forest and falls in with a group of bandits, who make him their leader because of his archery skills. In the name of righteousness, Xu, who now leads tens of thousands of followers, initiates an uprising against the greedy and cruel governor of the county. He acquires still more followers and a fiercer reputation and soon stages a rebellion. The rebels take numerous counties and cities. During the process, they abduct women, bring gold, jewels, and jade into their palace, and slaughter innocent people, drenching the streets in blood. The provincial governor cannot pacify them, so the emperor dispatches imperial troops to suppress the rebellion. They succeed, and Xu is sentenced to death.

After his death, Xu is chained up and dragged by ghosts into Hell. In the court, the king of Hell interrogates him sternly. When ghost runners confirm that Xu has killed and harmed thousands of people, the king of Hell pronounces a cruel and prolonged punishment. With full consciousness and all of his memories from his previous life, Xu is reborn numerous times. In the first life, he is a pig in the house of a landlord he once robbed. The butcher, as well as the customers in the butcher's shop, are all people he killed in their previous lives. Only after they have finished eating every part of the pig is Xu's spirit sent to see the king of Hell. In his second and third rebirths, Xu becomes an ox owned by someone he robbed in the past and a prostitute, respectively. In each life, Xu experiences great physical and emotional suffering, but in each is redeemed: from the life of an ox by saving the owner's child, and from that of a prostitute by being true to the lover.

In his final incarnation, Xu enters another life as a son in an affluent household. For the first time in all of Xu's rebirths, the author mentions that Xu has a new name: Fulang. Brilliant and handsome, he is particularly filial in serving his parents. When they die, he almost perishes from grief. The only thought that keeps him alive is that he needs to carry on the bloodline of the family. However, before long, Fulang, maligned by his political enemy, is imprisoned and sentenced to public execution. His beautiful and virtuous wife, by then pregnant, pulls every possible string to save him, but still fails. On the day of the execution, after bidding him farewell in tears, she cuts her throat in front of him using a poisoned knife. In tremendous agony, he cries out: "The sins from my previous life have been repaid through several lives. Now I have made the effort to cultivate myself unremittingly. Why has my suffering grown more and more severe, and yet the end is not in sight?" 某前生之罪，迭報数生。今刻意修行，似可稍从未减，何乃愈受愈苦，尚无已时耶.[82] At that moment, Fulang hears someone calling him, "Are you having a nightmare? Wake up!" Opening his eyes, Xu finds himself still in the room where the celebration had taken place. It is almost dawn. He hears the Daoist cooking millet porridge. When the porridge is ready, the Daoist sings two songs about emptiness and retribution. Enlightened, Xu follows him into the mountains and they both disappear.

The "yellow millet dream" of the story's title, "A Reversed Yellow Millet Dream," first appears in a Tang *chuanqi* story, "The World within a Pillow." Pu Songling picks up this theme in "A Sequel to the Yellow Millet Dream" ("Xu Huangliang" 續黃粱) and rewrites it.[83] Instead of making his protagonist experience a life full of fortune and accomplishment in the dream, as in the original Tang story, Pu Songling has him fall from grace shortly after some initial success. Pu Songling's adaptation of the story highlights "the dire consequences of unrestrained desire and the drama of inevitable retribution."[84]

In the title of Wang Tao's "A Reversed Yellow Millet Dream," the reversal refers to the protagonist's downward spiral from defender of the people to leader of a violent rebellion in his dream, where he also experiences great suffering. Xu's intention of "clearing up the realm under Heaven" recalls a famous statement by the historical figure Chen Fan 陳蕃 (?–168): "In his engagement with the world, a true man should clean the realm [of evil forces] under Heaven" 大丈夫處事，當掃除天下.[85] Chen Fan lived at the end of the Eastern Han dynasty (25–220 CE), an era characterized by political corruption and peasant rebellion.

82. Wang Tao, *SBSH*, 14b.

83. Wang Tao's other story titled "Huangliang xu meng" is found in his *SYML*. Its storyline resembles that of Pu Songling's "Xu Huangliang," in *Liaozhai zhiyi*, 1:518–27.

84. Wai-yee Li, *Enchantment and Disenchantment*, 146.

85. Fan Ye 范曄, *Hou Han shu*, 65:1a.

The echo, which would certainly have been heard by Wang Tao's audience, suggests that the world Xu inhabits also needs a capable leader to put it in order. Ironically, Xu's high-minded ambition is fulfilled as he becomes a rebel leader in the dream—at least, until the rebellion turns vicious. With his well-to-do family background and excellent martial arts skills, Xu fits the stereotypical character of the gentry-turned-rebel of vernacular fiction and historical reality. A character of this kind in *Water Margin* is Chai Jin; the Northern King of the Taiping Rebellion, Wei Changhui, also came from a gentry family. In Wang Tao's story, the rebellion is suppressed and its instigator severely punished, in both flesh and in spirit, by the weight of political and religious order. Wang Tao thus effectively unleashes both the wish to rebel and the desire to suppress this wish. In this sense, Wang Tao's evocation and suppression of rebellion brings to mind the treatment of this theme in *Quell the Bandits*, as these conservative adaptations of *Water Margin* can hardly suppress the "volatile semantics" of the original.[86] Unlike *Quell the Bandits*, however, Wang Tao's story is an allegory of the radical breakdown of ideological and moral order.

Xu's rebirths metaphorically represent the process of a Confucian student's moral cultivation, except that it ends, for him, in disillusionment. The climactic and melodramatic end of his last incarnation, Fulang, is reminiscent of the Tang story "Du Zichun" 杜子春, in which the eponymous protagonist helps a Daoist with his cultivation by keeping a vow of silence regardless of what he sees, hears, and experiences. Du Zichun breaks the vow only during a life as a woman who sees her husband killing their two-year-old son. Both "A Reversed Yellow Millet Dream" and "Du Zichun" reach a climax when the protagonist's intense feelings of horror, surprise, and agony are triggered by personal loss. The conclusions of their journeys, whether in dream or in rebirths, are marked by delusion and enlightenment. In "A Reversed Yellow Millet Dream," Xu achieves final Daoist enlightenment only after realizing that the Confucian path of self-cultivation has led him nowhere. This ending peels back the numerous layers the Confucian ethical order

86. On how the "newness" of *Dang kou zhi* derives from the novel's engagement with the narrative tradition of *Shuihu zhuan*, see David Der-wei Wang, *Fin-de-Siècle Splendor*, 125–37.

established to suppress the desire for rebellion. This skepticism of Confucian cultivation brings to mind the author's own experiences: after Wang Tao's political ambitions were crushed, he adamantly defended himself as a Confucian student loyal to the Qing government. Xu's ruthless punishment is therefore analogous to the writer's, as one who has submitted to Qing political authority and suffered for it. The fact that the Confucian path proves so illusory to Xu in the story deconstructs the moral order the author submitted to in real life.

Despite their opposing political stances, Xuan Ding and Wang Tao adopted the tradition of "stories about the strange" to transgress the boundary between the fantastic and the real, the remote past and the recent present, presenting a phantasmagoria of the destruction of political, moral, and social order during and after the Taiping War. Both authors treat the Taiping Civil War and the Ming-Qing dynastic transition (and even earlier political catastrophes) as traumatic events of comparable magnitude. Both blur the neat categories of traditional ethics and knowledge. One development that became a source of regeneration for Xuan Ding and Wang Tao's generation was the increasing use of various modern media—printed books, magazines, and newspapers. To describe this burgeoning literary environment, the nineteenth-century generation evoked the late Ming phrase "Ocean of Ink" (*mo hai* 墨海) to celebrate the wide dissemination of feelings and ideas through modern print technology. Xuan Ding used the term as the title of his painting manual, and the literal translation of the Chinese name of the London Missionary Society Press where Wang Tao worked was "Book House of Ocean of Ink" (*Mo hai shuguan* 墨海書館).[87] After all was said and done, a figurative ocean of writings and publications provided a kind of escape from the horrors of war.

87. The best-known seventeenth-century manual on ink is titled *Mohai* 墨海, comp. Fang Ruisheng 方瑞生 (fl. 1618).

# Conclusion

From the 1850s to the 1880s, the prevalent "sense of an ending" had broad repercussions in both political discourse and individual artistic expression. To those who initiated, experienced, and remembered the Taiping Civil War, the "collapse of Heaven" was not a dystopian fantasy but the reality they were living, caused and conditioned by violent sociopolitical disruptions and tragic personal encounters. The writers discussed in this book depicted a world of destruction and yearning for transcendence, the one arising in tandem with the other. This world was mediated through words, which could be employed to impose order but instead often unleashed such a destructive force that they further shattered an already imperiled reality, especially as they brought back traumatic memories of the Ming-Qing dynastic transition. Marshaling the evocative force of language across genres that include diaries, propaganda, poetry, fiction, and drama, writers on all sides of the conflict responded to the decay of the world once familiar to them and to the structures that upheld this world.

A summary of "Beiji Piye dao" and discussion of this text appeared in my article "The Multitude of Otherness During the Taiping Civil War," *Journal of Chinese Literature and Culture* 7.1 (2020): 215–31.

The writers I discuss were looking for a new vocabulary, frame-work, and aesthetics to articulate what was transpiring. For Hong Xiuquan and his followers, extreme poverty and inequality, together with stagnant social mobility, were signs of an ongoing or imminently pending catastrophe. For those on the Qing side, the Taiping rebels threatened not only the rule of the Manchus but also a Chinese civili-zation that had endured for thousands of years. As opposing ideolo-gies sought recourse to military violence, individual writers turned to narratives to make sense of what had happened and to reflect on the aftermath of the war. What characterizes the writings from this period is how various, sometimes radically different, standpoints and experi-ences are mediated through a conflation of language across multiple discourses. For instance, as I have shown, the imagery presented in the two excerpts from prose of "call to arms" (*xi wen* 檄文), quoted near the start of the introduction to this book, is broadly shared in personal accounts and artistic creations. In drawing from common traditions, the writers exhibit powerful and creative engagements with the past, during which process they exhibit the unraveling of late imperial lit-erary and cultural paradigms and the emergence of potentially new political, religious, and moral orders.

Taiping ideology and local interpretations of Qing ideology com-peted for the masses by promising different visions of moral and reli-gious certainty. Drawing inspiration from the West, the Taipings invoked the Christian god to build their religious and political legiti-macy and went further, to demonize the Manchu rulers. As the Taiping movement developed and their discourse evolved, Hong Xiuquan be-came the sole representative of God on Earth and embodied both po-litical and religious sovereignty. Faced with this ideological challenge from the Taiping rebels, local elites tried to rejuvenate Qing ideological discourse and to sustain social stability with Confucian morality. The fusion of popular religion and Qing ideology, however, inadvertently led to the introduction of divinities that endangered the Qing imperial authority's role as the representative for the Mandate of Heaven.

Individual writers, bearing the psychological, and sometimes physical wounds directly or indirectly inflicted by the Taiping Civil War, searched for the meaning of their existence in this state of chaos. As a result, personal accounts and artistic expressions challenged justifications for violence and destabilized the antitheses of "good" and "evil," "orthodox" and "heterodox," as well as "us" and "other" in political discourses. In diarists' witness accounts, vivid imageries of deaths and destruction brought about by various political parties and interest groups led to solemn reflections on the cause and consequences of the war. As Shen Zi's diary manuscript exemplifies, on the one hand, individual writers could claim authority stemming from their identities as witnesses and survivors of the war; on the other hand, editing and revising the accounts from the past revealed the precarity and instability of long-held moral and historical values. With their capacity to convey a deep sense of disturbance and disillusionment, personal accounts of the war found unexpected resonances in stories about the strange, where writers fully explored the ambiguous spaces between gender and political morality, imagination and reality as they utilized the lens of fantasy to mediate grotesque historical details and tragic personal encounters. For instance, Wang Tao's story "A Reversed Yellow Millet Dream" shows the coexistence of ideals and skepticism relating to karmic retribution and Confucian morality, as well as of desires for and fears of rebellious energy.

Fiction and drama, unlike other types of narratives discussed in the book, might be expected to follow more specific aesthetic conventions. One example is the customary "grand reunion" ending of traditional Chinese novels and plays, which reunites the family or community scattered over the course of the story. However, for the writers of the Taiping era, the challenge was whether it was even possible for the devastating tragedies of both individuals and communities to be convincingly reconfigured and reconciled through a wishful ending. Within fictional and theatrical space, individual writers tried to emulate models that had in the past offered consolation and transcendence through literary imagination and lyrical expression. Their innovative adaptations of literary conventions effectively called for new ways of coping with personal and national trauma. However, what the writers were able to salvage were merely the scraps and grimy residues of those past structures and practices; their creations were only remotely and fragmentarily reminiscent of what Heaven used to symbolize.

Xuan Ding's story "Beiji Piye Island" ("Beiji Piye dao" 北極毗耶島) epitomizes the ambiguous attitude of writers toward the war in its aftermath and ties together many of this book's topics.[1] In this story, a boat passenger's curiosity inspires him to explore the exotic islands that he sees now and then again over the ocean waves. The boatman, however, tells him that the greater the spectacle, the greater the chances that it is occupied by beasts and demons. To illustrate his point, the boatman tells the passenger the story of Zhu, a *juren* (student who succeeded in the provincial examination) who, after failing the capital examination, returns by sea to his hometown, Songjiang. After setting off from Tianjin, Zhu's boat is destroyed by a storm. He drifts for two days before being washed up on an island with strange birds and snakes. Starved and scared, Zhu advances deep into the woods where he sees a half-open gate, above which is an inscription in ancient script: "Beiji Piye Island." Zhu enters, and finds a village with houses made from stones and giant mollusk shells. He is told by a woodcutter that every three years, when extreme *yin* gives rise to *yang*, the gate opens. Zhu is welcomed by villagers who bring him drinks and bedding and inquire about the Heavenly Empire (China). The next morning, Zhu meets with the Daoist governor of the island. The Daoist, upon hearing that Zhu is a *juren*, is excited and invites him to tutor some students.

From then on, Zhu teaches the students every morning. He never catches a glimpse of their faces, however, because they are all locked in a cave sealed by an iron gate. Zhu expounds on canonical texts from the other side of the gate. From there, he hears the students speak in various voices, from old to young. After several months, Zhu is able to recognize the students by the sound of their voices. In the blink of an eye, two years pass, and the Daoist tells Zhu that he can return home. As happy as he is, Zhu still wonders why he could never see his students. The Daoist explains: the island features a large pothole where God imprisons monsters and entrusts them to the Daoist. In years of the red ram (*hong yang* 紅羊) and the red horse (*chi ma* 赤馬), God unleashes these creatures to cause disasters and afterward, imprisons them in the cave again. Hoping that the monsters will cause less harm

1. Xuan Ding, "Beiji Piye dao," in *YYQDL*, 2:314–18.

when released, the Daoist has been inviting teachers to educate them. After Zhu's repeated requests, the Daoist opens the gate to the cave. In the dim light, Zhu sees numerous strange creatures with human heads and bestial bodies. When a monster with nine human heads and a snake's body darts toward the gate, he is immediately made to go back. Zhu is sent off by the Daoist with a lavish banquet. After returning home, Zhu reunites with his family and becomes very rich because of the gifts bestowed on him by the Daoist.

The story continues. In the tenth year of the Xianfeng reign (1860), the Taiping rebels overrun the Suzhou and Songjiang area. By that time, Zhu has died and his offspring have moved to other regions. One day, a Taiping king attacks the city. Passing by Zhu's tomb and reading its inscriptions, the king is taken by surprise. He exclaims, "Isn't this Teacher Zhu?" The rebel king then summons his followers to offer sacrifices to Zhu and confer upon Zhu an official title. This act ends the story.

Full of political and cultural ambiguities, the story evokes the traditional Chinese vision of utopia, the Peach Blossom Spring, but concurrently suggests a dystopia. In the story of the Peach Blossom Spring, a fisherman stumbles upon a village where people lead an idyllic life, uninfluenced by and unaware of political chaos and dynastic changes beyond their borders.[2] Zhu's experience on the island alludes to, but ultimately subverts, the traditional topos: the fisherman is transformed into an unsuccessful student, and the entrance to the Peach Blossom Spring, originally covered by fragrant fallen flower petals and fresh grass, is now occupied by strange birds and snakes. In the original, the villagers are outside of the world of imperial administration and dynastic change, but on Beiji Piye Island they are subject to the administration and eager to learn about contemporary events in the "Heavenly Empire." The greatest difference is that the island serves as an eternal holding pen for monsters and demons. Xuan Ding produces a dystopian vision by inverting the Peach Blossom Spring. The boundary between dystopia and reality is porous: the monstrous creatures are periodically unleashed to create catastrophes such as the Taiping Rebellion. Unlike the island in *Traces of Flowers and the Moon*

2. See also the discussion in chapter 4.

(see chapter 3), Beiji Piye Island is no escape from reality, and the ocean through which one travels to reach it is a perilous rather than idealized passage. The Daoist who seems to have control over the demons is only fulfilling his Heaven-prescribed responsibilities. It is in this sense that the story sheds light on the perpetual cycle of catastrophes (*jie*) that will assume a multitude of forms in modern China.

The demons in the dark cave also reflect the tradition of *Water Margin* and foreshadow Lu Xun's famous analogy of the iron house in his preface to *Call to Arms* (*Nahan* 呐喊), an important collection of short stories in modern Chinese literature published in 1923. In Xuan Ding's story, the demonic creature that almost escapes symbolizes the barely containable power of subversion. This plot element resonates with the beginning of *Water Margin*, when the Heavenly spirits and the Earthly fiends are inadvertently freed and are subsequently incarnated as the 108 rebel heroes. The image of threatening demons locked in a cave with a metal gate is later echoed in Lu Xun's characterization of the Chinese as people locked inside an indestructible iron house, who, upon being awakened, destroy their confinement. Both authors acknowledge the rebellious energy the masses harbor. However, Xuan Ding and Lu Xun present starkly contrasting pictures: writing in the 1870s, Xuan Ding compared the members of the populace who constituted the Taiping force to savage demons that need to be kept under restraint until it is time for them to be released to disrupt the world; half a century later, Lu Xun imagined Chinese people as asleep in a dark, iron house, where they would soon die of suffocation but could also possibly be freed once awakened. The continuities and disjunctions between these two images reveal the extent of the changes among cultural elites and their understanding of the masses between the end of the nineteenth century and the beginning of the twentieth.

It is ironic that in the story "Beiji Piye Island," although the demons receive a Confucian education, once incarnated as the Taiping rebels, they cause catastrophic destruction. All they seem to have learned is a reverence for their teacher. Thus, the story invites a reading that questions the ultimate usefulness of knowledge—in this case of the Confucian classics—for the masses, who in the story live in metaphorical darkness. The possibility that communication exists between the orderly world of the "Heavenly Empire" and the demonic one in the cave, as evinced by the Taiping king's homage to Teacher Zhu, poses an even more provocative question: Is the Taiping king a product of Confucian teachings (no matter how mediated or twisted)? Given how the Taiping rebels first propagated Confucian moral values in their discourse to attract an audience, this question is particularly urgent, since it was precisely the abnormal transmutation of various traditions that gave rise to the Taiping Rebellion. The monstrous Other, as it turns out, is the result of the Confucian Self.

An unexpected parallel exists between "Beiji Piye Island" and Lu Xun's "A Madman's Diary" ("Kuangren riji" 狂人日記), the first short story in *Call to Arms*, as readings of Confucian classics in both stories inspire unruly spirits. First published in 1918, "A Madman's Diary" is widely acknowledged to be the first modern vernacular story, thus representing the dawn of modern Chinese literature. In Lu Xun's story, the madman is trying to read the Confucian classics, and among the lines he recognizes two characters: "Eat People." In having his madman interpret Confucianism as a cannibalistic tradition, Lu Xun in effect sabotages the old order and its moral authority on sociocultural, ideological, and linguistic levels. The insight Xuan Ding and Lu Xun share brings to mind the experiences of Hong Xiuquan, the rebel leader who was once a Confucian student.

At the end of "Beiji Piye Island," Xuan Ding recalls a custom of burning Confucian texts and scattering their ashes as a charm against monstrous sea creatures. Allegedly, once the monsters have swallowed Confucius's words, they will be born as human beings in China. Xuan Ding comments,

> Judging from this phenomenon, words seem to carry supernatural powers. However, the horror of the rebels, first and foremost, lies in their burning of the books. Why was that? For what reason were the collections of the three generations of my family all destroyed in the disaster of Zulong?[3] Now, holding the pen, I shed copious tears.

3. "The disaster of Zulong" (*zulong zhi jie* 祖龍之劫) was the destruction of "heterodox" books, including Confucian books, instigated by the First Emperor of Qin (r. 247–210 BCE).

觀此愈徵，文字若是靈異。然粵匪之猖獗也，首在燒毀書籍，又何故
與？余家三世所藏盡付祖龍之刼。秉筆至此，涕泗滂沱。[4]

Here, Xuan Ding laments how the Taipings destroyed books that ran
counter to their ideology. The destruction of the old books in the war,
however, happened in tandem with the proliferation of manuscripts,
newspapers, pamphlets, and books printed using both traditional and
modern technologies. The cultural and literary turbulence of the nineteenth century's second half was aided and abetted by the many kinds
of media available. The printing of the numerous personal accounts
and literary creations brought diverse voices and perspectives to a
broader audience, and thereby played an essential role in shaping Taiping history and the cultural and collective memories that revolve
around it. By producing extensive copies of various bodies of texts,
print technology served as a vehicle both for prosperity, and for transmitting a wide range of emotional and intellectual experiences to mass
consumers.

The Taiping Civil War penetrated not only the political and military
realms but also literary and cultural realms. Despite numerous efforts
to forestall the collapse of Heaven—whatever Heaven meant to the
different parties—the war led to destruction across the board. Writers
of the period appropriated topoi of transcendence and order to try to
reconstruct stability, only to reveal the unsustainability of those beliefs.
Both Taiping and Qing regimes imagined a populace that would submit willingly to their rule, but they did not completely succeed in either
case. However, the Taiping ideology and popular interpretations of the
Sacred Edict subverted the established connection between the Mandate of Heaven and Qing imperial legitimacy.

As the first Chinese utopian movement inspired by Western ideology, the Taiping movement had lasting, far-reaching repercussions,
from the Republican Revolution to the Tiananmen Incident and beyond.
Utopian aspirations, traumatic wounds, and collapsing illusions of

4. Xuan Ding, *YYQDL*, 1:218.

stability never ceased to be generated, endured, and remembered. Throughout the twentieth century, the discourses established in the Taiping period resurfaced to facilitate yet more rounds of rebellious, sometimes highly destructive energy on a grand scale. Again and again, people call upon Heaven in times of despair, but the opposition of "us" and "them" in people's struggles only aggravated myriad forms of suffering. Nevertheless, during this process, personal voices transcend conceptual dichotomies, giving rise to possibilities of imagination and innovation.

# Bibliography

Abe Yasuki 阿部泰記. *Hōkō densetsu no keisei to tenkai* 包公伝説の形成と展開. Tokyo: Kyūko shoin, 2004.

———. "Senkō seiyu: minshū bungaku tokushoku no enkou bun" 宣講聖諭：民眾文學特色の演講文. *Ajia no rekishi to bunka* 10 (2006): 77–81.

Ahern, Emily M. and Arthur P. Wolf, eds. *Religion and Ritual in Chinese Society*. Stanford: Stanford University Press, 1974.

Alexander, Katherine. "Conservative Confucian Values and the Promotion of Oral Performance Literature in Late Qing Jiangnan: Yu Zhi's Influence on Two Appropriations of Liu Xiang Baojuan." *CHINOPERL* 2 (2017): 89–115.

*The Analects of Confucius: A Philosophical Translation*. Translated by Roger Ames and Henry Rosemont. New York: Ballantine Books, 1998.

Anderson, Marston. *The Limits of Realism: Chinese Fiction in the Revolutionary Period*. Berkeley: University of California Press, 1990.

*Aodaliya cang Taiping tianguo yuanke guanshu congkan* 澳大利亞藏太平天國原刻官書叢刊. Edited by National Library of Australia. 4 vols. Beijing: Guojia tushuguan chubanshe, 2014.

Baiyun Shanren 白雲山人 [pseud.]. *Dangping fani tu ji* 蕩平髮逆圖記. Reprinted in *Jindai Zhongguo shiliao congkan xubian* 近代中國史料叢刊續編, vol. 29. Edited by Shen Yunlong 沈雲龍. 100 vols. Taipei: Wenhai chubanshe, 1974.

Barr, Allan. "A Comparative Study of Early and Late Tales in *Liaozhai zhiyi*." *Harvard Journal of Asiatic Studies* 45, no. 1 (1985): 157–202.

Bergson, Henri. *The Two Sources of Morality and Religion*. Translated by R. A. Audra and C. Brereton. New York: Doubleday Anchor, 1954.

Boardman, Eugene Powers. *Christian Influence upon the Ideology of the Taiping Rebellion, 1851–1864*. Madison: University of Wisconsin Press, 1952.

———. "Millenary Aspects of the Taiping Rebellion (1851–1864)." In *Millennial Dreams in Action: Studies in Revolutionary Religious Movements*, edited by Sylvia Thrupp, 70–79. New York: Schocken Books, 1970.

Bogue, Ronald. "Fabulation, Narration and the People to Come." In *Deleuze and Philosophy*, edited by Constantin V. Bounda, 202–23. Edinburgh: Edinburgh University Press, 2006.

Brokaw, Cynthia. *The Ledgers of Merit and Demerit: Social Change and Moral Order in Late Imperial China*. Princeton: Princeton University Press, 1991.

Brook, Timothy, ed. *Death by a Thousand Cuts*. Cambridge: Harvard University Press, 2008.

Butler, Judith. *Excitable Speech: A Politics of the Performative*. New York: Routledge, 1997.

Cao Daguan 曹大觀 (fl. 1850s). *Kou ting ji lüe* 寇汀紀略. Reprinted in *Taiping tianguo wenxian huibian* 太平天國文獻彙編, vol. 6.

Cao Xueqin 曹雪芹 (fl. 1717–1763). *The Story of the Stone: A Chinese Novel in Five Volumes*. Translated by David Hawkes and John Minford. New York: Penguin, 1973.

Chang, Kang-i Sun. "The Idea of Mask in Wu Wei-yeh (1609–1671)." *Harvard Journal of Asiatic Studies* 48, no. 2 (1988): 289–320.

Chang Ningwen 常宁文. "*Yeyu qiudeng lu* suo zhanshi de nüxing shijie" 《夜雨秋燈錄》所展示的女性世界. *Nanjing shida xuebao* 4 (1993): 67–71.

Chao Song 晁崧. "Wan Qing qujia Xu Shanchang yanjiu" 晚清曲家許善長研究. M.A. thesis, Nanjing Normal University.

Che Xilun 車錫倫. "Du Qingmo Jiang Yuzhen bian *Xing xin baojuan*" 讀清末蔣玉真編《醒心寶卷》. *Wenxue yichan* 2 (2010): 131–35.

———. *Xinyang, jiaohua, yule: Zhongguo baojuan yanjiu ji qita* 信仰，教化，娛樂：中國寶卷研究及其它. Taipei: Taiwan xuesheng shuju, 2002.

Chen Guoxue 陳國學. *Honglou meng de duochong yiyun yu Fo Dao jiao guanxi tanxi* 《紅樓夢》的多重意蘊與佛道教關係探析. Beijing: Zhongguo shehui kexue chubanshe, 2011.

Chen Li 陳理. "Taiping jun gongzhan Wuchang chengqu tu" 太平軍攻佔武昌城區圖. In *Taiping tianguo lishi ditu ji* 太平天國歷史地圖集, edited by Guo Yisheng 郭毅生, 56. Beijing: Zhongguo ditu chubanshe, 1989.

Chen Ling 陳嶺. "Zhixu bengkui: Xian-Tong zhi ji Jiangnan minzhong de zhanshi taonan yu richang shenghuo" 秩序崩潰：咸同之際江南民眾的戰時逃難與日常生活. *Junshi shi yanjiu* 32 (2018): 74–89.

Chen Qingyuan 陳慶元. "Wei Xiuren jiqi zazhu" 魏秀仁及其雜著. In *Wei Xiuren zazhu chaoben* 魏秀仁襍著鈔本, vol. 1, 1–23. 2 vols. Nanjing: Jiangsu guji chubanshe, 2000.

Chen Shanjun 陳善鈞 (fl. 1860s). *Guichou Zhongzhou libing ji lüe* 癸丑中州

罹兵紀略. Reprinted in *Taiping tianguo* 太平天國. Edited by Zhongguo shixue hui 中國史學會, vol. 5.

Chen Zuogao 陳左高. *Zhongguo riji shi lüe* 中國日記史略. Shanghai: Shanghai fanyi chuban gongsi, 1990.

Cheng Huaping 程華平. *Ming Qing chuanqi biannian shigao* 明清傳奇編年史稿. Jinan: Qilu shushe, 2008.

Cheng Junying 程俊英, ed. and comm. *Shijing zhuxi* 詩經注析. Beijing: Zhonghua shuju, 1991.

Chia, Lucille. *Printing for Profit: The Commercial Publishers of Jianyang, Fujian (11th–17th Centuries).* Cambridge, MA: Harvard University Asia Center, 2002.

Chien Yu-wen 簡又文. *Qing shi Hong Xiuquan zaiji* 清史洪秀全載記. Hong Kong: Jianshi mengjin shuwu, 1967.

———. *Taiping tianguo dianzhi tongkao* 太平天國典制通考. 3 vols. Hong Kong: Jianshi mengjin shuwu, 1958.

———. *Taiping tianguo quanshi* 太平天國全史. Hong Kong: Jianshi mengjin shuwu, 1962.

Clark, Philip. "New Technologies and the Production of Religious Texts in China, 19th to 21st Century." In *Modern Chinese Religion II, 1850–2015,* edited by Vincent Goossaert, Kiely Jan, Lagerwey John, vol. 1, 560–78. 2 vols. Leiden: Brill, 2016.

Cohen, Paul A. *Between Tradition and Modernity: Wang T'ao and Reform in Late Ch'ing China.* Cambridge, MA: Harvard University Asia Center, 1974.

Cui Zhiqing 崔之清, ed. *Taiping tianguo zhanzheng quanshi* 太平天國戰爭全史. 4 vols. Nanjing: Nanjing daxue chubanshe, 2002.

Dai Shunli 代順麗. "Dui Wang Tao Taiping tianguo xiaoshuo de zai renshi" 對王韜太平天國小說的再認識. *Hubei shifan xueyuan xuebao* 1 (2009): 45–48.

Dang Yueyi 黨月異. "Cong 'hou *Liaozhai*' kan jindai nüxing wenhua de yanbian" 從 "後聊齋" 看近代女性文化的演變. *Zhonghua nüzi xueyuan Shandong fenyuan xuebao* 4 (2003): 44–47.

———. "Lüelun Wang Tao wenxue guannian yu wenxue chuangzuo de jindai hua" 略論王韜文學觀念與文學創作的近代化. *Xueshu luntan* 10 (2009): 91–102.

Dawes, James. *The Language of War: Literature and Culture in the U.S. from the Civil War through World War I.* Cambridge: Harvard University Press, 2002.

Deng Shaoji 鄧紹基 and Lang Ying 郎櫻, eds. *Zhongguo wenxue tongshi* 中國文學通史. 12 vols. Nanjing: Jiangsu wenyi chubanshe, 2011.

Derrida, Jacques. *Specters of Marx: The State of the Debt, the Work of Mourning, and the New International.* New York: Routledge, 1994.

Ding Rouke 丁柔克 (fl. 1840s–1880s). *Liu hu* 柳弧. Reprint, Beijing: Zhonghua shuju, 2002.

Du Fu 杜甫 (712–770). *Du Fu quanji jiaozhu* 杜甫全集校注. Edited by Xiao Difei 萧涤非 and Liao Zhong'an 廖仲安. 12 vols. Beijing: Renmin wenxue chubanshe, 2014.

———. *The Poetry of Du Fu.* Translated by Stephen Owen. 6 vols. Boston: De Gruyter, 2016.

Du Weimo 杜維沫. "Jiaodian houji" 校點後記. In Wei Xiuren 魏秀仁, *Hua yue hen* 花月痕. Edited by Du Weimo 杜維沫. Beijing: Renmin wenxue chubanshe, 1982.

Du Zhijun 杜志軍. "*Honglou meng* yu *hua yue hen*"《红楼梦》与《花月痕》. *Honglou meng xuekan* 1 (1999): 186–202.

Duan Huaiqing 段懷清. *Wang Tao yu xiandai wenxue zhuanxing* 王韜與現代文學轉型. Shanghai: Fudan daxue chubanshe, 2015.

Duan Yuming 段玉明. "*Yuli zhibao chao*: jiu xi shuijia zhi shanshu" 玉歷至寶鈔：究系誰家之善書. *Zongjiao xue yanjiu* 2 (2004): 31–37.

Duara, Prasenjit. "Superscribing Symbols: The Myth of Guandi, Chinese God of War." *Journal of Asian Studies* 47 (1988): 778–96.

Ellul, Jacques. *Propaganda: The Formation of Men's Attitudes.* New York: Vintage Books, 1973.

Elman, Benjamin A. *From Philosophy to Philology: Intellectual and Social Aspects of Change in Late Imperial China.* Cambridge: Harvard University Press, 1984.

Engberg-Pedersen, Anders. *Empire of Chance: The Napoleonic Wars and the Disorder of Things.* Cambridge: Harvard University Press, 2015.

Eno, Robert. *The Confucian Creation of Heaven: Philosophy and the Defense of Ritual Mastery.* Albany: State University of New York Press, 1990.

Epstein, Maram. *Orthodox Passions: Narrating Filial Love During the High Qing.* Cambridge: Harvard University Press, 2019.

Esherick, Joseph. *The Origins of the Boxer Uprising.* Berkeley: University of California Press, 1987.

Fan Ye 范曄 (398–445). *Hou Han shu* 後漢書. 120 vols. Reprint, Beijing: Beijing tushuguan chubanshe, 2006.

Faust, Drew G. *This Republic of Suffering: Death and the American Civil War.* New York: Alfred A. Knopf, 2008.

Feng Menglong 馮夢龍 (1574–1646). *Qing shi* 情史. 4 vols. Reprint, Shanghai: Shanghai guji chubanshe, 1990.

Festinger, Leon. *When Prophecy Fails*. Minneapolis: University of Minnesota Press, 1956.

Gan Bao 干寶 (fl. 317–322). *Sou shen ji* 搜神記. 20 vols. Jiguge 汲古閣, 1640s edition.

Genette, Gérard. "Introduction to the Paratext." *New Literary History* 22 (1991): 261–72.

Geng Shuyan 耿淑燕. "Shengyu xuanjiang xiaoshuo: yizhong bei yanmo de xiaoshuo leixing" 聖諭宣講小說：一種被湮沒的小說類型. *Xueshu yanjiu* 4 (2007): 137–43.

Goldman, Andrea. *Opera and the City: The Politics of Culture in Beijing, 1770–1900*. Stanford: Stanford University Press, 2013.

Goossaert, Vincent. "1898: The Beginning of the End for Chinese Religion?" *Journal of Asian Studies* 65, no. 2 (2006): 307–35.

———. "Competing Eschatological Scenarios during the Taiping War, 1851–1864." In *The End(s) of Time(s): Apocalypticism, Messianism, and Utopianism*, edited by Hans-Christian Lehner, 269–306. Leiden: Brill, 2021.

———. *Making the Gods Speak: The Ritual Production of Revelation in Chinese Religious History*. Cambridge: Harvard University, 2022.

———. "Une théologie chinoise de l'au-delà. Visions des morts dans le *Yuli baochao* (xixe siècle)." In *Fantômes dans l'Extrême-Orient d'hier et d'aujourd'hui*, edited by Marie Laureillard and Vincent Durand-Dastès, vol. 1, 31–39. 2 vols. Paris: Inalco Presses, 2017.

Guo Jian 郭建. *Zhonghua wenhua tongzhi: falü zhi* 中華文化通志：法律志. Shanghai: Shanghai renmin chubanshe, 1998.

Guo Tingyi 郭廷以. *Taiping tianguo lifa kaoding* 太平天國曆法考訂. Shanghai: Shangwu yinshuguan, 1937.

———. *Taiping tianguo shishi rizhi* 太平天國史事日志. 2 vols. Reprint, Shanghai: Shanghai shudian, 1986.

Guo, Wu. "Recalling Bitterness: Historiography, Memory, and Myth in Maoist China." *Twentieth-Century China* 39 (2014): 245–68.

Guo Yingde 郭英德. *Ming Qing chuanqi shi* 明清傳奇史. Beijing: Renmin wenxue chubanshe, 2012.

Guo Yisheng 郭毅生 and Shi Shi 史式, ed. *Taiping tianguo da cidian* 太平天國大辭典. Beijing: Zhongguo shehui kexue chubanshe, 1995.

Haar, Barend Ter. *Guan Yu: The Religious Afterlife of a Failed Hero*. Oxford: Oxford University Press, 2017.

Hamberg, Theodore (1819–1854). "Taiping tianguo qiyi ji" 太平天國起義記. Translated by Chien Yu-wen 簡又文. In *Taiping tianguo ziliao* 太平天國

資料, edited by Deng Zhicheng 鄧之誠, vol. 36, 829–78. In *Jindai Zhong-guo shiliao congkan xubian* 近代中國史料叢刊續編, 100 vols. Taipei: Wenhai chubanshe, 1976.

———. *The Visions of Hung-Siu-tshuen, and Origin of the Kwangsi Insur-rection.* Hong Kong: China Mail Office, 1854.

Han Chunping 韓春平. "Liudu Nanjing dui Ming dai shenmo xiaoshuo liu-pai xingcheng de kaiduan yiyi" 留都南京對明代神魔小說流派形成的開端意義. *Qilu xuekan* 5 (2010): 133–38.

Hanan, Patrick. *Chinese Fiction of the Nineteenth and Early Twentieth Cen-turies: Essays.* New York: Columbia University Press, 2004.

———. *The Chinese Vernacular Story.* Cambridge, MA: Harvard Univer-sity Asia Center, 1981.

———. "Judge Bao's Hundred Cases Reconstructed." *Harvard Journal of Asiatic Studies* 40 (1980): 301–23.

Handan mengxing ren 邯鄲夢醒人 [pseud.]. *Meng zhong yuan* 夢中緣. 4 vols. Publisher unknown, 1885.

Hanson, Marta E. *Speaking of Epidemics in Chinese Medicine: Disease and the Geographic Imagination in Late Imperial China.* New York: Rout-ledge, 2011.

He Yan 何晏 (190–249), ed. *Lunyu zhu shu* 論語注疏. 20 vols. 1807.

Hegel, Robert. "Dreaming the Past: Memory and Continuity Beyond the Ming Fall." In *Trauma and Transcendence in Early Qing Literature*, edited by Wilt Idema, Wai-yee Li, and Ellen Widmer, 345–75. Cambridge: Harvard University Asia Center, 2006.

———. *The Novel in Seventeenth-Century China.* New York: Columbia University Press, 1981.

Heidegger, Martin. *Being and Time.* New York: Harper Perennial, 2008.

Heng He 恆鶴. "Qian yan" 前言. In *Yeyu qiudeng lu* 夜雨秋燈錄, edited by Heng He 恆鶴, vol. 1, 1–11. 2 vols. Shanghai: Shanghai guji chubanshe, 1987.

Hogan, Patrick C. *Cognitive Science, Literature, and the Arts: A Guide for Humanists.* Florence: Taylor and Francis, 2012.

Hu Hsiao-chen 胡曉真. *Cainü cheye weimian: Jindai Zhongguo nüxing xushi wenxue de xingqi* 才女徹夜未眠：近代中國女性敘事文學的興起. Taipei: Maitian renwen, 2003.

———. "Liluan Hangzhou: zhanzheng jiyi yu Hangzhou jishi wenxue" 離亂杭州：戰爭記憶與杭州紀事文學. *Zhongguo wenzhe yanjiu jikan* 36 (2010): 45–78.

Hu Sheng 胡勝. *Ming Qing shenmo xiaoshuo yanjiu* 明清神魔小說研究. Beijing: Zhongguo shehui kexue chubanshe, 2004.

Huang, Martin. *Literati and Self-Re/Presentation: Autobiographical Sensibility in the Eighteenth-Century Chinese Novel*. Stanford: Stanford University Press, 1995.

———. "Male Friendship in Ming China: An Introduction." *Nan Nü* 9 (2007): 2–33.

Hucker, Charles. *A Dictionary of Official Titles in Imperial China*. Stanford: Stanford University Press, 1985.

*Huizhou rongxiang yishu* 徽州容像藝術. Edited by Shi Gufeng 石谷風. Hefei: Anhui meishu chubanshe, 2001.

Huntington, Rania. "The Captive's Revenge: The Taiping Civil War as Drama." *Late Imperial China* 35, no. 2 (2014): 1–26.

———. "Chaos, Memory, and Genre: Anecdotal Recollections of the Taiping Rebellion." *Chinese Literature: Essays, Articles, Reviews (CLEAR)* 27 (2005): 59–91.

———. *Ink and Tears: Memory, Mourning, and Writing in the Yu Family*. Honolulu: University of Hawai'i Press, 2018.

———. "Singing Punishment and Redemption in the Taiping Civil War: Yu Zhi's Plays." *Frontiers of History in China* 13, no. 2 (2018): 211–26.

———. "The Weird in Newspaper." In *Writing and Materiality in China: Essays in Honor of Patrick Hanan*, edited by Patrick Hanan, Judith T. Zeitlin, Lydia He Liu, and Ellen Widmer, 341–92. Cambridge: Harvard University Asia Center, 2003.

Huters, Theodore. "Creating Subjectivity in Wu Jianren's *The Sea of Regret*." In *Dynastic Crisis and Cultural Innovation: From the Late Ming to the Late Qing and Beyond*, edited by David Der-wei Wang and Shang Wei, 451–78. Cambridge: Harvard Asia Center, 2005.

Idema, Wilt L. *Chinese Vernacular Fiction: The Formative Period*. Leiden: Brill, 1974.

———. "'Crossing the Sea in a Leaking Boat': Three Plays by Ding Yaokang." In *Trauma and Transcendence in Early Qing Literature*, edited by Wilt L. Idema, Wai-yee Li, and Ellen Widmer, 387–426. Cambridge: Harvard University Asia Center, 2006.

———. "Drama after the Conquest: an Introduction." In *Trauma and Transcendence in Early Qing Literature*, edited by Wilt L. Idema, Wai-yee Li, and Ellen Widmer, 373–85. Cambridge: Harvard University Asia Center, 2006.

———. *The Immortal Maiden Equal to Heaven and Other Precious Scrolls from Western Gansu*. Amherst: Cambria Press, 2015.

———. "Introduction." In *Judge Bao and the Rule of Law: Eight Ballad-Stories from the Period 1250–1450*. Singapore: World Scientific, 2010.

Ji Yun 紀昀 (1724–1805). *Yue wei caotang biij* 閱微草堂筆記. Shanghai: Shanghai guji chubanshe, 1980.

Jia Ping 賈平. "Lun Hanchuan shanshu de chuanbo" 論漢川善書的傳播. *Jiangxi shehui kexue* 6 (2008): 234–37.

Jiang Yan 江淹 (444–505). "Hen fu" 恨賦. In *Wen Xuan* 文選, edited by Xiao Tong 蕭統 (501–531) and annotated by Li Shan 李善 (630–689), vol. 1, 744–49. 6 vols. Reprint, Shanghai: Shanghai guji chubanshe, 1986.

———. "Rhapsody on Resentment." In *Wen Xuan, or, Selections of Refined Literature*, translated by David R. Knechtges, vol. 1, 193–200. 3 vols. Princeton: Princeton University Press, 1982.

Jiang Yubin 蔣玉斌. "Zhongguo gudai xiaoshuo de xinbian: lun Wang Tao de *Liaozhai zhiyi* fangzuo" 中國古代小說的新變：論王韜的《聊齋誌異》仿作. *Zhongguo wenyan xiaoshuo yanjiu* 20, no. 1 (2010): 151–60.

Jin, Huan 金環. "Authenticating the Renewed Heavenly Vision: *The Taiping Heavenly Chronicle (Taiping tianri)*." *Frontiers of History in China* 13, no. 2 (2018): 173–92.

———. "The Multitude of Otherness During the Taiping Civil War." *Journal of Chinese Literature and Culture* 7, no.1 (2020): 215–31.

———. "Stitching Words to Suture Wounds: A Manuscript Diary from the Taiping-Qing Civil War (1851–64)." *Late Imperial China* 40 (2019): 141–82.

———. "Violence and the Evolving Face of *Yao* in Taiping Propaganda." *Journal of Religion and Violence* 6, no. 1 (May 2018): 127–44.

*Jin shu* 晉書, edited by Fang Xuanling 房玄齡 (579–648). 130 *juan*. 8 *ce*. Reprint, Beijing: Zhonghua shuju, 1974.

Katz, Paul R. *Divine Justice: Religion and the Development of Chinese Legal Culture*. New York: Routledge, 2009.

Keulemans, Paize. "Onstage Rumor, Offstage Voices: The Politics of the Present in the Contemporary Opera of Li Yu." *Frontiers of History in China* 9, no. 2 (2014): 165–201.

———. *Sound Rising from the Paper: Nineteenth-Century Martial Arts Fiction and the Chinese Acoustic Imagination*. Cambridge: Harvard University Asia Center, 2014.

Kile, S. E. *Towers in the Void: Li Yu and Early Modern Chinese Media*. New York: Columbia University Press, 2023.

Ko, Dorothy. *Teachers of the Inner Chambers: Women and Culture in Seventeenth-Century China*. Stanford: Stanford University Press, 1994.

Kong Lingjing 孔另鏡. *Zhongguo xiaoshuo shiliao* 中國小說史料. Shanghai: Shanghai guji chubanshe, 1982.

Kong Shangren 孔尚任. *The Peach Blossom Fan*. Translated by Wai-yee Li, unpublished manuscript.

———. *Taohua shan* 桃花扇. Beijing: Renmin wenxue chubanshe, 2005.

Kuhn, Philip. "Origins of the Taiping Vision: Cross-cultural Dimensions of a Chinese Rebellion." *Comparative Studies in Society and History* 19 (1977): 350–66.

———. *Rebellion and Its Enemies in Late Imperial China: Militarization and Social Structure, 1796–1864.* Cambridge: Harvard University Press, 1980.

Lai Chi Tim. "Ming Qing Daojiao Lüzu jiangji xinyang de fazhan ji xiangguan wenren jitan yanjiu" 明清道教呂祖降乩信仰的發展及相關文人乩壇研究. *Zhongguo wenhua yanjiusuo xuebao* 65 (2017): 139–79.

Lai Xinxia 來新夏. *Zhongguo tushu shiye shi* 中國圖書事業史. Shanghai: Shanghai renmin chubanshe, 2009.

Lam, Ling Hon. *The Spatiality of Emotion in Early Modern China: From Dreamscapes to Theatricality.* New York: Columbia University Press, 2018.

Laub, Dori. "An Event without a Witness: Truth, Testimony, and Survival." In *Testimony: Crises of Witnessing in Literature, Psychoanalysis and History*, edited by Shoshana Felman and Dori Laub, 75–92. New York: Routledge, 1992.

———. "Bearing Witness or the Vicissitudes of Listening." In *Testimony: Crises of Witnessing in Literature, Psychoanalysis and History*, edited by Shoshana Felman and Dori Laub, 57–74. New York: Routledge, 1992.

Lee Fong-mao 李豐楙. "Chushen yu xiuxing: Mingdai zhefan xushu moshi de xingcheng jiqi zongjiao yishi—yi *Shuihu zhuan, Xiyou ji* weizhu" 出身與修行：明代謫凡敘述模式的形成及其宗教意識－以《水滸傳》、《西遊記》為主. *Guowen xuezhi* 7 (2005): 85–113.

———. *Xu Xun yu Sa Shoujian: Deng Zhimo Daojiao xiaoshuo yanjiu* 許遜與薩守堅：鄧志謨道教小說研究. Taipei: Taiwan xuesheng shuju, 1997.

Lee, Haiyan. *Revolution of the Heart: A Genealogy of Love in China, 1900–1950.* Stanford: Stanford University Press, 2007.

Legge, James. *The Chinese Classics: With a Translation, Critical and Exegetical Notes, Prolegomena, and Copious Indexes.* 5 vols. Hong Kong: Legge, 1861.

Li Bin 李濱 (fl. 1850s). *Zhongxing bieji* 中興別記. Reprinted in *Taiping tianguo ziliao huibian* 太平天國資料匯編, vol. 2. Edited by Taiping tianguo lishi bowuguan. 2 vols. Beijing: Zhonghua shuju, 1980.

Li Bo 李白 (701–762). *Li Bo quanji jiaozhu huishi jiping* 李白全集校注彙釋集評. Edited by Zhan Ying 詹鍈. 8 vols. Tianjin: Baihua wenyi chubanshe, 1996.

Li Chun 酈純. *Taiping tianguo junshi shi gaishu* 太平天國軍事史概述. Beijing: Zhonghua shuju, 1982.

Li Chunyan 李春燕. "Tang Minghuang you yuegong gushi de wenben yan-bian yu wenhua neihan" 唐明皇遊月宮故事的文本演變與文化內涵. *Tianzhong xuekan* 6 (2013): 20–23.

Li Hsiao-t'i. *Opera, Society, and Politics in Modern China*. Cambridge: Harvard University Asia Center, 2019.

Li Ji 李季. "Huangliang meng gushi ticai liubian kao" 黃粱夢故事題材流變考. *Yuwen zhishi* 1 (2011): 51–52.

Li Ji 李冀. "*Taishang ganying pian* wenben laiyuan jiqi chengshu shijian kao xi"《太上感應篇》文本來源及其成書時間考析. *Zongjiaoxue yanjiu* 1 (2017): 111–19.

Li Jinglin 李景林, ed. *Yili yizhu* 儀禮譯注. Changchun: Jilin wenshi chu-banshe, 2004.

Li Laizhang 李來章 (fl. 1660–1690). *Shengyu xuanjiang tiaoyue* 聖諭宣講條約. Cishutang edition, 1705.

———. "Shengyu xuanjiang xiangbao tiaoyue" 聖諭宣講鄉保條約. In *Shengyu guangxun jijie yu yanjiu*, edited and commented by Zhou Zhenhe, 535–42. Shanghai: Shanghai shudian chubanshe, 2006.

Li Li 李理. *Qingdai guanzhi yu fushi* 清代官制與服飾. Shenyang: Liaoning minzu chubanshe, 2009.

Li Shangyin 李商隱 (813–858). *Li Shangyin shige jijie* 李商隱詩歌集解. Edited by Liu Xuekai 劉學鍇 and Yu Shucheng 余恕誠. 5 vols. Beijing: Zhonghua shuju, 1988.

Li, Wai-yee. *Enchantment and Disenchantment: Love and Illusion in Chinese Literature*. Princeton: Princeton University Press, 1993.

———. "History and Memory in Wu Weiye's Poetry." In *Trauma and Transcendence in Early Qing Literature*, edited by Wilt Idema, Wai-yee Li, and Ellen Widmer, 99–148. Cambridge, MA: Harvard University Asia Center, 2006.

———. "Introduction." In *Trauma and Transcendence in Early Qing Literature*, edited by Wilt Idema, Wai-yee Li, and Ellen Widmer, 1–70. Cambridge, MA: Harvard University Asia Center, 2006.

———. "The Representation of History in the *Peach Blossom Fan*." *Journal of the American Oriental Society* 115, no. 3 (1995): 421–33.

———. *Women and National Trauma in Late Imperial Chinese Literature*. Cambridge: Harvard University Asia Center, 2014.

Li Yongping 李永平. "Fojiao wenhua dui Baogong wenxue de yingxiang" 佛教文化對包公文學的影響. *Shanxi shifan daxue xuebao* 37 (2008): 51–54.

Li Yu 李漁 (1611–1680). "Sheng wo lou" 生我樓. In *Shi'er lou* 十二樓. 12 vols. Xiaoxian ju edition, seventeenth century.

Lian Qiyuan 連啟元. *Mingdai de gaoshi bangwen: xunxi chuanbo yu shehui hudong* 明代的告示榜文：訊息傳播與社會互動. Taipei: Hua Mulan chubanshe, 2010.

Liang Qichao 梁啟超. *Zhongguo jin sanbainian xueshu shi* 中國近三百年學術史. Beijing: Shangwu yinshuguan, 2011.

Liang Shu'an 梁淑安. *Zhongguo jindai chuanqi zaju jingyan lu* 中國近代傳奇雜劇經眼錄. Beijing: Shumu wenxian chubanshe, 1996.

Liao Cho-Cheng 廖卓成. "Zizhuan wen yanjiu" 自傳文研究. Ph.D. dissertation. National Taiwan University, 1992.

Liao Yan 廖燕 (1644–1705). *Liao Yan quan ji* 廖燕全集. 3 vols. Shanghai: Shanghai guji chubanshe, 2005.

Lin Fan. "Knowledge, Power, and Technology." *Monumenta Serica* 69 (2021): 387–412.

Lin Shanwen 林珊妏. *Qingmo Shengyu xuanjiang zhi an'zheng yanjiu* 清末聖諭宣講之案證研究. Taipei: Wenjin chubanshe, 2015.

Lin Yu-ping 林宇萍. "'Hanchuan shanshu' de lishi bianqian jiqi guobao sixiang tantao"《漢川善書》的歷史變遷及其果報思想探討. *Xingda zhongwen xuebao* 23 (2008): 625–38.

Lindley, Augustus F. *Ti-ping Tien-kwoh: The History of the Ti-ping Revolution.* London: Day & Son, 1866.

Ling Shuowei 凌碩為. "Shenbaoguan yu Wang Tao xiaoshuo zhi zhuanbian" 申報館與王韜小說之轉變. *Qiushi xuekan* 34, no. 1 (2007): 106–10.

———. "*Yeyu qiudeng lu* yanben kao lun"《夜雨秋燈錄》贗本考論. *Ming Qing xiaoshuo yanjiu* 1 (2013): 144–50.

Liu Chiung-Yun 劉瓊云. "Ren, tian, mo—*Nü xian waishi* zhong de lishi quehan yu 'ta' jie xiangxiang" 天、人、魔—《女仙外史》中的歷史缺憾與'她'界想像. *Zhongguo wenzhe yanjiu jikan* 38 (2011): 43–94.

Liu Guizeng 劉貴曾 (transcribed by Liu Shouzeng 劉壽曾). *Yusheng ji lüe* 餘生紀略. Reprinted in *Taiping tianguo* 太平天國. Edited by Luo Ergang 羅爾綱 and Wang Qingcheng 王慶成, vol. 4.

Liu Guoxin 劉國新. *Zhongguo zhengzhi zhidu cidian* 中國政治制度辭典. Beijing: Zhongguo shehui chubanshe, 1990.

Liu Jingshu 劉敬叔 (fl. 417). *Yi yuan* 異苑. 10 vols. In *Yingyin Wenyuange Siku quanshu* 影印文淵閣四庫全書.

Liu Ping 劉平. *Zhongguo mimi zongjiao shi yanjiu* 中國秘密宗教史研究. Beijing: Beijing daxue chubanshe, 2010.

Liu Shouhua 劉守華. "Cong baojuan dao shanshu: Hubei hanchuan shanshu de tezhi yu meili" 從寶卷到善書：湖北漢川善書的特質與魅力. *Wenhua yichan* 1 (2007): 80–85.

Liu Xie 劉勰. *The Literary Mind and the Carving of Dragons*. Translated by Vincent Yu-chung Shih. Hong Kong: Chinese University Press, 2015.

Love, Harold. *Attributing Authorship: An Introduction*. New York: Cambridge University Press, 2002.

Lu, Tina. "Fictional Reunions in the Wake of Dynastic Fall." In *Trauma and Transcendence in Early Qing Literature*, edited by Wilt L. Idema, Wai-yee Li, and Ellen Widmer, 310–44. Cambridge: Harvard University Asia Center, 2006.

Lu Xun 魯迅. *Zhongguo xiaoshuo shi lüe* 中國小說史略. Hangzhou: Zhejiang wenyi chubanshe, 2000.

Luo Ergang 羅爾綱. *Taiping tianguo shi lunwen ji* 太平天國史論文集. Beijing: Shenghuo, dushu, xinzhi sanlian shudian, 1955.

———. *Taiping tianguo shigang* 太平天國史綱. Shanghai: Shanghai shudian, 1992.

———. *Tianli kao* 天歷考. In *Luo Ergang quanji* 羅爾綱全集, vol. 3, 7–190. 22 vols. Beijing: Shehui kexue wenxian chubanshe, 2011.

Lutz, Jessie Gregory. *Opening China: Karl F.A. Gützlaff and Sino-Western Relations, 1827–1852*. Grand Rapids: William B. Eerdmans, 2008.

Ma Tingzhong 馬廷中. "Qing wangchao de zhengce yu Jidu jiao zai xinan minzu diqu de chuanbo" 清王朝的政策與基督教在西南民族地區的傳播. In *Zhongguo nanfang minzu shi yanjiu wenji* 中國南方民族史研究文集, edited by Hu Shaohua 胡邵華, 224–32. Beijing: Minzu chubanshe, 2004.

Mair, Victor. "Language and Ideology in the Sacred Edict." In *Popular Culture in Late Imperial China*, edited by Andrew J. Nathan and Evelyn S. Rawski, 325–59. Berkeley: University of California Press, 1985.

Mann, Susan. *Precious Records: Women in China's Long Eighteenth Century*. Stanford: Stanford University Press, 1997.

Masschelein, Anneleen. *The Unconcept: The Freudian Uncanny in Late Twentieth-Century Theory*. Albany: State University of New York Press, 2011.

McDermott, Joseph. "Friendship and Its Friends in the Late Ming." In *Jindai jiazu yu zhengzhi bijiao lishi lunwen ji* 近代家族與政治比較歷史論文集, edited by Zhongyang yanjiuyuan jindaishi yanjiusuo 中央研究院近代史研究所, 67–96. Taipei: Zhongyang yanjiuyuan jindaishi yanjiu suo, 1992.

McMahon, Keith. *The Fall of the God of Money: Opium Smoking in Nineteenth-Century China*. Lanham: Rowman & Littlefield, 2002.

———. *Polygamy and Sublime Passion: Sexuality in China on the Verge of Modernity*. Honolulu: University of Hawai'i Press, 2010.

Meyer-Fong, Tobie. *Building Culture in Early Qing Yangzhou*. Stanford: Stanford University Press, 2003.

———. "Gathering in a Ruined City: Metaphor, Practice, and Recovery in Post-Taiping Yangzhou." In *Lifestyle and Entertainment in Yangzhou*, edited by Lucie Olivová and Vibeke Børdahl, 37–61. Oslo: Nordic Institute of Asian Studie, 2009.

———. "To Know the Enemy: The *Zei qing huizuan*, Military Intelligence, and the Taiping Civil War." *T'oung-pao* 104 (2018): 384–423.

———. "Urban Space and Civil War, Hefei 1853–1854." *Frontiers of History in China* 8, no. 4 (2013): 469–92.

———. *What Remains: Coming to Terms with Civil War in 19th-Century China*. Stanford: Stanford University Press, 2013.

Michael, Franz H. *The Taiping Rebellion: History and Documents*. 3 vols. Seattle: University of Washington Press, 1966.

Mink, Louis O. "Narrative Form as a Cognitive Instrument." In *The History and Narrative Reader*, edited by Geoffrey Roberts, 211–21. London: Routledge, 2001.


Ogaeri Yoshio 魚返善雄, ed. and comm. *Kanbun kago kōki kōtei ikun* 華語漢文康熙皇帝遺訓. Osaka: Yagō shoten, 1943.

O'Leary, Stephen. *Arguing the Apocalypse: A Theory of Millennial Rhetoric*. New York: Oxford University Press, 1994.

Orwell, George. *Seeing Things as They Are: Selected Journalism and Other Writings*. London: Harvill Secker, 2014.

Owen, Stephen. *The End of the Chinese "Middle Ages": Essays in Mid-Tang Literary Culture*. Stanford: Stanford University Press, 1996.

———. *The Late Tang: Chinese Poetry of the Mid-Ninth Century (827–860)*. Cambridge: Harvard University Asia Center, 2006.


Pan Jianguo 潘建國. "Wei Xiuren *Hua yue hen* xiaoshuo yinshi ji benshi xintan" 魏秀仁花月痕小說引詩及本事新探. *Wenxue pinglun* 5 (2005): 156–63.

Pan Zhongrui 潘鐘瑞 (1823–1890). *Sutai milu ji* 蘇臺麋鹿記. Reprinted in *Taiping tianguo* 太平天國, vol. 5. Edited by Zhongguo shixue hui 中國史學會.

Pankenier, David. "Temporality and the Fabric of Space–Time in Early Chinese Thought." In *Time and Temporality in the Ancient World*, edited by Ralph Rosen, 129–46. Philadelphia: University of Pennsylvania Museum of Archaeology, 2004.

Paperno, Irina. "What Can Be Done with Diaries?" *Russian Review* 63 (October 2004): 561–73.

Perry, Elizabeth. *Anyuan: Mining China's Revolutionary Tradition*. Berkeley: University of California Press, 2012.

———. "Taipings and Triads: The Role of Religion in Inter-rebel Relations." In *Religion and Rural Revolt*, edited by Gerhard Benecke et al., 342–53. Dover: Massachusetts University Press, 1982.

Plaks, Andrew. *Four Masterworks of the Ming Novel*. Princeton: Princeton University Press, 1987.

———. "Towards a Critical Theory of Chinese Narrative." In *Chinese Narrative: Critical and Theoretical Essays*, edited by Andrew Plaks, 163–202. Princeton: Princeton University Press, 1977.

———. "Where the Lines Meet: Parallelism in Chinese and Western Literatures." *Chinese Literature: Essays, Articles, Reviews (CLEAR)* 10 (1988): 43–60.

Platt, Stephen. *Autumn in the Heavenly Kingdom: China, the West, and the Epic Story of the Taiping Civil War*. New York: Knopf, 2012.

———. "Introduction: War and Deconstruction in 1860s Jiangnan." *Late Imperial China* 30, no. 2 (2009): 1–10.

———. *Provincial Patriots: The Hunanese and Modern China*. Cambridge: Harvard University Press, 2007.

Pu Songling 蒲松齡. Liaozhai zhiyi *huijiao huizhu huiping ben* 聊齋誌異會校會注會評本. Compiled and edited by Zhang Youhe 張友鶴. Shanghai: Shanghai guji chubanshe, 1986.

Pu Wenbin 濮文彬 (fl. 1850s–1880s). *Huangzhou huanyou cao* 黃州宦遊草. Huangzhou: publisher unknown, 1885/6.

*Puyuan zhi* 濮院志. Edited by Xia Xinming 夏辛銘 (fl. 1880s). Reprinted in *Zhongguo difangzhi jicheng: Xiangzhen zhi zhuanji* 中國地方誌集成：鄉鎮誌專輯, vol. 21. Edited by Shanghai shudian 上海書店. Shanghai: Shanghai shudian, 1992.

Qian Xiang 錢湘. "Xu ke *Dang kou zhi* xu" 續刻蕩寇志序. In *Shuihu zhuan ziliao huibian* 水滸傳資料匯編, edited by Zhu Yixuan 朱一玄, 517–18. Tianjin: Nankai daxue chubanshe, 2002.

Rankin, Mary Backus. *Elite Activism and Political Transformation in China: Zhejiang Province, 1865–1911*. Stanford: Stanford University Press, 1986.

Reilly, Thomas. *The Taiping Heavenly Kingdom: Rebellion and the Blasphemy of Empire*. Seattle: University of Washington Press, 2004.

Ricœur, Paul. "Narrative Time." In *On Narrative*, edited by W. J. Thomas Mitchell, 165–86. Chicago: University of Chicago Press, 1981.

———. *Oneself as Another*. Chicago: University of Chicago Press, 1992.

———. *Time and Narrative*. 3 vols. Chicago: University of Chicago Press, 1990.

Roddy, Stephen. *Literati Identity and Its Fictional Representations in Late Imperial China*. Stanford: Stanford University Press, 1998.

Rouzer, Paul. *Writing Another's Dream: The Poetry of Wen Tingyun*. Stanford: Stanford University Press, 1993.

Sakai Tadao 酒井忠夫. *Zōho Chūgoku zensho no kenkyū* 増補中国善書の研究. 2 vols. Tokyo: Kokusho Kankōkai, 1999.

Schechner, Richard. *Essays on Performance Theory, 1970–1976*. New York: Drama Book Specialists, 1977.

Schluessel, Eric. *Land of Strangers: The Civilizing Project in Qing Central Asia*. New York: Columbia University Press, 2020.

Scholes, Robert. *The Fabulators*. New York: Oxford University Press, 1967.

Shang, Wei. Rulin waishi *and Cultural Transformation in Late Imperial China*. Cambridge, MA: Harvard University Asia Center, 2003.

Shen Qifeng 沈起鳳 (1741–?). *Xie duo* 諧鐸. Reprint, Huhe haote: Neimenggu renmin chubanshe, 1999.

Shen Yue 沈約 (441–513). "Yu Xu Mian shu" 與徐勉書. In *Nan shi* 南史, edited by Li Yanshou 李延壽 (fl. seventh century). 80 vols. Reprint, Taipei: Dingwen shuju, 1992.

Shen Zi 沈梓. *Beishan biji* 北山筆記 (Manuscript). Jiaxing Library, Zhejiang. [ms. 1]

———. *Bikou riji* 避寇日記 (Manuscript). 2 vols. Jiaxing Library, Zhejiang. [mss. 2 and 3]

———. *Bikou riji* 避寇日記. Reprinted in *Taiping tianguo* 太平天國, vol. 8. Edited by Luo Ergang 羅爾綱 and Wang Qingcheng 王慶成.

———. "Jiefu Shi Jianshan qi Shen shi zhuan lüe" 節婦施兼山妻沈氏傳略. Reprinted in *Puyuan zhi* 濮院志, edited by Xia Xinming 夏辛銘. In *Zhongguo difangzhi jicheng: xiangzhen zhi zhuanji* 中國地方誌集成：鄉鎮誌專輯.

———. *Yangzhuo xuan biji* 養拙軒筆記. Reprinted in *Taiping tianguo shiliao congbian jianji* 太平天國史料叢編簡輯, vol. 2. Edited by Taiping tianguo lishi bowuguan 太平歷史博物館. 6 vols. Beijing: Zhonghua shuju, 1961.

Sheng Yang 盛洋. *Rushi yu chushi jian de jiujie: Xuan Ding jiqi Yeyu qiudeng lu* 入世與出世間的糾結：宣鼎及其《夜雨秋燈錄》. Xinbei: Boyang chubanshe, 2019.

*Shengyu lingzheng* 聖諭靈徵. 6 vols. Reprint, publisher unknown, 1885.

Sherman, Stuart. *Telling Time: Clocks, Diaries, and English Diurnal Form, 1660–1785*. Chicago: University of Chicago Press, 1997.

Shih, Vincent Y. *The Taiping Ideology: Its Sources, Interpretations, and In-fluences.* Seattle: University of Washington Press, 1972.

Shunzhi Emperor (r. 1643–1661). *Yuzhi quanshan yaoyan* 御製勸善要言. Publisher unknown, 1875.

Sima Qian 司馬遷. *Records of the Grand Historian.* Translated and edited by Burton Watson. 3 vols. New York: Columbia University Press, 1993.

———. *Shiji* 史記. Annotated by Wang Liqi 王利器 and Zhang Lie 張烈. 3 vols. Reprint, Taipei: Taiwan guji chubanshe, 1998.

Sommer, Matthew H. *Sex, Law, and Society in Late Imperial China.* Stanford: Stanford University Press, 2000.

Song Lian 宋濂 (1310–1381). "Yu Zhongyuan xi" 諭中原檄. In *Huang Ming wenheng* 皇明文衡, edited by Cheng Minzheng 程敏政, vol. 1, *juan* 1, 1a–2b. Reprint. 20 vols. Shanghai: Shangwu yinshuguan, 1929.

Song Xin 宋欣 and Yang Pu 楊蒲. "*Yeyu qiudeng lu, Yeyu qiu deng xu lu*" 夜雨秋燈錄，夜雨秋燈續錄. *Shehui kexue zhanxian* 1 (1987): 312–13.

Spence, Jonathan. *God's Chinese Son: The Taiping Heavenly Kingdom of Hong Xiuquan.* New York: Norton, 1996.

Struve, Lynn, trans. "Changshu in Chronicle, Storybook, Memoir, and Romance." In *Voices from the Ming-Qing Cataclysm: China in Tigers' Jaws*, edited and translated by Lynn A. Struve, 73–93. New Haven: Yale University Press, 1993.

———. "History and *The Peach Blossom Fan*." *Chinese Literature: Essays, Articles, Reviews (CLEAR)* 2, no. 1 (1980): 55–72.

———, trans. "'Horrid Beyond Description': The Massacre of Yangzhou." In *Voices from the Ming-Qing Cataclysm: China in Tigers' Jaws*, edited and translated by Lynn A. Struve, 28–48. New Haven: Yale University Press, 1993.

———. *The Ming-Qing Conflict: 1619–1683: A Historiography and Source Guide.* Ann Arbor: Association for Asian Studies, 1998.

———. "Self-Struggles of a Martyr: Memories, Dreams, and Obsessions in the Extant Diary of Huang Chunyao." *Harvard Journal of Asiatic Studies* 69, no. 2 (2009): 343–94.

Standaert, Nicolas. *Ke qin de Shangdi* 可親的上帝. Translated by He Lixia 何麗霞. Taipei: Guangqi chubanshe, 1998.

Stephenson, Barry. *Ritual: A Very Short Introduction.* New York: Oxford University Press, 2015.

*Taiping tianguo* 太平天國. Edited by Luo Ergang 羅爾綱 and Wang Qing-cheng 王慶成. 10 vols. Guilin: Guangxi shifan daxue chubanshe, 2004.

*Taiping tianguo* 太平天國. Edited by Zhongguo shixue hui 中國史學會. 8 vols. Shanghai: Shenzhou guoguang she, 1953.

*Taiping tianguo shiliao congbian jianji* 太平天國史料叢編簡輯. Edited by Taiping tianguo lishi bowuguan 太平歷史博物館. 6 vols. Beijing: Zhonghua shuju, 1961.

*Taiping tianguo wenxian huibian* 太平天國文獻彙編. Edited by Yang Jialuo 楊家駱. 9 vols. Taipei: Dingwen shuju, 1973.

*Taiping tianguo yinshu* 太平天國印書. Edited by Nanjing Taiping tianguo lishi bowuguan 南京太平天國歷史博物館. 2 vols. Nanjing: Jiangsu renmin chubanshe, 1979.

*Taiping zhaoshu* 太平詔書. In *Aodaliya cang Taiping tianguo yuanke guanshu congkan* 澳大利亞藏太平天國原刻官書叢刊, vol. 1, 33–72.

*Taiping zhaoshu* (*chong ke ben*) 太平詔書 (重刻本). In *Aodaliya cang Taiping tianguo yuanke guanshu congkan* 澳大利亞藏太平天國原刻官書叢刊, vol. 1, 73–104.

*Taishang ganying pian jishi* 太上感應篇集釋. Compiled and annotated by Li Changling 李昌齡 and Zheng Qingzhi 鄭清之. Beijing: Zhongyang bianyi chubanshe, 2016.

Tan Qian 談遷 (1594–1658). *Guo que* 國榷. In *Xuxiu siku quanshu* 續修四庫全書, vols. 358–63.

Tang Xianzu 湯顯祖. "*Mudan ting* tici"《牡丹亭》題詞. In Mudan ting *yanjiu ziliao kaoshi* 牡丹亭研究資料考釋, edited by Xu Fuming 徐扶明, 8–9. Shanghai: Shanghai guji chubanshe, 1987.

Tang, Xiaobing. *Chinese Modern: The Heroic and the Quotidian*. Durham: Duke University Press, 2000.

Tao Qian 陶潛 (?–427). *Tao Yuanming ji* 陶淵明集. Edited by Wu Zeshun 吳澤順. Reprint, Changsha: Yuelu shushe, 1996.

Teiser, Stephen. *The Scripture on the Ten Kings and the Making of Purgatory in Medieval Chinese Buddhism*. Honolulu: University of Hawai'i Press, 1994.

Theiss, Janet M. *Disgraceful Matters: The Politics of Chastity in Eighteenth-Century China*. Berkeley: University of California Press, 2004.

Thompson, Laurence. *Chinese Religion: An Introduction*. Belmont: Wadsworth, 1996.

Tian Gensheng 田根勝. *Jindai xiju de chuancheng yu kaituo* 近代戲曲的傳承與開拓. Shanghai: Shanghai sanlian shudian, 2005.

*Tian tiao shu* 天條書. In *Taiping tianguo yinshu*, vol. 1, 25–34.

*Tian tiao shu* (*chong ke ben*) 天條書 (重刻本). In *Aodaliya cang Taiping tianguo yuanke guanshu congkan*, vol. 1, 295–316.

Tian, Xiaofei. "Translator's Introduction." In Zhang Daye, *The World of a Tiny Insect: A Memoir of the Taiping Rebellion and Its Aftermath* (*Weichong shijie* 微蟲世界). Translated by Tian Xiaofei. Seattle: University of Washington Press, 2013.

*Tianfu Tianxiong shengzhi* 天父天兄聖旨. Reprinted with preface and notes by Wang Qingcheng. Shenyang: Liaoning chubanshe, 1986.

*Tianfu xiafan zhaoshu: di yi bu* 天父下凡詔書：第一部. In *Taiping tianguo yinshu*, vol. 1, 95–104.

Ting Chao-Chin 丁肇琴. *Suwenxue zhong de Bao gong* 俗文學中的包公. Taipei: Wenjin chubanshe, 2000.

Tschanz, Dietrich. "Wu Weiye's Dramatic Works and His Aesthetics of Dynastic Transition." In *Trauma and Transcendence in Early Qing Literature*, edited by Wilt Idema, Wai-yee Li, and Ellen Widmer, 427–54. Cambridge: Harvard University Asia Center, 2006.

Tu, Ching-I. "The Chinese Examination Essay: Some Literary Considerations." *Monumental Serica* 31 (1974): 393–406.

Tuotuo 脫脫 (1314–1355). *Jin shi* 金史. 8 vols. Reprint, Beijing: Zhonghua shuju, 1975.

Turner, Victor. "Are There Universals of Performance in Myth, Ritual, and Drama?" In *By Means of Performance: Intercultural Studies of Theatre and Ritual*, edited by Richard Schechner, 8–18. New York: Cambridge University Press, 1990.

Übelhor, Monika. "The Community Compact (Hsiang-yüeh) of the Sung and Its Educational Significance." In *Neo-Confucian Education: The Formative Stage*, edited by William Theodore de Bary and John W. Chaffee, 371–88. Berkeley: University of California Press, 1989.

Wagner, Rudolf. "Operating in the Chinese Public Sphere: Theology and Technique of Taiping Propaganda." In *Norms and the State in China*, edited by Chun-Chieh Huang and Erik Zurcher, 104–41. Leiden: Brill, 1993.

———. *Reenacting the Heavenly Vision: The Role of Religion in the Taiping Rebellion*. Berkeley: University of California Press, 1982.

Wang Ayling 王璦玲. *Xiqu zhi shenmei gousi yu qi yishu chengxian* 戲曲之審美構思與其藝術呈現. Taipei: Zhongyang yanjiuyuan zhongguo wenshi yanjiu suo, 2005.

Wang, C. H. "The Double Plot of *T'ao-hua shan*." *Journal of the American Oriental Society* 110, no. 1 (1990): 9–18.

Wang, David Der-wei. *Fin-de-Siècle Splendor: Repressed Modernities of Late Qing Fiction, 1849–1911*. Stanford: Stanford University Press, 1997.

———. *The Monster That Is History: History, Violence, and Fictional Writing in Twentieth-Century China*. Berkeley: University of California Press, 2004.

Wang Ermin 王爾敏. "Qing ting Shengyu guangxun zhi banxing ji minjian zhi xuanjiang shiyi" 清廷聖諭廣訓之頒行及民間之宣講拾遺. *Zhongyang yanjiu yuan jindaishi yanjiusuo jikan* 22 (1993): 257–76.

Wang Fansen 王汎森. *Wan Ming Qing chu sixiangshi lun* 晚明清初思想史論. Shanghai: Fudan daxue chubanshe, 2004.

Wang Guojun. *Staging Personhood: Costuming in Early Qing Drama*. New York: Columbia University Press, 2020.

Wang Haiyang 王海洋. *Qingdai fang* Liaozhai zhiyi *zhi chuanqi xiaoshuo yanjiu* 清代仿聊齋誌異之傳奇小說研究. Hefei: Anhui renmin chubanshe, 2009.

Wang Heming 王鶴鳴 and Wang Deng 王澄. *Zhongguo citang tonglun* 中國祠堂通論. Shanghai: Shanghai guji chubanshe, 2013.

Wang Jianchuan 王見川 and Lin Wanchuan 林萬傳. "Ming Qing minjian zongjiao jingjuan wenxian daoyan" 明清民間宗教經卷文獻導言. In *Ming Qing minjian zongjiao jingjuan wenxian* 明清民間宗教經卷文獻, vol. 1, edited by Wang Jianchuan 王見川 and Lin Wanchuan 林萬傳. Taipei: Xin wenfeng chubanshe, 1999.

Wang, Jing. *The Story of Stone: Intertextuality, Ancient Chinese Stone Lore, and the Stone Symbolism in Dream of the Red Chamber, Water Margin, and The Journey to the West*. Durham: Duke University Press, 1992.

Wang, Lawrence. "Legacy of Success: Office Purchase and State-Elite Relations in Qing China." *Harvard Journal of Asiatic Studies* 73 (2013): 259–97.

Wang Pijiang 汪辟疆. *Wang Pijiang shixue lunji* 汪辟疆詩學論集. 2 vols. Nanjing: Nanjing daxue chubanshe, 2011.

Wang Qingcheng 王慶成. *Taiping tianguo de wenxian he lishi* 太平天國的文獻和歷史. Beijing: Shehui kexue wenxian chubanshe, 1993.

Wang Tao 王韜. *Dunku lanyan* 遁窟讕言. 12 *juan*. 4 vols. Shanghai: Shenbaoguan, 1880.

———. "Shang Taiping tianguo shu" (A letter to the Taiping King) 上太平天國書. Reprinted in *Taiping tianguo wenshu* 太平天國文書, edited by Shen Jianshi 沈兼士. Beiping: Gugong bowu yuan, 1933.

———. *Songbin suohua* 淞濱瑣話. 4 vols. 12 *juan*. Reprint of 1893 edition, Taipei: Guangwen shuju, 1991.

———. *Songyin manlu* 淞隱漫錄. 12 vols. Shanghai: Dianshi zhai shuju, 1887.

Wang Yangang 汪燕崗. "Lun Qingdai Shengyu xuanjiang yu baihua xuanjiang xiaoshuo: yi Sichuan diqu wei kaocha zhongxin" 論清代聖諭宣講與白話宣講小說——以四川地區為考察中心. *Wenxue yichan* 6 (2014): 105–14.

*Wang zhang ci xiong qinmu qin'er gongzheng Fuyin shu* 王長次兄親目親耳共證福音書. In *Taiping tianguo yinshu*, vol. 2, 709–16.

Weller, Robert. *Resistance, Chaos, and Control in China: Taiping Rebels, Taiwanese Ghosts, and Tiananmen*. Seattle: University of Washington Press, 1994.

Wei Xiuren 魏秀仁. *Hua yue hen* 花月痕. Reprint of 1888 edition, edited and compiled by Du Weimo 杜維沫. Beijing: Renmin wenxue chubanshe, 1982.

———. *Wei Xiuren zazhu chaoben* 魏秀仁襍著鈔本. 2 vols. Reprint, Nanjing: Jiangsu guji chubanshe, 2000.

Wei Xiyuan 魏熙元 (1830–1888). *Ru suan fu* 儒酸福. Publisher unknown, 1884.

White, Hayden. "Introduction: Historical Fiction, Fictional History, and Historical Reality." *Rethinking History* 9 (2005): 147–57.

———. "The Value of Narrativity in the Representation of Reality." In *On Narrative*, edited by W. J. Thomas Mitchell, 1–24. Chicago: University of Chicago Press, 1981.

Widmer, Ellen. *Fiction's Family: Zhan Xi, Zhan Kai, and the Business of Women in Late-Qing China*. Cambridge, MA: Harvard University Asia Center, 2020.

———. *The Margins of Utopia: Shui-Hu Hou-Chuan and the Literature of Ming Loyalism*. Cambridge, MA: Harvard University Asia Center, 1987.

Wiener, Wendy J., and George C. Rosenwald. "A Moment's Monument: The Psychology of Keeping a Diary." In *The Narrative Study of Lives*, edited by Ruthellen Josselson and Amia Lieblich, vol. 1, 30–58. Newbury Park: Sage, 1993.

Wooldridge, Chuck. "Building and State Building in Nanjing after the Taiping Rebellion." *Late Imperial China* 30, no. 2 (2009): 84–126.

———. *City of Virtues: Nanjing in an Age of Utopian Visions*. Seattle: University of Washington Press, 2015.

Wu Cuncun 吳存存. *Xi wai zhi xi: Qing zhong wan qi jingcheng de xiyuan wenhua yu liyuan siyu zhi* 戲外之戲：清中晚期京城的戲園文化與梨園私寓制. Hong Kong: Hong Kong University Press, 2017.

Wu Dazheng 吳大澂 (1835–1902). *Wu Qingqing taishi riji* 吳清卿太史日記. Reprinted in *Taiping tianguo* 太平天國, vol. 5. Edited by Zhongguo shixue hui 中國史學會.

Wu Hanchen 武漢臣 (fl. thirteenth century). *Bao shizhi zhizhuan shengjin ge zaju* 包待制智賺生金閣雜劇. Maiwang guan gujin zaju, seventeenth century.

Wu, Pei-yi. *The Confucian's Progress: Autobiographical Writings in Traditional China*. Princeton: Princeton University Press, 1990.

Wu Renshu 巫仁恕. "Taoli chengshi: Ming Qing zhiji Jiangnan chengju shiren de taonan jingli" 逃離城市：明清之際江南城居士人的逃難經歷. *Jindaishi yanjiusuo jikan* 83 (2014): 1–46.

Xie Jiehe 謝介鶴 (fl. 1850s). *Jinling guijia jishi lüe* 金陵癸甲紀事略. In *Taiping tianguo wenxian huibian* 太平天國文獻彙編, vol. 4.

Xie Xingyao 謝興堯. *Taiping tianguo shi shi luncong* 太平天國史事論叢. In *Minguo congshu* 民國叢書, vol. 4. Reprint, Shanghai: Shanghai shudian, 1992.

Xie Zhangting 謝章鋌. *Duqi shanzhuang wenji* 賭棋山莊文集. *7 juan*. Taoyan Nanchang shixie, 1884.

Xin Ping 忻平. *Wang Tao pingzhuan* 王韜評傳. Shanghai: Huadong shifan daxue chubanshe, 1990.

Xu E 徐鄂 (1844–1903). *Lihua xue* 梨花雪. In *Song di zhai qu* 誦荻齋曲. 5 vols. Reprint, Shanghai: Shanghai shuju, 1895.

Xu Shanchang 許善長 (fl. 1875). *Yi yun yan* 瘗雲巖. Bisheng guan yin edition, 1877.

Xuan Ding 宣鼎. "Ti zeng Li Dudu huace hou" 題贈李都督畫冊後, vol. 12. In *Huanyu suoji* 寰宇瑣紀. 12 vols. Shanghai: Shenbaoguan, 1876.

———. *Yeyu qiudeng lu*. Edited by Heng He 恆鶴. 2 vols. Shanghai: Shanghai guji chubanshe, 1987.

*Xuxiu siku quanshu* 續修四庫全書. Edited by Xuxiu siku quanshu bianzuan weiyuan hui 續修四庫全書編纂委員會. 1800 vols. Shanghai: Shanghai guji chubanshe, 2002.


Yang Bojun 楊伯峻, ed. and comm. *Chunqiu Zuozhuan zhu* 春秋左傳注. 4 vols. Beijing: Zhonghua shuju, 1990.

———, ed. and comm. *Liezi jishi* 列子集釋. Beijing: Zhonghua shuju, 1979.

Yang Enshou 楊恩壽. *Gui hua feng* 姽嫿封. *Tanyuan* edition, 1870.

———. *Liling po* 理靈坡. *Tanyuan* edition, date unknown.

———. *Matan yi* 麻灘驛. *Tanyuan* edition, 1875.

———. *Tanyuan conggao*. 坦園叢稿. Nineteenth-century edition.

———. *Yang Enshou ji* 楊恩壽集. Edited by Wang Jingzhi 王婧之. Changsha: Yuelu shushe, 2010.

Yang Jianbo 楊建波. *Daojiao wenxueshi lungao* 道教文學史論稿. Wuhan: Wuhan chubanshe, 2001.

Yao Dadui 姚達兌. *Xiandai de xiansheng: wan Qing hanyu Jidujiao wenxue* 現代的先聲：晚清漢語基督教文學. Guangzhou: Zhongshan daxue chubanshe, 2018.

Yao Hongchou 姚鴻疇 (fl. 1850s). "Ba" 跋 to *Xiao cangsang ji* 小滄桑記. Reprinted in *Taiping tianguo* 太平天國, vol. 6. Edited by Zhongguo shixue hui 中國史學會.

Ye Chucang 葉楚傖. *Xiaoshuo zazhu* 小說雜著. Shanghai: Xinmin tushuguan, 1919.

Yeh, Catherine. *Shanghai Love: Courtesans, Intellectuals, and Entertain-ment Culture, 1850–1910*. Seattle: University of Washington Press, 2006.

*Yingyin Wenyuange Siku quanshu* 影印文淵閣四庫全書. 1500 vols. Taipei: Shangwu yinshu guan, 1983–86. Reprint, 1800 vols. Shanghai: Shanghai guji chubanshe, 1987.

You Zi'an 游子安. "Cong xuanjiang Shengyu dao shuo shanshu: jindai quanshan fangshi zhi chuancheng" 從宣講聖諭到說善書：近代勸善方式之傳承. *Wenhua yichan* 2 (2008): 49–58.

———. *Quanhua jinzhen: Qingdai shanshu yanjiu* 勸化金箴：清代善書研究. Tianjin: Tianjin renmin chubanshe, 1999.

———. *Shan yu ren tong: Ming Qing yilai de cishan yu jiaohua* 善與人同：明清以來的慈善與教化. Beijing: Zhonghua shuju, 2005.

Yu Shihao 于師號. "Wan Qing xiaoshuo xiqu zuojia Xuan Ding jiaoyou kaolun" 晚清小說戲曲作家宣鼎交遊考論. *Wenjiao ziliao* 7 (2012): 19–21.

Yu Xun 俞蟲. "*Dang kou zhi* xu xu" 蕩寇志續序. In *Shuihu zhuan ziliao huibian* 水滸傳資料匯編, edited by Zhu Yixuan 朱一玄, 515–16. Tianjin: Nankai daxue chubanshe, 2002.

Yu Zhi 余治. *De yi lu* 得一錄, 16 *juan*. Suzhou: De jian zhai, 1869.

———. *Jiangnan tielei tu* 江南鐵淚圖. Reprint, Taipei: Guangwen shuju, 1974.

———. Preface to *Shuji tang jin yue* 庶幾堂今樂. In *Zhongguo lidai qulun shiping* 中國歷代曲論釋評, edited by Cheng Bingda 程炳達 and Wang Weimin 王衛民, 531–32. Beijing: Minzu chubanshe, 2000.

Yuan Jin 袁進. "Chenfu zai shehui lishi dachao zhong: lun *Hua yue hen* de yingxiang" 沈浮在社會歷史大潮中：論《花月痕》的影響. *Shehui kexue* 4 (2005): 112–18.

Yuan Mei 袁枚. *Zi bu yu* 子不語. Edited by Cui Guoguang 崔國光. Reprint, Jinan: Qilu shushe, 1986.

*Yuli zhibao chao quanshi wen* 玉曆至寶鈔勸世文. Reprint, Shanghai: Hongda zhihao, 1920.


Zarrow, Peter. "Historical Trauma: Anti-Manchuism and Memories of Atrocity in Late Qing China." *History and Memory* 16, no. 2 (2004): 67–107.

Zeitlin, Judith. *Historian of the Strange: Pu Songling and the Chinese Classical Tale*. Stanford: Stanford University Press, 1993.

———. *The Phantom Heroine: Ghosts and Gender in Seventeenth-Century Chinese Literature*. Honolulu: University of Hawai'i Press, 2007.

———. "Spirit Writing and Performance in the Work of You Tong (1618–1704)." *T'oung Pao* 84 (1998): 102–35.

Zeng Guofan 曾國藩. *Zeng Wenzheng gong jiashu quanji* 曾文正公家書全集. Beijing: Jincheng chubanshe, 2013.

———. *Zuben Zeng Wenzheng gong quanji* 足本曾文正公全集. Edited by Li Hongzhang 李鴻章. 8 vols. Reprint, Changchun: Jilin renmin chubanshe, 1995.

Zeng Xianhui 曾憲輝. "Wei Xiuren nianpu" 魏秀仁年譜. *Ming Qing xiaoshuo yanjiu* 4 (1988): 174–87.

———. "Wei Zi'an lun lüe 魏子安論略." *Fujian shifan daxue xuebao* 4 (1988): 54–60.

Zhang Boxing 張伯行 (1651–1725). "Shenchi xiangyue baojia shi" (excerpt) 申飭鄉約保甲示(節錄). In *Shengyu guangxun jijie yu yanjiu*, edited and commented by Zhou Zhenhe, 542–45. Shanghai: Shanghai shudian chubanshe, 2006.

Zhang Dejian 張德堅 (fl. 1850s). *Zei qing huizuan* 賊情汇纂. 2 vols. Reprint, Taipei: Huawen shuju, 1969.

Zhang Erjia 張爾嘉 (fl. 1850s). *Nan zhong ji* 難中紀. Reprinted in *Taiping tianguo* 太平天國, vol. 6. Edited by Zhongguo shixue hui 中國史學會.

Zhang Fan 張帆. "Yeyu qiudeng lu yu Liaozhai zhiyi zhong nüxing xingxiang zhi bijiao" 《夜雨秋燈錄》與《聊齋誌異》中女性形象之比較. *Huazhong shifan daxue yanjiusheng bao* 21, no. 2 (2014): 81–85.

Zhang Hailin 張海林. *Wang Tao pingzhuan: fu Rong Hong pingzhuan* 王韜評傳：附容閎評傳. Nanjing: Nanjing daxue chubanshe, 1993.

Zhang Jian 張鑑. *Ruan Yuan nianpu* 阮元年譜. Beijing: Zhonghua shuju, 1995.

Zhang Jinchi 張錦池. "Lun *Shuihu zhuan* he *Xiyou ji* de shenxue wenti" 論《水滸傳》和《西遊記》的神學問題. *Renwen zhongguo xuebao* 4 (1997): 33–60.

Zhang Lei 張蕾. "Cong Wei Zi'an dao Lin Qinnan: lun Yao Yuanchu xiaoshuo de shicheng" 從魏子安到林琴南：論姚鵷雛小說的師承. *Zhongguo xiandai wenxue yanjiu congkan* 5 (2016): 134–46.

Zhang Runan 張汝南. *Jinling xingnan ji lüe* 金陵省難紀略. In *Taiping tianguo wenxian huibian* 太平天國文獻彙編, vol. 4. Taipei: Dingwen shuju, 1973.

Zhang Ting. *Circulating the Code: Print Media and Legal Knowledge in Qing China.* Seattle: University of Washington Press, 2020.

Zhang Tingyu 張廷玉 (1672–1755). *Ming shi* 明史. 28 vols. Beijing: Zhonghua shuju, 1978.

Zhang Xiaolan 張曉蘭. *Qingdai jingxue yu xiqu: yi Qingdai jingxuejia de xiqu huodong he sixiang wei zhongxin* 清代經學與戲曲：以清代經學家的戲曲活動和思想為中心. Shanghai: Guji chubanshe, 2014.

Zhang Xiumin 張秀民. *Taiping tianguo ziliao mulu* 太平天國資料目錄. Shanghai: Xinhua shudian, 1957.

Zhang Yichen 張禕琛. "Qingdai Shengyu xuanjiang lei shanshu de kanke yu chuanbo" 清代聖諭宣講類善書的刊刻與傳播. *Fudan xuebao* 3 (2011): 134–40.

Zhang Yongjian 張永健, ed. *Zhong Wai sanwen cidian* 中外散文辭典. Beijing: Zhongguo wenlian chuban gongsi, 1997.

Zhang Yuanyue 張袁月. "Cong baokan meiti yingxiang kan Wang Tao de xiaoshuo" 從報刊媒體影響看王韜的小說. *Ming Qing xiaoshuo yanjiu* 98, no. 4 (2010): 145–56.

Zhang Zhenguo 張振國. "Wang Tao xiaoshuoji zhong bufen zuopin zhu-zuoquan zhiyi" 王韜小說集中部分作品著作權質疑. *Nanjing shifan daxue wenxueyuan xuebao* 4 (2009): 73–78.

Zhao Dingxin. "The Mandate of Heaven and Performance Legitimation in Historical and Contemporary China." *American Behavioral Scientist* 53 (2009): 416–33.

Zhao Erxun 趙爾巽 (1844–1927). *Qing shigao liezhuan* 清史稿列傳. In *Qing-dai zhuanji congkan* 清代傳記叢刊, edited by Zhou Junfu 周駿富, vol. 7 in bk. 7. 205 vols. Taipei: Mingwen shuju, 1985.

Zhao Liewen 趙烈文 (1832–1894). *Nengjing ju riji* 能靜居日記. Reprinted in *Taiping tianguo*, vol. 7. Edited by Luo Ergang and Wang Qingcheng.

Zheng, Xiaowei. "Loyalty, Anxiety, and Opportunism: Local Elite Activism during the Taiping Rebellion in Eastern Zhejiang, 1851–1864." *Late Imperial China* 30, no. 2 (2009): 39–83.

Zheng Youxi 鄭由熙 (?–1898). *Muxi xiang* 木樨香. Publisher unknown, 1890.
———. *Wu zhong ren* 霧中人. Publisher unknown, 1890.

Zheng Zhenduo 鄭振鐸. *Wenxue dagang* 文學大綱. Beijing: Shangwu yin-shu guan, 1927.

*Zhongguo tongshi* 中國通史. Edited by Bai Shouyi 白壽彝. 12 vols. Reprint, Shanghai: Shanghai renmin chubanshe, 2013.

Zhou Bangfu 周邦福 (fl. 1850s). *Meng nan shu chao* 蒙難述鈔. Reprinted in *Taiping tianguo* 太平天國, vol. 5. Edited by Zhongguo shixue hui 中國史學會.

*Zhou li zhengyi* 周禮正義. Annotated by Zheng Xuan 鄭玄 (127–200). 6 vols. 86 *juan*. Reprint, Taipei: Taiwan zhonghua shuju, 1981.

Zhou Weichi 周偉馳. *Taiping tianguo yu* Qishi lu 太平天國與啟示錄. Beijing: Zhongguo shehui kexue chubanshe, 2013.

Zhou Zhenhe 周振鶴, ed. and comm. *Shengyu guangxun jijie yu yanjiu* 聖諭廣訓集解與研究. Shanghai: Shanghai shudian chubanshe, 2006.

Zhu Fuqing 朱福清 (fl. 1850s–1860s). *Yuanhu qiu jiu lu* 鴛湖求舊錄. Re-printed in *Yilin daoyou lu* 藝林悼友錄, edited by Wu Xiangzhou 吳香洲. Nanjing: Fenghuang chubanshe, 2010.

Zhu Shaoyi 朱紹頤 (fl. 1850s). *Hong yang jie* 紅羊劫. Reprint, publisher and date unknown.

Zhu Tianshun 朱天順. *Zhongguo gudai zongjiao chutan* 中國古代宗教初探. Shanghai: Shanghai renmin chubanshe, 1982.

Zhu Yixuan 朱一玄. *Shuihu zhuan ziliao huibian* 水滸傳資料匯編. Tianjin: Nankai daxue chubanshe, 2002.

*Zhuangzi nanhua zhenjing* 莊子南華真經, 5 vols. Printed between 1621 and 1644.

Zuo Pengjun 左鵬軍. *Wan Qing Minguo chuanqi zaju shigao* 晚清民國傳奇雜劇史稿. Guangzhou: Guangdong renmin chubanshe, 2009.

# Glossary-Index

Abe Yasuki, 78, 88n55, 90n58

*Account of Ten Days in Yangzhou, An (Yangzhou shiri ji* 揚州十日記), 10, 113–15

"accounts" (*ji* 記, *lu* 錄), 113. *See also* oral accounts; personal accounts

*Accounts of Falling into Rebel Hands (Mengnan shuchao* 蒙難述鈔), 112

*Admonitions to Awaken the World by Seeking the Fundamental Way (Yuan Dao xing shi xun* 原道醒世訓) (Hong Xiuquan), 35, 36

*Admonitions to Enlighten the World by Seeking the Fundamental Way (Yuan Dao jue shi xun* 原道覺世訓) (Hong Xiuquan), 35, 36

Alexander, Katherine, 88n53

allegory, 13, 166, 183, 200, 284, 290–91; animal and, 258; historical reality and, 180–81; Ming-Qing dynastic transition and, 182n82

*Analects, The (Lun yu* 論語), 4n7, 99

*Anatomy of Qing (Qing shi* 情史) (Feng Menglon), 210

"Ancient Spearhead, The" ("Gu jiantou" 古劍頭) (Xuan Ding), 278

Anderson, Marston, 275

An Lushan Rebellion (755–763), 160, 198, 238

anti-Christianity, 68n6, 88, 98–102

anti-Taiping, 101, 138n62, 179–80, 215–16, 222–24

apocalypse: images of God and devil, 59; of Ming-Qing dynastic transition, 9; religious meaning and, 10; sentiments of, 69; Taiping vision and, 41–43; the Taiping war and, 4, 14, 16, 247. *See also jie*

artifacts, texts as, 30–34

authority: authorship and, 27n5; construction of, 26–27, 101, 103, 106; crisis of, 55–56, 115–16, 141, 235–36; imperial, 19, 26–27, 71–72, 235–36, 287; omnipresent and omnipotent, 39, 47–48, 61–62, 103; religious, 14, 26, 61, 63n79, 69, 83, 98, 108

authorship: construction of, 80–81; "declarative," 27n5, 104–6; editorial influence and, 120n25; literary market and, 247n3, 254n17, 254n19, 254n21, 254n80; pseudonymity and, 105, 218–19, 251, 255

autobiography: development in the seventeenth century, 169, 170; divinity

autobiography (*continued*)
and, 249; historical distance and, 113; literati fiction and, 164; plays and, 170, 207, 220; *Traces of Flowers and the Moon* with details of, 152, 152n4, 153n6, 157–59, 161, 163–64, 175, 213

*Bai Shangdi hui* 拜上帝會. *See* "God-worshipping Society"
banished immortals (*zhe xian* 謫仙): fiction and, 194, 194n109, 197, 198; plays and, 209, 222; trope of, 11
*baojuan* 寶卷 (precious scroll): in comparison with *xuanjiang*, 87–89, 88n54; definition, 87n50; storytelling and, 68, 88nn52–53
*bazhai fei xian* 拔宅飛仙. *See* "uprooting the household and becoming immortal"
beasts: Manchus as, 226; Taiping rebels as, 110–11, 211–12, 216, 218, 222–23; violence and, 110–11, 257–59
"Beiji Piye Island" ("Beiji Piye dao" 北極毗耶島) (Xuan Ding), 286n, 289–93
"Being Unfilial toward One's Foster Parents" ("Buxiao fuyang fumu" 不孝撫養父母), 92
Bergson, Henry, 247–48
*biansai shi* 邊塞詩. *See* "frontier poetry"
Bible, the: Hong Xiuquan's reception of, 58; Hong Xiuquan's vision and, 60; as sacred Taiping texts, 34; Taiping emulation of, 64–65, 64n82. *See also* Christianity
"Biheng" 碧衡 (Wang Tao), 276, 277
*biji* 筆記. *See* "miscellaneous notes"
*Bitter "Blessings" for a Pedantic Scholar* (*Ru suan fu* 儒酸福) (Wei Xiyuan), 205–6
"Blood-Drenched Torches Illuminate Silver" ("Xue ju zhao yin" 血炬照銀) (Xuan Ding), 279–80
Boardman, Eugene, 6n11, 25–26
body, 128–29

"Book House of Ocean of Ink" (*Mohai shuguan* 墨海書館), 285
*Book of Odes, The* (*Shi jing* 詩經), 167n47
books: as cultural legacy of, 194; fragility of, 30n12, 205, 292; moral credit and, 76n27; mythical function of, 292; Taiping control of, 30, 34, 49–50, 55
"Boshu buci zizhi" 伯叔不慈子侄. *See* "Uncles Not Being Kind to Their Nephews"
bound feet: exoticized objects and, 215; violence and, 140, 215; women's limited mobility and, 116. *See also* women
Boxer Rebellion (1899–1901), 14, 81n39, 261
*Brief Accounts in Jinling During the Guijia Years* (*Jinling guijia jishi lüe* 金陵癸甲紀事略) (Xie Jiehe), 187
*Brief Notes on Encountering Militaries in Zhongzhou in the Year of Guichou* (*Guichou Zhongzhou libing ji lüe* 癸丑中州糧兵紀略) (Chen Shanjun), 116–17
Brokaw, Cynthia, 67n1, 68n4, 75n23
brotherhood, 43, 95, 129, 221–24, 232–36
Buddhism: *baojuan* and, 87n50, 88; character design and, 233n63; image of Hell and, 90; influences of, 1, 220, 248; *jie* in, 10; late Ming biography and, 169; morality books and, 75, 77n29, 249; Taiping ideology and, 6n11, 28; *yuan* in, 220n40

"calamity of the red ram" (*hong yang jie*) (紅羊劫), 10
*Calamity of the Red Ram, The* (*Hong yang jie* 紅羊劫) (Zhu Shaoyi), 11, 205, 205n3, 209–10, 218
calendars: diary and, 138–39, 147; sexagenary cycle, 10, 10n20, 156n11; Taiping calendar, 12, 31, 34, 62–63, 63n79. *See also* time

*Call to Arms* (*Nahan* 吶喊) (Lu Xun), 291, 292

cannibalism: in drama, 21; in "A Madman's Diary," 292; personal accounts and, 109–10, 140n69; portrayals of, 214–15

Cao Xueqin 曹雪芹 (1715?–1763?), 165–66, 168. See also *Dream of the Red Chamber*

censorship: Qing, 108, 111, 111n6; self-, 136–37; Taiping, 30, 60n74

Chang Ming 常明 (d. 1817), 80

Che Xilun, 88n52, 88n54

Chen Bingwen 陳炳文 (fl. 1860–1864), 141

Chen Daiyun 陳岱雲 (fl. 1850), 211

Chen Fan 陳蕃 (?–168), 162n29, 283

Chen Shanjun 陳善鈞 (fl. 1853), 116–17

Chen Weisong 陳維崧 (1625–1682), 189n103, 192

Chen Yucheng 陳玉成 (1837–1862), 172, 172n62

Chen Zilong 陳子龍 (1608–1647), 202

Chinese Communist cultural strategies, 12, 33, 119n24

Christianity: "Heaven" and, 17n36, 26; historical influence in mid-nineteenth century, 5–7; legal status in the Qing, 5n9; missionary proselytization of, 5, 29n11, 30, 98; morality books against, 88, 99; pamphlets and their dissemination, 30n14; Qing Sacred Edicts and, 68n2; Taiping ideology and, 25n1, 42, 69, 101, 287; Taiping portrayal of God and Jesus Christ, 39, 41, 59; Wang Tao and, 250–51. See also anti-Christianity; Bible, the

*Chronicle of Zuo* (*Zuo zhuan* 左傳), 74–75, 107, 196

*chuanqi* plays: characteristics of, 204; early-Qing, 183; post-Taiping, 11, 188, 188n100, 205, 211–15, 211n21, 234, 259. See also *Karmic Ties in a Dream*; *Peach Blossom Fan, The*; *Peony Pavilion, The*

*citang. See* shrines

civil service examination: disillusionment with, 154, 250; failures at, 16, 96, 98–99, 151–52, 157, 168, 250; Hong Xiuquan's participation in, 6; *juan na* system and, 235n67; literati and, 152n4; Lü zu and, 79n33

Clark, Philip, 15

*Classic of Mountains and Seas, The* (*Shan hai jing* 山海經), 269

*Cliff for Burying Clouds, The* (*Yi yun yan* 瘞雲巖) (Xu Shanchang), 207, 237

community: ghosts and, 267, 273–75; playwriting as reinvention of, 237–44; Puyuan, in chaos, 114–17, 137–42; Taiping creation of, 38, 52–53; Taiping vision of, 36, 41–43, 48; of transgressors in *Miraculous Proofs*, 89–98, 108; *xiangyue* and, 71n12, 73n19

Confucian traditions: brotherhood and, 232–33; drama and, 207–9; ideals of, 195–96; *jiaohua* and, 70–72; literati novels and, 164; loss of, 292; moral codes of, 83–84, 92–93, 95; moral cultivation and, 75n23, 169, 284–85; supports for, 3, 17, 224, 287; Taiping ideology and, 6n11, 28, 60n74; women and, 134

Confucius: statement of, 4n7; status of, 83; in Taiping vision, 58, 60

*Contemporary Music of the Shuji Studio* (*Shuji tang jin yue* 庶幾堂今樂) (Yu Zhi), 208

"contemporary plays" (*shishi ju* 時事劇), 216n32

"Credulous Man on Bad Terms with His Brother" ("Xin renyan buhe dixiong" 信人言不合弟兄), 103

"daily accounts" (*riji* 日記), 10, 112–15

*Daily Jottings from the End of the Ming* (*Mingji riji* 明季日記), 116

Daoist traditions: "banished immortals" and, 194, 209, 222; *baojuan*

Daoist traditions (*continued*)
and, 87n50, 88; deities and, 69, 78, 79n33, 105, 180; enlightenment and, 175, 219; Heaven and, 4n7; *jie* and, 10; liminal figures of, 76, 173–74, 233n63, 281–82, 289–90; morality books and, 75, 75n23, 77n29; spirit writing and, 10, 79, 197; Taiping ideology and, 6n11, 28; texts and, 82n42; transcendence and, 156, 173, 197, 275–77; *yin/yang*, 110, 181, 181n80, 231, 289. *See also* Guan Yu; Lü Dongbin; Wenchang di

Deleuze, Gilles, 248

deliverance plays (*dutuo ju* 度脫劇), 209–10, 220, 222, 228

"Denunciation of the Yue Rebels" ("Tao Yue fei xi" 討粵匪檄) (Zeng Guofan), 2–3, 3n4, 224, 224n42

Derrida, Jacques, 184

dialectics between heterodox and orthodox, 3, 14, 26, 36, 288; anti-heterodox, 72, 100n84; heterodox and, 36, 82, 98–102, 292n3

*Diamond Sutra, The*, 249

*Dianshi zhai Pictorial* (*Dianshi zhai huabao* 點石齋畫報), 254

diaries: "daily accounts" and, 112–13; manuscripts, 20, 117–25; revisions of, 135–46, 151, 288; self-continuity and, 113n9; time and, 113, 138; war and, 117. See also *Diary of Escape from the Rebels*

*Diary of Escape from the Rebels* (*Bikou riji* 避寇日記) (Shen Zi): fragility of manuscripts, 117–25, 120n25; moral judgement, 143–47; narrative and, 137–39; reconstruct and restore, 119–20, 135–47; revisions, 20, 129, 132–33; self-identity and, 126–29, 288; testimony of women, 130–31

*Diary of the Historian Wu Qingqing* (*Wu Qingqing taishi riji* 吳清卿太史日記) (Wu Dazheng), 15

*Diary of the Unperturbed Studio* (*Nengjing ju riji* 能靜居日記) (Zhao Liewen), 109–11, 215

"disaster of Zulong, The" (*zulong zhi jie* 祖龍之劫), 292n3

disenchantment (with Heaven), 17, 127–28, 262–63, 289

disillusionment: illusion and, 168; long-held beliefs and, 11n21, 21, 184; models of dynastic changes and, 20; personal writings and, 288; printing technology and, 18; tropes and, 247, 284

divinity: audience of, 51–52; mediation of, 45–46, 56–57, 84, 100–101, 105–7; morality books and, 74–78; narratives of, 53–54, 61, 65; political legitimacy and, 2, 4n7, 41, 108, 287; time and, 51, 62–64. *See also* spirit writing

*Draft History of Qing* (*Qing shi gao* 清史稿), 187

*Dream of the Red Chamber* (*Honglou meng* 紅樓夢) (Cao Xueqin): Lin Siniang in, 217; reinventions of, 20, 153n6, 164–68, 233n63, 258n26; romance in, 165, 169; *Story of the Stone*, 165n42, 166n43

dreams: in fragments, 158–59, 165–68, 243–44; Hong Xiuquan's, 6; mediation of divinity, 105–6; as metaphors, 240–42; of yellow millet, 281–85

Du Fu 杜甫 (712–770), 159–60, 241–42

"Du Zichun" 杜子春, 284

Duan Yuming, 75n25

Duke Dao of Jin (586–558 BCE), 104

*duoduo*, 179n77

*dutuo ju* 度脫劇. *See* deliverance plays

dystopia, 14, 90, 103, 108, 286, 290

"Edge of Sea and River" (*haishui jiangya* 海水江涯), 30–31

edicts, 26, 27. See also *Miraculous Proofs of the Sacred Edict*; Sacred Edict, Qing; Taiping edicts

"Elementary Tutor Who Did Not Rectify Students' Behavior, The" ("Mengshi buduan shixi" 蒙師不端士習), 95–96

Ellul, Jacques, 28

emotions, feelings, attachments. See *qing*

Engberg-Pedersen, Anders, 5

Epstein, Maram, 259

escape: boat and, 127, 136, 138–39, 232; to countryside, 116–17; ethical dilemma of, 127, 132, 232–33; fantasy and, 273–78; physical challenges of, 117, 128; women and, 116–17, 130–31. See also *Diary of Escape from the Rebels*

*Essential Summaries of the Proclamation* (*Xuanjiang jiyao* 宣講集要), 78–79

"establishing words" (*li yan* 立言), 195

"evil books" (*yao shu* 妖書), 30

fabulation, 21, 247–48

*Fanciful Stories from My Hideaway* (*Dunku lanyan* 遁窟讕言) (Wang Tao), 188n100, 245–46, 246n2, 254–55, 261

Fang Ruisheng 方瑞生 (fl. 1618), 285n87

Fang Zhi 方芷 (fl. seventeenth century), 174, 175n70

fantasy: antifantasy, 281–85; escape and renunciation, 275–78; fabulation, 21, 247–48; ghosts, 180–81, 184–85, 196, 264–75; moral solutions, 256–64; uncanny, 274; for war-torn populace, 253–55. See also *Fanciful Stories from My Hideaway; Random Jottings of a Wusong Recluse; Records under the Autumn Lamp on Rainy Nights; Tales of Trivia from the Banks of the Wusong*

"Father and the Son, The" ("Sheng wo lou" 生我樓) (Li Yu, 1611–1680), 260

Feng Menglon 馮夢龍 (1574–1646), 210

"Feng Peibo" 馮佩伯 (Wang Tao), 265–67

Feng Yunshan 馮雲山 (1815–1852), 38, 39, 46, 58, 65

*fengliu* 風流. *See* unrestraint

fiction: autobiographical echoes, 152, 153n6, 164, 167; literati identity and, 20, 164; printing and, 154, 246–47; Taiping Rebellion and, 42–43

filial piety: bloodline and, 127; in *Miraculous Proofs* and, 83–84, 92–93; passion and, 259–60; in Sacred Edicts, 72; women and, 132–33, 245, 259–60

First Emperor of Qin (r. 247–210 BCE), 292n3

First Opium War (1839–1842), 5

forgeries, 254, 254n17

*Fragrant Osmanthus* (*Muxi xiang* 木樨香) (Zheng Youxi), 212

friendship: dream and, 175; Han Hesheng and, 153, 161, 175, 194–96; lineage and, 133; poetry and, 162–63, 238–42

"frontier poetry" (*biansai shi* 邊塞詩), 157

"Fu Luanshi" 傅鸞史 (Wang Tao), 266–67

Fu Shanxiang 傅善祥 (fl. 1853): as a fictional character, 266–67; as a historical figure, 186n91, 266

*Garden of the Strange* (*Yi yuan* 異苑), 269

gender: fluidity of, 190, 262–63; morality books and, 91, 94, 96–97, 103; politics of, 45, 190–91; social norms and, 134n50, 263; violence and, 217–18, 245–46, 272–74; as wartime metaphor, 181–82

ghosts (*gui* 鬼): female, 180, 184–93, 196n116, 245–46, 259–60, 264–67, 270–73; headless, 269, 270n57, 272–74; male, 196–97, 267–68, 273–74; Manchus as evil, 42; punishment and, 94, 97, 102, 282

God (Taiping): authority and, 25–26, 37, 39, 41, 45; Heaven and, 31–32,

God (Taiping) (*continued*)
35–36; Hong Xiuquan and, 6–7, 46,
57–58, 60, 287; image of, 38n27, 59,
59n71; inscription of, 137; sentiments
of, 41; time and, 51; truth and, 2; visual alignment of, 31–32, 33n15. *See
also* "God-worshipping Society"; *Sacred Decrees of the Heavenly Father,
The*; *Taiping Heavenly Chronicle, The*;
Yang Xiuqing
Goddess of Disenchantment, 165, 257
gods (non-Taiping): Daoist, 79n33;
Heaven and, 4n7, 103, 106; sentiments
of, 105; visual alignment and, 83. *See
also* Guan Yu; Wenchang di
"God-worshipping Society" (*Bai Shangdi
hui* 拜上帝會), 38
*Good Words to Admonish the World*
(*Quan shi liang yan* 勸世良言) (Liang
Fa), 6, 58, 61–62, 64
Goossaert, Vincent, 10n19, 15, 69n7,
75n23, 81n39
"grand reunion" (*da tuanyuan* 大團圓),
177, 234, 234n65, 288
*Great Imperial Mandate* (*Da gao* 大誥),
70
Guan Yu (Guandi 關帝), 69, 69n7, 79–
80, 83, 105–7, 142
*gui* 鬼. *See* ghosts
Guo Hama 郭虾蟆 (1192–1236), 192
Gützlaff, Karl (1803–1851), 30, 30n14

*haishui jiangya* 海水江涯. *See* "Edge
of Sea and River"
Hamberg, Theodore (1819–1854), 59, 60
Hanan, Patrick, 15, 90n60, 171n59
Han dynasty (202 BCE–9 CE, 25–
220 CE), 7n12, 193
happiness (*kuaihuo* 快活), 101, 101n86
"Headless Female Ghost, The" ("Wutou
nügui" 無頭女鬼) (Wang Tao), 272,
273
Heaven: authority of, 106; "banished
immortals" and, 193–94, 222; collapse of, 4–5, 17, 21, 111, 203, 247, 286,

293; historical trauma and, 110, 127–
28, 146; in Qing discourse, 83, 104–8,
176; as a realm, 2, 58–60, 193, 197; in
Taiping ideology and practice, 2,
31, 35–36, 41, 45n41, 51, 63–64; *Tian*,
4n7, 26, 63n79. *See also* Mandate of
Heaven; *Sacred Decrees of the Heavenly Brother, The*; *Sacred Decrees of
the Heavenly Father, The*; *Taiping
Heavenly Chronicle, The*
Heavenly Brother. *See* Xiao Chaogui
Heavenly Father. *See* Yang Xiuqing
Heavenly King. *See* Hong Xiuquan
Heavenly Tribunal (*Tiancao* 天曹), 75
Hell: judgement in, 84–85, 90, 92, 94–
96, 99–103, 105–6; punishment in, 73,
76–78, 86, 89, 92, 93, 93n66, 94, 282;
in Qing discourse, 19, 67–68, 84–87;
retribution and, 75–78
*Hemp Beach Post Station* (*Matan yi*
麻灘驛) (Yang Enshou), 206
"Heroic Young Martyr Fulfilling Her
Filial Piety, The" ("Lie shang jinxiao"
烈殤盡孝) (Xuan Ding), 257–58
*History of Ming, The* (*Ming shi* 明史),
227
Hong Canal, the (Hong gou 鴻溝),
191–92
Hong Rengan 洪仁玕 (1822–1864),
35n20, 56, 58–60
Hong Sheng 洪昇 (1645–1704), 183
Hong Xiuquan 洪秀全 (Heavenly King)
(1814-1864): divine family and, 27n5;
early life experiences, 6; echoes with
contemporary writers, 193–94, 198,
243, 250, 287, 292; millenarian vision
and, 17, 25, 99, 106; Taiping texts and,
35, 41, 46, 48, 52–55, 57–65; the Taiping movement and, 9, 38, 49, 52–
56, 186; textual visual alignment of,
33. See also *Sacred Decrees of the
Heavenly Brother, The*; *Sacred Decrees of the Heavenly Father, The*; *Taiping Heavenly Chronicle, The*
Hongwu Emperor (r. 1368–1398), 41, 70, 74

Hou Fangyu 候方域 (1618–1654), 155–56

Hsia, C. T., 165n40

Hu, Hsiao-chen, 137n58

Huang Chao 黃巢 (?–884), 198

Huang, Martin, 164

Huang Shuhua 黃淑華 (1847–1864), 207, 207n8

Huang Wan 黃畹, 251

Huang Zhongze 黃仲則 (1749–1783), 160n25

"Huangliang xu meng" 黃粱續夢 (Wang Tao), 283n83

Huntington, Rania, 8n15, 15, 188n100, 197n120, 208n14, 246n2, 260

Idema, Wilt L., 171n59

ideology. *See* Qing ideology; Taiping ideology

*Idle Tales from the Bean Arbor* (*Doupeng xian hua* 豆棚閒話), 170, 171

illusory world: in *Dream of the Red Chamber*, 165–66, 168, 257, 258n26; dreams and, 243; in *Traces of Flowers and the Moon*, 165–68, 175–76

*Imperial Placard of Instructions to the People* (*Jiaomin bangwen* 教民榜文), 70

*In Accord with the Imperial Edict* (Zhou Han), 68n6

"In Discordance with the Sister-in-Law Because of Rumors" ("Wei renyan buhe zhouli" 為人言不和妯娌), 94

*In Search of the Supernatural* (*Sou shen ji* 搜神記), 219n38, 269

"Inspector of the Offerings for the Five Mountains and the Four Rivers, The" ("Jicha tianxia wuyue duxianghuo shi" 稽查天下五岳瀆香火使) (Xuan Ding), 277, 281

"Instant Retribution on Learning the Heterodox" ("Xixie xianbao" 習邪顯報), 102–3

*Jade Records* (*Yuli zhibao chao* 玉歷至寶鈔), 75–79, 89, 91, 93n66

"Jar of Silver under the Pagoda Tree, The" ("Huai gen yinweng" 槐根銀甕) (Xuan Ding), 260

Jesus Christ: authority and, 27n5; the Bible and, 64n82; Hong Xiuquan's vision and, 57; mediation of, 38, 65; violence and, 44; visual alignment of, 31–33. *See also Sacred Decrees of the Heavenly Brother, The*; Xiao Chaogui

*ji* 記. *See* "accounts"

Jia Sidao 賈似道 (1213–1275), 192

"Jia Yong" 賈雍, 269

"Jia Yunsheng" 賈芸生 (Wang Tao), 245–46

*jiang daoli* 講道理, 29, 29n11

Jiang Lingzhong, 104–6

"Jiang Yuanxiang" 江遠香 (Wang Tao), 261

*jiaohua* 教化 (teaching and transforming): drama and, 209; method of, 70; Qing ideology and, 70–89. *See also* Sacred Edict, Qing

Jiaqing Emperor (r. 1796–1820), 5n9, 79n33

*jie* 劫: "banished immortals" and, 11; Buddhism and, 10; Daoism and, 10; drama and, 209; Ming-Qing dynastic transition and, 183; Taiping Civil War and, 11, 17, 110, 111, 117; time, 13

Jing Ke 荊軻 (?–277 BCE), 263

*jiren* 雞人 (literarily, chicken man), 191n106

John, Griffith, 68n6

journeying (historical): Hong Xiuquan and, 58–62; Ming-Qing dynastic transition and, 159n18; proselytization and, 58; Wei Xiuren and, 152, 201

journeying (religious and metaphorical): banished immortals and, 194; Hell and, 90; illusory realm and, 165, 193, 284; time, 65, 113

*Journey to the West*, 164n34

*juan na. See* regular remittance

Judge Bao, 90, 90n58

"Judge Lu" 陸判 (Pu Songling), 269n54
judgment: Hell and, 84–85, 90, 92, 94–
    96, 99–103, 105–6; moral, 136, 143–47,
    280; Taiping ideology and, 45–48;
    *Tian* (Heaven) and, 4n7, 146; women
    and, 145
"Just Like the Man from Qi" ("Yanran
    Qi ren" 儼然齊人) (Xuan Ding), 260

*kanguan* 看官. *See* readers
Kangxi Emperor (r. 1661–1722), 67, 71–
    73, 72n14, 82, 83, 86, 107
*Karmic Ties in a Dream* (*Meng zhong
    yuan* 夢中緣) (Pu Wenbin): author-
    ship of, 219; "banished immortals,"
    209; brotherhood in, 221, 232–36;
    community and, 237–43; dream and,
    240–44; *The Peach Blossom Fan* and,
    221, 228–32; political injustice in, 235;
    Taiping Civil War and, 207; violence
    and, 212–13; *Water Margin* and, 233–
    34; *xi wen* and, 224
*Kechuang xianhua* 客窗閒話 (Wu
    Chichang), 246n2
Keulemans, Paize, 116, 138–39
Ko, Dorothy, 185n89
Kong Shangren 孔尚任 (1648–1718), 156,
    170, 173, 228–29. See also *Peach Blos-
    som Fan, The*
*kuaihuo* 快活. *See* happiness
Kuhn, Philip, 6

Lady Fei, 189, 189n103
Lady Yu, 225–27, 226n47
*lan ding* 藍頂 (blue button made of
    precious stone or glass on a Qing
    official's cap), 142n76
Laub, Dori, 125
"Learning Deviant Practices Out of
    Greed" ("Tancai xixie" 貪財習邪),
    99
Lee, Haiyan, 210
Legge, James (1815–1897), 251
Li Bo 李白 (701–762), 158n15, 161
Li Hongzhang 李鴻章 (1823–1901), 248

Li Shangyin 李商隱 (813–858): criticism
    about, 202; poetry of, 158n16, 198–201
Li, Wai-yee, 16n34, 217n34
Li Xiangjun 李香君 (fl.1640), 156, 173–
    74, 175n70, 263
Li Xiucheng 李秀成 (1823–1864), 251,
    276
"Li Yangeng" 李延庚 (Wang Tao), 267
Li Yu 李漁 (1611–1680), 260
Li Yu 李玉 (fl. seventeenth century),
    159n18
Li Zhi 李贄 (1527–1602), 89n56
Li Zicheng 李自成 (1606–1645), 189, 267
*li* 離 and *he* 合. *See* separation and union
Liang Fa 梁發 (1789–1855), 6, 58, 61–62,
    64
Liang Yannian 梁延年, 73n18
Liao Changming 廖長明 (fl.1885), 81
Liao Cho-cheng, 169n52
Liao Yan 廖燕 (1644–1705), 170n55
*Liaozhai* tradition, 255
*Liezi jishi* 列子集釋, 196n113, 243n88
*Liling Mountain, The* (*Liling po* 理靈坡)
    (Yang Enshou), 215–16, 217
Lin Shanwen, 68n3
Lin Siniang 林四娘, 206, 217–18
Lin Wanchuan, 75n25
Lin Yunming 林雲銘 (fl.1658), 217n34
Lindley, Augustus (1840–1873), 30n14
Ling Hon Lam, 205
*Lingwa shi* 靈媧石 (Xu Shanchang),
    237n69
literacy: Ming publishing industry,
    71; Taiping Rebellion and, 29n10,
    188n98; women and, 185n89, 186n91;
    *xuanjiang* and, 89n57
*Literary Mind and the Carving of
    Dragons, The* (*Wen xin diao long* 文心
    雕龍) (Liu Xie), 27
literary tropes, 5, 20, 90, 151, 177, 211,
    219n38, 247
literati identity: crises of, 6, 126–28, 249;
    ideals of, 194–95
literati novels 文人小說. See *wenren
    xiaoshuo*

literature of persuasion. See *jiaohua*; *xi wen*

lithography, 17, 154

Liu Bang 劉邦 (247–195 BCE), 192, 193

Liu Huankui 劉煥奎 (fl. 1879), 240, 241, 242

"Liu Jianxiang's Stone Coffin" ("Liu Jianxiong shiguo" 柳建雄石椁) (Xuan Ding), 278–79

Liu Xie 劉勰 (fl. 465–522), 27

Liu Zhongzhou 劉宗周 (1578–1645), 208

"Liu yu" 六諭. See "Six Edicts"

*li yan* 立言. See "establishing words"

"Lodging a False Accusation out of Resentment" ("Xiefen wugao" 挾忿誣告), 95

London Missionary Society Press, 251, 285

*Lotus Sutra, The*, 249

Love, Harold, 27n5

"Loyal and Virtuous Woman, The" ("Yilie nüzi" 義烈女子) (Wang Tao), 272, 273

"Loyal Spirit Enters a Dream, The" ("Zhonghun rumeng" 忠魂入夢) (Xuan Ding), 267–68

*lu* (錄). See "accounts"

Lü Dongbin 呂洞賓, 79n33

Lu, Tina, 260n31

Lü Xiong 呂熊 (fl.1674), 182–84, 194

Lu Xun 魯迅 (1881–1936), 152n5, 254n18, 274, 291, 292

Luo Ergang, 56n67, 63n79

Ma Zhiyuan 馬致遠 (fl.1251–1321), 219

"Madman's Diary, A" ("Kuangren riji" 狂人日記) (Lu Xun), 292

Magic arts, 181, 193, 276–78

Mair, Victor, 71n13, 73n17

"Male Heir, The" ("Feng xian lou" 奉先樓) (Li Yu, 1611–1680), 260–61

Manchus: God and, 39; Ming-Qing transition and, 256, 268; Taiping ideology and, 2–3, 25, 41–42

Mandate of Heaven: imperial politics and, 4n7; Qing literati and, 17, 19, 69, 104–8; Taiping ideology and, 2, 39–42

Manuscripts: fragility, 205; Ming-Qing transition and, 189n103; modern library preservation of, 120n25; Taiping ideology and, 43n38, 50n47; Taiping war and, 18, 112. See also *Diary of Escape from the Rebels*

Mao Qiling 毛奇齡 (1623–1716), 169, 206n6

Mao Xianglin 毛祥麟 (fl. 1850s), 246n2

mass audience, 17, 26, 28, 69, 81, 287, 291, 293

Masschelein, Anneleen, 274n64

"Match of Kalavińka, The" ("Jialing pei" 迦陵配) (Xuan Ding), 277

McMahon, Keith, 15, 155, 155n10, 181

Medhurst, Walter Henry (1796–1857), 251

media: form vs. content, 30–34, 254n19; genres as, 27, 112–13; human as, 29n10, 188n98; mass audience, 285; modern, 18, 254–55; propaganda and, 28; religious, 15; Taiping Civil War and, 293; Taiping use of, 17, 30–34. See also manuscript; printing; propaganda; *Shenbao* publisher (Shenbaoguan)

*Melodious Golden Pavilion, The* (*Sheng jin ge* 生金閣), 269–70

memoir: history writing and, 118; nature of, 113n10; the Taiping Civil War, 13, 112; Zhu Jiumei and, 187

memories: cultural, 206; drama and, 213; dream and, 243; ghosts and, 184–85; Ming-Qing dynastic transition and, 20, 184–85; pliability and, 124; reconstruction of, 147, 156; repository of, 20, 155. See also *Diary of Escape from the Rebels*

metatheater, 169–76

Meyer-Fong, Tobie S., 1n2, 7–8, 12, 14, 21n11, 112n7, 118

millenarian movement, 6, 56

millenarian vision, 7n12, 12–13, 54–55, 98, 250

"Millet, The" ("Shu li" 黍離), 167n47

Ming-Qing dynastic transition: diaries and, 111–12; drama and, 206; ghosts and, 264–68; literary legacies and reinventions of, 20–21; moral criticism and, 279; national trauma and supernatural, 182–84; personal accounts and, 123; Taiping Civil War and, 9–10, 14; women and, 185n90, 189. See also *Peach Blossom Fan, The*; *Unofficial History of a Female Immortal, An*

*Miraculous Proofs of the Sacred Edict* (*Shengyu lingzheng* 聖諭靈徵): *baojuan* and, 88n54; contents of, 83–89; drama and, 208; Heaven's will and, 104–8; imagined community of transgressors in, 89–98; language of, 73; moral retribution and, 69, 74–78; overview of, 19, 67–70; physical characteristics of, 79–83; prefaces, 68n3, 80–81, 104–6; punishment and retribution, 93–98; Taiping discourse and, 98–104; *xuanjiang* and, 89n57

"miscellaneous notes" (*biji* 筆記): *Beishan biji* and, 120n25; journeying and, 112–13; Shen Zi's, 121, 123; Taiping Civil War and, 246n2; Zhu Jiumei and, 185

*Miscellaneous Notes from the Studio of Cultivating Austerity* (*Yangzhuo xuan biji* 養拙軒筆記) (Shen Zi), 121, 123

"Mocking the Recluse of the Wood of Red Leaves on the Seventh Day of the Seventh Month" ("Qixi chao Lindan jushi" 七夕嘲林丹居士) (Wei Xiuren), 162–63

*Mohai* 墨海 (Fang Ruisheng 方瑞生), 285n87

Mongols, 41, 192

moon goddess, 182, 183, 184, 199

morality: ambiguity of, 125, 288; Confucian, 95–96, 208, 282, 284; drama and, 207–8; fantastic stories and, 256–64; judgement and, 143–45, 147; political, 179–80, 206, 225–27. *See also* filial piety

morality books (*shanshu* 善書): definition of, 68n4; *Jade Records*, 75–79, 89, 93–94, 93n66; literati and, 75n23, 96; production of, 73n17, 76n27; spread of, 68n6; Taiping Civil War and, 11n21; *Tract on Divine Action and Response*, 74–75, 78, 79, 249. See also *Miraculous Proofs of the Sacred Edict*

moral retribution: drama and, 208; popular beliefs and, 67; Qing ideology with *jiaohua* and, 70–89; schemes of, 145, 208n14, 279. See also *Miraculous Proofs of the Sacred Edict*

*Mo yu lu* 墨餘錄 (Mao Xianglin), 246n2

"Mrs. Pigs" ("Hai shi furen" 亥氏夫人) (Xuan Ding), 257–59

Napoleonic Wars (1803–1815), 5

narrative frame, 11n21, 46, 58, 170–71

Neo-Confucianism, 70–71, 75n23, 134n50, 164, 169, 233

*nü bushu* 女簿書. *See* women

Ogaeri Yoshio, 71n13

"On *Traces of Flowers and the Moon*" ("*Hua yue hen* tici" 花月痕題詞) (Wei Xiuren), 198–202

oral accounts, 29n10, 43n38

Orwell, George, 70n9

Other: animal and, 257–59; discourse of, 288; ethnicity and, 39–42; ideologies and, 98–102; monstrosity of, 179, 289–90; otherness, 286n

Owen, Stephen, 258n26

*Palace of Eternal Life, The* (*Changsheng dian* 長生殿) (Hong Sheng), 183

pamphlets, 2, 5–7, 30n14, 31, 61–62, 67, 81, 102, 208

Pan Jianguo, 160n24

Pan Zhongrui 潘鐘瑞 (1823–1890), 115–16

parallel prose, 167–68

paratext, 21, 30, 205, 237–38

parody, 100, 102, 226

"Path of Rejuvenation, The," 12

*Peach Blossom Fan, The (Taohua shan 桃花扇)* (Kong Shangren): *Karmic Ties in a Dream* and, 221, 228–32; Taiping Civil War and, 9–10, 19–20; *Traces of Flowers and the Moon* and, 155–56, 169–75, 184, 197

Peking opera, 208–9

*Peony Pavilion, The (Mudan ting 牡丹亭)* (Tang Xianzu), 210, 259

Perry, Elizabeth, 33

personal accounts, 2, 13, 109–12, 215, 288, 293

*Person in the Mist, The (Wu zhong ren 霧中人)* (Zheng Youxi 鄭由熙), 207, 211–12

*pihuang* 皮黃, 208–9

placards: Taiping, 2–4, 39–42, 39nn29–30, 44, 139, 226, 287; traditions of, 70, 71n12

Plaks, Andrew, 164n34, 164n37

Platt, Stephen, 12

plays: aesthetic conventions of, 288; brotherhood in, 232–36; communities and, 237–43; *dutuo ju*, 209–10, 220, 222, 228; ferocity and violence in, 210–18; *jiaohua* and, 207–8; *jie* and, 209–10; paratext of, 21, 228–29, 231–32, 237–44, 237nn69–70; playwrights and, 205–10; *shishi ju*, 216n32; Taiping Civil War in, 207, 210–13, 218–36; women in, 216–18, 225. See also *chuanqi* plays; *Karmic Ties in a Dream*; *Peach Blossom Fan, The*; *zaju* plays

*Plum in the Golden Vase, The (Jin Ping Mei)*, 164n34, 172n60, 226n47

poetry: autobiographical writings and, 169–70; community building and, 238–42; drama and, 208; "On *Traces of Flowers and the Moon*," 198–202; repository of memories, 161–63. See also *Traces of Flowers and the Moon*

*Poetry Notes from the Gainan Mountain Studio (Gainan shanguan shihua 陔南山館詩話)* (Wei Xiuren), 179, 179n77, 185–86, 190

preaching (*xuanjiang* 宣講), 88nn54–55, 89, 89nn56–57, 208

"preaching the principles." See *jiang daoli* 講道理

*Precious Admonishment on Saving People from Calamity (Jiujie baoxun 救劫寶訓)*, 100

precious scroll performance 寶卷. See *baojuan*

*Precious Scrolls of Ten Kings, The (Shi wang baojuan 十王寶卷)*, 87

Princess Rui'an 瑞安公主 (1569–1629), 267

"Principle Guidelines of *The Peach Blossom Fan*, The" ("*Taohua shan gangling*" 桃花扇綱領) (Kong Shangren), 228

printing, 49n46, 68n6, 76n27, 78, 80, 82n41, 147, 293; Taiping design of, 19, 27, 30–33; technology, 18, 82, 246, 251, 253; woodblock, 15, 17, 18, 44, 112, 246n2

*Promulgated Edicts (Banxing zhaoshu 頒行詔書)*, 35, 38–44

propaganda, 28, 33, 70n9, 81, 103, 154n8

"prophecy in retrospect," 277

proscriptions, 30, 71

Pu Songling 蒲松齡 (1640–1715), 246, 255–56, 255n20, 283, 283n83. See also *Stories about the Strange from Liaozhai Studio*

Pu Wenbin 濮文彬 (fl. 1850s–1880s), 219–20, 219n37, 243, 263. See also *Karmic Ties in a Dream*

punishment: "abandoned immortals" and, 193; in Hell, 73, 76–77, 86, 93n66; retribution and, 93–98

Puyuan 濮院, 1, 118, 118n23, 121, 123, 126–28, 131n45, 135–41, 143

Qian Xiangkun 錢象坤 (1569–1640), 280

"Qidao suoming" 七盜索命 (Yuan Mei), 270n57

Qin empire (221–207 BCE), 192–93

"Qin Erguan" 秦二官 (Xuan Ding), 256–57

qing 情 (emotions, feelings, attachments): Feng Menglon and, 210; illusory realm and, 165–66, 166n43; morality and, 256–60; *Peach Blossom Fan* and, 173; violence and, 210–18

Qing ideology, 70–89, 287. See also *Miraculous Proofs of the Sacred Edict*; Sacred Edict, Qing

*Quell the Bandits* (*Dang kou zhi* 蕩寇志) (Yu Wanchun), 44, 233–34, 236, 284

"Random Composition" ("Man cheng" 漫成) (Li Shangyin), 201–2

*Random Jottings of a Wusong Recluse* (*Songyin manlu* 淞隱漫錄) (Wang Tao), 254, 283n83

"Random Notes of Divine Revelation on the Planchette" ("Jixian yishi" 乩仙逸事) (Wang Tao), 264–65

readers (*kanguan* 看官), 171–72, 172n60

"Receiving the Mandate of Heaven to attack the barbarian" ("Fengtian taohu" 奉天討胡), 2, 41–42

"Receiving the Mandate of Heaven to Extinguish Demons" ("Fengtian zhuyao, jiushi anmin" 奉天誅妖, 救世安民), 39–41

*Record of Military Subjugation in [the land of] the Yu Hills and the Sea* (*Haiyu beibing ji* 海虞被兵記), 123

*Records from within Disaster* (*Nan zhong ji* 難中紀), 114–15

*Records of Escapes and the Remaining Life* (*Zhuanxi yusheng ji* 轉徙餘生記), 112

*Records of Handan*, 219, 242

*Records of Pondering Pain* (*Sitong ji* 思痛記), 112

*Records of the Grand Historian* (*Shi ji* 史記) (Sima Qian), 225–26

*Records on Deer of the Gusu Terrace* (*Sutai milu ji* 蘇臺麋鹿記) (Pan Zhongrui), 115–16

*Records under the Autumn Lamp on Rainy Nights* (*Yeyu qiudeng lu* 夜雨秋燈錄) (Xuan Ding): dystopia, 289–90; escapes, 273–75, 277–78; ghost, 267–68, 273–74; moral themes, 256–60; publication, 254. See also Xuan Ding

"red ram" (*hong yang* 紅羊), 10, 10n20, 11, 289

"Red Ram and the Red Horse, the," 277

regular remittance (*juan na* 捐納), 235n67

Reilly, Thomas, 7n12, 26

religious authority, 14, 35, 83. See also authority

religious tracts: Qing, 17, 67; Taiping, 2, 208

restoration: of causal relationship, 135–39, 142–45; of Confucian morality, 90–98; of local order, 133–34; of the rhythm of everyday, 113, 147; of Taiping's "fundamental way," 35–37

retribution, 19, 78, 87n50, 93–98. See also moral retribution

"Returning to the Human World to Recount His Sins" ("Huanyang suzui" 還陽訴罪), 100–102

*Reunion across Millions of Miles* (*Wanli yuan* 萬里圓) (Li Yu, fl. seventeenth century), 159n18

"Reversed Yellow Millet Dream, A" ("Fan Huangliang" 反黃粱) (Wang Tao), 281–84, 288

revisions: personal accounts and, 113, 119–20, 124–25, 129, 132, 135–47, 155; poetry and literati fiction, 161–63; power struggles and, 36–37, 46n2

"Rhapsody on Resentment" ("Hen fu" 恨賦) (Jiang Yan), 160

rhetoric: Taiping ideology and, 26, 29, 36; war and, 3–5, 14; *xi wen*, 224

rhetorical device, of breaking "fourth wall," 171–72, 171n59, 185

Ricci, Matteo (1552–1610), 26

Ricoeur, Paul, 13n23

right and wrong (*shi* 是 and *fei* 非), 176–77

*riji* 日記. *See* "daily accounts"

Roberts, Issachar J. (1802–1871), 58

*Romance of the Three Kingdoms (Sanguo yanyi* 三國演義), 43, 164n34, 232

*Romance to Awaken the World, A (Xing shi yinyuan zhuan* 醒世姻緣傳), 172n60

Rosemont, Henry, 4n7

rotten mouths (*lan yaba* 爛牙吧), 85, 85n45

*Sacred Decrees of the Heavenly Brother, The (Tianxiong shengzhi* 天兄聖旨), 49–55

*Sacred Decrees of the Heavenly Father, The (Tianfu shengzhi* 天父聖旨), 49, 55

Sacred Edict, Qing, 71n13, 73nn18–19, 80, 86, 89, 105, 208n12; with anti-heterodox agenda, 72, 100, 100n84; Christian missionaries and, 68n2; of Kangxi Emperor, 67, 71–73; morality books and, 73n17, 81, 95, 96; proselytizing, 98, 208; retribution and, 19, 78; teaching, 70–74; women and, 96–97, 96n76. *See also Miraculous Proofs of the Sacred Edict*

*Sai Shang'e* 賽尚阿 (1794–1875), 47

Sakai, Tadao, 68n4, 70n11

Sanli battle (1851), 53

"Saving All Chinese People Born of Heaven and Nourished by Heaven" ("Jiu yiqie Tiansheng Tianyang Zhongguo renmin" 救一切天生天養中國人民), 42

Schluessel, Eric, 70n8

Scholes, Robert, 247

*Sea of Regret (Hen hai* 恨海) (Wu Jianren), 261

Second Opium War (1856–1860), 173n64

self: censorship, 136, 147; continuity of, 113, 113n9; cultivation of, 67, 71–72, 75, 75n23, 164, 276, 284

"Self-Strengthening Movement" (1860s–1880s), 9

separation and union (*li* 離 and *he* 合), 176–77

*Sequel to Records under the Autumn Lamp on Rainy Nights, The (Yeyu qiudeng xu lu* 夜雨秋燈續錄) (Xuan Ding), 249n9, 254, 255

"Sequel to the Yellow Millet Dream, A" ("Xu Huangliang" 續黃粱) (Pu Songling), 283, 283n83

sex: desire and, 186n91, 215, 256–57, 258; as metaphor, 181, 258; punishment and, 91n62; Zhu Jiumei and, 185

sexagenary cycle, 10, 10n20, 153n7, 156n11

*Shadows of the Paired Purities (Shuang qingying* 雙清影) (Yang Enshou), 210–11

Shang, Wei, 195n111

*shanshu* 善書. *See* morality books

Shen Congwen 沈從文 (1902–1988), 274

Shen Fen 沈芬 (d. 1860), 131–35, 131n45

Shen Tao 沈濤 (?–1850s), 121

Shen Yunying 沈雲英 (1624–1660), 206n6

Shen Zi 沈梓 (1833–1888), 2, 20, 117, 120n25, 121n28, 151, 155, 288; with ancestral tombs, 143–44; as historian,

Shen Zi (*continued*)
    144–45, 146; playwriting and, 237;
    with self-censorship, 147; in Taiping
    Civil War with personal losses, 1, 121,
    127–29, 132–33. See also *Diary of Es-
    cape from the Rebels*
*Shenbao* newspaper, 247n3, 252, 254n17
*Shenbao* publisher (Shenbaoguan 申報
    館), 18, 188n100, 253–54, 254n17, 255
*Shengyu helü zhijie* 聖諭合律直解
    (Chen Bingzhi), 73n19
*Shengyu xiangjie* 聖諭像解 (Liang
    Yannian), 73n18
*shi* 是 and *fei* 非. *See* right and wrong
Shi Dakai 石達開 (1831–1863), 39, 56, 223
Shih, Vincent, 6n11, 42, 43n36
*shishi ju* 時事劇. *See* "contemporary
    plays"
*Short Record to Settle My Thoughts, A*
    (*Dingsi xiaoji* 定思小記), 116
shrines (*citang*), 59, 101, 196, 196n112, 237
Shunzhi Emperor (r. 1643–1661), 74, 82
"Silver Transformed into Toads" ("Yin
    bian hama" 銀變蛤蟆) (Xuan Ding),
    273–74
Sima Qian 司馬遷, 225–26
"Six Edicts" ("Liu yu" 六諭), 74
*Six Records of a Floating Life* (*Fu sheng
    liu ji* 浮生六記), 164n37
*Snow on the Pear Blossom* (*Lihua xue*
    梨花雪) (Xu E), 140n69, 188, 188n100,
    207, 207n8, 209, 215–17, 265
social disorder: personal accounts and,
    141; women and, 145
Song Lian 宋濂 (1310–1381), 41n32
"Song of Lasting Regret" ("Chang hen
    ge" 長恨歌) (Bai Juyi), 238–39
"Song of Lin Siniang, The" ("Lin Siniang
    ge" 林四娘歌) (Chen Weisong), 192
"Song of One Hundred Virtues" ("Bai
    zheng ge" 百正歌), 37n24
*Song of Saving the World by Seeking the
    Fundamental Way, The* (*Yuan Dao
    jiu shi ge* 原道救世歌) (Hong Xiu-
    quan), 35, 36

"Son Who Failed to Be Filial, A" ("Erzi
    buxiao" 兒子不孝), 92
Spence, Jonathan, 25, 75–76
spirit possessions: Qing, 106; Taiping,
    38, 45, 51–52, 106
spirit (planchette) writing, 10, 79, 197,
    264
stage directions, plays, 211, 216, 228
stone steles (*bei* 碑), 158n17, 166–67
*Stories about the Strange from Liaozhai
    Studio* (*Liaozhai zhiyi* 聊齋誌異)
    (Pu Songling), 19, 21, 184–85, 246,
    246n2, 255–56, 255n20, 259
storyteller's manner, rhetorical device
    of, 171–72, 171n59, 185
"Summoning Souls" ("Shehun" 攝魂)
    (Wang Tao), 193, 276, 277
supernatural: courtesans with powers
    of, 180–83; elements of, 75, 81, 98,
    106, 255; magic, 181, 190, 193, 276, 277–
    78; national trauma and, 182–84; *In
    Search of the Supernatural*, 219n38,
    269; spirits, 10, 38, 45, 51, 79, 197, 221–
    22, 264; in *Traces of Flowers and the
    Moon*, 153. *See also* ghosts
*Surviving Chronicle from the [Yangzi]
    Cape* (*Haijiao yibian* 海角遺編), 123

Taiping: ballads, 27, 35–36, 37n24, 43;
    calendar, 12–13, 30–31, 34, 62–63,
    63n79; censorship, 30, 60n74; pam-
    phlets, 102; placards, 2–4, 39–42,
    39nn29–30, 44, 82, 139, 226, 287. *See
    also* textual universe, Taiping
Taiping civil service examination,
    women's participation in, 186n91,
    266
Taiping Civil War (Rebellion) (1851–
    1864), 15, 118n23, 141n73, 247, 286n; col-
    lapse of Heaven and, 4–9, 293; deaths,
    1, 1n2, 2; escape and renunciation,
    275–81; with escape to countryside,
    116–17, 127, 128; foreign involvement,
    8; Heaven and, 127–28, 146, 147; *hong
    yang* and, 10, 11; *jie*, 17, 117; late Tang,

198–201; legacy, 12; Ming-Qing dynastic transition and, 9–10, 111–16; personal accounts, 2, 109–17, 215, 288; personal writings during, 111–17; in plays, 207, 210–13, 218–28; women in, 116n18, 121, 121n28, 127, 129–35, 140, 143, 145, 159, 179–83, 185–92, 207, 210, 212–13, 224–28, 245, 265; writing after, 178–203; writing from within, 151–78; *xi wen* and, 2–4, 39, 41–42, 44, 287. See also *Diary of Escape from the Rebels*; *Karmic Ties in a Dream*; *Traces of Flowers and the Moon*

Taiping edicts, 26, 33n15; of the Heavenly Father, 186; with imperial authority, 19, 27; in manuscript form, 50n47; moral codes and, 34n18; *Promulgated Edicts*, 35, 38–44; *The Taiping Edicts*, 35–37, 37n24, 41; *The Taiping Heavenly Chronicle*, 25n, 35n20, 49, 55–65, 151, 193, 198; texts listed as approved, 35–49

*Taiping Edicts, The* (*Taiping zhaoshu* 太平詔書), 35–37, 37n24, 41

*Taiping Heavenly Chronicle, The* (*Taiping tianri* 太平天日), 25n, 35n20, 49, 55–65, 151, 193, 198

Taiping Heavenly Kingdom, 7, 9, 12, 37, 39, 56–57, 186n91, 223

Taiping ideology, 6n11, 28, 29n10, 59n71, 104, 137, 208; Christianity and, 25n1, 69, 101, 287; context and function, 29–30; Hong Xiuquan and, 60–61, 64; novels and, 42, 43n36

Taiping movement, 6, 7n12, 12, 25–26, 43n38

Taiping Rebellion. *See* Taiping Civil War; Taiping movement

Taiping (Yue) rebels, 7n13, 60, 215; ambivalent political morality, 179–80; as beasts, 111, 211–12, 216–18, 221–25; brotherhood of, 43, 232; flag of, 129, 136, 136n54; long-haired, 126, 126n34, 142; Qing government and, 2–3, 3n4, 7, 15, 224, 224n42. See also *Diary of Escape from the Rebels*; Taiping Civil War

*Taishang baofa tushuo* 太上寶筏圖說, 82n42

*Tales of Trivia from the Banks of the Wusong* (*Songbin suohua* 淞濱瑣話) (Wang Tao), 254

Tang Xianzu 湯顯祖 (1550–1616), 210, 219, 219n38, 259

Tang *chuanqi* stories, 219, 275, 283

"Tang Emperor Taizong's Visit to Hell, The" ("Tang Taizong you difu" 唐太宗遊地府), 90

*Tanyuan liuzhong qu* 坦園六種曲 (Yang Enshou), 211n21

Tao Qian 陶潛 (365–427), 197n119, 269n52

*Tears from a Man of Iron in Jiangnan* (*Jiangnan tie lei tu* 江南鐵淚圖) (Yu Zhi), 215

Terrace of Raining Flowers Mountain (Yuhua tai 雨花台), battle at, 180–81, 185

testimony, 4, 46, 103, 110n3, 111, 127, 135; of women, 130–31. *See also* witnessing

textual universe, Taiping: approved texts, 35–49; context and function, 29–30; edicts, 19, 25n, 27, 33n15, 34n18, 35–49, 35n20, 37n24, 55–65, 151, 193, 198; hybridity in, 19, 27, 30–31; publications, 28–34, 30nn12–14, 33n15, 34n17, 81; with texts as artifacts, 30–34; texts not listed as approved, 49–66

theater, 204, 205; metatheater in *Traces of Flowers and the Moon*, 169–76, 202–3; Peking opera, 208, 209. *See also* plays

theatricalization: of traumatic memories, 215, 218; of violence, 215, 215n30, 216–18

"Three Strange Occurrences in the Law Office of Guilin" ("Guilin nieshu sanyi" 桂林臬署三異) (Xuan Ding), 268

*Tian* 天 (Heaven), 4n7, 26, 63n79

Tian, Xiaofei, 130n10

*Tiancao* 天曹. *See* Heavenly Tribunal

Tianjing Incident, 48–49, 55, 223

Time: anticipatory nostalgia, 156; calendrical time, 62, 63; cyclical temporality, 62; different temporal axes, 155; linear temporality, 63; multiplicity of, 13; narrative and, 51

*Time and Narrative* (Ricoeur), 13n23

Tong Pass (Tong guan 潼關), 156, 157, 157n12

*tongsheng* 童生, 96, 96n74

traces (*hen* 痕), 178, 178n75; metaphor of, 176–78

*Traces of Flowers and the Moon* (*Hua yue hen* 花月痕) (Wei Xiuren), 20, 154, 155n10, 157n13, 181n80, 207, 215, 290–91; autobiographical details in, 152, 152n4, 153n6, 157–59, 161, 163–64, 167–70, 172, 174–75, 193–98, 202–3, 213; battle at Terrace of Raining Flowers Mountain, 180–81, 185; courtesans in, 153, 161, 161n28, 163, 165, 165n40, 174–75, 177, 180–84, 201; *Dream of the Red Chamber* and, 165, 165n41, 169, 184; framing in, 170–71, 176–77, 179; ghosts in, 196–97, 267; illusory world in, 165–68, 175–76; *Karmic Ties in a Dream* and, 243–44; metaphor of "traces," 176–78; metatheater, 169–76, 202–3; "On *Traces of Flowers and the Moon*" and, 198–202; *The Peach Blossom Fan* and, 155–56, 169–75, 184, 197; poetry in, 155–56, 158–63, 191–92, 197; prefaces, 153n7; reality and fictionality in, 155–64; romance in, 153, 163, 165, 165n40, 169, 175–76, 177, 201; temporal structure of, 155–57, 156n11, 163; *An Unofficial History of a Female Immortal* and, 182–84; Zhu Jiumei in, 181, 185, 188, 190–92, 196

*Tract on Divine Action and Response* (*Taishang ganying pian* 太上感應篇), 74–75, 78, 79, 249

Tracts. *See* pamphlets

trauma, 113n10, 118, 247; female ghosts and, 184–85, 190; historical, 16n34, 110, 156; of Ming-Qing dynastic transition, 203, 275, 286; narrative and lyricism to transcend, 152, 155, 160; national, 16n34, 152, 174, 182–84, 217, 217n34, 264, 288; personal accounts of wartime, 109–11, 215; plays and, 204, 206, 210, 215–18, 237

"Uncles Not Being Kind to Their Nephews" ("Boshu buci zizhi" 伯叔不慈子侄), 97n79

*Unconcept, The* (Masschelein), 274n64

*Unofficial History of a Female Immortal, An* (*Nüxian waishi* 女仙外史) (Lü Xiong), 182–84, 194

*Unofficial History of the Scholars* (*Rulin waishi* 儒林外史), 164n37

unrestraint (*fengliu* 風流), 101, 101n86

"uprooting the household and becoming immortal" (*bazhai fei xian* 拔宅飛仙), 275

*Useless Words Written in Exasperation* (*Duoduo lu* 咄咄錄) (Wei Xiuren), 179, 180

utopia, 14, 16–17, 103, 197, 274, 290, 292

vernacular, 83, 86, 97, 103; fiction, 81, 171, 171n59, 174n68, 284; stories, 88, 104, 171n59, 282

village compact (*xiangyue* 鄉約), 70

violence, 16, 21, 110, 187, 190, 191; communal, 275; plays with ferocity and, 210–18; rhetoric of, 3–4; sexual abuse, 179–80, 213, 272; theatricalization of, 215, 215n30, 216–18; witness accounts of, 113, 114, 115; *xi wen* and, 2–4, 39, 41–42, 44, 287. *See also* Taiping Civil War; trauma

"Virtuous and Heroic Woman, The" ("Zhenlie nü" 貞烈女) (Xuan Ding), 260, 261

"Vying for Lands and Being in Discord with His Brothers" ("Zheng tianchan buhe dixiong" 爭田產不合弟兄), 95

Wagner, Rudolf, 25
Wan Changzuo 萬長祚 (?–1644), 267
Wan Wei 萬煒 (?–1644), 267
Wang, David Der-wei, 16, 154–55, 155n9, 184
Wang, Jing, 166
Wang Lawrence, 235n67
Wang Qingcheng, 27n5, 34n18, 50nn47–48
Wang Shiduo 汪士鐸 (1882–1889), 123–24
Wang Tao 王韜 (1828–1897), 188–90, 188n100, 191, 247, 247nn3–4, 283n83, 288; antifantasy and, 281–85; as author, 251–55, 252n14, 254n19, 281n80; with escape and renunciation, 276–77; ghosts and, 264–67, 269–73, 274–75; morality and, 256, 261–64
Wang Xianzhi 王仙芝 (?–878), 198
Wang Xiuchu 王秀楚 (ca. mid-seventeenth century), 111n6
Wang Yangming 王陽明 (1472–1529), 71, 71n12, 208
Wang Zhi 王直 (1379–1462), 169
Wanli yuan 萬里圓. See Reunion across Millions of Miles
Water Margin (Shuihu zhuan 水滸傳), 19, 20–21, 36n43, 43n36, 164n34, 172n60, 284; brotherhood in, 43, 236; Call to Arms and, 291; kanguan in, 172n60; Qing cultural elites and, 44; Quell the Bandits and, 233–34
Wei Changhui 韋昌輝 (1823?–1856), 38–39, 46, 49, 52–53, 55, 65, 223
Wei Xiuren 魏秀仁 (1818–1873), 20, 151n1, 177, 179n77; autobiographical details in works of, 152, 152n4, 153n6, 157–59, 161, 163–64, 167–70, 172, 174–75, 193–98, 202–3, 213; civil service examination and, 151–52, 157, 168; female ghosts and, 185–86, 190; illusory

world and, 164–66, 168; as poet, 154n8, 160–63, 178–79, 180, 195n111, 198–202; trauma of, 152, 155, 156, 160, 203. See also Traces of Flowers and the Moon
Wei Xiyuan 魏熙元 (1830–1888), 205–6
"Wei renyan buhe zhouli" 為人言不和妯娌. See "In Discordance with the Sister-in-Law Because of Rumors"
Weller, Robert, 25n1
Wenchang di 文昌帝 (god of literature and culture), 78, 79n33
wenren xiaoshuo 文人小說 (literati novels), 18, 20, 152, 152n4, 155, 164, 172. See also Traces of Flowers and the Moon
"Wenxin King" 文信王 (Yuan Mei), 270
What the Master Would Not Discuss (Zi bu yu 子不語) (Yuan Mei), 270, 270n57
White, Hayden, 13n27, 51
Widmer, Ellen, 15, 15n33, 247n3
"Wife of Liu, The" ("Liu shi fu" 劉氏婦) (Wang Tao), 261
"Wife Who Fails to Respect Her Husband, A" ("Bujing qifu" 不敬其夫), 94–95
Winsome General, The (Guihua feng 媿嬅封) (Yang Enshou), 206, 217–18
witnessing, 110n3, 179, 241, 271; of communal violence, 275; testimony and, 4, 46, 103, 110n3, 111, 125, 127, 130–31, 135; wartime and different levels of, 125–35
"Woman Who Aborted Her Baby or Drowned Her Daughter, A" ("Furen datai ninü" 婦人打胎溺女), 96–97
women, 97n78, 131n45, 134n50, 174, 189n103, 229, 256, 261; abduction of, 145, 179, 186, 189, 207, 207n8, 216–17, 266, 282; with bound feet, 116n18, 140n69; with civil service examination, 186n91, 266; copy clerks, 185, 186, 186n91; female ghosts, 180, 184–93, 186n91, 196, 196n116, 245, 246, 255,

women (*continued*)
260, 264–67, 270–73; literacy and, 185n89, 186n91, 187; as metaphorical site with judgment, 145n87; morality and, 121, 131–35, 159, 175, 188–90, 192, 207, 210, 226–27, 245, 259–60, 262, 265–66, 271–72, 283; in "Mrs. Pigs," 257–58; Sacred Edict and, 96–97, 96n76; social disorder and, 145; in Taiping Civil War, 116n18, 121, 121n28, 127, 129–35, 140, 143, 145, 159, 179–83, 185–92, 207, 210, 212–13, 224–28, 245, 265; testimony of, 130–31; warriors, 180–83, 216–18, 262; writers, 97n78, 131n45

Wooldridge, Chuck, 15

"World within a Pillow, The" ("Zhen zhong ji" 枕中記), 219, 283

writers: personal accounts, 109–17; plays and playwrights, 205–10; playwriting and community, 237–44; women, 97n78, 131n45

Wu Chichang 吳熾昌 (fl. 1850s), 246n2

Wu Dazheng 吳大澂 (1835–1902), 115

Wu Jianren 吳趼人 (1866–1910), 261

Wu Weiye 吳偉業 (1609–1671), 170, 202

*xiangyue* 鄉約. *See* village compact

Xiao Chaogui 蕭朝貴 (Heavenly Brother) (fl. 1820–1852), 38–39, 38n28, 53–54, 56–57, 59; Heaven and, 45n41; Jesus Christ and, 41, 100, 106; as shaman, 45

Xie Jiehe 謝介鶴 (fl. 1853–1856), 187

Xie Zhangting 謝章鋌 (1820–1903), 152n5

Xingtian 刑天, 269

*xi wen* 檄文 (call to arms): fictional imitation of, 224; as a genre, 2; Qing, 3; Taiping, 2, 39–42

Xu E 徐鄂 (1844–1903), 188n100, 207. See also *Snow on the Pear Blossom*

Xu Junde 徐駿德 (fl. 1880s), 242

Xu Shanchang 許善長 (1823–1889?), 207, 237, 237n69

Xuan Ding 宣鼎 (1832–1880), 21, 246–47, 246n2, 249n9, 254nn17–18, 285, 286n, 289–93; as author, 247n3, 248–55, 254n16; with escape and renunciation, 277–81; ghosts and, 264, 267–69, 273–75; morality and, 256–63. See also *Records under the Autumn Lamp on Rainy Nights*

*xuanjiang* 宣講. *See* preaching

"Yan Exian" 嚴萼仙 (Wang Tao), 264

Yang Enshou 楊恩壽 (1835–1891), 206, 206n6, 208, 210–11, 211n21, 215–18

Yang Xiuqing 楊秀清 (Heavenly Father) (1821?–1856), 38n28, 45, 51, 186n91, 189; God and, 60n74, 65; as leader, 11, 38, 39, 46–49, 55, 223; Zhu Jiumei and, 186–87, 188

*yang* troop formation, 181n80. See also *yin/yang*

*yao shu* 妖書. *See* "evil books"

"Yao Yunxian" 姚雲仙 (Wang Tao), 262–63

Ye Chucang (1887–1946), 154n8

Yeh, Catherine, 252n14

yellow millet, dreams of, 241, 242, 247, 281, 283–84, 288

Yellow Turban Rebellion, the (184–200s), 7n12

*yin* troop formation, 181, 181n80, 182

*yin/yang*, 181, 231

Yongzheng Emperor (r. 1722–1735), 73n18, 83, 277

You Tong 尤侗 (1618–1704), 170

Yu Wanchun 俞萬春 (1794–1849), 44, 233–34, 236, 284

Yu Yue 俞樾 (1821–1907), 8n15

Yu Zhi 余治 (1809–1874), 208–9, 208n12, 208n14, 215

Yuan Mei 袁枚 (1716–1798), 270, 270n57

"Yuanhun suoming" 冤魂索命 (Yuan Mei), 270n57

*Yuefei jishi* 粵匪紀事, 112n7

*yuefu* poems, 158n17

"Yuejiao" 月嬌 (Wang Tao), 262

"Yu Zhongyuan xi" 諭中原檄 (Song Lian) (1310–1381), 41n32

*zaju* 雜劇 plays, 204–5

Zarrow, Peter, 16n34

*Zei qing huizuan* (Zhang Dejian), 112n7

Zeitlin, Judith, 184

Zeng Guofan 曾國藩 (1811–1872), 8, 9, 16, 109, 112n7, 237; as leader, 56, 56n67; proclamation against Taiping rebels, 2–3, 3n4, 224, 224n42

Zeng Guoquan 曾國荃 (1824–1890), 8–9, 180

Zhang Daye 張大野, 113n10

Zhang Dejian 張德堅 (fl. 1850s), 7n13, 30n14, 112n7

Zhang Ting, 73n19

Zhang Xianzhong 張獻忠 (1606–1647), 206n6

Zhang Yichen, 73n18

"Zhao Biniang" 趙碧孃, 262

Zhao Liewen 趙烈文 (1832–1894), 109–10, 111, 215

Zheng Youxi 鄭由熙 (?–1898), 207, 211–12, 237, 237n69

Zheng Zhenduo 鄭振鐸, 154n8

*zhe xian* 謫仙. *See* banished immortals

"Zhixian" 芝仙 (Wang Tao), 270–72, 273, 274

Zhou Qiong 周瓊 (ca. mid-seventeenth century), 239

Zhou Weichi, 38n27, 59n71

Zhou Wenzao 周雯藻 (fl. 1860), 240, 241–42

Zhou Xineng 周錫能 (d. 1851), 46, 47

Zhou Zhenhe, 71n13, 73n17, 79n35

"Zhu Huixian" 朱慧仙 (Wang Tao), 188–89, 262

Zhu Jiumei 朱九妹 (fl. 1853), 45, 180–81, 185–92, 186n91, 188n97, 196, 262

Zhu Shaoyi 朱紹頤 (1833–1880), 11, 205, 205n3, 209–10, 218

*Zōho Chūgoku zensho no kenkyū* (Sakai), 70n11

Zou Tao 邹弢 (1850–1931), 281n80

Zuo Pengjun, 219n37

# Harvard-Yenching Institute Monographs
## (most recent titles)

94. *Savage Exchange: Han Imperialism, Chinese Literary Style, and the Economic Imagination*, by Tamara T. Chin

95. *Shifting Stories: History, Gossip, and Lore in Narratives from Tang Dynasty China*, by Sarah M. Allen

96. *One Who Knows Me: Friendship and Literary Culture in Mid-Tang China*, by Anna M. Shields

97. *Materializing Magic Power: Chinese Popular Religion in Villages and Cities*, by Wei-Ping Lin

98. *Traces of Grand Peace: Classics and State Activism in Imperial China*, by Jaeyoon Song

99. *Fiction's Family: Zhan Xi, Zhan Kai, and the Business of Women in Late-Qing China*, by Ellen Widmer

100. *Chinese History: A New Manual, Fourth Edition*, by Endymion Wilkinson

101. *After the Prosperous Age: State and Elites in Early Nineteenth-Century Suzhou*, by Seunghyun Han

102. *Celestial Masters: History and Ritual in Early Daoist Communities*, by Terry F. Kleeman

103. *Transgressive Typologies: Constructions of Gender and Power in Early Tang China*, by Rebecca Doran

104. *Li Mengyang, the North-South Divide, and Literati Learning in Ming China*, by Chang Woei Ong

105. *Bannermen Tales (Zidishu): Manchu Storytelling and Cultural Hybridity in the Qing Dynasty*, by Elena Suet-Ying Chiu

106. *Upriver Journeys: Diaspora and Empire in Southern China, 1570–1850*, by Steven B. Miles

107. *Ancestors, Kings, and the Dao*, by Constance A. Cook

108. *The Halberd at Red Cliff: Jian'an and the Three Kingdoms*, by Xiaofei Tian

109. *Speaking of Profit: Bao Shichen and Reform in Nineteenth-Century China*, by William T. Rowe

110. *Building for Oil: Daqing and the Formation of the Chinese Socialist State*, by Hou Li

111. *Reading Philosophy, Writing Poetry: Intertextual Modes of Making Meaning in Early Medieval China*, by Wendy Swartz

112. *Writing for Print: Publishing and the Making of Textual Authority in Late Imperial China*, by Suyoung Son

113. *Shen Gua's Empiricism*, by Ya Zuo

114. *Just a Song: Chinese Lyrics from the Eleventh and Early Twelfth Centuries*, by Stephen Owen

115. *Shrines to Living Men in the Ming Political Cosmos*, by Sarah Schneewind

116. *In the Wake of the Mongols: The Making of a New Social Order in North China, 1200–1600*, by Jinping Wang

117. *Opera, Society, and Politics in Modern China*, by Hsiao-t'i Li
118. *Imperiled Destinies: The Daoist Quest for Deliverance in Medieval China*, by Franciscus Verellen
119. *Ethnic Chrysalis: China's Orochen People and the Legacy of Qing Borderland Administration*, by Loretta E. Kim
120. *The Paradox of Being: Truth, Identity, and Images in Daoism*, by Poul Andersen
121. *Feeling the Past in Seventeenth-Century China*, by Xiaoqiao Ling
122. *The Chinese Dreamscape, 300 BCE–800 CE*, by Robert Ford Campany
123. *Structures of the Earth: Metageographies of Early Medieval China*, by D. Jonathan Felt
124. *Anecdote, Network, Gossip, Performance: Essays on the* Shishuo xinyu, by Jack W. Chen
125. *Testing the Literary: Prose and the Aesthetic in Early Modern China*, by Alexander Des Forges
126. *Du Fu Transforms: Tradition and Ethics amid Societal Collapse*, by Lucas Rambo Bender
127. *Chinese History: A New Manual (Enlarged Sixth Edition)*, Vol. 1, by Endymion Wilkinson
128. *Chinese History: A New Manual (Enlarged Sixth Edition)*, Vol. 2, by Endymion Wilkinson
129. *Wang Anshi and Song Poetic Culture*, by Xiaoshan Yang
130. *Localizing Learning: The Literati Enterprise in Wuzhou, 1100–1600*, by Peter K. Bol
131. *Making the Gods Speak: The Ritual Production of Revelation in Chinese Religious History*, by Vincent Goossaert
132. *Lineages Embedded in Temple Networks: Daoism and Local Society in Ming China*, by Richard G. Wang
133. *Rival Partners: How Taiwanese Entrepreneurs and Guangdong Officials Forged the China Development Model*, by Wu Jieh-min; translated by Stacy Mosher
134. *Saying All That Can Be Said: The Art of Describing Sex in Jin Ping Mei*, by Keith McMahon
135. *Genealogy and Status: Hereditary Office Holding and Kinship in North China under Mongol Rule*, by Tomoyasu Iiyama
136. *The Threshold: The Rhetoric of Historiography in Early Medieval China*, by Zeb Raft
137. *Literary History in and beyond China: Reading Text and World*, edited by Sarah M. Allen, Jack W. Chen, and Xiaofei Tian
138. *Dreaming and Self-Cultivation in China*, 300 BCE–800 CE, by Robert Ford Campany
139. *The Painting Master's Shame: Liang Shicheng and the Xuanhe Catalogue of Paintings*, by Amy McNair
140. *The Cornucopian Stage: Performing Commerce in Early Modern China*, by Ariel Fox
141. *The Collapse of Heaven: The Taiping Civil War and Chinese Literature and Culture, 1850–1880*, by Huan Jin